GERMAN PIETISM DURING THE EIGHTEENTH CENTURY

STUDIES

IN THE HISTORY OF RELIGIONS

(SUPPLEMENTS TO *NUMEN*)

XXIV

GERMAN PIETISM DURING THE EIGHTEENTH CENTURY

LEIDEN
E.J.BRILL
1973

GERMAN PIETISM DURING THE EIGHTEENTH CENTURY

BY

F. ERNEST STOEFFLER

Department of Religion
Temple University

LEIDEN
E.J.BRILL
1973

ISBN 90 04 03668 7

PRINTED IN BELGIUM

„*Even as one turns his hand,*
so all my doubts were gone."

August Hermann Francke

CONTENTS

Preface IX

List of Symbols XII

I. August Hermann Francke 1-38
His religious maturation 1
Francke the theologian. 7
Francke as educator 23
Francke's other roles 31

II. The Spener-Halle Movement in Germany . . . 39-87
The socio-political situation 39
The Halle theologians and their task 42
Controversies 57
Expansion 71

III. Characteristic Manifestations of Pietism in Württemberg 88-130
The background. 88
The rise of Swabian Pietism 91
Bengel and his circle 94
Oetinger and the theosophical tradition 107
Pietistic fellowships. 120
An over-view of Swabian Pietism. 128

IV. Zinzendorf and the Rise of the Renewed Moravian Church 131-167
Zinzendorf's early years 131
The establishment of Herrnhut 137
An interpretation of Zinzendorf 140
Renewed Moravianism on its way 159
The increasing appreciation of Zinzendorf. 166

V. Radical Pietism 168-216
The mystical background 168
Major voices 175
Other radicals 202
German Philadelphianism 208

VI. German Reformed Pietism and Prominent Neo-Pietists 217-265
German Reformed Pietism 217
Introductory considerations 217
Lampe, Mel, and Hottinger 224
Neo-Pietism 236
Theological transition 236
Early representatives 243
Jung-Stilling 253

Selective Bibliography of Secondary Sources . . . 266

Index 276

PREFACE

In a previous volume (*The Rise of Evangelical Pietism*, 1965) we have attempted to do two things, namely, to project an historically valid concept of evangelical Pietism and to trace the development of Pietism down to Philipp Jakob Spener. In doing this we found that the religious emphases which Spener and his early followers regarded to be of basic importance may be summarized as follows : The need for, and the possibility of, an authentic and vitally significant experience of God on the part of individual Christians; the religious life as a life of love for God and man, which is marked by social sensitivity and ethical concern; utter confidence, with respect to the issues of both life and death, in the experientially verifiable authenticity of God's revelation in Christ, as found in the biblical witness; the church as a community of God's people, which must ever be renewed through the transformation of individuals, and which necessarily transcends all organizationally required boundaries; the need for the implementation of the Reformation understanding of the priesthood of all believers through responsible lay participation in the varied concerns of the Christian enterprise; a ministry which is sensitized, trained, and oriented to respond to the needs and problems of a given age; and finally, the continual adaptation of ecclesiastical structures, practices, and verbal definitions to the mission of the church.

During the eighteenth century these hopes and aspirations came to full fruition within Continental Protestantism, bringing about what may be regarded as the golden age of the Pietistic Movement. The result was a new religious vitality which manifested itself upon all levels of man's life before God. For multitudes of men and women, who had been alienated from the church by its ever growing detachment from life's concerns, the Christian faith became once again a viable religious option. Though naively, perhaps, they now looked to the future with confidence, praying and working for a day when the institutions of church and state would be more fully expressive of the divine design. and would thus provide a more suitable environment for man's fulfillment.

Quite contrary to contemporary misconceptions, therefore, Pietism as it developed on the European Continent during and after the days of Spener was a religious movement which had its face turned to the future. It was profoundly critical of the present, its adherents being not infrequently called upon to suffer the consequences of such criticism in terms of discrimination, banishment, and imprisonment. As a movement it looked to the past only in the hope of finding models and mentors which would help men to face responsibly the problems which lay ahead. Strange as that may seem to some of us today, Pietists were preeminently the advocates of change in their day. Secretly, and sometimes not so secretly, they hoped to complete the Reformation, which, they felt, the sixteenth century reformers had only begun. And, significantly, many of them chose to regard true reformation not merely as a renewal of doctrine and ecclesiastical practice, but as a thoroughgoing renewal of man's entire life, including his social institutions.

In time this religious perspective was transplanted to North America by a substantial number of immigrants from Continental Europe. In its new environment it was merged with the impulses, quite similar in nature, which originated in the earlier Puritan tradition and the Evangelical Revival stemming from the Wesleys. Thus it became an important aspect of the total matrix of religious beliefs, values, understandings, and attitudes in which Protestant church life in America had its origins. For Americans, therefore, to understand the nature and development of Continental Pietism means, among other things, a fuller understanding of their own religious traditions, and hence of themselves in the context of a culture which is notoriously pluralistic in its historical development.

The present study, then, is an attempt to give a comprehensive, and, hopefully, a readable account, of German Pietism during its period of greatest vitality, which roughly covers the eighteenth century. As seen from a contemporary perspective it constitutes, at the same time, one chapter in the history of modern man's religious self-understanding. The temporal limitation which has been mentioned was imposed because toward the end of the century in question German Pietism's rival approaches to religious reality, namely rationalism, moralism, and romanticism, were in the ascendancy, and hence helped to reduce it gradually to a movement of secondary importance. Geographically our study is limited to Germany for two reasons : In the first place, an effort to reach out into all of Continental Europe would necessitate the writing of another full volume. In the second place, a knowledge of this phase of German Pietism affords the reader an insight into the heart of the movement, as it were, and thus presents a reasonably representative image of the entire phenomenon. The problem of Pietism's interaction with other intellectual movements of the time has consciously been treated as peripheral to our present interests. The reason is, of course, that a really serious attempt to say anything significant on that topic will necessitate another study of the same magnitude.

It should also be pointed out that, in undertaking such a comprehensive treatment as this, one must necessarily take into serious consideration the work of a great many scholars who are interested in pietistic developments within certain localities, or in particular aspects of German Pietism. Our debt to all such devotees of historical research, whose findings have been reported in numerous monographs and local journals, is readily acknowledged.

One hopes that the present volume may provide the general reader with an account of a significant segment of relatively recent religious history which hitherto has not been readily accessible to him. For the more serious student copious references have been included, which should open up many avenues of further research. It is hardly necessary to point out that in a study of this kind the matter of bibliography presents a major problem. The available material is overwhelming in extent. Under the circumstances only the most important secondary sources are mentioned at the end of the book. For original materials and relevant items in periodic literature the references should be consulted.

The author wishes to acknowledge gratefully the enthusiastic cooperation of the librarians of the University of Tübingen in Germany, of Mr. Charles Willard and his staff of the Speer Library at Princeton, N.J., as well as of Dr. Henry Scherer and his staff of the Krauth Memorial Library in Philadelphia. In all of these and other centers many months of research were required. Grateful acknowledgement should also be made to Temple University for granting the author the study leaves necessary to complete this work, to Miss Erna Müller and to Mrs. Luise Steele who spent long hours in typing this material, and to my wife, Marie Anna Stoeffler, who worked arduously in getting it ready for the printer.

F. Ernest Stoeffler

LIST OF SYMBOLS

ADB	*Allgemeine deutsche Biographie*
AGL	Jöcher, C.G., *Allgemeines Gelehrten-Lexicon*
AGLF	Jöcher, C.G., *Allgemeines Gelehrten-Lexicon, Fortsetzung und Ergänzungen*
BbKG	*Beiträge zur bayerischen Kirchengeschichte*
BFcT	*Beiträge zur Förderung christlicher Theologie*
BKGP	*Blätter für Kirchengeschichte Pommerns*
BMC	*British Museum General Catalogue of Printed Books*, Photolithographic Edition to 1955
BwKG	*Blätter für württembergische Kirchengeschichte*
EvTh	*Evangelische Theologie*
GBL	Goebel, M., *Geschichte des christlichen Lebens in den rheinisch-westphälischen evangelischen Kirchen*, 1862
HPE	Heppe, H., *Geschichte des Pietismus und der Mystik in der Reformierten Kirche, namentlich der Niederlande*, 1879
JbKG	*Jahrbuch für brandenburgische Kirchengeschichte*
JsKG	*Jahrbuch für schlesische Kirchengeschichte*
JsKK	*Jahrbuch für schlesische Kirche und Kirchengeschichte*
JVwKG	*Jahrbuch des Vereins für westfälische Kirchengeschichte*
MI	Meusel, J.G., *Lexikon der vom Jahr 1750 bis 1800 verstorbenen Teutschen Schriftsteller*
MrKG	*Monatshefte für rheinische Kirchengeschichte*
RE	*Realencyklopädie für protestantische Theologie*, founded by J. J. Herzog and continued by A. Hauch, 1896-1913
RI	Stoeffler, F.E., *The Rise of Evangelical Pietism*, 1965
RTL	Ritschl, A., *Geschichte des Pietismus*, 1880-1886
SSoKG	*Schriften der Synodalkommission für ostpreussische Kirchengeschichte*
SVshKG	*Schriften des Vereins für schleswig-holsteinische Kirchengeschichte*
ThLZ	*Theologische Literaturzeitung*
ZbKG	*Zeitschrift für bayerische Kirchengeschichte*
ZGnKG	*Zeitschrift der Gesellschaft für niedersächsische Kirchengeschichte.* Also *Jahrbuch der Gesellschaft für niedersächsische Kirchengeschichte*
ZKG	*Zeitschrift für Kirchengeschichte*

CHAPTER ONE

AUGUST HERMANN FRANCKE

The city of Lübeck is situated some 40 miles northeast of Hamburg. Once the head of the powerful Hanseatic League, it had fallen on evil days during the Thirty Years War and some decades thereafter. Yet, during the late seventeenth century its proud traditions were still very much in the mind of its citizenry. It was in this city, on March 22, 1663, that August Hermann Francke was born. Kramer[1] assumes that his grand-father, Hans Francke, had come from Thüringia to Lübeck as journeyman baker and remained there. Through marriage the older Francke found himself in very comfortable economic circumstances and was thus in a position to give his son, Johannes, a most excellent education. The latter, the father of August Hermann, studied at the universities of Königsberg and Rostock. Thereafter he undertook various journeys, as was the custom of the time. He established contact with some of the famous teachers of Europe and was finally awarded the degree of doctor of jurisprudence at the University of Basel. Little wonder that in 1651, three years after his return to Lübeck, he was able to marry Anna Gloxin, the daughter of another jurist who later became the mayor of the city. August Hermann Francke thus had the good fortune of having been born into a family with strong intellectual traditions and in which, therefore, a university education was a matter of course.

In 1666 Francke's father was employed by Herzog Ernst the Pius of the Thüringian house of Gotha as his legal counsel. Gotha at this particular time had become a center of religious and moral reform in the spirit of men like Sigismund Evenius, whose posthumously published *Speculum intimae corruptionis* (1640) attempted to link together Orthodoxy and morality.[2] Francke thus grew up in an environment in which Lutheran Orthodoxy and a progressive understanding of a Christian's ethical obligations were officially promoted to set the standard for both public and private life. That this kind of religious

[1] G. Krämer, *August Hermann Francke*, 1880, p. 1.

[2] H. Leube, *Die Reformideen in der Deutschen lutherischen Kirche zur Zeit der Orthodoxie*, 1924, pp. 113-114.

atmosphere pervaded Francke's home is without question, insofar as both his father and his mother were of the same mind with his employer, Ernst the Pius.

At this point it should be mentioned that one of the most pervasive religious influences among earnest Lutherans at this time was that of Johann Arndt, who through his *Wahres Christentum* helped to mold the thought and life of several generations after him.[1] At the beginning, of course, and several times thereafter Arndt's orthodoxy was questioned. Thus shortly after his death, Lucas II Osiander, Tübingen's defender of "true" doctrine, found his *Wahres Christentum* full of papistical, monarchistic, enthusiatic, Pelagian, Calvinistic, Schwenckfeldian, Flaccian, and Weigelian errors. As a result of such suspicions, however, a long list of seventeenth century theologians, among them J.V. Andreä of Schwaben,[2] Johann Konrad Dannhauer of Strassburg, and Solomon Glassius of Gotha, went to some length to declare him orthodox. Through the influence of Glassius and others the religious life of Gotha was largely shaped by Arndt. Arndt's *Wahres Christentum* was thus the companion of Francke's childhood, its meaning being impressed upon the boy by his favorite older sister Anna, whom he seems to have held in the most profound affection. It is quite understandable, therefore, that for the rest of his life Francke felt that deep indebtedness to Arndt which is evidenced in a host of references. It is interesting, too, that, as Koepp points out,[3] Francke's recommendation helped Arndt's popularity to grow until, during the first part of the eighteenth century, his *Wahres Christentum* was translated into a host of modern languages, including those of missionary territories.

From the point of view of his religious maturation Francke's educational opportunities are also of considerable significance. At the age of 16 he went to the University of Erfurt, which happened to be nearby. As he informs us in his autobiography, he there began his academic studies by concentrating on logic and metaphysics. His friend, Conrad

---

[1] For a discussion of his piety see RI, p. 202f. For a discussion of his influence see W. Koepp, "Johann Arndt und sein 'Wahres Christentun': Lutherisches Bekenntnis and Ocumene," in *Aufsätze and Vorträge zur Theologie und Religionswissenschaft*, 1959, Heft 7.

[2] Andreä himself owed a great religious debt to Arndt. He says : "Arndt danke ichs dass ich von der oberflächlichen Theorie der Religion und dem freien Leben, das sich in den unfruchtbaren Glauben hüllt, zur wahren Praxis und einem tätigen Glauben durch Gottes Gnade mich erhob." (Quoted from his *Selbstbiographie* by Leube, *op. cit.*, p. 87)

[3] Koepp, *op. cit.*, p. 19.

Rudolph Hertz, an older student, also gave him some instruction in Hebrew. The academic atmosphere at Erfurt does not seem to have been congenial to him. Thus after one semester he moved on to the University of Kiel, a move which had been made possible for him by his uncle, Anton Henry Gloxin, who was able to obtain a stipend for him. There he became a house guest for three years at the home of Christian K. Korthold (1633-1694).[1]

Korthold had both studied and taught at the University of Rostock, which was one of the prominent intellectual centers of the reform party within Lutheranism.[2] Through a series of tracts he had become known for his reform spirit throughout Germany. Because of his interest in shaping the life of the Lutheran Communion in the direction in which the reform group meant to go he had been called to the University of Kiel upon its opening in 1665. At the time Francke was matriculated at Kiel Korthold had been advanced to professor primarius and pro-chancellor. Under these circumstances his influence at Kiel was of major importance and helped to set the tone for the university's theological enterprise. Francke not only attended Korthold's lectures in historical theology but lived from day to day under his teacher's close supervision. Of the latter he says that he endeavored "diligently and earnestly to warn the students against the offensive character of the world, and to make them fully aware of the difficult calling of a preacher."[3] It was through these efforts of Korthold, Francke informs us, that the religious spark in his soul was frequently fanned into a blaze. Hence he made repeated resolutions to separate himself from "the world and its vanities," though, at this time, he did not seem to succeed. Korthold's influence did, however, move him toward a most serious quest for the reality of a personal religious faith.

At Kiel Francke had not only studied theology, but physics, philosophy, and history as well. After three years he left abruptly and went to Hamburg to give some attention to his Hebrew studies under Esdras Edzardus (1629-1708), who was willing to give free lessons to all

---

[1] For a discussion of Korthold see W. Halfmann, "Christian Korthold. Ein Bild aus der Theologie und Frömmigkeit im Ausgang des orthodoxen Zeitalters," SVshKG, series 1, vol. 17, 1930, pp. 1-82. The dates relating to his career are variously given. Compare ADB, vol. 16, pp. 725-726 with AGL-II, columns 2149-2151.

[2] See Leube, *op. cit.*, p. 63f; also RI, p. 217f.

[3] G. Kramer, ed., *Beiträge zur Geschichte August Hermann Francke's, enthaltend den Briefwechsel Franckes und Speners*, 1861, p. 35. This work will hereafter be referred to as *Beiträge*.

serious students of Hebrew. After two months under the tutelage of this distinguished orientalist he spent some time in private study at Gotha, hoping to perfect his linguistic skills in Hebrew, Greek, and English.

Shortly before Easter in 1684 Francke entered the University of Leipzig, which, in close fraternal relation with Wittenberg, constituted the universally recognized bastion of Lutheran Orthodoxy. Here he sat at the feet of the leading theological lights of the day, men like Adam Rechenberg, Johann Cyprian, Johann Olearius, Johann B. Carpzov, and Johann Dornfeld. Beyond this, so he tells us in his *Vita*, he studied the works of Johann Hülsemann, one of the defenders of Arndt, and others. He also immersed himself in the study of French, English, and Italian.

According to his own testimony the most meaningful institution at Leipzig was the *collegium philobiblicum*, which had come into existence on July 18, 1686 under the inspiration of Carpzov, and in which Francke quickly assumed a leading role. Here the more serious students, as well as some of the professors, came together on Sunday afternoon for the purpose of studying the Bible in the original languages. Initially the interest in such study seems to have been dominantly linguistic. When Philipp Jacob Spener, who had just come to Dresden, heard of it he advised the masters of the *collegium philobiblicum* that they should study the Bible devotionally and refrain from spending an excessive amount of time on difficult passages. As a result of this suggestion the original intention of the institution was modified. The primary interest of the members of the *collegium* now became religious rather than linguistic. This change was of major importance for Francke, insofar as the *collegium* sharpened most markedly his interest in, and appreciation for, the intensive, devotional study of Scripture. In reference to it he says, "I can assure anyone, that, if I consider the benefit which has come to me as a result of it, I must regard this *collegium* as the most useful and best which I have ever held at any university."[1] Hereafter Francke's interests were turned from systematics to exegesis.[2]

It was at Leipzig, too, that Francke began to pay some attention to mysticism. As we shall point out in our discussion of radical Pietism, it was especially the study of Quietism which had come into vogue, and

---

1 *Ibid.*, p. 42.

2 See H. Weigelt, *Pietismus-Studien*, 1. Teil, in *Arbeiten zur Theologie*, ed. by T. Schlatter, 2. Reihe, Band 4, pp. 57-58.

Francke was not immune to its subtle attractions. Though he repudiated it later as a reliable guide to religious experience he felt that there is in it much that is good and helpful. He was especially impressed by the emphasis of mystics like Molinos upon humility, Christ-centeredness, and the trials associated with the religious life.[1] It is interesting to find that in connection with Molinos, whose writings he translated from Italian into Latin, Francke speaks also of Daniel Dyke's *Mystery of Self-Deceiving*[2] and Immanuel Sonthom's *Golden Gem.*[3] Both of these men were what we called Pietistic Puritans with whose writings Francke was evidently acquainted. We may assume that Francke had become aware of these, and other devotional books, which had come out of the Reformed Tradition, through Korthold, whose roots were in Rostock. It is well known that the faculty at Rostock had long been open to the claims of Reformed piety.

Francke's autobiographical observations would lead us to believe that his experiences at Leipzig had done more than serve only his scholarly interests. They awakened within him the strong desire for a new religious orientation. His main aim, he tells us, was now to become a true child of God.[4] He was deeply grateful to his uncle, Anton Henry Gloxin, for getting him once again the *stipendium Schabbelianum*, which made it possible for him to go to Lüneburg in order to continue his exegetical studies. It was in October of 1687 that he undertook the journey from Leipzig to Lüneburg. Soon after he had arrived at his destination he experienced that sudden religious crisis, his "conversion," which is basic to his system of theological understandings, and which will, therefore, be treated later.

From the time of his conversion to the Spring of 1690 Francke was drawn increasingly into the Spenerian circle. This was the case especially at Hamburg, where he spent some time as the house guest of Johann W. Winckler (1642-1705). Upon Spener's recommendation Winckler had become pastor of St. Michael's Church in the city of Hamburg in 1684. Here Franke lived in close association with the other leading lights of Spenerian Pietism, Johann Heinrich Horb (1645-1695) and Abraham H. Hincklemann (1652-1695), The former had been elected pastor of St. Nicolas Church in 1684, while the latter became pastor of St. Catherine's Church in 1688. Because of the fanatical oppo-

---

1 *Beiträge*, p. 44.

2 See RI, p. 74.

3 *Ibid.*, pp. 189, 231.

4 *Beiträge*, p. 47.

sition to all things pietistic of men like J.F. Mayer, Hamburg's outstanding champion of Orthodoxy, these men emerged as the leaders of Pietism in its acrimonious controversy with Orthodoxy, a controversy which ensued at Hamburg during Francke's stay in that city.

Already at Lüneburg Spener's influence upon Francke had been considerable. At the time it was exerted through Superintendent Caspar Hermann Sandhagen (1639-1697), under whose guidance Francke had carried on exegetical studies. Sandhagen was not only a personal friend of Spener but moved decidedly in the latter's theological orb. As has been indicated, Spener's influence upon Francke was intensified at Hamburg. We are not surprised to find, therefore, that toward the end of 1688 he traveled via Leipzig to Dresden to visit Spener and stayed with him until February of 1689. From here on a common bond united the two men and they were animated by the common purpose of furthering the pietistic understanding of Protestant Christianity. In his letters Francke now referred to Spener usually as "my dear father" and he signed himself as "your dutiful son." He made sure that he absorbed thoroughly the Spenerian understanding of Christianity and that he devoted his energies to its propagation by word and deed.

During his stay with Spener Francke appears to have become sure of himself and of his theological presuppositions. This is indicated by the fact that upon his return to Leipzig (February 1689) Francke's lectures quickly developed into the major attraction for students. Three hundred strong they came out to hear him as he lectured in the great hall under the auspices of the *collegium philobiblicum*. In addition, Francke preached whenever the opportunity presented itself. The result of his activity was an increasingly noticeable change in the religious and intellectual atmosphere of the university. This is made apparent by the curious complaints which the theological faculty lodged with the ruling authorities. Students are seriously beginning to neglect lectures on systematic theology, they lamented, as well as disputations about the symbolical books, and if one mentions philosophical studies, logic, or metaphysics students only smile. If one announces a lecture on one of these subjects the auditors are so few that one cannot even begin.[1] In short, Francke had now emerged as the intellectual leader of Pietism in central and northern Germany and was soon destined to become the political leader of the same movement

---

[1] Krämer, *op. cit.*, p. 46.

as well. The movement which he led, furthermore, was to occupy the main stage of religious interest within Continental Protestantism for a generation to come.

Under these circumstances, it becomes necessary to take a reasonably careful look at both the thought and the activity of this man, who has so often been dismissed in a few lines, or a brief paragraph, as a kind of amenuensis to Spener. We begin by speaking of Francke the theologian.

Francke the Theologian

Because of the determined opposition of Johann Benedict Carpzov II (1639-1699), professor of theology at Leipzig, and his orthodox friends, Francke moved on to Erfurt, where he briefly held a deaconate at the Church of St. Augustine. Carpzov's opposition followed him, however, so that he lost his position in the fall of 1691, spent some time with Spener, and upon Spener's intercession became pastor at Glaucha and professor of oriental studies at the newly established University of Halle. When he thus arrived at Halle on January 7, 1692 the thought that was perhaps furtherest from his mind was that of becoming a professional theologian. Francke was preeminently a man of affairs, and insofar as he busied himself with theology it was for reasons of practical concern. This is not difficult to understand if we are aware of the historical situation in which Francke labored. In a relatively short time he found himself to be in a position of intellectual leadership within a rapidly developing movement, the champion of a new and ever more pervasive religious perspective, a reformer both loved and disliked by great numbers of people, and perhaps the most widely consulted educator of his day in Germany.

It was these circumstances, then, which for Francke defined the outer limits of his theological interest. The content of his theology was strongly influenced by his relation to Lutheran Orthodoxy. While he still shared the basic theological convictions of Orthodoxy, he had become a stranger to its primary task, which was conceived to be polemical. For him the basic theological concern was no longer *reine Lehre* but *das Nützliche*, or that which has immediate relevance for the Christian life. Lives changed, a church renewed, a nation reformed, a world evangelized — these were the great objectives in the realization of which he meant to employ his energies. Theologizing, therefore, was of interest to him only insofar as it served to orient the Pietistic Movement toward these ends. For this reason his theological insights are embodied chiefly in sermons and tracts directed to specific ends.[1]

Implied in this shift of theological interest is the fact that to Francke the theological task was essentially connected with a new understanding of the meaning of religion. While to his orthodox contemporaries Christianity was preeminently a matter of assent to received understandings concerning essential Christian doctrines, to Francke it was primarily a new state of being expressed in a new life. At this point Francke has been generally misunderstood by his interpreters. His central concern was not the experience of conversion and the *Busskampf* which leads up to it.[2] His real interest was in the individual's new relation to God which must lead to a progressive amendment of life. "True faith," he says, "is a divine work in us, which transforms us and bestows upon us the new birth from God, which kills the old Adam, and fashions us into a man who is entirely different in heart, soul, mind, and in all his powers."[3] To initiate this new life conversion is necessary, of course, but the emphasis is not on the means but on the result. That this was Francke's primary interest is indicated also by his basic educational aim which, as will be pointed out, was essentially that of a life progressively conformed to the will of God.

Since Ritschl's attempt to discredit Pietism by associating it with medieval piety[4] much time and effort has been invested in trying to track down Francke's theological ancestry.[5] While confessional Lutheranism has often attempted to put as much distance as possible between Francke and Luther it should be pointed out that the former thought of himself as being essentially Lutheran. As such he adhered to Luther's Christocentrism and to the Reformer's basic insights concerning sin,

---

[1] A good working bibliography on Francke, consisting of both primary and secondary sources, is available in E. Beyreuther, *August Hermann Francke, 1663-1727*, 1956, pp. 244-246.

[2] For this wide-spread misunderstanding see, for instance, the otherwise very fine discussion of Pietism in K.D. Schmidt's *Grundriss der Kirchengeschichte*, 5th ed., 1967, pp. 414-431.

[3] E. Beyreuther, *Selbstzeugnisse August Hermann Franckes*, 1963, p. 64. This work will hereafter be referred to as *Selbstzeugnisse*.

[4] A. Ritschl, *Geschichte der Pietismus*, 1884. For section on Francke see vol. 2, pp. 249-294.

[5] See E. Peschke, *Studien zur Theologie August Hermann Franckes*, 1964, vol. 1, p. 142f; also "Zur Struktur der Theologie A. H. Franckes," ThLZ, vol. 86, 1961, p. 882f; Weigelt, *op. cit.*, p. 46f; H. Stahl, *August Hermann Francke. Der Einfluss Luthers und Molinos aufihn*, 1939.

justification, the means of grace etc.[1] All of this was modified, however, insofar as he understood Luther through the Arndtian tradition.[2] Whether or not this can be called "a thoroughgoing transformation"[3] of Luther's basic theological insights is a matter of interpretation. Perhaps it would be more accurate to speak of a new emphasis, which in part is the result of the Arndtian influence, and in part the result of a changed historical situation. The combined testimony of Peschke, Stahl, and Aland seems to be that the quietistic mysticism of Molinos had no profound effect upon the structure of Francke's theology, though it probably helped to move him toward the psychologizing tendency which we find in his theological thought.[4] His Lutheran regard for the objective authority of Scripture prevented him, however, from permitting Quietism to enter constitutively into his thinking.[5] Furthermore, there can be little doubt that Peschke is right when he sees Reformed elements in Francke's emphasis upon ethics, discipline, self-control, and love for the neighbor.[6] Since, as has been said above, Francke had read at first hand some of the outstanding devotional

---

[1] Peschke, *op. cit.*, p. 149.

[2] Of considerable interest here is Peschke's summary of the Arndtian influence upon Francke. He says : "Of mystical origin and transmitted especially by Arndt is the *Urbild-Abbild* idea and the emphasis upon the identification of man's will with that of God—. Francke speaks of humility, of following Christ under the cross, of Christ dwelling in us, and of searching for the Ground. Furthermore, Arndt's influence becomes apparent in the doctrine of order, the times and hours of God, in the emblematic understanding of the process of salvation as developing upon different levels, in the high estimate of prayer, trials and the temporary withdrawal of grace, in the insistence upon self-analysis, the negative judgment upon one's relation to the sensuous, material reality, with reference especially to the so called *adiaphora*, and finally in the criticism of a merely theoretical knowledge of the truths of faith, as well as in the emphasis upon experiencing and feeling." (*Ibid.*, pp. 150-151).

[3] *Ibid.*, p. 150.

[4] *Ibid.*, p. 151; K. Aland, *Kirchengeschichtliche Entwürfe*, 1960, p. 563f. Reluctantly H. Stahl (*op. cit.*, p. 70) makes a similar concession. Peschke summarizes Molinos' influence on Francke as follows : We have reference here "to the ideas of mortification, trial, and forsakenness, as well as doubt concerning one's own state of grace, fear of illusion, self-analysis, the testing of one's own soul, the seeking for signs indicative of being in a state of grace, the mystical prayer technique, and the interest in confession are reminiscent of quietistic mysticism." (p. 151).

[5] Perhaps it should be mentioned here that we are not very much concerned about the question of the genuineness of Francke's Lutheranism, on which confessional historians have spent considerable energy. In our contemporary American setting this problem generates little more than academic interest.

[6] E. Peschke, *op. cit.*, p. 151.

books of Puritanism it must be assumed that his knowledge of Reformed piety was direct rather than mediated only by Spener, who is also indebted to that tradition.

Whether Spener's insights were more faithfully perpetuated at Halle or through the Pietism found in Württemberg is difficult to say. Francke's close association with the older man has been mentioned above. Like Spener, and in contradistinction to Orthodoxy, he emphasized the subjective effects of salvation rather than the objective ground for it. In both men the primary concern has to do with what God does now for a sinner in need, rather than with God's salvatory acts in history, though the latter are accepted as absolutely essential. The practical effect of this is that both in Spener and in Francke we read more about regeneration than about justification. The latter followed the former also in the general understanding of the *ordo salutis*, and the primary effect of divine illumination upon the will rather than the intellect,[1] with a resulting emphasis upon man's own effort in his salvation. Here Francke would say that even continuation in the state of grace depends on the set of a man's will.[2] One of Spener's assertions, which actually involved him in the so called terministic controversy, was that after repeated efforts God may withhold his saving grace from man. Francke developed this into his doctrine of *Gnadenstunden*, or special times of grace, on which a person is alleged to be dependent all through his life.[3] That Francke is preeminently concerned about the life of the Christian has already been mentioned. In this, too, he followed Spener, as he did in his doctrine of religious growth.[4] With Spener Francke emphasized the devotional use of Scripture and the need for daily prayer. While he shared his mentor's controversial hope for the betterment of the church he refrained from saying much about Spener's more abstruse eschatological speculations.[5] Thus whenever he speaks of the Kingdom of God he interprets it as a present

---

[1] See RI, pp. 240-241.

[2] *Selbstzeugnisse*, p. 37.

[3] A.H. Francke, *Predigten und Tractätlein* etc., 1723, vol. 1, pp. 58-59. This is a collection of homilies in four volumes which will hereafter be referred to as PT-1 — PT-IV.

[4] A.H. Francke, *Sonn- und Festtagspredigten* etc., 1728, p. 220. This is a collection of occasional sermons which will hereafter be referred to as SEP.

[5] A.H. Francke, *Busspredigten, darinnen gezeignet wird wie nicht nur Unbekehrte zur wahren Busse kommen* etc., 1848 ed., vol. 1, p. 191f. This is a collection of evangelistic sermons in two volumes which will hereafter be referred to as BP-I or BP-II.

reality in those who have faith,[1] and hence as an increasingly visible reality in history.

In speaking about Francke the theologian it is not our intention to present an exhaustive catalogue of his theological insights. In view of the wealth of material which is available such an attempt would be a major undertaking in itself. Within the framework of this study our attention will be confined to the central theological issues to which he addressed himself. All of these revolve around the new state of being, the quality of life which may be expected to result therefrom, and the conditions in church and society in which the new life is to be lived. While the last of these major concerns will be treated in connection with Francke's educational work, the first two need to be taken up here. Related theological issues will be discussed with reference to these primary concerns.

There is no doubt about the fact that Francke's theology, like Luther's, is grounded in his own religious experience. What Beyreuther calls "the great change in Lüneburg"[2] was as significant to Francke as was the experience on the road to Damascus to St. Paul, the experience in the garden at Cassisiacum to St. Augustine, and the experience in the tower of the monastery of the Black Friars to Luther. It seemed to prescribe for him the way in which men ordinarily enter upon a really meaningful relation to God, and it constituted for him the incontrovertible ground of personal religious certainty. For that reason he not only referred to it ever and again, but he gives us a most detailed description of what transpired. Here are the basic features of that experience as he wrote it down at Erfurt in 1690-1691 : "I had hardly arrived (at Lüneburg) when I was asked to preach a sermon at St. John's Church. Already I was in such a frame of mind that I aimed not merely at the exercise of preaching but at the edification of the listeners. While I was thinking about this I came upon the text, 'These are written that you may believe that Jesus is the Christ, the Son of God, and that believing you may have life in his name' (Jo. 20:31). With reference to this text I hoped to take the opportunity of speaking about a true, living faith and how such faith is to be distinguished from a mere human and imagined faith in the sense of assent to truth. While with all earnestness I was bent upon this intention I began to realize that I myself did not have the kind of faith for which I was asking. Thus I

---

[1] SEP, p. 524f.

[2] E. Beyreuther, *August Hermann Francke, 1663-1727*, 1956, p. 43.

was diverted from my meditation about a sermon and found that I had enough to do with myself."

Here follows an account of various experiences the narrator had and then he continues : "On the afore mentioned Sunday while in such great fear I went down upon my knees again and implored the God, whom I did not yet know and whom I did not believe, that, if there really is a God, he should save me from this wretched condition. Then the Lord, the living God, as I was still upon my knees, heard me upon his holy throne. So great was his fatherly love, that he did not relieve me gradually of such doubt and inquietude of heart, which would have been enough for me. But in order that I might be the more fully convinced, and in order that my reason might be bridled so as not to gainsay his power and faithfulness, he heard me suddenly. Even as one turns his hand, so all my doubts were gone. In my heart I was assured of the grace of God in Jesus Christ. I was able to call God not only God, but Father. All sadness and restlessness of heart was taken away at once. On the other hand, I was suddenly overwhelmed by a flood of joy, so that audibly I paised and magnified God, who had manifested such great grace to me. Upon standing up I was minded entirely differently from the way I had been when I knelt down. — That, then, is the time which I may really regard as my true conversion, for from that time on my Christianity has had substance. From that time on it was easy to deny ungodliness and worldly lusts, and to live righteously and joyfully in this world. — And since I had once made an idol of erudition, I now realized that faith as big as a mustard seed is worth more than a hundred bags of erudition, and that all knowledge acquired at the feet of Gamaliel is to be accounted as dung as compared with the glorious knowledge of Jesus Christ, our Lord."[1] This, then, is the experience which constitutes the foundation stone of Francke's theology.

As such it is the basis also of his understanding of man. It was, in fact, an analysis of his own religious condition before Lüneburg which seemed to him to confirm the understanding of man he read out of Luther and of the Lutheran symbols. In order to emphasize the difference between the old and the new state, however, he tended to state the Reformation doctrine of the inability of man to help himself religiously in the most radical terms. Peschke is quite right, therefore, when he says that Francke does not think about man in the context of creation but

---

[1] *Selbstzeugnisse*, pp. 18-25.

within the framework of man's radical sinfulness.[1] This is the reason why he sees man before his conversion as having upon him the "shameful yoke of sin" and as being a slave and servant of the devil.[2] Natural man carries within him the seed of moral corruption and is, therefore, capable of performing every evil deed unless God in his grace somehow keeps him from it.[3] Not only does the corruption of sin involve every aspect of man's nature but it also applies to everything he touches. In the whole sphere of history man's sinfulness is visible in innumerable instances of corruption and distortion. In deepest essence history, apart from those influences which result from men's conscious commitment to God's revealed will, is the realm of Satan.[4]

Over against this Kingdom of Satan, which is found wherever man resists the renewing influences of divine grace, is the Kingdom of God. It is a reality only where men have been truly born of God and have thus passed from death to life.[5] It is a Kingdom created and sustained by God's undeserved grace. Its locus is the heart of those who have freely accepted the salvation in Christ which God offers all men. Regnant within it is God's Law which is by no means abrogated for the Christian but which, quite to the contrary, now orders every relationship in which the Christian stands. In fact, the Christian's obedience to the divine Law makes the difference between the Kingdom of Satan and the Kingdom of God. Of course, to the converted Christian the Law no longer has the force of a commandment. For him the motivational force is the voice of the Spirit within, a voice which he obeys freely and gladly.[6] From day to day he remembers, too, that this is the Kingdom in which God's free and unfathomable love may be trusted utterly in relation to everything life has to offer, and that, for that reason, life in this Kingdom alone is one of overflowing joy and utter fulfillment.[7]

Because of Francke's understanding of the antithetical nature of the two kingdoms, or, from another perspective, the two states, and because of his overpowering conviction that man finds his true destiny

---

1 Peschke, *op. cit.*, p. 18.

2 A.H. Francke, *Catechismuspredigten* etc., 1729 ed., p. 284. This is a collection of sermons on the catechism which will henceforth be referred to as CP.

3 CP, p. 159.

4 See his sermon "Von den Kindern des Reichs und den Kindern der Bosheit," SEP, p. 367f.

5 *Ibid.*, p. 372.

6 CP, p. 123.

7 See his sermon "Christi Lust bei uns, und unsre Lust bei Christo," SEP, p. 151f.

only in God's Kingdom much of his preaching is concentrated upon helping to move men from one to the other. Involved here, of course, is his pastoral concern which cannot be divorced from his theology. It shows itself, on the one hand, in the fact that almost every sermon, no matter what the subject, contains passages which are calculated to effect this transition. It is apparent also in his tremendous emphasis on what man must do in order to enter this new state of being. His great fear in this connection was that the traditional Lutheran insistence upon the divine initiation of human salvation, which he accepted in principle, might be used as an excuse for not trying to take hold of God's gift. This, in fact, is the burden of a tract he wrote in 1709 to which he gave the following title : *A Short Instruction Concerning the Possibility of True Conversion to God and Active Christianity, Being a Scriptural Answer to the Frequent but Meaningless Excuse That — in One's Own Strength One Cannot be Converted or Become More Pious.*[1] His pastoral interest is also revealed in his use of Luther's concept of God's *Stündlein,* which he focused mainly, though not exclusively, upon the moment of conversion. The presupposition here is that God is utterly sovereign and thus gives his gifts when he chooses.[2] Man, therefore, must take these gifts when they are offered or suffer the consequences.

The widespread impression that Francke's chief contribution to Pietism was a rigid schematization of the Spenerian insistence upon a conscious conversion is not born out by the facts. In trying to combat this notion Beyreuther says : "The fable that Francke held to a conversion methodology in a way that was completely legalistic and insufferable, with a rigid sequence of *Busskampf* and acceptance of grace, and with a fixing of day and hour, appears ..., of course, to be ineradicable. August Hermann Francke was different !"[3] Actually he does not seem to have been interested in any given methodology. What he hoped to accomplish through his preaching was that the sinner, as well as the saint, might find the fullness of the life which Francke felt God had intended for him. Human nature being the same everywhere, he simply took for granted that ordinarily a radical change of religious

[1] In the preface he explains that there are three classes of people who use the necessary divine initiative as an excuse, namely, the unconverted, those on the way to conversion, and the converted who should be making progress. The tract is meant for all three groups.

[2] BP-I, p. 6.

[3] *Selbstzeugnisse,* Intr., pp. 11-12. For a similar judgment see also F. W. Kantzenbach, *Orthodoxie und Pietismus* in *Ev. Enzyklopädie,* 1966, vols, 11-12, p. 152.

orientation, the necessity of which he taught in common with Spener, is accompanied by appropriate feeling tones. Francke would most profoundly wish to grant God full freedom to deal with every person in his own way. In conceptualizing the process, however, and in thus making himself understood by his hearers he felt he had to set forth certain items of special moment.

In faithfulness to Reformation theology he pointed out that the transition from one kingdom to another, or from a "state of nature" to a "state of grace," is initially effected by God's prevenient grace.[1] Nothing can possibly happen apart from it. On the other hand, nothing will happen unless man in his God-given freedom accepts this gift in genuine repentence. In analyzing the psychological nature of repentance Francke, after much experience with great numbers of people, found that it was frequently accompanied by a decided inner struggle, the *Busskampf*. By this he did not mean the artifically stimulated emotional state which we associate with some forms of later revivalism. His positive model here was David who, in a moment of earnest religious resolution prays, "Create within me a clean heart, O God" (Ps. 51); while his negative model was the conventional eighteenth century Lutheran who thoughtlessly rattled off the formula of confession and then received absolution.[2] Such an earnest attempt to lay hold of a personally meaningful religious reality, to which neither St. Paul, nor Luther, nor Calvin were strangers, was fully recognized as legitimate by Lutheran Orthodoxy. For that reason even Valentin Ernst Löscher, its last great champion, never dared to question it. Francke's novelty, then, consists not in a new doctrine or a new methodology but in a new emphasis, an emphasis which must be explained by the fact that many of his contemporaries had been beaten into religious insensitivity by the wooden-headed preaching and ecclesiastical practice of the day.

In his sermons Francke frequently speaks of repentance and faith in the same sentence. The reason is that in both of these he saw essentially a human response to divinely offered grace. While upon occasion he quotes with approbation Luther's insistence upon faith as a gift of God[3] he treats it throughout as something for the posssession and increase

---

[1] PT-IV, pp. 7, 14.

[2] On this whole subject one should consult especially Francke's sermon "Kampf eines bussfertigen Sünders," BP-I, p. 76f, notably p. 82.

[3] SEP, p. 303.

of which the real responsibility is borne by man. It is interesting to find that in his sermons even Luther tends to move in this direction, while in his theological tracts he insists more radically on divine initiative in the generation of saving faith. Francke, on the other hand, wrote mostly sermonic literature. Hence we are not surprised to find that the emphasis is decidedly on what man must do in order to come into right relationship with God.[1] In repentance and faith man responds to God's grace, the result being the new birth.

In contradistinction to Luther, Francke tends to speak more of the new birth than of justification. The reason is that the emphasis here is not so much on the forgiveness of sins as it is upon a new life which ensues. "Thus the new birth must be a real birth," he says, "and it must initiate within us something that is real and true."[2] The certainty of forgiveness, which was of such over-riding significance to Luther, is assumed, of course, and, in Lutheran fashion, the new life is treated as a gift of God's free grace. Yet, at this point also Francke's pastoral concern led him to put primary emphasis on man's responsibility to take hold of this gift. For this reason he used upon occasion a term borrowed from Christian mysticism, namely *Durchbruch*. This has no Pelagian implications, however, as his opponents generally alleged. It simply puts the accent upon man's need to open himself to God's gracious influences. The difference between Luther and Francke here is that Luther is still residually predestinarian, while Francke simply decided to affirm and live with the irreconcilable paradox of God's absolute sovereignty and man's full responsibility for his religious and moral choices. In fact, much of the polemic which Francke, and especially his followers, directed against orthodox Lutheranism was focused upon its alleged unwillingness to treat man as a fully responsible agent.

The means ordained by God to bring about the new birth are, first of all, the Word. Following the Reformers Francke divided this into the Law and the Gospel. "God's Word," he says, "is Law and Gospel. Law is that which God commands, namely, what we are to do or leave undone. Gospel is the saving grace of God, which is in Christ Jesus, in which is promised the good that God wants to give us."[3] In emphasizing

---

[1] For Francke's paradoxical understanding of faith see especially his sermon "Der Glaube an Jesum Christum," SEP, p. 288f.

[2] *Selbstzeugnisse*, p. 39.

[3] *Ibid.*, p. 52.

equally the Law and the Gospel Francke unwittingly departed from Luther, however, and approached the Calvinistic Tradition. The reason is probably again his pastoral insight into the human situation. Without the hammer of the Law, he felt, the sinner tends to overlook God's *Gnadenstunden*, and without the Law the Christian cannot know what the conditions of the new life are meant to be. For these reasons Francke was able to rejoice in the Law as well as in the Gospel. He was certain that in the divine economy both have their ordained function, the one preeminently to convict and instruct, the other to give comfort and hope.[1]

In faithfulness to his Lutheran heritage Francke also spoke at times of baptism as a means toward the new life. Following Spener, however, he made very sure not to introduce any *ex opere operato* concepts into his theology of baptism. For that reason he always speaks of baptism and faith together and makes it a very special point to say that the promise of salvation is not connected with baptism only.[2] Actually he treated baptism as being both a gift and a responsibility, a sign of God's promise, as well as an occasion for self-examination. It appears to have been his belief that the baptized infant finds himself in a relation of special divine solicitude, which, however, never precludes the absolute necessity of a personal decision for God either on the part of a child or an adult.[3] At some point in the maturation of the individual personal faith must be added to baptism. In view of the ambiguity which hangs over Luther's understanding of baptism it is difficult to say just how Lutheran Francke is in this connection. It goes without saying, of course, that his understanding of this sacrament gave the Orthodoxists of his day considerable cause for anxiety.

The nature of the new state of being, into which one enters by the new birth, Francke sometimes tries to make explicit by the use of terminology borrowed from mysticism. Thus he speaks of being "united with Christ"[4] or of being "a bride of the Lamb."[5] Even Ritschl, admits, however, that such expressions do not occur frequently,[6] and beyond that, it should be stated that when they do occur they must be interpreted within the context of the Lutheran perspective.

---

[1] *Ibid.*, pp. 52-53. See also his sermon "Nexus Legis et Evangelii," SEP, p. 1495f.

[2] See his sermon "Über die Lehre von der heiligen Taufe," CP, p. 521f.

[3] *Selbstzeugnisse*, p. 26f.

[4] CP, p. 117.

[5] SEP, pp. 647, 1088.

[6] RTL, vol. 2, p. 264.

As in both Arndt and Spener there is no thought here of ontological, but only of psychological union. It is true, however, that Francke speaks perhaps more often of love for Christ than of faith in Christ. By these and a variety of other expressions he wants to emphasize that there is a radical, qualitative disjunction between the old state and the new. The new being is really a new creation in the sense of a complete existential re-orientation. He is a person who has wholly given up his "earthly, fleshly mind" (*Sinn*) and is now minded like Christ. His sins are forgiven and the power of sin is broken in his life. If he really wills to do so he has the power to follow Christ and the sensibilities to appreciate the affective rewards of such discipleship.[1] These are the gifts of the Spirit who now "dwells" in him.

The new being must manifest itself, of course, in a new pattern of life. In reading Francke one cannot be sure whether he puts more emphasis on the new birth or on the kind of daily life in which it must result. His preaching constantly revolves around both of these foci, since he was sure that one invariably involves the other.

Perhaps the outstanding thing about Francke's understanding of the life of faith is that here, as at various other points in his theology, he is closer to the Reformed Tradition than to Luther.[2] Accordingly he is wholly given to the dynamic conception of the life of faith which we find in Calvin. His tireless exhortation is that his hearers must grow in faith, grow in wisdom, grow in dedication, grow in good works, and, by the same token, that they must dissociate themselves increasingly from the "world" and from the pleasures of the "flesh." Nor can this be the result of an occasional attempt to amend one's life. It must, rather, be a constant, a daily effort.[3]

The guiding principle of the life of faith is that it must be wholly unselfish, or, to state it positively, it must be oriented completely toward doing the divine will as that will is revealed in Scripture. Francke is totally uncompromising in his application of the New Testament ethic to man's daily relationships. He did not recognize any *adiaphora* because they may lead to temptation.[4] A line of action either serves the self and is, therefore, sinful, or it serves God and is,

---

[1] See Francke's sermon on "Die Nachfolge Jesu," SEP, p. 1185f.

[2] This could be said of Spener as well. For an initial indication of it see RI, p. 231.

[3] See his sermon on "Die tägliche Erneuerung, PT-I, last sermon. Also BP-II, p. 103.

[4] A. H. Francke, *Sonn-Fest-und Aposteltagspredigten* etc. 1746 ed., vol. 3, p. 214. This is a collection of occasional sermons in three volumes which will hereafter be referred to as SFA-I — SFA-III.

therefore, acceptable in his sight. The basic criterion of moral action is what he calls the "honor of God." Thus he begins his tract on the education of children with these solemn words, "The honor of God must in all things — remain before our eyes." Then follows the instruction that the whole educational process must be informed by this concern.[1] The same attitude pervades his preaching. Anything which has to do with the "lust of the eyes," or the "lust of the flesh," or the "pride of life" needs to be resolutely rejected.[2] The judgment of Hirsch is perhaps too harsh when he says that Francke regarded all natural desires as evil.[3] It would be more correct to say that according to Francke all of man's wants and endeavors are evil unless they can honestly be regarded as serving God's honor either directly or indirectly. It is quite obvious, of course, that in the application of this principle a certain casuistry is unavoidable and that the scope of the pietistic morality will differ according to the personal inclinations of the individual interpreter. By and large Francke himself was a man of broad sympathies, of irenic temper, and of massive insight into human nature and its attendant problems.

There are five marks of the life of faith of which Francke speaks ever and again in a great variety of ways. They are "trials" (*Anfechtungen*), cross-bearing, obedience to God's Law, trust in God, and joy. It would be difficult to say which of them comes first in the order of importance, insofar as his emphasis here depends on the circumstances under which he is preaching.

In his treatment of *Anfechtung* he seems to be heavily indebted again, not only to the mystical element within sixteenth century Lutheranism, but to the Reformed Tradition.[4] In the concept of "trials" the *Busskampf* has no place. They are occasions for testing and strengthening a Christian's resolve to live the life of faith which are deliberately sent by God.[5] If he stands the test he will be a better Christian for having done so. Related to this is Francke's constant reference to

---

[1] A.H. Francke, *Kurzer und einfältiger Unterricht wie die Kinder zur wahren Gottseligkeit und christlichen Klugheit anzuführen sind* etc., 1748, pp. 1-2. This important little tract will hereafter be referred to as KEU.

[2] See especially his sermons "Die Lehre von der Bekenntnis der Sünden," BP-II, p. 272f, and "Väterliche Ermahnung" etc., BP-I, p. 21f, which details his moral prohibitions.

[3] E. Hirsch, *Geschichte der neueren evangelischen Theologie*, 1949-1954, vol. 2, p. 159.

[4] See RI, p. 193f and p. 157f.

[5] See the sermon "Der Kampf wider die Sünde," SFA-I, p. 464f, especially 478f.

suffering and cross-bearing as being an inescapable part of a Christian's calling. In a sense the cross must become the central symbol of the Christian's existence. It stands not only for the above mentioned occasions for testing, which include sickness, misfortune etc., but it must express the most fundamental attitude of the Christian toward his vocation.[1] The Christian life is one essentially of self-denial in the service of active love. God's Law has not done its work when it helps to move the individual Christian toward the experience of the new birth. Francke feels that in his new state it now confronts him at every moment of his life with God's holy demands. Yet, it is not the tyrant which Luther tended to see in it. It is essentially God's call to active love, expressed both toward him and toward the neighbor.[2] For him, therefore, in whom such love has become a settled *modus vivendi* God's Law is in reality the way to freedom. Thus Francke thinks of the Christian life as a life of freedom which compares most favorably with that of the "natural" man who is subject to the tyrannies of sinful desires.

Throughout Francke's sermons we find the repeated admonition that faith in God must be absolute, or, as he puts it, "childlike."[3] This was not simply a theologumenon with him but a principle upon which he acted in the midst of the ambiguities and uncertainties which constantly attended his career. It was his firm belief that if one door closes God in his providence can find a thousand others which he may open, and that the opening and closing is finally controlled by a love so unfathomable that man can appreciate it best on his knees. Hence anxiety simply has no rightful place in Christian experience. In its place should be joy. By this he did not mean a momentary affective response to a pleasant situation, but an attitude toward God and his world which is profoundly appreciative of all the good that is and will be. Such joy will make one's daily life almost literally a song.[4] It is this element in much of the Pietistic Movement which frequently led to the charge of enthusiasm, though in Francke, the critical professor and sober administrator, it remained an undertone rather than a goal.

It should be pointed out especially that to Francke one of the most important aspects of the life of faith was a new and profound concern

---

[1] See the sermon "Übung des Glaubens im Kreuz," SFA-I, p. 321f.

[2] See the sermon "Das vollkommene Gesetz der Freiheit," SFA-II, p. 536f.

[3] See especially his sermon "Die geistliche Seelen-Cur," SFA-II, p. 552f.

[4] See his sermon "Das rechte Lob Gottes," SFA-III, p. 151f.

for the neighbor. As a child of the Reformation he thought of such concern as being motivated preeminently by the Christian's thankfulness to God. This he states at the beginning of his sermon regarding the poor.[1] Then he mentions twenty-four manifestations of God's solicitude for men which should elicit on the part of the Christian a constant disposition of gratitude. This gratitude in turn should dispose the Christian to a constant, unvarying concern for his neighbor, and especially his underprivileged neighbor. Francke was existentially identified with the poor. So deeply did he feel about their plight that when he thought of Christ he thought of him invariably as doing good; when he walked through the fields and noticed the harvest he wondered how in the presence of such manifestations of God's love anyone could close his heart against a needy brother. Out of such considerations as these grew his renowned institutions. They are simply the concretion of a theology of the life of faith which revolved around what he called *tätige Liebe.*

One of the most incisive criticisms of the Christian life as conceived by Lutheran Orthodoxy, which was made by Spener and Francke alike, was its conspicuous lack of ethical urgency. All these people do, Francke charged, is go to confession and then take communion every three months. Thereafter they go back and burden their consciences with the same wrong-headed way of life.[2] In place of this relatively passive approach to personal Christianity the Pietists advocated what they called an "active" (*tätig*) approach. They meant to advocate an understanding of the life of faith which requires complete dedication and an investment of all one's energies. Francke was one of the foremost representatives of this concept. Hence he insisted constantly on the faithful and diligent use of those means which had long since proved helpful toward that end within the Pietistic Tradition. These are self-examination, daily repentance, prayer, hearing the Word, and participating in the Sacrament.

Relatively little needs to be said about each of these. In his insistence upon self-examination Francke almost matched the Pietistic Puritans.[3] Both self-examination and the attendant repentance for sins committed, or moral weaknesses tolerated, needs to be a daily exercise.[4] Shades of

---

1 "Vierundzwanzig Berwegungs-Gründe zu Beobachtung der Pflicht gegen die Armen," SEP, p. 1258f.

2 SFA-I, p. 732.

3 See RI, pp. 74-75.

4 See his sermon "Von der täglichen Busse der Bekehrten," BP-II, p. 1f.

the Mystical Tradition, especially Quietism, are detectable in his emphasis on prayer. In deepest essence it is an intimate concourse of the soul with Christ.[1] In Christ God is thought to meet the Christian as a friend with whom the most intimate problems can be discussed. All of it must take place, however, in the attitude of worship rather than in that of petitioning for favors. In his opposition to Orthodoxy Francke deliberately emphasized the psychological as over against the objective efficacy of Scripture and preaching. In reading Scripture or hearing a sermon the worshiping believer is brought face to face with the revelatory activity of the divine Spirit, for the Word is God's means to communicate to a receptive human being his Law and Gospel.[2] While in his understanding of the Lord's Supper Francke did not depart from the Lutheran concept of the real presence he speaks of it only rarely. His overriding concern was that of the effect of a Christian's participation upon his own psyche.[3] In order that this subjective effect may be as fruitful as possible he counseled frequent communion and intensive personal preparation for it.

Francke's understanding of the church is closely related to his major theological insights which have been detailed. With sixteenth and seventeenth century Lutheranism in general he accepted the idea of the established church. Repeatedly he let it be known, especially in the presence of separatistic tendencies, that inspite of its massive faults some good is accomplished by it. At the same time, however, he was profoundly critical of it. Upon occasion he refers to it as Babel because it lacks any kind of effective discipline.[4] In extreme agitation over its imperfections he may even call it a pigsty, citing Luther as the author of such an uncomplimentary idea.[5] Generally he seems to have felt that this "external" church is in need of a thorough-going renewal. Hence the responsible and earnest pastor must concentrate his efforts upon establishing within it the "invisible church," which is constituted of truly converted people. In this way a new reformation will take place in heart, home, and church.[6] Because Pietism as a movement had become aware of its power Francke no longer needed to depend exclusive-

[1] See his sermon "Das liebliche Gespräch der Seelen mit Christo," SFA-III, p. 99f.

[2] CP, pp. 93-94.

[3] See his sermon "Die Lehre von dem Heiligen Abendmahl," CP, p. 549f.

[4] SFA-I, p. 613.

[5] *Ibid.*, p. 605.

[6] See his sermon "Die höchstnötige Kirchen-Haus und Herzensreformation," SFA-II, p. 313f.

ly on the institution of conventicles to bring this about. The enterprise of theological education, to which he devoted much of his energy, was calculated to make it possible for the Pietists to establish Halle trained pastors in many local congregations. Thus all pastoral work within an increasing number of local churches was aimed at the ideal of reformation through conversion. Even if the church were reformed, however, it would be far from perfect. In it, Francke believed, there will inevitably be levels of dedication. On the one hand, there always is a group of church members who at best have the form of godliness but lack the substance, as Francke conceived that substance.[1] Much smaller is the group wich has made a good beginning but does not find the will to enter fully into the implications of the new state.[2] Smaller yet is the circle in which one finds "true and living faith,"[3] and which, therefore, constitutes the "true" church. Francke's major aim in life was the extension of this inner circle.

There can be no doubt about the fact that in northern and central Germany the theological insights of Spener were not only conserved but compacted by Francke into a clear-cut body of ideas which could be communicated to the younger generation with relative ease. It is this, rather than any doctrinal innovation that he may have made, which constitutes Francke's main theological contribution. In doing this he helped to shift the religious emphasis of his entire age. It was a shift from "true" doctrine to right action, from theological speculation to devotional earnestness, from ontological to psychological interest, from an intellectualized to an experiential approach to the Christian Faith, from systematic theology to biblical exposition, from that which God has done in history to that which he wants to do in every human being now, from passive reliance on God's initiative to human responsibility. Thus we find that in Francke the Arndt-Spener development had come into its own and constitutes a comprehensive re-orientation of Lutheranism toward the concerns of the modern age.

Francke as Educator

August Hermann Francke cannot be understood apart from his very impressive contribution to the field of education, and his achievements in this area must be seen in the light of his vision of the future, which

[1] SFA-II, pp. 628-630.

[2] *Ibid.*, pp. 630-633.

[3] *Ibid.*, pp. 633-638.

shaped his educational philosophy.[1] Francke was one of the few men of his day whose interests were not confined to Germany, or even to Europe, but were beginning to encompass the entire world. Thus he begins his *Great Essay* by describing the deplorable state in which the world finds itself and which is visible in all three "estates," in government (*Regier-Stand*), in civil life (*Haus-Stand*), and in the educational establishment (*Lehr-Stand*). While he found various reasons for these difficulties the chief blame, he felt, must be laid upon the educational establishment, and particularly upon the universities. In the past the latter have been places, he says, "where under the name of academic freedom every kind of wild, arrogant, and raw conduct have been both permitted and excused. And through such false freedom," he continues, "they have, so to speak, become the source of all indecency and horror — so that understanding people are afraid to send their children there, since the latter need to fear for their lives, and can hardly be sheltered from the general seduction and moral decay."[2]

Against such an impressive portrayal of both personal and institutional corruption, centered in a faulty educational system, Francke set his dream of a new reformation. It is a reformation, however, which is no longer confined to the church, but which must reconstitute all of society throughout the world. What he had in mind was nothing less than a religious and moral renewal of every segment of private and public life, or, as he puts it, "a true and thorough reformation (*Verbesserung*) of life in all estates."[3] In this call for betterment one hears echoes of Theophilus Grossgebauer's *Voice of a Watchman Out of the Devastated Zion* and Spener's *Pia Desideria*,[4] although Francke went beyond both of these men by his emphasis upon reconstituting the life of the whole community. In this he would again seem to be closer to Geneva than to Wittenberg.

With regard to the means to be employed for the purpose of achieving

---

[1] Francke's educational vision is embodied most fully in a tract to which Gustav Krämer gave the title *Der grosse Aufsatz* in 1882, and which since that time goes under that name. Francke himself gave it the title *Offenherzige und gründliche Nachricht von der inneren Beschaffenheit und Wichtigkeit des Werks des Herrn zu Halle — sowohl — als was unter dem ferneren Segen Gottes davon zu hoffen*. It was written in 1704 and most painstakingly edited by Otto Podczeck in *Abhandlungen der sächsischen Akademie der Wissenschaft zu Leipzig* in 1962. We refer to it as his *Great Essay*.

[2] *Great Essay*, p. 77.

[3] *Ibid.*, p. 48.

[4] See RI, pp. 218, 232.

such a transformation Francke also went beyond Spener. The latter still had hopes that the church could be renewed through the pastorate. For that reason he suggested special *collegia* for theological students at academic centers in which emphasis is put upon the devotional as well as the intellectual life. Francke, on the other hand, hoped for a thoroughgoing revision of the whole educational system from the university down to the folk schools. This alone, he felt, can bring the desired results. Hence his chief emphasis was on the proper training of both teachers and pastors. It was his profound conviction that if there is to be a religious and moral renewal of society the chief agencies through which this can be accomplished are the school and the church. And since the trained personnel of both of these institutions ultimately comes from the universities, this is the place where the renewal must begin.[1]

With respect to Halle Francke's aim was, therefore, a twofold one. On the one hand, he meant to set up a model educational community on all levels of the educational enterprise. It was his hope that his vision might inspire other communities to undertake a similar venture. In this sense he refers to it as a "universal work" which is to be of help to many thousands.[2] On the other hand, he hoped that Halle might supply both teachers and pastors for other communities, which might be imbued with the same zeal for religious and moral renewal which was found at Halle.

In the present context it would lead us too far afield to give a detailed description of the educational institutions at Halle during Francke's lifetime. Hence a brief sketch must suffice. As a result of his deep conviction that education must be suited to the needs of the students a somewhat fluid system of schools evolved between 1695 and 1702, which in 1698 already included 500 children,[3] a number which at his death had alledgedly risen to nearly 2,300.[4] In general the schools followed the stratification of the society of his day. Various modifications aside, there were essentially four kinds of schools :

1. The *Paedagogium* in which the sons of the nobility were educated, and which, therefore, was meant to prepare future army officers and state officials.

[1] *Great Essay*, p. 88.

[2] *Ibid.*, p. 63.

[3] G. Krämer, ed., A.H. *Franckes pädagogische Sshriften*, 1885, p. 447. This work is hereafter referred to as PS.

[4] G.F. Hertzberg, *August Hermann Francke und sein hallisches Waisenhaus*, 1898, p. 64.

2. The Latin school, which was adjusted especially to the needs of the sons of the professional and merchant classes. It was meant to prepare students for the university and thus to supply future lawyers, doctors, theologians, and merchants.
3. The German schools in which the boys and girls of ordinary citizens were given the kind of education which would fit them to become good tradesmen and housewives.
4. The schools for the poor in which board and tuition was free.

Teachers for these schools were recruited from the students of the university, largely those who needed some support. In return for their teaching they were given free meals at the orphanage. Thus the system made it possible, on the one hand, for poor students to attend the university, and, on the other, for people of moderate means, to give their sons and daughters an excellent education.

Since the Halle institutions were private schools, supported in the main by an ever growing number of interested people,[1] Francke had a free hand in instituting whatever changes he felt would be helpful. Under the circumstances this extremely resourceful educator made any number of innovations in the educational process which were meant to improve that process. One of these, namely, the close cooperation between the university and the other educational institutions has alreday been mentioned. Another was Francke's earnest attempt to bridge educationally the social stratification of his day, which, at this particular time, required both vision and courage. Thus there were always sons of ordinary burghers, and sometimes a substantial number of them, in the *Paedagogium*. Furthermore, it was Francke's instruction to the inspectors of the orphanage that the orphans are to be given every opportunity to advance according to their ability. Under the circumstances we find that in 1706 no less than 60 out of 96 orphans were preparing themselves for the university in a special Latin school, while only 36 of them were apprenticed to learn a trade. Related to this is a third innovation of Francke, namely his insistence upon giving every child an opportunity to move ahead according to its "God-given" ability. In the implementation of this policy the lines between the various schools remained fluid, many of the gifts being used as scholarships for especially deserving students.

---

[1] Francke gives considerable insight into this support in his lengthy account called *Segens-volle Fusstapfen des noch waltenden — Gottes* etc., 1709. This work is henceforth referred to as SF-1709.

Innovations were made also with respect to the various curricula and extra-curricular activities. Here Francke's fertile imagination combined with his strongly pragmatic interests in order to make Halle stand for an education that was preeminently relevant to his day. Under the circumstances the teachers at the orphan school, for instance, were not satisfied to instruct their pupils in the customary reading, writing, and arithmetic. They also had to have at least a rudimentary acquaintance with astronomy, physics, history, geography, as well as public law. The students at the *Paedagogium* were given a really varied fare.[1] In addition to the usual subjects such as Latin, Greek, and Hebrew, emphasis was put on French. Furthermore, there was to be an introduction to the principles of jurisprudence, medicine, history, geography, botany, and public speaking. For recreational as well as instructional purposes the students were to visit regularly various workshops and art studios in the community.[2] They were to have some insight into the physical sciences related to animals, herbs, trees, metals, stones, minerals, water, air, fire, etc. Furthermore, a certain elementary knowledge of basic trades such as carpentry, optics, etc. was mandatory. Not to be neglected were the elements of astronomy, music, drawing, and calligraphy. In all schools Francke counseled considerable emphasis upon good manners in keeping with the various levels of society. The value he placed upon such instruction is evident in his *Instruction in Good Manners* which he published in 1709.

For bringing about a desirable learning experience Francke relied less upon a meticulously planned curriculum than upon a core of dedicated teachers. One of his basic assumptions was that instruction without a good example was not sufficient. "True godliness," he says, "is best imparted to tender youth by the godly example of the teacher himself.[3] For that reason theological students were preferred as teachers. According to Francke's understanding of things theologues were expected to live, as well as to study, the Christian faith. Hence their teaching experience was, at the same time, an opportunity to put their Christianity into practice. Since qualified teachers were scarce, however, Francke instituted in 1707 the so-called *Seminarium selectum praeceptorum*, the function of which was to prepare teachers especially for the upper schools. Its members were young men who obligated themselves to

---

1 For details see Francke's *Verbesserte Methode des Pädagogiums*, PS, p. 289f.

2 *Ibid.*, p. 347f.

3 *Ibid.*, p. 19.

stay with the seminary for five years, the first two of which were spent in studying especially the humanities in preparation for teaching. During the last three years study and teaching were combined. Here too, of course, an *Exercitium pietatis,* at which both conversation and prayers had to be in Latin, was part of the weekly routine.

The fiction that Francke's educational philosophy was essentially oriented toward the *Busskampf* is nowhere borne out in his pedagogical tracts. What he aimed at essentially was the formation of Christian character, or, in secular terms, the development of adults who are responsible, moderate, sensitive to the needs of others, aware of every aspect of their world and its problems, honorable in their dealings with all men, devout if possible, and eminently concerned about the public good. It is quite true that in his educational writings two expressions occur ever and again, namely, "godliness" (*Gottseligkeit*) and "Christian wisdom" (*christliche Klugheit*). Yet, a careful analysis of his understanding of these concepts would seem to indicate that along with the sharpening of the intellect Francke primarily expected an education to produce the kind of person described above. "True wisdom," he says, "is nothing else but the eye in man, through which he sees what keeps him from harm and what serves the best ends."[1] To bring about a specifically religious experience, Halle style, he regarded it as "a special purpose"[2] of the educational experience of children, which, of course, the teacher should also be interested in. To that end, as well as for the building of character, religious instruction was prescribed for every educational level.

The picture of Francke as a stern task-master and spoil-sport for young people has hardly any basis in fact. All accounts seem to indicate that Halle's *esprit de corps* was excellent, that administrators and teachers lived together in a spirit of mutual appreciation and confidence. Staff and students alike were caught up in Francke's astonishing vision of world renewal, which was thought to be taking concrete form at Halle. Most noteworthy is Francke's profound insight into human nature, his sensitivity to the needs of youth of all age levels, and his constant attempt to insure individual attention to student problems. While he himself did not teach below the university level, he wrote his educational tracts in order to give direction and guidance to the entire Halle enterprise. Perhaps the best of these is his *Kurtzer — Unterricht.*

---

[1] KEU, p. 85.
[2] KEU, p. 86.

Through it speaks an eminently humane and kindly man whose chief reliance is not on the harsh school discipline of his day, but upon concerned and sensible teachers who will attempt to lead each child into a satisfying and useful existence.

Before we leave behind Francke's educational role a word needs to be said about his understanding of theological education. The reason is, of course, that he regarded the pastorate as being an essential part of his endeavor at societal reform through education. Hence, he tried to implement Spener's suggestions regarding the training of pastors and theologians by devoting much thought and effort to this enterprise.

In 1708 he decided to write down his thoughts on the subject in three Latin tracts.[1] Perhaps even more important than these, however, are his *Idea studiosi theologiae* etc. of 1712[2] and his *Lectiones paraeneticae.*[3] In the very center of his understanding of theological education was the idea that the study of theology cannot be divorced from a life of piety. "For," he says, "it is not enough that you become learned; the basis of it must be a rightly formed being in Christ."[4] He was convinced that a pastor or a theologian without such an existential religious foundation is an anachronism. In fact, he believed that the deplorable state of the church of his day was largely the result of such leadership. Hence, he advocated throughout his life that for students of theology a rigorous intellectual discipline must be supplemented by a constant, conscious striving to bring every aspect of life into harmony with God's Law.[5] To this end candidates for ecclesiastical office must not permit themselves to be tyrannized by any moral weakness. They must attempt day by day to correct their own faults. They must be becomingly grave. generous, honorable, truthful, kind, patient, flexible, mild mannered, friendly, and honest, With regard to their external appearance they need to be clean, unaffected, punctual, courageous,

---

1 They are : *Definitio studii theologici una cum adhortatione* etc.; *Definitio methodi studii theologici* etc.; and *Institutio brevis de fine studii theologici* etc.

2 This is found in PS, pp. 375-435.

3 These constitute his Thursday lectures to all theological students of the University of Halle, which he started in 1693 and continued to his death. From 1695 on they were written down. In 1726 he began to publish selections and brought out two volumes. Five other volumes were published by his son, the last one in 1736. Francke thought a great deal of these lectures, insofar as they constituted the means through which he set the tone of the university.

4 PS, p. 388.

5 See his definition of Christianity as a matter of suffering, dying, and rising with Christ, *Ibid.*, pp. 391-392.

good conversationalists, happy, and well able to order their own households. They should, in other words, be Christian gentlemen in every respect, and their theological education should help them toward that end. Hence, there must be ample opportunity for devotional practices — the reading of Scripture, of books like those of Arndt, meditation, and prayer. At times in his Thursday lectures Francke went so far as to counsel that for this reason other studies may be temporarily neglected.[1] The primary purpose of these lectures, in fact, was that of the cultivation of Christian character.

It would be a mistake to think, however, that as a result of such educational goals Francke relaxed the intellectual requirements of Halle students of theology. Before they came to the university they were already well equipped by the Latin schools with the necessary linguistic tools — Latin, Greek, and Hebrew. The center of the theological curriculum was the minute and careful study of the Bible in the original languages, a study which he called "the foundation" on which all theological learning rests. For the purpose of engaging in such study students were not only expected to take in lectures in hermeneutics and exegesis, but to further such study privately by becoming a member of one of the *collegia biblica.* In addition to biblical studies the theological curriculum consisted of dogmatics, including a careful study of the symbolical books of Lutheranism, polemics, and church history. Philosophy is to be handled circumspectly, since it can lead too far afield. Theological professors will adjust their lectures on philosophy to the needs of theological study and will guide their students into the reading of helpful philosophical discussions.[2]

Generally speaking Francke was given to the idea that the intellectual content of theological education should be restricted to a thorough knowledge of religion, specifically Christianity. Conspicuously absent from the curriculum is any mention of the classical, humanist tradition, or of any kind of literature which would tend to afford the student greater insight into human nature and problems. This very serious lack is somewhat compensated for, however, by the fact that theological students had an opportunity to teach in the various schools, and were also expected to help in the catechetical instruction of children. Francke was aware of the educational advantages of this and makes quite a point of the fact that theological education must be thus related to

---

[1] *Lectiones Paraeneticae* etc., III, 1729, p. 152.

[2] PS, p. 409.

practical concerns.[1] In this combination of the theoretical and the practical he prepared the way for the theological seminary of the future and the inclusion of "practical theology" among its educational concerns.

Francke's other Roles

While Francke made his chief contributions to the history of Pietism in setting out theological and educational goals, his other roles should, at least, be touched upon briefly. By no means unimportant is the fact that he was the originator, founder, and life-long head of a charitable enterprise which has caught the imagination and elicited the admiration of people the world over. Nothing like it could be found in the long history of the Christian church. Spener's disciple, Johann Winckler, in whose home Francke had stayed, had made only a beginning in this direction by establishing a number of schools for the poor in Hamburg. In 1694 Francke appears to have followed Winckler's example by establishing a school for the poor with seven sixteen-groschen pieces which someone had given him.[2] From this modest beginning the work grew until it comprised the institutions already mentioned. Merely to administer this whole enterprise and to supervise the constant expansion in buildings and personnel was a considerable achievement.[3] More important, however, was the fact that Francke was solely responsible for the financial support of the expansion program, as well as the day to day operational costs. In order to bring the undertaking to the attention of the moneyed classes of Europe he wrote his *Fusstapfen* in which he reported the gifts that kept coming in. Through his charitable undertakings he has supplied Pietism with the prototype of all future so called "faith" ventures, as well as with the model for the vivid expectation of concrete answers to prayer. He established a pattern, furthermore, which was gradually copied all over Germany, especially after the King himself, upon consultation with Francke, opened his orphanage for sons of the militia at Potsdam (1724).

Since Francke was undoubtedly one of the great pastors of Protestantism mention must also be made of his pastoral role. The only reason so little is said of it as a rule is that his success as an educator

[1] *Ibid.*, p. 428f.

[2] SF-1709, p. 11.

[3] A description of the ground plan of the various institutions, as it was in 1708, is found in SF-1709, pp. 3-8.

has been so dramatic. His pastoral work began at Erfurt, where on April 21, 1690, he preached his first sermon. Strangely enough it was his extraordinary success which aroused unbelievable opposition and cut short his pastorate in that city. Thus he came to Halle and became pastor at the neighboring town of Glaucha, where he first preached on February 7, 1692. Both the political and ecclesiastical circumstances at Glaucha were such that Francke, who initially was the only pastor in town, was relatively free to put his ideas into practice. It was here, therefore, where his characteristic work as pastor developed. He remained in this parish of about 200 families to 1715, and ended his pastoral career at St. Ulrich's Church at Halle (d. 1727).

Almost immediately after his installation as pastor he began catechising the children of the parish, whose religious instruction, he felt, had been sadly neglected. He also abolished group confession by the mere repetition of the prescribed formula and put into its place an individual religious interview with the pastor. Having thus gained some insight into the state of his congregation he preached a series of sermons on the training of children, in which he stressed the cooperation between home and church for the purpose of building character. His congregation realized very quickly that a new spirit was beginning to make itself manifest in the community. Yet, the charm of Francke's personality and his transparent sincerity were such that it rallied around him during a period of sharp opposition on the part of the Halle Ministerium.[1] The need to defend himself against the oral and written attacks of Orthodoxy consumed a considerable amount of his time and energy.[2] Not until the spring of 1693 did it at last become clear that his opponents would not succeed in dislodging him as they had done at Erfurt, though their attempts to do so continued.

Francke was now in a position to take up his pastoral work in earnest. It was only one and one-half years after his arrival when he published his *Glauchisches Gedenkbüchlein* and saw to it that every home in his parish was given a free copy. It outlined what he expected to accomplish at Glaucha through his pastoral activity. The preaching program which he adopted was strenuous indeed, including three sermons during the week and two on Sunday, with two sermons on repentance

---

[1] *Beiträge*, p. 277.

[2] For a running account of this opposition, and his efforts to keep his post, see his correspondence with Spener, *Beiträge*, p. 202f; also his *Apologia*; *oder Defensions-Schrift an ihre churfürstl. durchl. zu Sachsen*, 1692, to which he refers in a letter to Spener on July 19, 1692.

thrown in during every quarter. For the latter a special service of preparation was arranged the day before, which put emphasis on Bible study and prayer. To the young people, as well as the adults, catechetical instruction was available almost daily. Adults were generally catechised early in the morning and children in the evening. In conjunction with such instruction morning and evening prayer meetings were held. The evening meetings for instruction and prayer might be attended by as many as 500 young people and children. Theological students were expected to help in this instructional program. In addition to this, an hour for Bible study at the parsonage from 11 AM to 12 AM was part of the usual fare, in which children of both sexes, as well as adults, were welcome. To this must be added the many meetings for the purpose of prayer and Bible study which were held in the homes of various church members during the week. Sometimes these were attended by as many as 50 or 60 people. A rather new feature of Francke's pastoral program had to do with pastoral visits in the homes of his parishioners. These were made according to a pre-announced schedule and were again occasions for instruction, Bible reading, and prayer for the entire family group, including servants. In order to reach the men of the parish three so called *citizens-collegia* were held at stated times. The devotional literature used in all of these meetings consisted chiefly of the Bible and Arndt's *Wahres Christentum*, while the instructional literature consisted of the catechism. In order to help people prepare themselves for Holy Communion, a special hour of preparation was designated on Friday evening after the usual prayer meeting.

Until 1694 Francke bore the entire burden of the pastoral work which has been described. As his responsibilities at Halle increased, however, he gradually handed them over to others, keeping for himself only the general supervision of the congregation and the work of preaching. As a preacher he appears to have been eminently successful. Everywhere he went crowds strained to hear him.[1] This seems the more remarkable, since the sermons which have come down to us appear to lack all sparkle and originality. They are hastily put together, insufferably repetitious discourses on a selection of themes which remains endlessly the same. There are few illustrations, no interesting turns in phraseolo-

[1] The author found a manuscript at Tübingen in which Francke recorded his visit to that city. Item 15, which has reference to Nov. 29, 1717, records about a certain Mrs. Schwartz as follows : "She came over from Stuttgart, since, as result of the great commotion, she had been unable to speak to the professor (Francke) in that place." (Manuscript : *Aus dem Tagebuch August Hermann Franckes*).

gy, no startling insights. In fact, they seem to be consciously following the model of Puritan sermons, which were designed not to be "witty." Thus the appeal of Francke's sermonic effectiveness must be sought, on the one hand, in his transparent sincerity, which gave everything he said an utterly authentic ring. His hearers invariably felt that the message he brought them came directly from God. On the other hand, Francke was an uncommonly kind and gentle man, who seemed to be concerned personally about everybody's problem, without ever creating the impression of wanting to meddle in other people's business. For this reason the dirty alleys of Glaucha, with the accumulated filth of its 2,000 inhabitants, suddenly seemed brighter when the "Pastor" passed by, while its many establishments for making whiskey, and its innumerable and ill-reputed taverns, seemed a little more like the portals of hell which Francke thought they were. Thus, to a most unusual degree the Pastor of Glaucha was his own message.

Francke's interest in world missions and his ecumenical vision cannot be separated from each other, since they are simply a part of his vision of world reform. He saw the world in need of the Christian witness and felt it was the joint responsibility of European Protestantism to supply that need. Being a thoroughgoing realist, however, he was aware of the fact that any worthwhile achievement in this direction necessitated the effective penetration of the centers of political power. As a result of this insight he followed Spener's example, endeavoring to win followers among the nobility and even in the royal palaces. Thus Frederick III of Prussia, as well as a substantial number of influential men in his government, were either kindly disposed toward, or outright followers of Francke.[1] This inspite of the fact that the ruling house of Prussia was officially Reformed. After an initial period of suspicion toward Francke Frederick Wilhelm I, too, became his friend, as is indicated by the considerable correspondence between them. In fact, when in 1717 Frederick Wilhelm I instituted the Prussian school system it was based on the Halle model. A similar story could be told about Francke's influence upon many important officials in various state governments throughout Germany. Beyond the borders of Germany several ministers of Peter the Great in Russia, as well as people close to Scandinavian royalty, were among Francke's friends. One of Francke's students, Anton Wilhelm Böhme (1673-1722), was made court preacher of Prince

---

1 K. Deppermann, *Der hallesche Pietismus und der preussische Staat unter Friedrich III*, 1961, pp. 29-31.

George of Denmark, who became the husband of Queene Anne of England in 1705. Francke's correspondence with the SPCK was usually handled on the English side by Heinrich Wilhelm Ludolf, friend of Francke and secretary to Prince George.

Such a system of personal relations with the nobility of Europe had been almost accidentally established by Spener. As the older man's mantle of pietistic leadership fell increasingly on Francke the latter expanded it and used it consciously to move the world toward the reformation which he felt was needed.[1]

The awakening of Francke's interest in foreign missions as such came almost by accident, or, from Francke's point of view, by providence. In 1705 the King of Denmark was looking for two missionaries for his colonies. His attention was directed to two of Francke's students, Batholomäus Ziegenbalg from Saxony, and Heinrich Plütschau from Mecklenburg. On July 9, 1706, both of them arrived in the East Indies. Soon their letters were received back home, the first nine of them being published by Joachim Lange, a devoted disciple of Francke. Presently Francke put notices into the newspaper at Halle which he had founded. He also began to use his immense system of important connections to spread the zeal for foreign missions throughout Europe. Anton Wilhelm Böhme translated the letters into English so as to enlist English support for the same work.[2] Soon a stream of missionary gifts poured into Halle from all over Europe, and Francke had become one of the outstanding personalities connected with the rise of Protestant missions. More than that, however, he had established missionary work in the East Indies as one of the first and really dramatic ecumenical endeavors of Christianity, which revolved around a kind of Halle-Copenhagen-London axis.[3]

Francke's ecumenical concerns have been written up by Beyreuther.[4] It will be sufficient to point out here that his ecumenism must be seen, as has been said, in the light of his endeavor to reform the world by transforming individuals. For that reason he had no interest in the

---

1 Francke had approximately 5,000 addresses. He corresponded more or less regularly with over 300 people.

2 They came out under the title *Propagation of the Gospel to the East.*

3 For greater detail see R. Kammel, "A.H. Francke's Tätigkeit für die Diaspora des Ostens," *Auslandschristentum und evangelische Kirche,* Jahrbuch 1939.

4 E. Beyreuther, *August Hermann Francke und die Anfänge der ökumenischen Bewegung,* 1957.

union efforts of the ruling house of Prussia between the Lutheran and the Reformed communions, which, he felt, was politically motivated. Nor did he enter into the breath-taking plans of his famous contemporary Leibnitz, who actually envisioned the eventual union of all religions in the ultimate harmony of all mankind. While Francke and Leibnitz corresponded and felt attracted to each other, Francke believed that union in itself is not necessarily good, and that it cannot be achieved at the expense of truth. Instead of union he envisioned unified efforts of various communions for the purpose of supporting missionary, educational, and charitable endeavors.

One other achievement needs to be mentioned here. It was Francke who, above all others in the history of later Protestantism, supplied the initial inspiration to make the Bible really a book of the people. In 1710 his devoted disciple, Carl Hildebrand von Canstein, appealed for gifts for the purpose of putting out cheap editions of the Bible.[1] The result was that during the first year of publication approximately 10,000 New Testaments were sold at 2 groschen each. This work continued until in 1800 the Canstein Bible House alone had distributed over two and one-half million Bibles or parts of the Bible. More significant than the actual sales figures is the fact, of course, that Francke and his followers not only supplied the funds for this publishing venture, but they were to a substantial degree responsible for creating the market for it.

Francke is undoubtedly one of the most massive figures of the late seventeeth and early eighteenth centuries in Europe. As a religious genius he fashioned Spenerian Pietism into the most self-assured, theologically compact, as well as dynamic, religious movement of his day. In doing so he proved himself to be a man of large ideas and broad concerns, envisioning a world in which ignorance, religious and moral apathy, injustice and hunger, even war, could be progressively reduced through a determined effort to apply the Christian Gospel to man's individual and corporate needs. As an educator he inspired his generation with entirely new concepts of educational philosophy. Education was no longer to be book centered, but person centered; a school was no longer to be an institution primarily for the transmission of information, but for the transformation of human character, and for the alleviation of the evils of social caste; educational method

---

[1] *Ohnmassgebender Vorschlag, wie Gottes Werk den Armen zur Erbauung um einen geringeren Preis in die Hände zu bringen sei.*

was to be flexible and adapted to the needs of the individual; the curriculum was to be pragmatically determined, rather than based on merely traditional patterns; and above all, every child, even the sadly underprivileged orphan, was to be given a chance to grow according to his innate ability. It would be difficult, indeed, to over-estimate the potency of these educational ideas in Germany and beyond its borders. Last but not least, as a man of deep concern for the poor and the underprivileged he helped to inspire contemporary Christendom, and through it western society in general, with an entirely new understanding of their obligation to deal with social needs.

At the same time, however, it is necessary to point out that in the light of history Francke's approach to Protestant Christianity embodies various short-comings. There is truth in the frequent charge that he conceived the life of faith too narrowly when he insisted upon love for God and for one's fellowmen as being the only legitimate motivational springs for Christian conduct. Even though Francke was tolerant in the application of this norm, large segments of human experience, which make for personal happiness and fulfillment, were thus excluded in principle from the realm of man's rightful concerns. Theologically, too, Francke gave no impetus toward bridging the increasing estrangement between religious faith and secular culture, thus actually increasing this estrangement. As undisputed leader of the Halle movement he appears, furthermore, to have put too much emphasis on cultivating the favor of the very rich and powerful so as to be able to support the very poor. Because of this fundamental orientation Halle Pietism never succeeded in embracing fully the broad masses of those people who do a substantial share of the world's nitty-gritty work.

In many ways Francke stood on the boundary between the new and the old, with one foot in each of two different worlds. He still basked in the sunshine of royal favors and enjoyed the atmosphere of lordly castles, though his sympathies went out to the waif on the street; he still supported the repressive application of the principle of external authority, while intellectually be hegan to make room for a broader concept of individual rights; unconsciously he accepted the rigid class system of his day, though equally unconsciously he did much to break it down; theologically he adhered to the notion of the superiority of a particular denominational perspective, while pragmatically he regarded a certain type of religious experience among all Christians as a valid criterion for religious authenticity; he still accepted the idea that the main mission of the church is that of getting people to go to heaven, while he worked strenuously at the task of shaping earth more perfectly according to the divine design. Francke's eyes were indeed on the future, though existentially he was still rooted in an age which was destined soon to pass away.

CHAPTER TWO

THE SPENER-HALLE MOVEMENT IN GERMANY

In attempting to give an over-view of the movement with which we are concerned in this chapter it would be impossible to separate the impact of Spener from that of Francke. Theologically, as well as ideologically and politically, the lines of influence which eminated from Berlin and Halle were so blurred that it would be fruitless to try to separate Spenerian from Franckean elements, either within local communities or in the thinking of individual men. In fact, past attempts to do so seem to have been largely inspired by confessional interests which do not concern us here. As has been indicated before, Halle stands for the compacting of Spener's manifold religious insights into a sharply defined theological perspective. This being the case the present chapter will treat Halle as the main eighteenth century center of the Pietistic Movement begun by Spener.[1]

That during the period in question Halle occupied the leading position in European Protestantism needs little proof today. It would indeed be difficult to find an important Protestant development either in Germany or in Scandinavia which did not react either positively or negatively to Halle's leadership in theology and church politics. Its rise to eminence needs to be understood, of course, in the light of the political situation of the day.

The hegemony of Halle within Lutheranism is directly related to the political ascendency of Prussia. The latter began with the Elector Frederick Wilhelm (1640-1688). Motivated by a Calvinistic sense of destiny this energetic ruler determined to undo as quickly as possible the ravages of the Thirty Years War. He was convinced that, in order to accomplish this, political power had to be concentrated in a strong central government. As a result of his efforts the Prussian state gradually became a reality within the system of European states. Both internal and external security was guaranteed by a standing army. Subject rulers were expected to help in the maintenance of that army and in turn were given the necessary guarantees to secure their own positions.

---

[1] For the life and work of Spener himself see RI, p. 228f.

Essentially the same policy was continued by the son of Elector Frederick Wilhelm, whose coronation in 1701 as Frederick I, King of Prussia,[1] was the outward symbol of Prussia's rise to power. Frederick Wilhelm I (1713-1740), the soldier king, was thoroughly imbued with the political vision of both his grandfather and his father and continued their work by devoting his energies to the strengthening of the internal structure of the newly formed empire. Frederick the Great (Frederick II — 1740-1786) secured Prussia's position within the European system of states during the Seven Years War and generally led his country to unprecedented heights of internal stability and external prestige.

Of greatest moment to Halle was the religious policy of these Hohenzollern rulers.[2] It was a policy not only of religious toleration, but of trying to use religion as a cohesive force within the state. Thus the power of the state was exercised consistently on the side of the most irenical elements within both the Reformed and the Lutheran confessions. Halle having gained the reputation of being more interested in piety than in the customary polemics of Orthodoxy, it almost consistently enjoyed the favor of the court. Since the ruling family took for granted that its constituted authority within both the Reformed and the Lutheran confessions was absolute such favor had to be reckoned with.[3] A case in point is Francke's protection by the Elector Frederick III when he arrived at Glaucha in 1692. The orthodox pastors of Brandenburg were simply forbidden to preach against him. All differences of theological opinion had to be submitted to the consistory, which meant, in effect, that Frederick himself would make the final decision. Frederick, in turn, would rely heavily on the judgment of Spener, whom he had called to Berlin, thus giving Halle a direct line into the very citadel of political power. The result was, of course, that Francke's ministry at Glaucha came off to a most auspicious start.

---

[1] From 1688-1701 he was known as Frederick III, Elector of Brandenburg.

[2] For a discussion of the relation of the House of Hohenzollern to Pietism see C. Hinrichs, *Friedrich Wilhelm I*, 1941; W. Stolze, "Friedrich Wilhelm I und der Pietismus," JbKG, vol. 5, 1908, pp. 172-205; K. Deppermann, *Der hallesche Pietismus und der preussische Staat unter Friedrich III*, 1961; K. Wolff, "Ist der Glaube Friedrich Wilhelm I von A.H. Francke beeinflusst?" JbKG, vol. 33, 1938, pp. 70-102. The answer he gives to the question is negative.

[3] Frederick the Great summed up the Hohenzollern concept of church-state relations when in 1742 he told Cardinal Sinzendorf, a Roman Catholic, "In matters which do not touch upon articles of faith I am *summus episcopus* in the land, and I recognize neither papal, nor any other authority." (Quoted by H. Eberlein, *Schlesische Kirchengeschichte*, 3rd ed., 1952, p. 113).

Special mention needs to be made here of Frederick Wilhelm I, who from his accession to the throne in 1713 strongly preferred Halle's approach to the Protestant faith. At one time he is reported to have said, "I was born and raised in the Reformed religion and I shall live and die in it, but I love the Lutherans, too, and I rather go to their churches than to ours."[1] There can hardly be any doubt that by "Lutherans" he meant Lutherans of the Halle type, since he always preferred Halle pastors, and since in some sections all pastoral appointees had to have the Halle stamp upon them. Whether he followed this policy from religious conviction or as an attempt to undercut the power of Orthodoxy, the divisive mentality of which he intensely disliked, is a very much debated question. On the one hand, he insisted that he is not a Pietist. On the other hand, he preferred Halle's fervent preaching, as well as its austere way of life. Under the circumstances, he did all he could to restrain Orthodoxy. Even the most high-minded of the Orthodoxists, Valentin Ernst Löscher, was finally forced, upon the king's desire, to relinquish the editorship of *Unschuldige Nachrichten*, which had become the most distinguished voice of conservative theological opinion. It seems that after 1730 Frederick Wilhelm I came under the influence of the Wolffian philosophy and, therefore, became more restrained in his support of Halle. Even during this period, however, Halle-trained men such as Johann Gustav Reinbeck (1683-1741) continued to enjoy his confidence and were thus able to protect the Halle cause.

When Francke first came to Halle it was not a particularly inviting appointment for a young pastor.[2] The duchy of Magdeburg, in which Halle was located, had suffered heavily during the Thirty Years War. Only slowly did the salt industry, which was of major economic importance, recover from the war's aftermath. As economic and social conditions gradually began to improve the dreaded Black Death struck Halle's population in 1682 and reduced its inhabitants to approximately half their former number. As if this were not enough, two gigantic fires, one in 1683 and one the following year, reduced large segments of the town to ashes. The result of these successive catastrophes was an uncouthness in manners and morals which appears

[1] Quoted by W. Wendland, *Das Erwachen religiösen Lebens in Berlin*, 1925, p. 122.

[2] For accounts of its early religious history see W. Delius, "Die Reformationsgeschichte der Stadt Halle a/S," *Beiträge zur Kirchengeschichte Deutschlands*, 1953. For a fuller history consult K. Heldmann, *Vierhundert Jahre Hallescher Kirchen- und Kulturgeschichte*, 1923.

to have been widely known. Among Halle's ca. 200 houses 37 were establishments of prostitution. Recreation on Sunday frequently consisted of excessive drinking and brawling. The children of the poor grew up illiterate, their only playground being the narrow city streets with their open sewers and the accumulated garbage from all its kitchens.

In the hope of saving the town from complete ruin Elector Frederick III, who had acquired the duchy of Magdeburg in 1680, opened it to Huguenot refugees in 1685. After some months 23 French families arrived, to be followed by a considerable influx of others from the Palatinate and from Switzerland. These were industrious, capable people, who quickly introduced new life into Halle's sagging economy and who in the process of doing so achieved a measure of economic well-being. The result was that they were bitterly resented, both because of their relative wealth and because of their Reformed Faith, by the original members of the community. Lutheran Orthodoxy, motivated not only religiously, but also economically, unfortunately could not restrain itself from stoking the fires of jealousy and resentment.

It was under these circumstances that the Elector decided to open the fourth university within his domain at Halle (1694). This was done upon the advice and under the direction of the jurist Christian Thomasius (1655-1728), who after a bout with Orthodoxy at Leipzig had been called to Berlin as advisor to the Elector. The chief theological objective of this new seat of learning was to be that of fostering among the prospective clergy of the land the newer trends in the self-understanding of Protestantism which tended to regard religion primarily as a quality of life rather than a dogmatic system. In the mind of the court the dominant, though not the exclusive, symbol of this new approach was the name of Spener.

The Halle Theologians and Their Task

We are not surprised, therefore, to find that the first professor of theology appointed to the faculty was a friend of both Spener and Francke, namely, Joachim Justus Breithaupt (1658-1732).[1] Another

[1] Born at Nordheim, Braunschweig. Studied at Helmstädt and at Kiel under Korthold. Friend of Spener and Francke. Came to Halle in 1691 and was made the first theological professor after the establishment of the new university. Some of his major theological works are : *Institutiones theologiae de credendis atque agendis*, in three vols., 1694; *Theses credendorum atque agendorum fundamentales*, 1700, which was an extract of the

appointment was Paul Anton[1] (1661-1730, who in 1695 took the place of Johann Wilhelm Baier (1647-1695),[2] the one representative of Orthodoxy who briefly held a professorship of theology within the citadel of Pietism. In the meantime (1692) Francke had been appointed to the chair of oriental languages, only to become professor of theology in 1698. Perhaps the most prominent member of the Halle team next to Francke was Joachim Lange (1670-1744),[3] who was appointed professor of theology in 1709, to succeed Breithaupt. Of lesser importance among the first generation of Halle men were Johann Heinrich Michaelis[4] (1668-1738), who joined the faculty as professor of Greek and oriental languages in 1699 and became professor of theology the same year as Lange, and Johann Daniel Herrnschmid (1675-1723), who became

---

former work and was translated and published in 1702 by Johann Crasselius under the title, *Grundsätze christlicher Glaubens- und Lebenspflichten*; *de perfectione partium*, 1704, in which he develops especially his theology of the new birth. His many other writings are detailed in AGL-I, col. 1358.

[1] Was born at Hirschfeld, Oberlausitz. Studied at Leipzig and later at Halle. In 1692 became court preacher at Eisenach and joined the theological faculty at Halle in 1695. Among his most important works are his *Commentatis theologica de analogia fidei*, 1724; his *Harmonische Erklärung der heiligen vier Evangelisten*, 1737-1748, an exegetical work in 14 volumes. Other works by him are found in AGL-I, cols. 459-460.

[2] Baier was a mild, irenical man, whose posthumously published volume on moral theology indicates his affinity with the concerns of Pietism. So does his rather popular *Compendium theologiae positivae*. See especially pages 484-536 of the 1750 edition. His *Compendium* appears to have been highly regarded by the Lutherans of the Missouri Synod in America. Baier left Halle the year after he was appointed because of a disagreement with Thomasius.

[3] Born at Gardelegen in the Altmark. Studied at Leipzig, where he became acquainted with Francke, and at Halle. In 1697 became rector of the Friedrichs-Gymnasium at Berlin and remained professor of theology at Halle from the time of his appointment to his death. He was the most prolific writer of the Halle group, coming into print with one or two pieces every year. Because of his incessant writing his popularity as a lecturer waned after 1730. Nevertheless, he must be considered one of the outstanding Halle theologians, and the chief polemicist of the Spener-Halle theological perspective. His polemics were directed against such diverse personalities as Löscher, Dippel, and Wolff. His *Oeconomia salutis dogmatica, oder, Ordentliche Verfassung aller zur christlichen und evangelischen Religion gehörenden Glaubenslehren und Lebenspflichten* etc., 1733, constitutes a basic theological text of the Halle school on which Rambach later based his greatly expanded systematic theology. With remarkable skill Lange spread himself, in fact, over a large segment of theological knowledge, including his very extensive commentaries, and a large number of sermons. A list of his works is found in AGL-II, cols. 2249-2251.

[4] For his life see AGL-III, cols. 514-516.

professor of theology in 1715.[1] Though he was not a member of the theological faculty at the university Johann Anastasius Freylinghausen[2] should also be regarded as a member of the original Halle circle, insofar as both his books and his hymns helped to solidify the theological position of Halle. Finally it would seem to be necessary also to add here the name of Johann Jacob Rambach (1693-1735),[3] though he did his major work at the University of Giessen. His massive tomes on dogmatic and moral theology may be considered the fullest systematic expression of the original Hallensian understanding of Protestantism.

This, then, is the group who must be regarded as mainly responsible

[1] Herrnschmid was the only South German on the faculty. He was born in Bopfingen in Schwaben and studied at Altorf and Halle. He held various positions at Halle and generally acted as Francke's aid. Herrnschmid was identified with the Halle enterprise to his death. Francke's high regard for him is indicated by the fact that Herrnschmid joined the former in the conversations with Löscher (1719) for the purpose of settling their theological difficulties. His most important works are his *Disputatio de peccato acediae*, 1712, and his *De natura et gratia*, 1700. A lengthy account of his other works is given in J.A. Myer's preface to the translation of Herrnschmid's *Disputatio de peccato acediae* (*Unterricht von der geistlichen Trägheit* etc.) which was published in 1724.

[2] Freylinghausen was born at Gandersheim in Wolfenbüttel. He studied at Jena, Erfurt, and Halle. In 1695 he was made assistant to Francke at Glaucha and in time became the latter's son-in-law. Upon the death of Francke, Freylinghausen became his successor at St. Ulrich's Church and director of the orphanage. His most important theological work is his *Grundlegung der Theologie, darinn die Glaubenslehren aus göttlichem Wort deutlich fürgetragen* etc., 1703. His *Einleitung zur rechten Erkenntnis — des Leidens und Sterbens Jesu Christi* was translated into Russian. Freylinghausen is especially important as a hymn-writer. For a list of other writings by him, see AGL-II, col. 750.

[3] Rambach was born at Halle. He studied at Jena and Halle, became adjunct professor at Halle in 1726, and in 1727 was appointed as full professor to the theological faculty in Francke's place. Because of the more restrictive operational philosophy of Francke's son, on whom the mantel of general leadership had fallen, Rambach left Halle and went to Giessen in 1731. His most important works, published after his untimely death were : *Dogmatische Theologie oder christliche Glaubenslehr* etc.. 1744, ed. by E.L. Neubauer (who also edited much of Rambach's other literary output), and *Moraltheologie, oder christliche Sittenlehre* etc., 1738, ed. by C.C. Griesbach. In the light of these works Ritschl's contention that his theological method is Wolff's (Ritschl II, p. 388) is incomprehensible. He had an open mind, of course, and was, therefore, influenced rather profoundly by the Puritan tradition, having edited works by Watts, Baxter, Goodwin and others. He also edited a series of mystical tracts from both within and without the Lutheran tradition, including Jakob Boehme. In both instances, however, he evaluated these traditions critically. His literary output is breathtaking. For a list of works written by him see AGL-III, cols. 1836-1839, and especially AGLF-VI, cols. 1285-1293. See also I. Büttner, *Der Lebenslauf des — Johann Jakob Rambachs — nebst einer historischen Nachricht von allen seinen Schriften*, 1736.

for the Halle point of view. Their influence may be thought of as radiating out from Halle in concentric circles. On such a model Francke would have to be regarded as being in the center, with the two most prominent theologians, Breithaupt and Lange, being next to him. Somewhat farther out would be the rest of the first generation Halle team, and on the periphery would be the theological leadership of other religious centers which were essentially under the Halle aegis.

Having previously discussed the theology of Francke, a detailed presentation of the nuances of difference between him and the men with whom he surrounded himself would be beyond the scope of this study. Since, however, Halle was by all accounts the most famous theological center in all of Continental Europe at this particular time a relatively brief summary of its major emphases would seem to be in order.

Halle's theological accomplishment must be seen, of course, as a conscious reaction against Orthodoxy, and, by the same token, as an effort to systematize the more or less inchoate mass of Spenerian insights and suggestions. Its originality, therefore, must not be sought in a creative relation with an emerging secular culture. As yet, the latter was regarded, by Orthodoxy and Halle alike, as an intruder into German church life, alien and insidious, which can and must be vanguished by vigorous theological confrontation. The real enemy, as perceived by the early Halle circle, was Orthodoxy, which it deemed to be essentially an uninspiring, woodenheaded preoccupation with largely irrelevant theologumena, and which it, therefore, held responsible for the deplorable state of the Lutheran churches in both Germany and Scandinavia. On the basis of these presuppositions the Halle theologians viewed their task as being one of simplification, on the one side, and of intensification on the other.

The simplification was accomplished under the guidance of Francke's concept of *das Nützliche.* This stern criterion of theological relevance required that all aspects of traditional theology which were not strictly oriented toward the Christian life were either not treated at all, or given only peripheral attention. The first systematic outline of this new understanding of the theological task is Breithaupt's *Theses credentorum* (1700),[1] the whole burden of which is to show the need for a new life in Christ, how it can be had, and how it manifests itself in

---

[1] This was available to me in the 1702 ed. of Johann Crasselius under the title *Grundsätze christlicher Glaubens- und Lebenspflichten* etc.

human conduct once it has become a personal reality. "All theology," he says, "is oriented toward the end that man may regain, first of all, the divine image, and that at last he may reach the glory of eternal life."[1] He then defines this restored image as follows : It consists of the "spiritual affections of a regenerated person, i.e., the stirrings caused by the Holy Spirit in the heart and mind, as well as in the understanding and will of such a person, which prove effective in this, that God is rightly known and honored."[2] When functioning theologically, therefore, Breithaupt put the human mind under rigid restraint to admit nothing which is not rather directly relevant to the progressive and full restoration of this image. In thus straining for relevancy Halle was temporarily in the forefront of theological thinking. In fact, it set the theological enterprise of Protestantism upon a new course which has never been fully abandoned. Needless to say, under the impact of the Enlightenment the concept of relevancy was later altered.

As a result of this simplification of the theological task, the above mentioned intensification regarding the accepted aspects of theology becomes a matter of course. All Halle theology, wherever one dips into it, is an endlessly varied repetition of a few basic theological themes. If it is true, therefore, that repetition and effective communication are related, it is not surprising to find that the Halle theologians were by far the most effective religious communicators of their day. Halle's was truly a "simple" Gospel, uncomplicated by ontological speculation, epistomological frustations, or theological superfluities. Yet, the intensification was not merely related to a narrowing of content, but to a profound deepening of religious conviction. This is a factor which needs to be given further attention.

Actually the Halle approach to Protestant Christianity required not only a new understanding of the theological task, but a new kind of theologian. Spener had already suggested that a theologian ought to be a "Christian," thus introducing the distinction between natural knowledge of God and knowledge unto salvation, which was especially characteristic of Calvin. At Halle Spener's application of the doctrine of two kinds of knowledge to the professional theologian was hardened into dogma. In his *Theses credentorum* Breithaupt insists unequivocally on the necessity of inner renewal and the resulting divine illumination for the theologian. "Such inner, spiritual change," he says, "is so essen-

[1] *Op. cit.*, p. 24.
[2] *Ibid.*, p. 30.

tial that, in matters theological, nothing can be truly comprehended and put into practice, or properly and rightly executed" without it.[1] Freylinghausen illucidates the concept of illumination as follows : "Illumination consists in this, that, in his light and by means of the Word of God, the Holy Spirit represents the heavenly truth to the human understanding, and he does so clearly, powerfully, and convincingly.[2] In his lengthy section on the sentence, *Impii non sunt vere illuminati*, Rambach applies the word *impii* to teachers as well as listeners.[3] The implication that there is a distinction between theology and "true" theology, and that orthodox theologians and pastors are among the *impii* caused great unhappiness in the camp of Orthodoxy and continued unpleasantness for the Halle party. On the other hand, it made Halle an almost impregnable theological fortress, since no one among its followers felt moved to read the works of the unenlightened except for purposes of refutation.

The concept of "true knowledge" which is not the result of ratiocination, but which is the gift of the Spirit, subtly influenced also Halle's attitude toward the Lutheran symbols. Thus operating with the model of "living" faith, as over against Orthodoxy's "dead" faith, Lange insisted that only those aspects of the historic Lutheran symbols are of prime importance which are clearly related to "living" (experienced) faith. Related to this is Breithaupt's understanding of heresy, which constitutes the burden of his *De haeresi* (1697). In this work it is Breithaupt's point that mere deviation from historically approved doctrine is not heresy. The latter consists, rather, in the willful neglect or distortion of truth which enables man to be in right relationship with God. In line with this Rambach characterizes a heretic as follows : "Not any error makes one a heretic, but only the kind of error, which, directly or indirectly, damages, or, what is worse, overturns, the ground of faith and the way of salvation."[4] Thus when Halle theologians use the term "basic truths" (*Hauptwahrheiten*) their primary reference is not to historically defined dogma, but to experientially verified biblical truth. On this basis they could be quite liberal in their interpretation of the Lutheran symbols. Such liberality was a constant source of irritation

---

1 *Ibid.*, p. 34.

2 *Grundlegung der Theologie, darinn die Glaubenslehren aus göttlichem Wort deutlich fürgetragen* etc., 1712 ed., p. 166.

3 *Dogmatische Theologie oder christliche Glaubenslehr* etc., 1744 ed. by E. Neubauer, vol. 2, p. 1557f.

4 *Ibid.*, vol. 1, p. 281.

to the Orthodoxists who insisted that these symbols had to be accepted *in toto* and without any such vague distinction between truths of primary and truths of secondary importance.

As Halle's understanding of the nature of the Christian faith required a new definition of the theological task, and a new kind of theologian, it appealed to a new source of religious certainty. To it the Halle theologians refer ever and again, usually under the caption *analogia fidei*, or, as Breithaupt does, by the words *Gleichheit geistlicher Erkenntnis und Erfahrung*.[1] Lange tries to make it concrete by means of the following simile: "As is — the harmonious connection of all internal and external members of the body, so, in revealed theology, is the analogy of faith."[2] The classic exposition of this understanding of religious authority was given by Paul Anton in his *Commentatio theologica de analogia fidei* (1724). The idea seems to be that an honest, diligent, exhaustive, systematic, and experientially verified exposition of all lucid passages of Holy Scripture must yield a common understanding, and hence an incontrovertible criterion, of saving truth. The reason given, of course, is that the Spirit who inspired such a community-wide set of convictions cannot contradict himself. In modesty, however, the Halle team averred that because of the defects of human judgment even a regenerated theologian must not regard himself as being favored with the complete understanding of such a system of religious insights. Anton himself insisted unequivocally that the *analogia fidei* does not coincide with any known theological system, including his own. Nor was this Halle criterion conceived as having its primary locus in the comparative biblical studies of the theologians, which is essentially an intellectual exercise, but rather in the experiential verification of the truths obtained by the theologians within the life of the entire regenerated community of believers. As a result of such verification it was regarded to yield enough practical certainty for all regenerated Christians, theologians included, to face confidently their religious responsibilities.[3] Needless to say, this insistence that all "true Christians," which in this context meant Christians inspired by Halle, experience religious truth essentially the same way and can, therefore, utterly trust its valididy, made for deep conviction and enthusiastic witness wherever the Halle influence reached.

---

[1] *Grundsätze, op. cit.*, p. 20.

[2] *Oeconomia salutis dogmata, oder, ordentliche Erfassung aller zur christlichen und evangelischen Religion gehörenden Glaubenslehren und Lebenspflichten* etc., 1738, p. 44.

[3] Rambach, *Dogmatische Theologie*, vol. 1, p. 283.

Furthermore, Halle's redefinition of the theological task made for a new language. Like all other communities, the Christian community has, of course, early generated its characteristic language forms. This tendency has been accentuated by Pietism, however, and specifically by the Halle theologians. While this is evident even in their theological works it is especially pronounced in the sermonic literature produced by the adherents of the Halle perspective.[1] Wherever one dips into this literature one finds characteristic terms and phrases, such as "new birth," "illumination," "living faith," "spiritual growth," "active Christianity," etc., by which Halle communicated its characteristic emphases, and which served the members of the Halle group as symbols of self-identity.[2] Part of the reason for this distinctive linguistic development is the deliberate attempt on the part of the theologians of Halle to get away from the abstract language of the schools, with which orthodox preachers regularly dazzled and mystified their audiences, and to use representational, symbolical language forms. In the preface to his *Grundsätze* Breithaupt states this principle explicitly. Because of his adherence to it he uses no Latin words, though this was common practice, unless he gives the German equivalent.[3] Behind such linguistic change, of course, is Halle's religiously felt need to communicate the Gospel. The Orthodoxist, who characteristically waited for God to deal with men, could afford to display his erudition in the language of the schools while he waited for divine action. The Halle preacher, on the other hand, who felt himself to be God's chosen agency to rescue the sinner from the fires of hell, had to use a more persuasive approach. Thus in the language of Halle we find once again the unembellished directness and the burning urgency of the Puritan[4] sermon, an urgency which had all but gotten lost under the weight of Orthodoxy's *ex opere operato* concept of the efficacy of the divine Word.

As has been pointed out in the chapter on Francke the basic emphasis of Pietism, and of Halle Pietism in particular, has been misconstrued so long that it is difficult, indeed, to combat the distortions which have accrued through the years, For too long the words *Halle* and *Buss-*

[1] For a careful comparison of all aspects of orthodox and pietistic preaching see M. Schian, *Orthodoxie und Pietismus im Kampfe um die Predigt*, 1902.

[2] For a study of the language of German Pietism see A. Langen, *Der Wortschatz des deutschen Pietismus*, 1954.

[3] In this practice he is generally supported by his colleagues, though in his theological treatises Rambach falls back again into the old linguistic mishmash of the universities.

[4] See RI, p. 25f.

kampf have been juxtaposed in the minds of people, much like the words "male" and "female," the one inevitably recalling the other. Yet, as in Francke so in Breithaupt, and in Anton, and in Freylinghausen, and in Lange, and in Rambach one looks in vain for the emphasis upon a rigid methodology of religious conversion suggested to twentieth century interpreters by the word *Busskampf.* They are all one in their judgment, of course, that there must be a conscious break between the old and the new life. There is little attempt, however, at a sharp theological definition of this break, or at pressuring the individual toward a given order of psychological events. Breithaupt says simply, "The new birth is necessary" and then quotes the appropriate passages in Jo. 3, I Peter 1, and Titus 3. With regard to the "how" of it he quotes the *Apology* to the *Augsburg Confession,*[1] and then ends the section with a conscious disclaimer about describing the actions of the Spirit in the process of moving a man from the old to the new life.[2] Freylinghausen dispenses with the matter of the *Busskamp* in one sentence which has reference to I Jo. 5:4, 18.[3] Lange does not use the word at all but reverts to the term *contritio,* which he defines as "earnest and felt repentance."[4] In his whole section on conversion (p. 250f) there is nothing to support the contention in question. Rambach follows strictly in the footsteps of Lange, but adds the warning against an artificial effort at reaching the deepest levels of spiritual regret.[5]

With regard to the major themes there is a surprising unanimity between Francke and the entire Halle group of theologians. They are the new state of being and the new pattern of life which must result from it. Because of the remarkably close correspondence between the content of Francke's theology and that of his associates a detailed exposition of them at this point would be needlessly repetitious. It would seem, therefore, that an analysis of the main characteristics of the theological perpective of Halle would best serve our purpose.

---

[1] *Grundsätze, op. cit.,* pp. 276, 282. The article quoted from the apology is the following : "Likewise the faith of which we speak exists in repentance, i.e., it is conceived in the terrors of conscience which feels the wrath of God against our sins, and seeks the remission of sins to be freed from sin. And in such terrors and other afflictions, this faith ought to grow and be strengthened. Wherefore, it cannot exist in those who live according to the flesh, who are delighted by their own lusts and obey them." (*The Book of Concord,* ed. H.E. Jacobs, 1911, pp. 106-107).

[2] *Ibid.,* p. 286.

[3] *Compendium, oder kurzer Begriff der ganzen christlichen Lehre* etc., 1739, p. 63.

[4] *Oeconomia, op. cit.,* p. 253.

[5] *Dogmatische Theol.,* vol. 2, *op. cit.,* p. 1526.

Perhaps the most apparent characteristic of Halle theology, and by the same token, one of its outstanding achievements, was its shift from the systematic to the biblical way of doing theology. Freylinghausen states the point of view of all of his associates when he says in his preface : "With regard to the content of the matters treated the Christian reader will find nothing in this little book, but that which is founded upon the themes of God's Word itself."[1] Thus we have here a conscious attempt to get away from the domination of theology by philosophy and dogma, and in that way to permit the Reformation to speak once again to the eighteenth century. This was done, however, with the most critical tools available, namely, John Fell's 1702 edition of the New Testament, and it was done by the world's most highly trained experts in the ancient languages. To speak of the dearth of Halle scholarship simply indicates ignorance of the facts, or, perhaps an attempt to measure Halle by what passes for scholarship in later ages.[2] In keeping with the times Halle's critical method was confined to linguistic comparisons, of course. This, however, constituted a considerable step forward and was possible only because of the Halle introduced distinction between the *Kern* and the *Schale* of Holy Scripture. The Biblical languages, being of the nature of *Schale,* could be approached critically, while the *Kern* had to be treated after the manner of the *analogia fidei* mentioned above. What the Halle theologians meant to do was to avoid the possible extremes of biblical study. On the one hand, they did not want to treat such study as an end in itself with all the attending futility of this approach, and on the other, they did not wish to compress it into mere devotional exposition. By means of meticulous study they hoped to make the Bible a sure and certain guide to the Christian life.

A further, and a very noticeable, characteristic of Halle theology was its recognition of the individual. This heritage of the Protestant Reformation had been rather successfully submerged by the ecclesiastical reaction which followed it. The latter had succeeded in enveloping the major Protestant communions on the Continent in an atmosphere in which the dominant theological emphasis was on more or less irrelevant

---

[1] *Grundlegung, op. cit.,* n.p.

[2] Among the Halle achievements in biblical interpretation are Michaelis' annotated *Old Testament* and especially Lange's *Biblisches Licht und Recht,* 1729-1738, in seven folio-volumes, as well as Rambach's much used *Instutitiones hermeneuticae sacrae,* 1723, 3rd ed. 1729, and his *Erläuterung über seine eigene Institutiones,* posthumously published by E.F. Neubauer in 1738.

systems, and the socio-political emphasis on concern for the welfare of aggregates. It is interesting to find that almost all the polemical missives thrown at the Pietists by the defenders of Orthodoxy were motivated by the fear that these people might somehow upset the apple-cart by departing from traditional systems and commonly accepted values. Because of the fear of the Radical Reformation, post-Reformation Protestantism on the Continent, perhaps with some assist from the later Luther, had begun to worship the sacred cow of objectivity. Hence, the Protestant scholastics' *ex opere operato* interpretations of Word and Sacrament, which radically de-emphasized human effort in the appropriation of salvation. Hence, also the almost neurotic fear of "active" Christianity, which was thought somehow to detract from the glory of God, and to offend against the established order, while giving the individual a chance to do something for himself and his neighbor.

With their feet solidly in the present, and with their eyes upon the future, the theologians of Halle set themselves resolutely against these apprehensions, and fetishes of the immediate past, in order to put into the center of their effort the individual and his religious need. In this they were simply in tune with the times, while their opponents were not. Hence most of them could quietly ignore the vehement polemics of their detractors.[1] This aspect of historic Pietism, namely its progressivism, needs to be emphasized, since the present tendency is to equate it with the various reactionary trends in contemporary Protestant Christianity. That in its subsequent confrontation with the Enlightenment Halle eventually did become quite as reactionary as Orthodoxy had been in its initial bout with Pietism is part of the record, and an inevitable part, perhaps, of the sociology of history.

Related to what has already been said is the close association in Halle's thinking between theology and morality. Such an association had been much neglected by post-Reformation Lutheranism. Because of its well known insistence upon that which God must do in personal renewal, and because of its abhorrence of religious legalism, the development of moral theology during this period is exceptionally meager. Melanchthon had made some efforts in this direction in his *Unterricht der Visitatoren*, as did Baduin in his *Tractates on Cases of Conscience* (1628).

---

1 We have an example of this in Freylinghausen's reaction to criticisms published of him in Löscher's *Unschuldige Nachrichten*. (See Freylinghausen's preface to his *Compendium*, n. p.). He simply acknowledges Löscher's criticisms, but feels that they are not sufficiently significant to compel any changes.

To this were later added the voices of the Rostock theologian J.F. König (1619-1664),[1] and of J.K. Dannhauer (1603-1666), one of Spener's teachers.[2] Down to the time of Spener, however, Lutheran Orthodoxy shows little enthusiasm to move in this direction. Within the Lutheran Communion, therefore, the history of moral theology, or of Christian ethics as it is now called, begins in earnest only with the advent of Pietism. There can be no question about the fact that when Johann Olearius (1639-1713) wrote his reasonably popular tract on this subject he was already under the influence of Spener. The same must be said about Johann Franz Buddeus (1667-1729), whose *Institutiones theologiae moralis* (1711) really began to herald the new age of moral sensitivity among Lutherans, of which Pietism then became the chief bearer within that communion.

It is amazing to find that the positive achievements which the Halle school made in this area within Lutheranism have not been recognized. Already in his *Grundsätze* Breithaupt, in conscious indebtedness to John Arndt, assumes that, since Christian doctrine revolves essentially around faith and love, Christian theology must be divided into two parts, dogmatic theology and moral theology. He than defines moral theology as setting forth one's duty to God and to the neighbor.[3] Schematically, however, he does not yet separate the two "parts" of theology. This is done by Buddeus who assumes the essential relationship between *Glaubenslehre* and *Sittenlehre* and then, in a long methodological discussion tries to establish the latter as an important discipline for university study.[4] It constitutes the first serious attempt in this direction by one who shares fully most of the basic Halle assumptions.[5] Breithaupt's and Buddeus' understanding of the situation was held by all the Halle theologians. It eventuated in Rambach's lectures on moral theology, which for some years appear to have been the star

---

[1] König's tract was called *Theologia positiva acroamatica*, 1664. For the theological environment of Rostock see RI, p. 217f.

[2] Dannhauer's *Theologia casualis* was edited by J.F. Mayer in 1706.

[3] See p. 27f.

[4] See the preface to his *Einleitung in die Moraltheologie* etc., 1719, n. p. This is a translation of his *Institutiones theologiae moralis*, 1711.

[5] Buddeus defines moral theology as follows : "Strictly speaking, under moral theology we understand an active discipline (*Wissenschaft*), which according to the testimony of Scripture teaches how the regenerated are to make progress in the spiritual life for the purpose of the progressive restoration of the image of God." (*Einleitung, op. cit.*, p. 6).

attraction at Halle.[1] Both Buddeus and Rambach make a careful distinction between *philosophia moralis* and *theologia moralis*, insisting that the former is based on reason, the latter on revelation. Thus it is only moral theology which has the final word for the Christian, though moral philosophy should be treated as an handmaid. In setting out the pietistic way of life in all its details Rambach proceeds on that basis.[2] It hardly needs to be pointed out that through their characteristic emphasis, for better or for worse, the Halle theologians helped to establish a moralizing trend within modern Protestantism which has gained ever greater momentum with the passing of the years.

A further characteristic of Halle theology was its relatively optimistic view of history. This was in the main a legacy of Spener. Specifically, Spener had refused to interpret the Book of Revelation historically, as had been customary in the Lutheran Communion. He had regarded all the events mentioned in chapter 16f as being future. Thus combining the millenium of Rev. 20 : 6 with Paul's idea of the fullness of the Gentiles (Rom. 11) Spener had looked to a great future for the church. He had interpreted the millenium as an era of greatest development for Protestant Christianity, since the Lutheran (Protestant) Church will have been cleansed from its evils through God's judgments, the Jews will have been converted, and the Roman Church (the "whore" of *Revelation*) will have been vanguished by God's legions. By comparison with other millenial speculations, before, as well as during, and after Spener's time, these were relatively mild, of course. Nevertheless, they involved him in considerable controversy with Orthodoxists who were irritated by the very notion that the church ought to be as pure as Plato's Republic.[3] They felt, too, that Spener was playing into the hands of an increasing crop of separatistic enthusiasts, who in disaffection with the established church, were prophesying all manner of divinely inflicted catastrophes upon it.

It is to the credit of the Halle theologians that with the exception of Lange, they did not follow Spener with regard to the details of his eschatological speculations. In general they seem to have taken seriously the

---

[1] See C.C. Griesbach's preface to his edition of Rambach's lectures under the title *Moraltheologie oder christliche Sittenlehre*, 1738, n.p. Griesbach says that when Rambach lectured, people crowded into the large lecture hall as if the church bells had been rung. Rambach's lectures were originally based on Buddeus' *Institutiones theologiae moralis*, 1711.

[2] See his *Prolegomena* in his *Moraltheologie*, *op. cit.*, p. 6f.

[3] See P. Grünberg, *Philipp Jakob Spener*, 1893, vol. 1, p. 303f.

criticisms hurled at Spener, and, in any case, did not wish to become embroiled in a similar polemical hassle.[1] Furthermore, since eschatology is only obliquely related to what they felt was central to the Christian faith they could afford to be reticent. Hence, they treated the future with great restraint, simply setting forth Scripture passages which seemed to indicate what God had in store for his church.

Still, it was an existential necessity for the Halle group to take an optimistic view of the future of the church. With Spener they still felt that they were completing the Reformation, and that their work, therefore, had significance not only for individual, but also for corporate renewal. In fact, the tremendous drive behind the Halle movement can only be explained on the basis of this twofold objective. Because of such interest in corporate renewal the possibility of progress, both in church and society, had to be assumed. This assumption underlies the writings of all of them and becomes especially explicit in Lange. In his commentary on *Revelation*,[2] based on the famous *Anakrisis apocalypseos Joannis apostoli* (1705) of Campegius Vitringa (1659-1722), the Reformed theologian at Franeker, Lange came out with essentially the same program for the future as Spener had done — a vanguished Rome, a converted Jewry, a purified church, and a glorious age for Protestantism. His whole work is carried along by the profound assurance that light must triumph over darkness, right over wrong, and that after God's judgments have been visited upon the church, it will enter into a sabbatical period, which he describes as a holy, blessed, and flowering state.[3]

The last characteristic of Halle theology to be mentioned here is its  profound conviction that the devotional aspects of the religious life are of prime importance to both the individual and the church. This is the reason for the fact that within the space of one hundred years Halle printed ca. two million Bibles and one million New Testaments, thus for the first time in Protestant history making the Bible really a book of the people. The agency which accomplished this was the Canstein Bible House, inspired by Francke and instituted in 1710 by Carl

[1] Unfortunately they did not fully succeed in this attempt, insofar as some of the orthodox animus against Spener rubbed off on them. See preface to Freylinghausen's *Compendium*, *op. cit.*, n.p.

[2] Lange's work is called *Apocalyptisches Licht und Recht, das ist richtige und erbauliche Erklärung des — Buchs der — Offenbahrung* etc., 1730. It must be considered the most explicit eschatological statement of the Halle school.

[3] *Ibid.*, preface, n.p.

Hildebrand von Canstein (1667-1719). This is the reason, too, for the massive number of hymns, which were written under Halle inspiration, and which were meant for group as well as private worship. To a greater or lesser degree all of the Halle theologians engaged in this enterprise.[1] The most prominent and most gifted of the Halle hymn writers was Freylinghausen, who not only composed forty-four hymns of his own, but who edited his famous, and often revised and republished *Geistreiches Gesangbuch.*[2] Some of his hymns and those of his friends have permanently enriched Protestant hymnody in various languages.

The Halle emphasis on the devotional life is responsible, furthermore, for the very great amount of sermonic literature which issued from its press. Since its theology was oriented toward preaching, and since preaching was meant to be preeminently a means to personal devotion all the Halle theologians felt under obligation to preach frequently and to have their sermons published for home use.[3] No less important here are the various biblical commentaries of Halle origin, which were meant as aids to the popular understanding of the Bible. In this connection mention must be made especially of Rambach's exceedingly popular meditations on Christ's passion, which was translated into various languages and read avidly both in the old and the new world.[4]

Besides hymns, sermons, and popular Bible commentaries Halle produced a large number of edificatory tracts which had to do with specific aspects of the religious life. A case in point is Francke's little

---

[1] For a discussion of Halle's contribution to Protestant hymnody see E.E. Koch, *Geschichte des Kirchenlieds und Kirchengesangs der christlichen, insbesondere der deutschen evangelischen Kirche*, 1852, vol. 2, pp. 36-127.

[2] The first part was printed in 1704 under the title *Geistreiches Gesangbuch, der Kern alter and neuer Lieder* etc. It contained 683 hymns. The second part was printed the following year with an additional 75 hymns. (For a further history of this hymnal, see Koch, *op. cit.*, vol. 2, p. 53).

[3] Francke's sermons were mentioned with reference to his theology. Among other rather popular collections of the Halle theologians were : Anton's *Erbauliche Betrachtungen über die sieben Worte Christi am Kreuz*, 1734; Breithaupt's *Sieben Kreuzpredigten*, 1702; also his *Fünf Erläuterungspredigten über die Sonn- und Festagsepisteln*; Freylinghausen's *Predigten über die Sonn- und Festagsepisteln*, 5th ed. 1744; Rambach's sermon series on various themes, including the catechism.

[4] Its title is: *Betrachtungen über das ganze Leiden Christi — nach der harmonischen Beschreibung der vier Evangelisten abgehandelt*, parts of which were published in 1722, 1728, 1729, and 1730. The ed. available to me was that of J.P. Fresenius, 1750. Also available was a Dutch ed. of 1741, as well as the second American ed. (English) of 1833, reprinted from an earlier London edition.

book on right and wrong fear[1] and his instruction regarding the wrong use of the Lord's supper.[2] Very interesting in this connection is Herrnschmidt's four hundred page discussion of spiritual sluggishness, which is reminiscent of Daniel Dyke's *Mystery of Self-Deceiving* in its thorough analysis of the pitfalls of the personal religious life.[3] Mention should also be made of Rambach's repeated attempts to put religious insights into poetic form, in the hope that they may the better serve the edificatory needs of the community.[4] Much of the edificatory literature of the Spener-Halle movement during the eighteenth century was written away from Halle itself and will be alluded to in connection with a discussion of the expansion of that movement.

Controversies

One of the most unfortunate chapters in the history of Continental Protestantism has to do with the controversies which were occasioned within the Lutheran Communion by the rise of Pietism. In their day they were bitter indeed, being carried on with a vehemence which to the contemporary Protestant seems almost incomprehensible. The time and energy consumed by such polemics is incredible. One surmises that this is at least part of the reason why in the past historians have given considerable prominence to these controversies.[5] At the present moment they are of limited interest only. They are part of the record, of course, and they bring into focus certain differences in theological perspective. For that reason they can hardly be ignored. Yet, a detailed account of them would not serve the end which is being pursued in this volume.

---

[1] *Ein Traktätlein von der Menschenfurcht und nützliche Lehren zur Pflanzung der wahren Furcht Gottes* (available to me in the 1818 ed.).

[2] *Der unverantwortliche Missbrauch des hl. Abendmahls*, etc., 1699.

[3] Herrnschmidt's book is called *Unterricht von der geistlichen Trägheit* etc., 1724. It was translated from the Latin by J.A. Majer and published in 1724. For Dyke see RI, p. 74.

[4] Rambach's first attempt in this connection was published in 1720 under the title *Geistliche Poesien, davon der erste Teil zwei und siebzig Kantaten — der andere Teil einige erbauliche madrigale — in sich fasset* etc. It was subsequently revised and republished several times.

[5] The major work here is J.G. Walch's *Einleitung in die Religionstreitigkeiten der evangelisch-Lutherischen Kirche* etc., 1733 and 1739, which constitutes the basic source for all subsequent discussions. For extensive references to these controversies see also H. Schmid, *Die Geschichte des Pietismus*, 1863. For a contemporary discussion of certain aspects of these controversies see Deppermann, *op. cit.*, and H.M. Rotermund, *Orthodoxie und Pietismus*, 1959, which deals specifically with Löscher vs. the Halle school.

Since the Spener-Halle Movement arose in reaction to Lutheran Orthodoxy our concern here is with the controversies which ran their course between these two parties.[1] The controversial period actually began in 1679 with the publication of Georg Conrad Dilfeld's *Theosophia Horbio-Speneriana*, an attack upon Spener's insistence on spiritual illumination for theologians. Since we are primarily interested in Halle, however, only the last decade of the seventeenth century will be given attention. To all intends and purposes the period of controversy ended in 1722 when Löscher, cognizant of a situation which had wholly changed, refused to answer Lange's *Abermahliges Zeugnis*. After this there were only sporadic exchanges between the two schools, which now faced a common enemy, namely, Wolffian thought.

As one sees this controversy in retrospect it is not possible to say that both parties were equally responsible for the highly charged theological atmosphere and for the recrimminations, including banishments, which frequently punctuated religious argument. While the Halle Pietists are not free from occasional outbursts, and even personal attacks, their tracts do not remotely approach the venomous vilifications which representatives of Orthodoxy often accorded their opponents. Nor do we find among Pietists the tendency toward actual persecution of theological opponents, which, unfortunately, was the stock-in-trade in many places where Orthodoxy was in a position to wield political power. Historically, of course, the state of mind of Orthodoxy, which unquestionably caused it to be the attacking party, is understandable. As has already been pointed out, the Spener-Halle Movement was in tune with the times and thus challenged many of the most precious values for which Orthodoxy stood. Under the circumstances every passing year made it more clear that Orthodoxy was fighting for its very life. As in other ages so here, it was but a step from such collective frustration to heresy hunts and worse.

In line with what has been said it is not surprising to find that the first phase of the controversy in which Halle became involved is essentially a struggle for survival. Inspite of more than ten years of vigorous attack upon Spener the latter had succeeded not only in adroitly defending himself, but in helping his movement to penetrate one bastion of Orthodoxy after another. When it began to look, therefore, that in the newly established University of Halle, and under the direct

[1] Controversies arising between the older representatives of Halle and the school of Wolff will be referred to in a later chapter.

protection of the Prussian government, Spener's movement might gain an intellectual center the apprehensions of Orthodoxists knew no bounds. Hence an all-out effort was made right from the beginning to forestall such an eventuality.

To the sharp-eyed defenders of the *status quo* within Lutheranism the extraordinary talents of Francke to promote Spenerian Protestantism had already become evident at Leipzig. After having been there only a few months students by the hundreds flocked to hear his lectures, while other lecture rooms were nearly empty. This was an unheard-of success among universities of the day and promptly caused Johann Benedict Carpzov II, who had turned against Spener and what he stood for, to censure the new movement at Leipzig which seemed to be spear-headed by Francke. He did this, of all things, in a funeral sermon at the grave of a student who had been close to Francke. Under Carpzov's inspiration the faculty of Leipzig, furthermore, took steps to close the university to the young intruder, an action which came under blistering attack by the lawyer Christian Thomasius. Because of this animosity of the Leipzig faculty, and the threat of its political implementation, Francke left the city (1690), came eventually to Erfurt, and then to Halle (1692).

At Halle, as previously at Leipzig and at Erfurt, Francke's talents soon attracted students and towns-people alike. The result was that here, too, the immediate and vigorous opposition of Orthodoxy became apparent. Its early champion at Halle was Albrecht Christian Rothe, pastor at St. Ulrich's Church. It is generally taken for granted that he was the author of the *Imago Pietismi*[1] in which Pietists are pictured as a dangerous sect, and which, therefore, was vigorously refuted by the Halle group as it struggled for its right to exist. Rothe had published his attack the year before Francke and Breithaupt came to Halle. In a sermon he had also castigated Christian Thomasius for holding that Lutheran and Reformed Christians should have social contacts with each other and that they might even listen to one another's sermons. Thus the atmosphere at Halle was electrical with controversy from the beginning. What made matters worse was that the town fathers, as well as the local consistory, tended to side with Rothe, while the ruling

---

[1] *Imago Pietismi : Ebenbild des heutigen Pietismi, das ist : Ein kurzer Abriss der Missbräuche und Irrtümer auf welche sich der Pietismus gründen soll* etc. 1691. For the controversy this scurrilous piece of hearsay caused see J.G. Walch's *Einleitung, op. cit.*, vol. 1, p. 599f.

house of Prussia, for reasons of its own, regarded itself forthwith as the protector of Pietism.

During the month when Francke arrived at Halle (Jan. 1792) Veit Ludwig von Seckendorf (1626-1692), one of the most learned and influential men of his age, had published what turned out to be probably the most effective refutation of Rothe.[1] His effectiveness lay not only in his sane and balanced refutation of the major points of Rothe's attack, but in the fact that Frederick III had great respect for his erudition and character, and had previously made him his adviser. When his tract was reviewed and favorably received in Berlin, therefore, Rothe's cause received a set-back. Presently the clergy of Halle were directly enjoined by the Elector not to speak publicly against Breithaupt and Francke, and to bring any grievances they might have before the consistory in Berlin. In this way the local authorities in both church and state were effectively circumvented, and the way to the rapid development of Pietism in Halle was at least initially assured.

Francke's energetic program continued to arouse very severe opposition, however, on the part of the neighboring pastors. Enraged by the fact that among the people their own popularity was in inverse proportion to that of Francke, they seized upon every opportunity to hurt the cause of Pietism. Thus in July of his first year at Halle Francke felt himself forced into a counter-attack. Against his usual custom he preached a polemical sermon in which he made Orthodoxy responsible for the religious ignorance and moral degredation of the laity in the churches.[2] Though the sermon named no names and was meant to be only a general indictment of Orthodoxy, the clergy of Halle regarded it as an insult and hence a new call to theological arms. In righteous indignation Rothe hastily put together a manuscript against the major leaders and errors of Pietism and distributed handwritten copies locally. He was prevented from rushing it at once into print only by a direct prohibition from the consistory of Berlin which Francke had informed of his new difficulties. Inspite of this prohibition, however, the missive was eventually published at Leipzig under the title *Eilfertiges Bedenken*. In the meantime a controversy had ensued both at Hamburg and at Halle about certain prophetesses who claimed to

[1] *Bericht und Erinnerung auf eine neulich im Druck lateinisch und deutsch ausgestreute Schrift* etc.

[2] The sermon, preached on July 3, 1692, bore the title "Der Fall und die Wiederaufrichtung der wahren Gerechtigkeit." See G. Krämer, *August Hermann Francke*, vol. 1, p. 110.

have personal revelation.[1] Francke's original judgment upon the doings of these women was mild. Hence Rothe accused him in the above mentioned tract of being a Quaker, which, on the theological level, was about the worst accusation that could be brought against a Lutheran. Tempers began to rise until finally von Seckendorf, chancellor in Berlin, engineered an investigation by the consistory of Berlin of the allegations made against the Pietists. Francke and Breithaupt thus had an opportunity to clear themselves of the charges of heterodoxy, insisting at the same time on their main emphases — the right to hold conventicles in a home without the presence of a pastor, the right to preach "active" faith, and the need for the spiritual illumination of a theologian (or pastor). Seeing in advance that things were not going to go well for him Rothe decided to leave town.

During the closing days of Spener's life Johann Friedrich Mayer (1660-1712), one of the most fanatical Orthodoxists of the day, had carried on a vigorous controversy with him, and especially with his friend and disciple Johann Heinrich Horb (1645-1695).[2] It had been occasioned by Horb's local distribution of a tract whose authorship he did not know, but which turned out to have been by the French mystic Peter Poiret.[3] Mayer decided that it was heretical and that an issue should be made of it.[4] The controversy finally died down when Horb was forced to look for a pastorate elsewhere. This, however, left Mayer free to turn his boundless energy for polemics in a different direction. The victim was Francke, who in his magazine *Observationes biblicae* (Jan. to Sept. 1695) had dared to correct Luther's translation

[1] Surreptitiously some letters sent to Francke by such prophetesses had been pilfered and published in such a way that the impression had been created that Francke approved of illuminism. Francke finally dissociated himself from such illuminism in his *Entdeckung der Bossheit* etc., 1692.

[2] The controversy stirred up the whole city. Ca. 200 pieces of controversial litterature were produced, many of which are found in a massive volume called *Mayer-Horbianische Acten*, which has neither continuous pagination nor date of publication. Most of the tracts are dated 1693 or 1694.

[3] The name of the tract, translated from the French into German, was *Die vertädigte Klugheit der Gerechten, die Kinder nach den wahren Gründen des Christentums von der Welt zu dem Herrn zu erziehen* etc., 1693. It is included in the first part of the volume mentioned above.

[4] This he did in his *Warnung an die werte Stadt Hamburg* etc., 1693, also included in the same volume. Mayer could bleat like a lamb and roar like a lion, depending on the desired effect. The "lamb" side of his dual personality is evident on the title page of his *Warnung*, the "lion" side in his mean-spirited preface. For an insight into his copious literary activity see F.L. Hoffmann, *D. Johann Friedrich Mayer* etc., 1865.

of the Bible. Francke had done this against the advice of Spener and Kaspar Schade who agreed with him, but who felt that it would stir up more controversy. Francke, more interested in truth than in peace, had proceeded anyway. Presently Mayer became aware of the enterprise and condemned the venture as inspired by Satan and as another effort to attack the precious Lutheran faith.[1] In the May number of his *Observationes* Francke answered Mayer, defending his position and clarifying his attitude toward Luther and the Lutheran symbols. This led to other attacks upon the theological perspective of Halle, which were intensified by Spener's death in 1705. In brief succession Mayer wrote two tracts against Francke, in one of which he deliberately tried to equate the theological position of Halle with that of people like Eva von Buttlar and J.C. Dippel.[2] This was such a scurrilous attack that the faculty of Halle commissioned Breithaupt to answer it.[3] Mayer, of course, was under the inner necessity to respond. Nevertheless, Breithaupt's answer may be considered the terminus of the first phase of the controversy in which Halle was involved. The main champions had been Rothe, Mayer, and Francke, though others had joined in the fray, such as Johann Heinrich Knoblach, Christian Serpilus, and Theodor Sassov on the orthodox side, and Breithaupt, Michaelis, and Johann Melchior Krafft on Francke's side.[4]

In following this initial phase of the theological battle between Orthodoxy and Halle one becomes convinced that behind Orthodoxy's various accusations of heresy and irregularity there is the desparate struggle for retention of power by cultivating the good will of the secular authorities. Halle, on the other hand, was equally bent upon establishing itself by the same means. This is born out by the fact that both sides constantly appealed to the secular government for a justification of their position and submitted elaborate theological statements in order to substantiate their point of view. It becomes especially explicit in the crisis which developed in 1699 when the very existence of Halle developed into a test of political strength between the authori-

---

[1] His tract bore the title *Anweisung zum recht lutherischen Gebrauch der Psalterbücher*. See H. Schmid, *Geschichte der Pietismus*, 1863, p. 314f.

[2] This was done in his *Eines schwedischen theologi kurzer Bericht von Pietisten*, 1705, republished by him with a new preface in 1707.

[3] This was done in *Der theologischen Fakultät auf der Universität Halle Verantwortung* etc., 1707, mentioned by Schmid, *op. cit.*, p. 319.

[4] For a more detailed account of this phase of the controversy see especially Walch, *op. cit.*, vol. 1, p. 719f; also vol. 5, p. 43f.

ties of the County of Magdeburg and the government at Berlin.[1] The straining for such political advantage was inevitable, of course, because of the church-state relationship which obtained. No theological perspective could maintain itself without political backing. Even Halle's success must in part be attributed to its relations with the Prussian government, which, as has been said, were generally amicable.[2]

In the second phase of the controversy the champions were Valentin Ernst Löscher (1673-1749)[3] and Halle's chief controversialist Joachim Lange. Both men were superbly equipped for the task of being spokesman for their party. Löscher excelled especially in general and historical knowledge, while Lange was the better linguist. Actually the contest between the two was unfortunate, even on a personal level, because they had so much in common. Löscher was a deeply sincere man, who honestly held that the rise of Pietism was a profound tragedy, an insidious illness of the spirit, which for traditional Lutheranism could spell nothing but trouble. "What is the saddest thing of all," he laments in 1711. "is that it looks more and more like a schism, or some other, similar disaster," and then he details the "serious weaknesses" of Pietism which cause him such concern.[4] Coupled with such genuine interest in the welfare of his communion was a life of piety which had adopted many of the features of Pietism. His sense of restraint and propriety even entered into his polemics, so that he compares well with Lange who does not always succeed in hiding his arrogance. The latter, on the other hand, was equally convinced that without the Halle corrective Lutheranism will be lost. In saying this he was less disciplined than his opponent, but possibly more effective. It was his honest belief that Löscher was essentially a ruthless troublemaker, whose irresponsible allegations against the Pietists were the main

[1] For the full story see Deppermann, *op. cit.*, p. 119f.

[2] For an account of the critical period between Halle and Berlin see Deppermann, p. 155f. Berlin's major disagreement with Halle had to do with Halle's lack of enthusiasm for the union schemes of the king. It would seem to speak well, however, of Francke's independence in matters of religious conviction.

[3] Löscher became professor at Wittenberg in 1707 and superintendent and head of the consistory at Dresden in 1709. He is generally considered the last, and perhaps the greatest, representative of Lutheran Orthodoxy. For his life and work see M. Von Engelhardt, *Valentin Ernst Löscher nach seinem Leben und Wirken*, 2nd ed., 1856; and F. Blankmeister, *Der Prophet von Kursachsen*, 1920.

[4] *Unschuldige Nachrichten von alten und neuen theologischen Sachen* etc., 1711, pp. 681, 687-710.

cause for contemporary ecclesiastical unrest.[1] To the mind of Lange Löscher no longer represented Protestantism in general, or Lutheranism in particular, but only a clique of conservative die-hards, who made up in stubbornness what they lacked in religious substance. Both men tried hard to get away from the type of *argumentum ad hominem*, which had previously been so prominent. Because of the emotionally charged atmosphere, however, they did not always succeed.

As over against the first phase of the controversy the contest between Löscher and Lange was essentially theological.[2] Moreover, the whole conflict was deeply tragic, since both men shared the convictions of traditional Lutheranism — emphasis on the Word as found in a thoroughly trustworthy Scripture, on God-given faith relative to human salvation, on the dominical sacraments as means of grace, on the hermeneutical need for the judgment of the community as espressed in the Lutheran symbols, on the necessity of a reliable doctrinal expression of religious insights, and on the legitimacy of the voice of the secular authority in church affairs. Amazingly enough, they shared many of the same fears as well. This becomes quite evident when one compares Löscher's catalogue of pietistic weaknesses with Lange's understanding of the "middle way."[3] The difference between them, therefore, was essentially one of theological perspective conditioned by differences in temperament — Löscher being dominantly a traditionalist, Lange a pragmatist; Löscher tending to put his trust in what he thought were objectively demonstrable certainties, Lange in what he regarded as experientially verifiable truths; Löscher preferring to stand by what had been proved true in corporate experience, Lange preferring to give more room to individual predilection and conscience; Löscher finding repose in the validity of a painfully constructed system, Lange in the consensus of like-minded men; Löscher looking for the golden age in the past, Lange in the future. Unfortunately, both men did not understand the nature of their differences, any more than did their followers.

---

[1] See especially his introduction to his *Apologetische Erläuterung der neuesten Historie*, 1719, p. 6f.

[2] For a thorough discussion of this contest see H.M. Rotermund, *Orthodoxie und Pietismus; Valentin Ernst Löschers "Timotheus Verinus" in der Auseinandersetsung mit der Schule August Hermann Franckes*, 1959.

[3] See *Unschuldige Nachrichten*, 1711, pp. 687-710, and Lange's *Die richtige Mittelstrasse zwischen den Abwegen der Absonderung von der äusseren Gemeinschaft der Kirche, wie der pabstischen Ketzermacherei*, 1712, an abstract of which he gives in his *Apoligetische Erläuterung, op. cit.*, pp. 85-198. See especially his various sections on *Abwege zur Linken.*

Hence they kept on detailing and "refuting" individual "errors" of their opponents, without ever coming to grips with the fundamental issue of theological perspective. The result was, of course, that they succeeded only in convincing themselves and their followers of the obstinacy and wrong-headedness of their opponents.

The substance of the controversy comes into view if we try to understand what seemed to be the major fears on each side. A careful review of Löscher's allegations and criticisms regarding Pietism reveals that either consciously or unconsciously he was at war with what he felt were three major enemies of his church and its faith. First among these was what he took to be an inexcusable indifference toward the inherited norms of faith, thought, and practice. Since he saw such indifference in the unionism eminating from Berlin, in Pietism, and later on in Wolffian philosophy, he opposed all three, though at this time he regarded Pietism as the chief offender. This is the reason why he did not treat Pietism as a heresy, but rather as a sickness, calling it *malum Pietisticum*. This is why he was so disconcerted about Pietism's tendency to "mix together things dissimilar," its habit of stressing piety rather than doctrinal correctness, its apparent degrading of the pastoral office by recognizing the charisma of the laity etc. Through Pietism the rising indifference of his age to inherited norms seemed to him to infiltrate the thinking and the life of the church.

A second major fear of Löscher as he watched the goings on of his day is related to what has been said. It was the fear of a constantly rising individualism. This individualism, which came to full bloom in the Enlightenment, was already sending ahead its shock waves in the reports of philosophical developments coming from England and France, as well as in the philosophy of Leibnitz. Again it seemed to find its way into the church preeminently through Pietism. This explains why during the early issues of *Unschuldige Nachrichten* Löscher pays considerable attention to the illuministic, radical, mystical segment of Pietism, which appeared to put subjective revelations in the place of corporately approved interpretations. This explains, too, why the Spener-Halle Movement's somewhat irresolute rejection of mystical books of devotion seemed to him to be such a serious indication of the structural defects of its theology. In fact, Halle's basic approach to theology, which was biblical rather than systematic, seemed to be an unfortunate aberration from this point of view. Through a contextual approach to the meaning of individual passages, as well as through the unprecedented use of linguistic tools, the Halle theologians seemed to open the door to a pandoras box of individualistic hermeneutical vagaries. If one adds to this Halle's reconstitution of the basic rules of homiletics and pastoral practice one need not even look beyond it to Gottfried Arnold's redefinition of heresy, or Dippel's disdain for the organized church, to realize why a man like Löscher meant to give his all to check such rampant individualism.

Löscher's third major fear was that of reckless enthusiasm, or the tendency of his age to substitute emotional satisfaction for reasoned positions. This incipient romanticism, which tends to think psychologically rather than ontologically, which prefers to look for the locus of certainty in religious experience rather than in what the Puritans had called "godly logic," seemed like a very special source of mischief to the observer at Wittenberg. Thus the very warmth with which the Pietists spoke and wrote, their concrete emphasis on love for God and man, their well publicized charitable endeavors, their direct concern for human need seemed like a melody sung off key — not really wrong, yet grating on the sensibilities of one who expects true pitch. More than that, however, to Löscher the note of enthusiasm in pietistic theology seemed to distort much of what Pietists said. After all, they had inverted the traditionally recognized order. Instead of adapting life to the System, they really seemed to be hell-bent upon adapting the System to life. "They teach—," he complains, "that the necessity of good works for salvation must not be denied but granted." Such a doctrinal stance "is highly dangerous, and is in opposition to the clear words of the Formula of Concord."[1] In this he echoed the constant carping of his party against "active faith." Behind it is the obvious fear that pietistic enthusiasm for Christian conduct might play havoc with the established understanding of the temporal succession of events in the *ordo salutis*, thus giving man the initiative in salvation. What Löscher did not realize, of course, was that the Halle men, against whom he constantly polemicizes, had no such intention. The fact was that they operated essentially with psychological rather than ontological categories and hence felt the orthodox distinction to be nothing but needless pedantry, it being clearly impossible to distinguish between divine and human agency in the human psyche.

Lange's fears and goals, on the other hand, are implicit in the pietistic understanding of the Protestant faith which has been variously discussed. Hence they need not be detailed here.

---

1 *Unschuldige Nachrichten*, 1711, pp. 698, 699.

The Löscher-Lange controversy as such grew out of the severe tension which had developed between Orthodoxists and Pietists. Actually Lange had written several polemical tracts before he began to cross swords with Löscher.[1] Being aware of the same tension Löscher decided in 1701 to put out a yearly volume called *Altes und Neues aus dem Schatze theologischer Wissenschaft*, the title of which he changed the following year to *Unschuldige Nachrichten von alten und neuen theologischen Sachen*. From the beginning it was profoundly censorious of Pietism. In addition Löscher decided to subsume under the title of "Pietist" practically all the people whose theology he did not like. Thus he mixed together indiscrimminately Dippel and Spener, Arnold and Breithaupt, Lange and Rosenbach, etc. That this was done with the deliberate intention of spreading confusion and fear can hardly be doubted. Not only did he attack Pietism directly in a series of articles included in the volumes for 1711 and 1712,[2] but he made it a point to slant all of his literary reviews and recensions against the same movement. The result was, of course, that the Halle theologians quickly began to recognize in Löscher their chief opponent. For that reason they entrusted Lange with the task of being their chief spokesman.

The immediate occasion for Löscher's decision to take up the sword against Halle Pietism in particular appears to have been a twofold one. Having been notoriously successful in expanding the total Halle enterprise, Francke and his friends tended to treat this expansion as a sign of divine favor,[3] a mental habit which was especially annoying to the Orthodoxists because it was difficult for them to know how to deal with it. Furthermore, in 1701 the *Orthodoxa vapulans*,[4] a pietistic

---

[1] See W. Gass, *Geschichte der Protestantischen Dogmatik*, 1862, vol. 3, p. 26.

[2] To this series of articles against Pietism he gave the title *Timotheus Verinus*. Löscher published an enlarged edition of them in a separate volume in 1718. To it he gave the same title. The *Timotheus Verinus* is generally considered Löscher's major work.

[3] See Francke's *Segensvolle Fusstapfen*, first published in 1701. Various later accounts of the Halle venture, and always written by Francke, appeared from time to time. For further information about reports concerning the work at Halle see R. Krämer, *op. cit.*, vol. 2, pp. 32f, 72f. For Francke's attempt to attribute the success of Halle to a special (*sonderbare*) divine providence see his preface to the 1909 edition of *Segensvolle Fusstapfen*, p. 28.

[4] The *Orthodoxa vopulans* was attributed to Lange by Löscher, as well as by the anonymous defender of Orthodoxy, who answered it under the following title : *Eines anonymi Antwort auf das unverschämte und gottlose scriptum M. Joachim Langens* etc., 1716. Lange, however, never acknowledged authorship.

attack upon Orthodoxy, was published anonymously. These signs of pietistic vigor moved Löscher to pay increasing attention to Halle, ending in his major assault through his *Timotheus Verinus*. Lange, on the other hand, began his counter-offensive in earnest in 1707 when he decided to publish his *Aufrichtige Nachrichten*, which, as the full title indicates, is set directly against Löscher.[1] In 1709 and 1711 he began to put the "pseudo-orthodoxi" on the defensive.[2] In order to introduce the proper distance between Halle and the enthusiasts, with whom Löscher deliberately had tried to equate the Halle theologians, Lange published his tract on the middle way in 1712 and 1714.[3] The following year he answered the first publication of Löscher's *Timotheus Verinus* in a point by point refutation.[4] After Löscher's expanded version of the *Timotheus* Lange more or less concluded the exchange by three more tracts.[5] A characteristic illustration of Lange's tone is found in the preface to his *Apologetische Erläuterung*.[6] His polemics are, on the one hand, not as objectionable as they have frequently been made out to be; nor are they as irenical as Spener's. He generally assumes the stance of a deliberately injured party, and it would be difficult, indeed, to maintain that such deliberate injury had not been Löscher's unvarying objective for some twenty years.

The substance of the controversy has been carefully analyzed and documented by Rotermund.[7] For that reason a mere summary of the major themes on which the two contestants took characteristic positions will be sufficient here. The themes were : The relationship of the Word to doctrine; the nature of faith and its relation to piety; imputed or inherent righteousness; whether or not Christian perfection (in an ethical sense) is attainable in this life; whether or not ethical holiness is a necessary characteristic of the church; whether or not theologians and pastors need the illumination of the Spirit to interpret the faith

---

[1] *Aufrichtige Nachrichten von der Unrichtigkeit der Unschuldigen Nachrichten* etc., 1707f.

[2] *Antibarbarus orthodoxiae dogmatico hermeneuticus* etc., 1709-1711.

[3] *Richtige Mittelstrasse* etc.

[4] This was done in his most intemperate tract : *Die Gestalt des Creuzreichs Christi in seiner Unschuld mitten unter den falschen Beschuldigungen* etc., 1713.

[5] *Abgenöthigte völlige Abfertigung des sogenannten vollständigen Timotheus Verinus* etc., 1719. *Apologetische Erläuterung, op. cit.*, 1719. *Abgenöthigtes abermaliges Zeugnis der Wahrheit und Unschuld,* 1722. The latter was Lange's response to Löscher's continuation of the *Timotheus Verinus* in 1722.

[6] 1719 ed., p. 4f.

[7] Rotermund, *op. cit.*

meaningfully; whether or not ordination confers a special charisma; whether or not one should work and hope for better times; and finally, the place of mystical thought forms in the Christian approach to personal religious reality.

One of the central points of divergence, which has not been directly touched upon previously, had to do with the matter of Christian perfection. Both camps were satisfied with the traditional doctrine of imputed righteousness and hence with the idea that the believing Christian is eschatologically perfect in the sight of God. The question, however, which caused incessant disagreement was related to the possibility of ethical (motivational) perfection in this life. Löscher was strongly given to the Lutheran insistence that the Christian always remains a sinner. Even during the sixteenth century the widespread abuse of this doctrine had brought a strong censure of Lutherans from men like Caspar Schwenckfeld and the radical reformers in general. They felt that, however correct it may be theoretically, it was the main excuse for ethical insensitivity and moral indifferentism. Pietism generally shared such a critical stance toward this particular theologumenon. Hence some Pietists tried to get rid of it altogether, while the Spener-Halle group took the position that the Christian must come as close as possible to a state of being in which all of his actions are motivated only by the Spirit of God.[1] Because Löscher had serious reservations about this position[2] Lange spoke of Löscher's "impietism,"[3] and of the "theologia concupiscentia de Verini" which plays into the hands of libertines.[4] Thus we have here an interesting example of two equally sincere men talking past each other because they are motivated by different fears, one by the fear of reckless enthusiasm, the other by the fear of ethical sterility of religious belief.

After the Löscher-Lange debate all that really could be said had been said. Hence the occasional efforts at polemics during the following two decades, especially on the periphery of the Spener-Halle Movement, are, in the main, of local import only. In the past these controversies have usually been blamed on the one side or the other, depending on the bias of the historian who wrote about them. Perhaps it is better to think of them as an inevitable clash which always occurs in history

1 See Lange *Apologetische Erläuterung, op. cit.*, p. 510f.

2 For Löscher's whole series of mental reservations regarding the pietistic emphasis on ethical relevance see *Unschuldige Nachrichten*, 1711, p. 898f.

3 *Ibid.*, p. 515.

4 *Ibid.*, p. 365.

when old values and perspectives are seriously challenged. Nor is this confrontation wholly unfortunate. The debate cleared the issues and gave the rest of the clergy of eighteenth century Lutheranism an opportunity to choose intelligently the side which they preferred. From a contemporary point of view the unfortunate element involved in this dialogue is not that it occurred, but that each side arrogated to itself the exclusive right to speak for God. It is mainly for this reason that both parties presently lost the respect of intellectuals, who found in Wolff what neither Wittenberg nor Halle seemed to offer them.

It is especially to the credit of Löscher that in 1718-1719 he sought a conference with the theologians of Halle at which their differences might be discussed. Part of the reason for this desire must be sought in the fact that by this time it was becoming quite clear that Orthodoxy was on the defensive. This explains also the self-assured attitude of the Halle men which is evident in their initial conditions regarding the conference, namely, that Löscher must first be converted, that he must confess to having treated the Pietist's unfairly, and that he must acknowledge his errors and ignorance.[1] After considerable sparring they finally met, however, on May 10, 1719. Having done so they quickly came to feel that the central differences between them had to do with the already mentioned differences concerning the doctrine of illumination and the pietistic conviction that in the area of personal religion there are no *adiaphora*. Francke and Breithaupt, who represented Halle, felt that their insistence upon the need for spiritual illumination of theologians and pastors is both biblical and necessary for their program of church renewal, while Löscher insisted that such an understanding of things militates against the doctrine of the objective validity of the Word. The Halle representatives also held that adiaphoristic practices, such as dancing, are intrinsically sinful, since they are not motivated by the Spirit, while Löscher insisted that they are sinful only if misused, since motivations originating in the realm of nature are also good. Finally they made some concessions, Francke granting that the Word keeps its objective power in man's mind, and Löscher conceding that activities such as dancing may be "dangerous." In the end both parties left the conference wondering whether or not the other side could really be trusted. Just what its significance was

[1] For an account of this conference, which, however, is strongly biased in Löscher's favor, see M. von Engelhardt, *Valentin Ernst Löscher*, p. 246f. See also Walch, *op. cit.*, vol. 5, pp. 279-306.

remains a question. The controversy did continue afterwards, each side blaming the other for not fully respecting the agreements reached.

Expansion

It now remains to give some indication of the geographical dimensions of the Spener-Halle Movement during the period of Halle hegemony. Because of the direct political and excclesiastical dependence upon Berlin this would seem to be the logical place to begin. The attitude of the House of Hohenzollern toward Pietism has already been discussed.

Because of the Prussian policy of religious toleration the representatives of rigid Orthodoxy never felt comfortable in Berlin. Partly for that reason, and partly because of Spener's irenical temper, the rise of the Spener-Halle Movement to a dominant position in that city and its surroundings was relatively uneventful. Its rapid ascendency began with the coming of Spener to Berlin in 1691. Because of the interest of the Elector Frederick III the former was immediately given the influential position of prior and inspector of the Church of St. Nicholas and member of the consistory. While his direct contacts with the court were few he had various highly placed friends in government circles. Among these was D. G. von Natzmer (1654-1739), the successful general, who all through his adult life stood in highest favor at the Prussian court. Spener made it one of the chief objectives of his carrer to fill all pastorates within the sphere of Prussian influence with pietistic, usually Halle trained, pastors. This applied to Berlin and its environs as well. As Halle's reputation grew, Spener and Francke both had the ear of the reigning house. Hence no pastoral appointment was made in Berlin unless it had Spener-Halle approval, a practice which was extended in 1717 to cover all of Prussia and in 1729 to apply to the entire realm.

Under these circumstances we are not surprised to find that the Spener-Halle Movement grew in Berlin until it dominated the religious life of the city. In an interesting letter to Herrnschmid, which Francke wrote on his Berlin trip (Dec. 1702), he reports with great satisfaction that he preached before the king and the queen and "from one end of the city to the other." In a postscript to the same letter he adds : "Among the preachers in Berlin are now actually ten who do the work of the Lord single-mindedly, and who come together weekly in order to awaken one another in prayer."[1] Little wonder that in time all

[1] A. Nebe, "Neue Quellen zu August Hermann Francke," in BFcT, vol. 31, book 1, 1927, pp. 68-69. Other interesting letters are printed in the same volume, pp. 1-94.

positions of ecclesiastical influence were filled with Piestists, and the devotional books flowing from the press at Halle found their way not only into the royal palace but into church life everywhere.

Among the leaders of the Spener-Halle Movement in Berlin was Johann Kaspar Schade (1666-1698),[1] who held a distinguished pastorate in the city. He was a most effective preacher and highly esteemed by those who agreed with him. In contrast to his close friend and colleague Spener, however, he appears to have been a somewhat impulsive, even reckless, zealot, who tended to speak first and think later. Looking upon Berlin as a city which was both corrupt and corrupting he poured out his soul in condemnation of the evils it tolerated. The ecclesiastical institution which, he felt, was chiefly responsible for the ineffective ministry of the church was the confessional as then practiced among Lutherans. As a result he wrote a tract demanding its reform,[2] which the following year was answered by Johann Deutschmann of the faculty at Leipzig. This began a theological wrangle which caused Spener no mean concern.[3] It seems, however, that the rumor of the loss of Schade's pastorate as a result of this controversy is unfounded. Even though the zeal of the Lord threatened to consume him at times, his friends regarded him as a man of blameless life and almost irresistible religious persuasiveness.

Even more influential then Schade was Johann Porst (1688-1728),[4] who came to Berlin in 1695 and was led into a religious experience by Spener and Schade. With the help of these men he rose rapidly to a

---

[1] Born at Kühndorff. Studied at Leipzig, where together with Francke he was involved in the hassle concerning the holding of the *collegium philobiblicum* (Walch, *op. cit.*, vol. 1, pp. 566-593). In 1691 he was called to the church of St. Nicholas in Berlin. Schade wrote a long series of devotional books, which were published posthumously at Leipzig (1720) in five octavo volumes. See AGL-IV, col. 207.

[2] *Praxis des Beichtstuhls und Abendmahls*, 1697.

[3] For details see Walch, *op. cit.*, vol. 1, pp. 762-763; vol. 5, pp. 80-99.

[4] Porst was born at Oberkotzau, Vogtland. In 1698 he was recommended by Spener to a pastorate at Malchow near Berlin. He wrote a long series of tracts, mostly of an edificatory nature. His most important works are his *Theologia viatorum practica*, 1722, his *Theologia practica regenitorum*, 1723, and an extract of these, called *Compendium theologiae viatorum et regenitorum practica*, 1723. All of these were frequently reprinted. References here are to the 1723 ed. For a list of his works see AGL-III, cols. 1708-1709; also AGLF-VI, cols. 667-669. For a detailed account of the content of his *Compendium* see RTL, vol. 2, pp. 463-472. For an analysis of the mystical element in Porst's writings see B. Altenberg, "Die Mystik im lutherischen Pietismus. Dargetellt auf Grund der Erbaungsschriften Johann Porsts, 1668-1728," ZbKG, vol. 26, 1931, pp. 53-78; vol. 27, 1932, pp. 92-102; vol. 28, 1933, pp. 128-145; vol. 29, 1934, pp. 61-75.

position of eminence until in 1709 he became confessor to the queen and three years later prior at St. Nicholas Church, as well as first pastor and inspector. In 1716 he joined the consistory. Porst's theology moves within the circle of ideas characteristic of the Spener-Halle Tradition. While he used such mystical terms as *Vereinigung* (p. 713) and *gleichförmig* (p. 714), it would be difficult to sustain Ritschl's attempt to explain Porst's piety on the model of St. Bernard (Ritschl II, p. 468f). Porst remained faithful to the Lutheran understanding of the theology of salvation and uses such terms mainly to underscore his emphasis upon the Christian's love for God. In this he followed basically the long-standing Arndtian tradition within Lutheranism. As a result a profoundly devotional spirit pervades everything Porst has written.

The third of the great trio of pietistic preachers at Berlin was Johann Gustav Reinbeck (1683-1741),[1] who in 1717 became first pastor, prior, and inspector of St. Peter's Church in Berlin. In 1727 he joined the consistory. In time he had the distinction of being confessor to two Prussian queens, and the personal friend of two successive kings. Thus he was close, indeed, to the centers of power and hence one of the political main-stays of the Spener-Halle Movement. In time Reinbeck became involved in the very considerable controversy which raged around the publication of the so called *Wertheim Bible*, printed in four parts in 1735.[2] It consisted of a free, annotated translation into German of the Pentateuch, executed by Johann Laurentius Schmid, who had studied theology at Jena and at Halle. By this time the philosophy of Wolff was beginning to make itself felt, and the feeling of Orthodoxists as well as many Pietists, was, that this translation was the first effort of Wolffianism to insinuate itself into the very citadel of Protestantism, namely biblical exegesis. The result was a major theological storm, which was first raised by Lange,[3] and which badly buffeted the nonplused Schmid. Reinbeck jumped into the fray against the Schmid translation. This is remarkable, indeed, since at

---

[1] Reinbeck was born at Zelle, studied at Halle, and upon Halle's recommendation became assistant to Probst at Dorotheen-Stadt in 1709. Beginning with 1715 he edited the magazine *Freiwilliges Hebopfer von allerhand theologischen Materien*, which came out in five annuals. He was a prolific writer, 79 pieces by him being mentioned in AGLF-VI, cols. 1663-1667. See also AGL-III, cols. 1985-1987.

[2] For a detailed account of the substantial amount of polemical literature generated by this publication see Walch, *op. cit.*, vol. 5, pp. 1276-1374.

[3] In *Den philosophischen Religionsspöttern in dem ersten Teile des wertheimischen Bibelwerks verkappt*, 1736.

that time he himself was deeply impressed by Wolff and insisted that between Christian theology, by which he meant the theology he had imbibed at Halle, and the philosophy of Wolff there is no inner contradiction. Whether or not this otherwise very irenical man had anything to do with the royal confiscation order of the *Wertheim Bible* (Jan. 1737) is a question. That he was close enough to the throne to accomplish this is indicated by the fact that by royal decree his main work had to be put into all church libraries in the realm.[1]

Because of the sane and vigorous theological leadership which the Spener-Halle Movement enjoyed in Berlin it maintained considerable strength in that city throughout the century. As the professional theological leadership began to yield to the influence of Leibnitz and Wolff lay leadership in the movement became stronger. The result was that conventicles led by laymen became a prominent feature of Berlin church life.[2] The heart of this lay movement toward the end of the century consisted of the nobleman Ernst von Kottwitz (1757-1843) and the merchant Samuel Elsner (1778-1856). Among the clergy, too, however, an effective minority group of Pietists maintained itself. Most prominent among them were Johann Esaias Silberschlag (1716-1791), pastor at Trinity Church, student of Baumgarten at Halle, and avowed enemy of the Enlightenment, Theodor Carl Georg Woltersdorf (1727-1809), a popular, if not very learned preacher, who has the dubious distinction of having petitioned the king in 1790 to stop Immanuel Kant from further publication; and Johann Jaenicke (1748-1829), preacher at Bethlehem Church, who carried on a bilingual ministry in German and Bohemian.[3] Even toward the end of the century there was enough vigor in this group to prevent the rationalizing hymnal of 1790 from being prescribed for exclusive use in Lutheran churches.

A second center of Spener-Halle influence was East Prussia, including the University of Königsberg. Its spirit of ethical concern was represented by the éxceptionably able Johann Jakob Quand (1686-1772), one of the most eloquent preachers Germany ever produced. Listeners have reported that if he merely read the words of the liturgy, "Have

---

[1] The title was : *Betrachtungen über die in der augsburgischen Confession enthaltenen — Wahrheiten* etc., 1731-1741. It is an early indication of the later alliance of Pietism and the philosophy of Wolff.

[2] See W. Wendland, "Siebenhundert Jahre Kirchengeschichte Berlins," *Berlinische Forschungen*, vol. 3, p. 133.

[3] For further information see W. Wendland, "Studien zur Erweckungsbewegung in Berlin," JbKG, vol. 19, 1924, pp. 5-77.

mercy, have mercy upon us," some people in his audience felt as if he were taking their breath away.[1] Being a friend of the court Quand held some of the most influential ecclesiastical posts in the kingdom. In 1714 he became professor of theology at Königsberg. During the years 1721-1730 he gave Lithuania a translation of the Bible, a catechism, and a number of edificatory books. His interest in the public schools would be a chapter in itself. Though Quand had studied oriental languages at Halle, however, and though he agreed in principle with Halle's ethical emphasis, he was opposed to Pietism as a political party in the church. Hence he should not be considered as being unqualifiedly in the pietistic camp.

Lutheran Pietism as such had come to East Prussia toward the end of the seventeenth century, when Spener's influence was beginning to be felt.[2] One of its early promotors was the layman Theodor Gehr[3] (d. 1705), who held Spener-oriented conventicles and then went to Halle (1697) to look over Francke's institutions. He came back full of zeal for similar educational ventures, beginning first a school for the wealthy and then a school for the poor. Violently opposed by Orthodoxists as a "papistical" venture, Gehr's educational work was saved from ruin only by the fact that Elector Frederick III, who presently became King Frederick I, put it under the protection of a royal commission in 1701.

Very quickly Lutheran Pietism in East Prussia, and specifically at Königsberg, came under the theological leadership of a number of very able men. The first of these who needs to be mentioned here is Heinrich Lysius (1670-1731). In contradistinction to the retiring Gehr he was a strong, courageous man, and a ready match for the continuing opposition of Orthodoxy. His accomplishments are many, of which only a few can be mentioned here.[4] Lysius was a confirmed Pietist of the Spener-Halle School, had received his doctor's degree at Halle in 1702 and been recommended to become inspector of the newly established

---

[1] For my information about Quand I am indebted to A. Nietzki, "D. Johann Jakob Quand, Generalsuperintendent von Preussen und Oberhofprediger in Königsberg," SSoKG, vol. 3, 1905, pp. 1-161, and to MI, vol. 2, pp. 574-576.

[2] For a more detailed account see W. Borrmann, "Das Eindringen des Pietismus in die ostpreussische Landeskirche," in SSoKG, 1913, vol. 15, pp. 1-142.

[3] See J. Horkel, *Der Holzkämmerer Theodor Gehr*, 1855.

[4] See Borrmann, *op. cit.* See also "Heinrich Lysius in Litauen und Masuren," *Altpreussische Monatschrift*, vol. 18, p. 127f. For Pietism's long success in Lithuania see W. Gaigalat, "Die evangelische Gemeinschaftsbewegung unter den preussischen Litauern," SSoKG, vol. 1, 1904.

Fredericks Collegium at Königsberg. He rose rapidly to a position of eminence and became first professor of the theological faculty of Königsberg in 1721. His crowning academic achievement was the reformation of the University of Königsberg, which was undertaken under order of the king and along the lines of Halle, a move bitterly opposed by representatives of Orthodoxy. The work of Lysius was ably continued by his successor at the Fredericks-Collegium and on the theological faculty of Königsberg, Abraham Wolf (1680-1731).[1] When Georg Friedrich Rogall (1701-1733), who was close to Francke, was promoted to an extraordinary position on the Königsberg faculty, over the head of four Orthodoxists, the Spener-Halle hegemony with respect to the religious life of East Prussia was established. By royal decree no candidates were accepted for any pastorates except upon recommendation of Wolf and Rogall. The result was that the lectures, even of men like Quand, were notoriously neglected. Pietism in this section was further enhanced by the very great success of Rogall's hymnal, first printed in 1731, of which within the first seven years alone ca. 50,000 copies were sold.[2]

Very special mention needs to be made in this connection of Franz Albert Schultz (1692-1762), who may well have the distinction of having been the most powerful ecclesiastic in Prussia between 1730 and 1742,[3] even Quand being pushed aside by his somewhat younger rival. Schultz had studied at Halle, remained in uninterrupted communication with Halle, and was strictly committed to its major emphases (rebirth, new life, no concession to *adiaphora* etc.). At the same time, however, he was favorably disposed toward Wolff, under whom he had also studied at Halle, and insisted that between Halle theology and Wolffian philosophy there is an inner bond. He was an enemy of all narrowness and every manifestation of what he regarded as fanaticism, a man of broad vision and irenical temper. In 1731 he was called to a pastorate at Königsberg, where he quickly gained the confidence of

---

1 See : AGL-IV, col. 2044.

2 See Ruth Fuehrer, "Die Gesangbücher der Stadt Königsberg," SSoKG, vol. 26. For further information on Rogall see J. Wotschke, "George Friedrich Rogalls Lebensarbeit nach seinen Briefen," SSoKG, vol. 27, 1928, pp. 1-191, and "Der Pietismus in Königsberg nach Rogalls Tode in Briefen," SSoKG, vol. 28, 1929-1930.

3 See Borrmann, *op. cit.*; P. Kalweit, "Kants Stellung zur Kirche," SSoKG, vol. 2, 1904, pp. 1-88; G. Zippel, *Geschichte des königlichen Friedrichskollegiums zu Köngisberg*, 1898; and W. Wendland, "Ludwig Ernst von Borowski" etc., SSoKG, vol. 9, 1910, pp. 1-104 for various references to Schultz and his influence.

Frederick Wilhelm I. The king's favorable impression of him is evidenced by the fact that he wanted to promote him to first professor on the theological faculty of Königsberg, though he should have been in eighth place. Schultz's character, on the other hand, is revealed by the fact that he declined and reluctantly took third place, and then also the directorship of the Fredericks Collegium. Nietski holds that the revised church order of 1734 was entirely Schultze's work and that between 1732 and 1740 every royal decree regarding church life in Prussia was inspired by Schultz.[1] Beyond this he should perhaps be given credit also for actually beginning the Prussian folk school system of public education.

In Schultz and his close associates the kind of Lutheran Pietism associated with the City and University of Königsberg is epitomized. It was inspired by the Spener-Halle Tradition and remained essentially true to its emphases. Yet, it remained free of the narrowness which tended to descend upon Halle under the leadership of Francke's son, August Gotthilf. As graduates of the University of Königsberg increasingly entered the pastorates of the surrounding area they diffused the spirit of their teachers throughout the province. By the succeeding generation of teachers, however, notably T.C. Lilienthal who was a student of Schultz, the Halle element was gradually reduced in favor of Wolff.

The entrance of the Spener-Halle influence into Pommerania was closely connected with the shifts of political sovereignty.[2] In eastern Pommerania, which was under Prussian rule, such entrance was assured by the religious predilections of the court. Hence Pietism found its way into such centers as Stargard and Stolp, as well as Köslin, Neustettin, and Naugard. Through the efforts of Günther Heiler (1645-1707), friend of Spener and Francke, and since 1687 General Superintendent for eastern Pommerania, it was advanced as rapidly as was possible in a section where Orthodoxy was deeply entrenched. This was done through his influence with the court, as well as through devotional books which he wrote. His son-in-law, Johann Wilhelm Zierold (1669-1731), who was heavily under Spener's influence, became involved in a controversy on illumination and other typical

[1] Nietzki, *op. cit.*, p. 49f.

[2] For further details see H. Heyden, "Kirchengeschichte Pommerns," vol. 2, in *Osteuropa und der Deutsche Osten*, 1957; also T. Wotschke, "Der Pietismus in Pommern," BKGP, vol. 2.

emphases of the Spener-Halle Tradition, which lasted for some time.[1] In 1696 Zierold was appointed rector of the Gymnasium at Stargard and henceforth he was considered the leading Pietist in that city. The vitality of Pietism at Stargard is attested by the fact that in 1696 an orphanage was founded there on the Halle model, and that the so called *Stargard Bible*, a pietistic work, was published in that city in 1707. The voices of Zierold and Johann Heinrich Sprögel, who tried to defend in print his son-in-law Gottfried Arnold, are the most prominent coming out of Pietism in eastern Pommerania. Sprögel's sphere of influence was in the vicinity of Stolp, a town in the far north.

Because of Swedish resistance to anything that came out of Halle, central and western Pommerania were slow in accepting Pietism. As the region of Stettin came under Prussian rule, however, the first beginnings were made. Under Johann Christoph Schimmeyer, pastor of the Church of St. John, and others, it gradually established itself. Presently both an orphanage and a school for the poor were built upon the Halle model. In western Pommerania, on the other hand, which remained under Swedish sovereignty, the going was slow, partly so, because the opposition of Orthodoxy was deeply entrenched. Even after Pietism took hold it had to maintain itself against the most acrimonious controversy.[2] One of the citadels of Orthodoxy had been the University of Greifswald in western Pommerania. Only through a strange coincidence did the Spener-Halle perspective gain a foothood there. It was J.F. Mayer, Pietism's arch-enemy of Hamburg fame, who, of all people, recommended to the theological faculty of the University of Greifswald Brandanus Heinrich Gebhardi (1657-1729).[3] After his appointment, however, the latter came gradually under the influence of Spener, and upon Mayer's death became a convinced champion of the Spener-Halle theology. He was ably supported by Jacob Heinrich von Balthasar (1690-1763), another Pietist, who was appointed to the same faculty in 1719.[4] The incessant pulpit warfare carried on against Pietism was

---

[1] See Walch, *op. cit.*, vol. 5, pp. 159-165. Ritschl gives a lengthy criticism of his volume on church history, which is really a polemic against Lutheran scholasticism. (Vol. 2, pp. 393-395).

[2] See H. Lother, *Pietistische Streitigkeiten in Greifswald*, 1925; also Walch, *op. cit.*, vol. 5, pp. 307f and 392f.

[3] See ADB, vol. 8, pp. 481-482. For his controversial activities see Walch, *op. cit.*, vol. 5, pp. 307f, 311f, 314f, 317f. 412f.

[4] For a list of his writings, mostly on historical topics, see AGLF-I, cols. 1386, 1387.

finally halted by the government which had become sensitive to its decidedly divisive influence.

Generally speaking, Pommerania cannot be considered very fertile soil for the pietistic perspective. Whether or not Heyden is right in attributing this to the temper of the people[1] is difficult to say. Perhaps more important is the fact that the pastors of this region had been trained almost exclusively in the strongholds of Orthodoxy. The political factor, too, must not be forgotten. Since in the mind of many people the words "Pietism" and "Prussian" meant almost the same thing religiously, whatever resistance there was to Prussian political aspirations would tend to work in favor of Orthodoxy.

During the period in which we are interested Saxony remained the major bastion of rigid Orthodoxy. During Spener's earlier days there had been some leanings in his direction on the part of the nobility. For that reason Johann Georg III had called Spener to Dresden in 1686. The popular climate, however, was decidedly inhospitable to Spener's influence, and the clergy were generally hostile to him. As a result neither he nor Halle could establish much of a popular following. Amazingly enough, it was Zinzendorf who finally made at least a modest impression upon the religious life of the people.

In spite of this lack of popular appeal, however, the Spener-Halle understanding of Protestant Christianity did not leave the universities untouched. With the death of Johann Benedikt Carpzov II (1699) the University of Leipzig, for instance, ceased to present a solid orthodox front.[2] Johannes Olearius (1639-1713) had joined the theological faculty of the University of Leipzig in 1677. From the beginning he took a friendly attitude toward Pietism, though, being a retiring man, he was no match for the imperious and ruthless Carpzov, who continued to dominate the Leipzig faculty to his death. His gifted son, Gottfried Olearius (1672-1715), who joined the theological faculty in 1708, continued in the same spirit as his father. Both men were deeply sympathetic with both Spener and Francke, but did not wish to be part of Pietism as a political entity. More resolutely on the side of the Spener-Halle axis was Adam Rechenberg (1642-1721), who joined the Leipzig faculty in 1699. His fourth wife being a daughter of Spener, we are not

---

[1] Heyden, *op. cit.*, p. 133.

[2] For a fuller account of the influence of Pietism upon the University of Leipzig see O. Kirn, "Die Leipziger theologische Fakultät in fünf Jahrhunderten," *Festschrift zur Feier des 500-jährigen Bestehens der Universität Leipzig, chapter* 5.

surprised to find him defending repeatedly the Spener-Halle group in print. On the same faculty the irenical attitude of these men was continued later by Christian Friedrich Börner (1683-1753), and Johann Gottlob Pfeiffer (1668-1740). None of these men should be regarded as being unqualifiedly within the Spener-Halle orbit. Yet, on the faculty of Leipzig they constituted an effective barrier against the fervor of religious Orthodoxy which continued there. The same should be said about Johann Franz Buddeus at the University of Jena. On the other hand, the voices of Johann Caspar Haferung (1689-1744) and Johann Georg Joch (1685-1731) availed relatively little against Orthodoxy's vociferous representatives on the theological faculty of the University of Wittenberg.

In trying to be the spokesmen for a new approach to theology Rechenberg, Joch, and Haferung became involved in considerable controversy.[1] As always, the Saxon pulpits were used for the vigorous defense of the theological *status quo*. The devisive effect of this polemical activity was so serious that the ruling house of Saxony feared it might disrupt political relations with Prussia. Hence, a promulgation on August 20, 1727, inspired by the Saxon government, forbid all writing against Pietism. On September 8 this was read to the faculties. According to Kirn this promulgation sounds very much like an apology for Spener. On the practical level it accomplished that persecution of people touched by the Spener-Halle spirit became impossible,[2] though it remained equally impossible to call into being a popular pietistic movement in Saxony.

In Silesia, on the other hand, there was relatively little intellectual opposition to the rise of the Spener-Halle emphasis.[3] Francke's interest in that province had been elicited by Henrietta von Gerstorff, wife of one of the officials at the Saxon court. As a result a lively correspondence ensued between Halle and Silesia during the last decade of the seventeenth century. Presently a considerable number of Halle trained pastors and teachers found their way into the region. For this reason Halle Pietism gained a strong foothold in cities like Teschen, Sorau, and Züllichau.[4] This was the case in spite of the fact that Silesia was

[1] For details see Walch, *op. cit.*, vol. 1, p. 763f; vol. 2, p. 943f; vol. 5, pp. 431f, 474f.

[2] Kirn, *op. cit.*, p. 155.

[3] For some of the earlier difficulties see Walch, *op. cit.*, vol. 1, p. 853f.

[4] For at least an initial account of the Spener-Halle type of Pietism in Silesia see W. Schwarz, "August Hermann Francke und Schlesien," JsKG, 1957, pp. 106-113; M. Schian, *Das kirchliche Leben der evangelischen Kirche der Provinz Schlesien*, 1903;

under the sovereignty of the Catholic house of Austria, which, according to Schultze,[1] was by no means friendly toward such religious innovations. In the last mentioned centers institutions of learning patterned on the Halle model were founded while Teschen was considered the pietistic capital of the province. The most permanent representatives of Silesian Pietism of the Spener-Halle type are Carl Heinrich von Bogatzki (1690-1774)[2] and Ernst Gottlieb Woltersdorf (1725-1761).[3] Both of these men are considered among the most outstanding hymn writers of Continental Protestantism. Besides writing hymns Bogatzki was one of the very prolific writers of edificatory literature in the Spener-Halle Tradition. Having been relieved of the necessity of having to make a living by the younger Francke he devoted all of his energy during his later years to the creation of a devotional literature embodying the Halle perspective.

Religiously speaking the Hannover region, sometimes referred to as Lower Saxony, had been strongly under the influence of Johann Arndt and his followers during the seventeenth century.[4] This was at least part of the reason why the rigid Orthodoxy, which was found in other places, could not gain a footfold in most Hannoverian localities. Both Uhlhorn and Ruprecht hold that this is the reason also why Spener-

E. Schultze, "Der Missionsgedanke im schlesischen Kirchenlied," JsKG, 1956, pp. 88-105; E. Schultze, "Wie und wann erfasste der Missionsgedanke die schlesischen Gemeinden," in JsKK, 1957, pp. 169-176; H. Ebelein, *Schlesische Kirchengeschichte*, 1952.

[1] Schultze, *op. cit.*, "Wie and wann," etc., p. 170.

[2] See RE, vol. 3, pp. 279-280. Bogatzki was born in Silesia, came under the influence of Francke and then studied at Halle. Not being under great urgency to be gainfully employed, he spent much of his time in the households of the Silesian nobility. The last years of his life he spent at Halle, where he was given free board. His hymns were published first in 1750 under the title "*Übung der Gottseligkeit in allerlei geistlichen Liedern.* One of his most important devotional books is his *Tägliches Hausbuch der Kinder Gottes*, 1747, and perhaps his most beloved piece, available in many editions, is his *Güldenes Schatzkästlein der Kinder Gottes*, 1734.

[3] See RE, vol. 21, pp. 485-488. Woltersdorf was born near Berlin. He studied at Halle (1742f). In 1748 he became second pastor at Bunslau and in 1758 director of the orphanage which had been founded in that city four years before. He is often referred to as the "Silesian Asaph" because of the great number of popular hymns which he wrote (a total of 218). His hymns were first published in 1750. Though late in the century Woltersdorf was strongly committed to the original Halle perspective.

[4] For excellent discussions of the religious situation within the various localities of this region see G. Uhlhorn, *Hannoverische Kirchengeschichte*, 1902; R. Ruprecht, *Der Pietismus des 18 Jahrhunderts in den Hannoverschen Stammländern*, 1919; Bartels, "Mitteilungen zur Geschichte des Pietismus in Ostfriesland," ZKG, vol. 5, 1882, pp. 250f, and 387f.

Halle Pietism in this general section was at first not felt to be in opposition to the accepted theological perspective. Conventicle Protestantism was generally associated here with separatistic Pietism and was increasingly opposed, while Spener's ideas were welcome. It needs to be remembered, however, that no general statement applies to all local situations.

The center of Lutheran Pietism in Hannover was Wernigerode. There it had found entrance through Spener, and especially through the wife of G.A. von Münchhausen. Frau von Münchhausen had been brought to a personal religious experience by Frankce in 1727 and ever thereafter the Spener-Halle type of Pietism was disseminated from her home. Presently Count Christian Ernst von Stolberg (1691-1771) and his wife Sophie Charlotte (1695-1762) became its ardent supporters. Under their level-headed leadership the pietistic excesses associated with the Hart region were strictly avoided at Wernigerode. The rulers of Stolberg-Wernigerode had close relations, too, with the nobility in other sections, and in this way fostered their own understanding of Protestant Christianity in such sections as Schaumburg-Lippe and Hauber. Being related to the Danish king, Christian IV, the lines of influence from Wernigerode lead to Denmark as well.

A second center of such Pietism was Eastern Frisia (*Ostfriesland*).[1] Again the reason for it is found in the fact that the ruling family strongly favored it. Spener himself had been present at the wedding of George Christian. After his death his wife Christine Charlotte (1665-1699), her son Christian Eberhard (1699-1708), and her nephew Georg Albrecht (1708-1734) continued the same religious policy. Especially under the enlightened and tolerant rule of Christian Eberhard and Georg Albrecht pastorates were filled with men trained at Halle, rigid Orthodoxy and left-wing Pietism being both unwelcome. Under the reign of the latter the *Ostfriesisches Morgen-und-Abendopfer* was published (1708), a book of devotion based largely on Arndt and on Lewis Baily's *Practice of Piety*. Among the stalwarts of Pietism in this section was the Halle trained jurist Enno Rudolf Brenneysen (1669-1734), as well as Johann Friedrich Bertram (1699-1741). The latter had taught at Halle and wrote a considerable amount of devotional literature in the Halle spirit.

Because of the influence of Eleonore Charlotte von Schwiecheldt a Halle oriented type of Pietism was strong also at Hildesheim. Here

---

[1] See A. deBoer, *Der Piestismus in Ostfriesland*, 1938.

the moving spirits were Johann Heinrich Schmidt (1690-1741),[1] a student of Buddeus, and for a time, Henry Melchior Mühlenberg of American fame. The dukedoms of Bremen and Verden were less hospitable toward church-related Pietism, so that its chief representatives, Johann Diecmann (1683-1720) and especially Lukas Backmeister (1772-1748) were drawn into considerable controversy.[2] Unfortunately the province of Hannover itself became finally involved in the pangs of theological wrangling.[3] The reason for it must be sought in the doings of the separatists, which during the early thirties tended to bring even the Spener-Halle Tradition into ill repute. The trouble was stirred up by the fanatical Orthodoxist B. Menzers.[4] His charges were finally answered thoroughly by an anonymous author who signed himself D.M.[5] Ruprecht suspects, and with a good deal of justification, that the author was Henry Melchior Mühlenberg. However, the controversy raised a great deal of hard feeling, so that at a time when other sections of Germany moved toward gerater religious understanding Hannover came close to persecuting people who simply wanted to worship and pray in peace. The situation was alleviated as the irenical influence of the University of Göttingen gradually made itself felt.[6]

It might be mentioned in passing that in Schleswig and in the northern section of Holstein the Spener-Francke tradition was also strongly represented.[7] Schleswig, and later part of Holstein, was under Danish sovereignty at this time. The Pietism of Spener had found entrance during the last decade of the seventeenth century and in time came to

---

[1] See K. Thimme, "J.H. Schmidt aus Rudolstadt," ZGnKG, vol. 14, p. 136f.

[2] See R. Steinmetz, "Die Generalsuperintendenten in den Herzogtümern Bremen-Verden," ZGnKG, vol. 10, 1905, pp. 144-196; vol. 11, 1906, pp. 1-88.

[3] For details see Walch, *op. cit.*, vol. 5, p. 534f.

[4] In 1740 he brought out a most intemperate missive under the title *Worte der Ermahnung an die ihm anvertrauten Seelen* etc. In it all Pietists are branded "heretics."

[5] D.M. answered under the title *Sendschreiben*.

[6] See Götz von Selle, *Die Georg-August-Universität zu Göttingen*, 1737-1937, 1937; and especially J. Meyer, "Geschichte der Göttinger theologischen Fakultät," ZGnKG, vol. 42, 1937, pp. 7-107. Göttingen had been dedicated in 1737 and was to exclude atheists, naturalists, enthusiasts, and orthodoxists. The result was a most irenical theological faculty consisting at first of Joachim Aporin, Christoph August Heumann, Magnum Crusium, and later J.L. von Mosheim, and J.G. Walch. Aporin leaned strongly toward Pietism, while the rest were decidedly amenable to its emphasis on the Christian life.

[7] See M. Wittern, "Die Geschichte der Brüdergemeinde in Schleswig-Holstein," SVshKG, vol. 4, sections 1-5, pp. 271-414; also O. Scheel, "Pietismus, Christiansfeld und Dalleyhof," SVshKG, vol. 11, 1952, pp. 199-227, and vol. 12, 1953, pp. 59-82. For the usual controversy with Orthodoxy see Walch, *op. cit.*, vol. 1, p. 816f.

be strongly favored by the Danish court, which regarded it as a stabilizing force over against separatism and Moravianism. The strength of the Spener-Halle Movement in this section is pointed out by the fact that according to Scheel the *Konventikelplakat* of Christian IV (1741), himself a Pietist of Halle persuasion, heavily favored the Spener-Halle tradition. The two best known representatives of Lutheran Pietism in this section were J.K. Schrader and the hymn-writer H.A. Brorson.

Regarding northwestern Germany historians have usually given a good deal of prominence to the activities of the pietistic separatists. It should be pointed out, however, that in this region, comprised largely of Westphalia and the sections of the lower Rhine, several territories leaned very strongly toward the Spener-Francke axis. Among these was the county of Waldeck.[1] During the latter part of the seventeenth century the successive wives of Count Christian Ludwig had been very friendly toward Lutheran Pietism and exchanged letters with Francke. As a result the doors were open and the influence of Halle poured in, Count Ludwig employing only pietistic pastors. Unfortunately here as elsewhere an acrimonious debate ensued with Orthodoxy,[2] the latter gaining an ally in Count Friedrich Anton Ulrich, who took the reigns of government in 1706. As a result, all of the Halle men involved in the controversy were finally forced to leave the county. During the lifetime of Count Ludwig, however, and mainly through the efforts of O.H. Becker, the spirit of Halle had considerable influence upon church and state alike. Thus in 1703 public "excesses" were forbidden, in 1704 an orphanage was founded, and during the same year the school system was revised according to the Halle model. Furthermore, a *seminarium theologicum* was opened with Halle trained Hieronymus Brückner at the helm.

During the period in question, the county of Mark was especially notorious for various kinds of religious enthusiasm, which will be covered elsewhere. Here, too, however, the Spener-Halle tradition did not leave itself without eloquent witnesses.[3] The ground had been well

[1] See W. Irmer, *Geschichte des Pietismus in der Grafschaft Waldeck*, 1912.

[2] For details see Walch, *op. cit.*, vol. 1, p. 906f, and vol. 5, p. 222f. For a summary of the controversial literature see Irmer, *op. cit.*, footnotes, pp. 1-9. The outstanding names on the pietistic side were : Anton Wilhelm Böhme (b. 1673), Joh. Heinrich Marmor (b. 1684), J.F. Botterweck (b. 1669), and especially O.H. Becker (b. 1667). For a summary of the latter's work see Irmer, *op. cit.*, pp. 42-56.

[3] See H.W. Zur Nieden, *Die religiösen Bewegungen im 18. Jahrhundert und die lutherische Kirche der Grafschaft Mark*, 1910; W. Sauerländer, "Pietismus und Rationalismus

prepared for its coming by Johann Jakob Fabricius (1620-1673),[1] the dedicated and able disciple of Arndt, who became pastor in the city of Schwelm in 1644 and was forced out of office by his orthodox opponents six years later. By examining the records of the synod of Mark County Zur Nieden[2] found a great many evidences of the influence of the Spener-Halle Tradition. Thus all the pastors were exhorted to be exemplary not only in their teaching but in their life according to the pattern laid down in Spener's *Natur und Gnade*. Dancing was forbidden outright, bowling on Sunday was frowned upon, and the celebration of baptisms and weddings was to be observed in the spirit of Halle.

In other sections of northwestern Germany the Spener-Halle perspective was also making itself felt. This was the case in the cities of Essen and Dortmund, where Johann Merker (1659-1728),[3] who later became a separatist, and Johann Georg Joch (d. 1731),[4] were the respective leaders. At Düsseldorf Bartholomäus Crasselius (1667-1724)[5] was the heart of the movement. Egidius Günther Hellmund (1680-1749)[6] carried it to the cities of Wetzlar and Wiesbaden, and Israel Clauder (1670-1721)[7] to the county of Ravensberg. At Ravensberg-Minden[8] a number of pietistic superintendents strongly supported the movement under discussion. Similar influences were found at Schaumburg-Lippe,[9] where an orphanage was founded on the Halle

im Märkischen Sauerland," JVwKG, vol. 44, 1951, pp. 165-189; J. Wotschke, "Johann Friedrich Kopstadt," MrKG, vol. 24, 1930, pp. 80-89.

[1] Among the devotional books which Fabricius wrote were the following : *Von der Ursache alles Elends* etc., *Von der Wiedergeburt oder herzgründlichen Busse*, etc.; *Das vielgeplagte und doch verstockte Ägypten, das ist das jezige abtrünnige Maulchristentum*, etc.

[2] See Zur Nieden, *op. cit.*, pp. 13-15.

[3] GBL, vol. 2, p. 616f.

[4] *Ibid.*, p. 632f.

[5] *Ibid.*, p. 642f.

[6] *Ibid.*, p. 656f.

[7] *Ibid.*, p. 647f.

[8] See H. Rothert, "Die Minden-Ravensbergische Kirchengeschichte," sec. section, "Reformation und Pietismus," JVwKG, vol. 29, 1928, pp. 1-169. According to Rothert the chief representatives of the Spener-Halle movement in this county were : Matthias Dreckmann, who became superintendent of Ravensberg in 1695, Johann Henrich Kahnmann, who was made superintendent of Minden in 1717, and the Halle trained Israel Clauder, made superintendent at Ravensberg in 1718.

[9] For details see Heidkämper, "Schaumburg-Lippische Kirchengeschichte vom dreissigjährigen Kriege bis zur Gegenwart," ZGnKG, vol. 12, 1907, pp. 73-131. The pietistic development is covered specifically from p. 95 to p. 102. The moving spirit here was E. David Hauber (1695-1765).

model in 1738 and put in charge of the Halle trained Christoph Gottlob Schwartze. The persistence of the movement in this county is evidenced by the local hymnal of 1745,[1] which includes many typically pietistic hymns. That the same movement had found entrance into other sections of northwest Germany is evidenced by the considerable amount of correspondence of representatives of various locations with Spener and Francke.[2]

In central and southern Germany Württemberg developed its own characteristic brand of Pietism, so that there was relatively little need for the Spener-Halle Movement to gain a foothold. The latter did manifest considerable vigor, however, in Hesse-Darmstadt and in Bavaria. At Hesse-Darmstadt Lutheran Pietism had been introduced by the able Johann Winckler (1642-1705),[3] who had been made court-preacher and assessor of the consistory in 1676. The seeds which he had sown were nurtured by Johann Heinrich Mai (1653-1719),[4] who was a member of the theological faculty of the University of Giessen. After Winckler left it was Mai who became the center of the movement and who carried on the controversy with Orthodoxy in which Pietism had become involved. In the Bavarian region the Spener-Halle influence was felt especially at Oettingen and Bayreuth, as well as at Dinkelsbühl, Nördlingen, Pappenheim, and Augsburg.[5] According to Schatten-

---

1 *Vollständiges Gesangbuch der lutherischen Kirchen in der Grafschaft Schaumburg-Lippe.*

2 See J. Wotschke, "Francke's rheinische Freunde in ihren Briefen," MrKG, vol. 27, 1933, pp. 241-249; "Zur Geschichte des westfälischen Pietismus," JVwKG, vol. 32, 1931, pp. 54-100; vol. 34, 1933, pp. 39-103; "August Hermann Francke's rheinische Freunde," MrKG, vol. 22, 1928, pp. 81-92, 103-123, 151-158, 175-189, 207-215, 236-251, 264-278, 308-320, 343-350, 366-373; vol. 23, 1929, pp. 23-29, 55-90; vol. 24, 1930, pp. 68-79; "Briefe vom Niederrhein an Spener und Francke," MrKG, vol. 21, 1927, pp. 129-154.

3 See ADB, vol. 43, pp. 365-373; also H. Heppe, *Kirchengeschichte beider Hessen*, 1876, vol. 2, pp. 414-417. Winckler, personal friend of Spener, spent most of his active life at Hamburg, where be became involved in the controversy with Mayer.

4 Heppe, *ibid.*, pp. 420-421; also AGL-III, cols. 65-66. Mai was a friend of Breithaupt at Halle.

5 For details see W. Gussmann, "August Hermann Francke in Bayern," ZbKG, vol. 3, 1928, pp. 17-40; F.P. Schaudig, *Der Pietismus und Separatismus im Aischgrunde*, 1925; P. Schattenmann, "Untersuchungen und Beiträge zur Kirchengeschichte der Grafschaft Oettingen im 17. und 18. Jahrhundert," ZbKG, vol. 28, 1959, pp. 97-118; *Georg Adam Michel, Generalsuperintendent in Oettingen, und sein gelehrter Briefwechsel*, 1962; J. Batteiger, "Zur Geschichte des Pietismus in Bayreuth," BbKG, vol. 9, 1903, pp. 153-189; H. Claus, "Untersuchungen zur Geschichte des Pietismus in der Markgrafschaft Ansbach," BbKG, vol. 26, 1920, pp. 97-138.

mann a great deal of correspondence between Halle and all of these localities is available down to almost the end of the eighteenth century. Orphanages on the Halle model were founded at Ansbach in 1709 and at Bayreuth in 1730. The latter was the work of Johann Christoph Silchmüller (b. 1694), one of the pillars of Pietism in this region, and a man who tried to combine the insights of Zinzendorf and Francke. It was his catechism, published in 1732, which brought the usual controversy with Orthodoxy to this region.

There can be little doubt about the fact that the Spener-Halle Movement in Germany was one of the most vigorous in the history of Protestantism. In many sections of the North its influence predominated in Lutheran church life, while elsewhere its representatives went as far as they could to mold Lutheranism according to the Halle pattern. Beyond the borders of Germany its force was felt in Scandinavia, in America, in Switzerland, and even in Russia. Our attempt has been to give some insight into its rise, its theological self-understanding, its leadership, and its general distribution within Germany. It is hoped that in this way a reasonably accurate image of the movement has been established. There remains, of course, the painful awareness that within the general scheme of this volume much that should be said had to be omitted.

CHAPTER THREE

CHARACTERISTIC MANIFESTATIONS OF PIETISM IN WÜRTTEMBERG

The Pietism which arose in the Duchy of Württemberg, like Pietism elsewhere in Germany, was related to the older reform party within Lutheranism, and especially to Spener. In its development, too, it manifested many affinities with pietistic Protestantism elsewhere. Nevertheless, its characteristic features were such as to make it a distinct segment of a larger movement. For that reason its discussion in a separate chapter would seem to be necessary.

The period which is of special interest to us in this connection extends from ca. 1680-1775. It was during the last two decades of the seventeenth century that the influence of Spener was beginning to make itself felt within Württemberg and the territories contiguous to it. From here on conventicles were held in various towns such as Tübingen, Mössingen, Herrenberg, and Altensteig, the first one presently on record having been convened in 1684 by Pastor Zeller at Göppingen. Perhaps largely because of the religious development described in this chapter the Enlightenment made relatively little headway within the established church of Württemberg. As a result, the Pietistic Movement in this section of Germany remained quite stable almost to the very close of the century.

Like other German territories this one had suffered cruelly under the ravages of the Thirty Years War. What is sometimes referred to as Old Württemberg (exclusive of the sections which were added from 1803-1809) found its population reduced by hunger and by the various military campaigns of that war from 450,000 to 166,000. Fritz[1] records that in the district of Weinsberg only two horses and one cow could be found in 1636. Whole villages were wiped out. Community life was often totally disrupted insofar as the peasants were compelled to seek refuge for long periods of time behind the walls of cities. In the wake of receding armies hunger and disease exacted their toll. The schooling

[1] F. Fritz, "Die evangelische Kirche Württembergs im Zeitalter des Pietismus," BwKG, vol. 55, 1955, pp. 68-116.

of children, especially of girls, became almost impossible in some localities. It took many decades, therefore, before even the physical effects of the war could be entirely erased. The situation was aggravated when Louis XIV of France instituted his ill-famed campaigns of plunder against this same region during the years 1688-1692,

Unfortunately for the people of Württemberg their government was frequently insensitive to their needs. During the first part of the eighteenth century three highly oppressive regimes succeeded each other. Duke Bernard Ludwig (1717-1733) was bent upon pleasure, regarding the court of Louis XIV as his model. The government of the country he left to his mistress, the universally disliked Wilhelmine von Grävenitz. Through excessive taxation she acquired great wealth for the court, while abject poverty was the rule in the villages. To the population in general the castles which he built for Wilhelmine, notably Ludwigsburg, were a symbol of frustration. Even today the latter is sometimes referred to as *Lumpenburg*. The situation was no better, perhaps even worse, under Duke Karl Alexander (1733-1737), a Catholic called upon to administer a preponderantly Protestant state during an age when religious intolerance was still rampant. Accordingly he gave free reign to his unscrupulous fiscal adviser, Süss Oppenheim, whose rapacity was so deeply resented that he was hanged after the duke's death. Perhaps the greatest spendthrift of all, at least during the first part of his reign, was Duke Karl Eugen (1737-1793), son of Karl Alexander. Having a mania for beautifying old castles and building new ones — Solitude, Hohenheim, Grafeneck, Einsiedeln — he not only increased taxes, but he pressed large numbers of peasants into involuntary servitude for long periods of time. Opposition was crushed by harsh prison terms and cruel treatment of opponents. Only at the age of fifty did he come to himself, possibly under the influence of his second wife, Franziska von Hohenheim, whom he had forced to dissolve her former marriage and to marry him. He now openly acknowledged regret for his former policy and gradually befriended some of the outstanding pietistic pastors. His regime, therefore, ended on a relatively high note of public concern. To him is attributed the famous last word, which was his dying confession to his pastor Christian Gottlieb Götz : "Pastor, dying is no child's play" ("*Sterben ist kein Kinderspiel*").

In Württemberg, as elsewhere, there was a close correlation between the social situation and the religio-ethical climate of the day. On the one hand, we come across many accounts of the moral degradation and the ethical insensitivity of the masses of people during the seventeenth, as well as the first part of the eighteenth centuries. The picture of their times, painted by many pietistic preachers during the age in question, is dark indeed. Even if we make proper allowances, however, for the overly pessimistic appraisals of contemporary manners and morals which have come down to us from these earnest guardians of treasured values, we must conclude that ethical and religious attitudes left much to be desired. During the early eighteenth century, especially, not only the court, but all classes of society, adopted a rather reckless, and often ruthless, attitude of self-indulgence. The state of public morality is perhaps most eloquently portrayed by requests of pastors for transfer (recorded in the minutes of consistories) for reasons such as the following : "Because of much tribulation resulting from thievery in the night."[1]

On the other hand, the influence of Arndt and the older reform party within Lutheranism was not lost upon Württemberg.[2] Arndt's books, in fact, were so widely read that already in 1623 the Orthodoxist Lucas II Osiander felt impelled to write against them, thus committing what was close to the unpardonable sin in the eyes of many Swabian people. The seeds sown by Arndt, Grossgebauer and others of the same frame of mind bore fruit especially in the concerns and writings of Johann Valentin Andreä (1586-1640),[3] who hoped to make religion a matter of life rather than merely of doctrine. The widely traveled, intellectually open, cosmopolitan Andreä was one of the most influential religious figures of his age and did much to keep the ethically insipid Orthodoxy of Saxony from engulfing Swabian Lutheranism. His attempt to apply the Christian ethic to individuals and society alike strongly influenced the development of Lutheran theology in Württemberg. Andreä's vision remained a live option for the theological faculty of Tübingen during the second part of the seventeenth century. To a degree, at least, it was shared by Tobias W. Wagner (1598-1680), Johann Adam Osiander (1622-1697), Balthasar Raith (1616-1683, and Wolfgang Jäger (1647-1720).[4] While these men conscientiously endeavored to be

[1] *Ibid.*, quoted on p. 79.

[2] See RI, p. 202f.

[3] A list of his writings was edited in 1793 by M.P. Burk. For his singular significance to the early development of Swabian Pietism see H. Scholtz, "Evangelischer Utopismus bei Johann Valentin Andreä; ein geistiges Vorspiel zum Pietismus," in *Darstellungen aus der württembergischen Geschichte*, vol. 42, 1957. See also H. Leube, *Die Reformideen in der deutschen lutherischen Kirche zur Zeit der Orthodoxie*, 1924, p. 86f.

[4] Wagner came to Tübingen in 1652, J.A. Osiander in 1653, Raith in 1656, Jäger initially as geography instructor in 1678.

orthodox, and at times defended their convictions vigorously, they incorporated in their concept of Lutheran Orthodoxy the ethical concerns, as well as the devotional emphasis, of the older reform party. At Tübingen University, therefore, and within its sphere of theological dominance, Lutheranism was significantly open to pietistic insights. Hence we are not surprised to find that the theological reconstruction which Pietism gradually effected in Württemberg eminated largely from Tübingen.

The Rise of Swabian Pietism

The story of Swabian Pietism actually begins with an extended visit of Philipp Jakob Spener to Württemberg, and especially to Tübingen, in 1662.[1] During that visit he was the guest of Johann Andreas Frommann (1626-1690), who two years before had joined the law faculty of Tübingen University. Spener remained in the home of Frommann from June to October. Making this his base of operations he entered into friendly relations with members of the theological faculty. With Raith he carried on extended discussions about Grossgebauer's *Voice of a Watchman.*[2] He succeeded in establishing a very special friendship with Johann Andreas Hochstetter (1637-1720), one of the prominent churchmen of his time who had joined the faculty of Tübingen as ordinary professor of languages and ephor in 1677.[3] While Hochstetter

[1] For further study of the general pietistic development in Württemberg see J. Rössle, *Von Bengel bis Blumhardt*, 1962; O. Schuster, *Schwäbische Glaubenszeugen*, 1946; C. Kolb, "Die Anfänge des Pietismus und Separatismus in Württemberg," *Württembergische Vierteljahrshefte für Landesgeschichte*, vols. 9-11, 1900-1902; W. Claus, *Württembergische Väter*, vol. 1, *Von Bengel bis Burk*, 1887; F. Fritz, *op. cit.*, BwKG, vol. 56, 1956, pp. 99-167; BwKG, vol. 57, 1957, pp. 44-68; F. Fritz, "Konventikel in Württemberg," BwKG, vol. 49, 1949, pp. 99-154; vol. 50, 1950, pp. 65-121; vol. 51, 1951, pp. 78-139; vol. 52, 1952, pp. 28-65; vol. 53, 1953, pp. 82-130; vol. 54, 1954, pp. 75-122; F. Fritz, "Die Wiedertäufer und der Württembergische Pietismus," BwKG, vol. 39, 1939, pp. 81-109; F. Fritz, "Württemberg in der Zeit des Pietismus," BwKG, vol. 55, 195,, pp. 117-124; H. Hermelink, *Geschichte der evangelischen Kirche in Württemberg von der Reformation bis zur Gegenwart*, 1949, p. 136f; A. Köberle, *Das Glaubensvermächtnis der schwäbischen Väter*, 1959; M. Leube, *Geschichte des Tübinger Stifts*, 1921, 1930; C. Palmer, *Die Gemeinschaften and Sekten Württembergs*, 1877; F.W. Kantzenbach, *Orthodoxie und Pietismus*, in *Evangelische Enzyklopädie*, vols. 11-12, p. 209f.

[2] See RI, p. 218.

[3] Hochstetter, like Pfaff, is difficult to classify. While he thought of himself as a representative of Orthodoxy he was so close to Spener in his understanding of Protestantism and so deeply sympathetic to the aims of both Spener and Francke, and so greatly

was a representative of Württemberg's brand of mild Orthodoxy he was so akin to Spener in spirit that Francke is said to have referred to him in 1717 as the Swabian Spener. He was famous for following the Puritan example of rising at 4 AM, spending the morning in prayer and meditation, giving the tenth of his income, and continuing his family devotions sometimes until 12 PM. Little wonder that Spener felt at home in his presence and free to make strategic use of his friendship.

Not only did Spener work for his projected church reform in Württemberg through personal contacts, but he conducted two *collegia* at the same time. The latter were attended by university personnel, as well as by members of the nobility. In the face of these facts, and others which might be cited, it is not true that the rise and early progress of Swabian Pietism is independent of the influence of the Spener-Halle Movement. Here as elsewhere in Germany the latter provided a motivational force which left few sections of German Protestantism untouched.

Yet, in speaking of the beginnings of Swabian Pietism one should be careful not to over-state the Spener-Halle impetus. As has been implied above there was in Württemberg a strong native inclination toward personal piety and social sensitivity which clearly extends through Lutheran Orthodoxy, as it flourished in this region, from the days of the earlier reform party. It was this native combination of Orthodoxy and piety which predisposed most of the members of the theological faculty of the University of Tübingen (the exceptions being Michael Müller, Gottfried Hoffmann, and Michael Förtsch) to look with favor upon Spener's primary concerns.

At the theological foundation (the so called *Stift*), which had been associated with the University of Tübingen since the days of the Reformation, the early Pietistic Movement manifested itself most dramatically in 1703. During that year three tutors at the *Stift*, S.C. Gmelin, J, Oechslin, and J. Rebstock, decided to gather on Sunday afternoons in a wine dresser's hut outside of the town of Tübingen in order to read and discuss the Bible. Soon they were joined by others. Out of this practice came a considerable religious revival, mostly among young people, which presently caused the ecclesiastical authorities at Stutt-

---

appreciated by both of these men, that one is perennially tempted to put him into the pietistic fold. Thus Spener's tract to a theologian in Württemberg (1683) was probably meant for Hochstetter. Furthermore, Hochstetter prevailed upon his son Andreas to live with Spener in Dresden for about six months.

gart grave concern.[1] While this particular conventicle eventually ceased to exist the idea of having a sodality for religiously awakened students long maintained itself at Tübingen. In 1705 Christoph Reuchlin (1660-1707), who had joined the theological faculty in 1699 and who was now dean of the *Stift*, began a pietistic conventicle in his own home. Hochstetter had previously defended the conventicle which had begun in the wine dresser's hut as being of divine origin, and continued to regard such meetings in this light. Equally unstinting support was given to the new movement by Johann Reinhard Hedinger (1664-1704), formerly professor at Giessen and now holding an influential position as court preacher and member of the consistory at Stuttgart.

Swabian Pietism thus had gained influential allies among the intellectuals who more or less set the tone for the University of Tübingen. It was warmly received also by Andreas Adam Hochstetter (1668-1717), the son of Johann, who made it his avowed aim to mediate between Orthodoxy and Pietism,[2] as well as by Andreas Adam's student, the church historian Christoph Eberhard Weissmann (1677-1747), who joined the theological faculty in 1721.[3] Somewhat enigmatic in this context is the position of Christoph Matthias Pfaff (1686-1760), successor to Jäger as chancellor of the university. Kolb points out that he was pietistic both in his understanding of theological method and of the purpose of theology. He held to the typical pietistic position on matters such as conversion, the need for confirmation, critique of existing conditions in the church, sharp differentiation between converted and unconverted church members, emphasis on biblical theology etc.[4] It is safe to say, therefore, that Pfaff was at least intel-

---

[1] Oechslin, one of the participants speaks of "a revival not only at the theological foundation, but in all of Tübingen, which moved many hundreds of souls." (Quoted among others'by F. Pfeil, *Christian Gottlob Pregizer und die Gemeinschaft der Pregnizerianer*, a dissertation at the University of Heidelberg, 1938, p. 8).

[2] He joined the theological faculty of Tübingen in 1707. His deeply devotional spirit is revealed especially in the hymnal he published in 1709. It came out under the title : *Neuvermehrte Seelenharfe, oder Württembergisches Gesangbüchlein.*

[3] C.E. Weissmann's best known work is his *Introductio in Memorabilia ecclesiastica historiae sacrae Novi Testamenti* etc., 1718-1719, in which he follows the historical method of Gottfried Arnold. He was one of the important bulwarks against the onslaught of the Leibnitz-Wolff philosophy.

[4] See C. Kolb, *Die Aufklärung in der Württembergischen Kirche*, 1908, pp. 2-3; also E. Hirsch, *Geschichte der neueren evangelischen Theologie*, 1949-1954, vol. 2, p. 336f. Pfaff's emphasis on the devotional life is evident in the titles of some of his devotional works : *Kurzer Abriss vom wahren Christentum*, 1720; *Kurzer Katechismus, oder die ersten Grundsätze der christlichen Lehre aus dem Grunde des innersten Christentums her-*

lectually on the side of the developing Pietistic Movement and for that reason helped to make the *Stift* at Tübingen its theological center. As a result, a long succession of Swabian Pietists, the so called *Schwäbische Väter*, began to issue from its halls.

BENGEL AND HIS CIRCLE

By far the most prominent of these was Johann Albrecht Bengel (1687-1752).[1] Bengel became the very soul of Swabian Pietism, and the center of a "school" of likeminded men. For that reason he and his circle of followers need to be given some attention.

By the ordinary standards of judgment the circumstances attending Bengel's youth left much to be desired. Throughout the tender years of his childhood calamity seemed to stalk him. He was not yet six years old when his father, who had been pastor at Winnenden, near Waiblingen, passed away. About that time the family homestead was destroyed by the plundering hordes of Louis XIV. Because of the dire circumstances in which the family found itself young Johann was put into the care of a friend of his father. Spindler, his foster father, took him to the town of Marbach, until it, too, was severly damaged by the French. Thus the

---

geleitet, 1720. *Zwölf Betrachtungen über unterschiedene Stücke des wahren und tätigen Christentums*, 1720. His biblicism is attested by his practical Bible commentary, in which he followed Hedinger. What makes all of this seem quite ambiguous, however, is that in his own personal life he did not seem to be as close to the pietistic ethic as he was to that of the Enlightenment. This in spite of the fact that he was suspicious of the insinuation of rationalism into the domain of theology.

[1] The literature on Bengel is distressingly plentiful. The following is an attempt to give a brief introduction to it. F. Baum, *Johann Albrecht Bengel, der Vater des schwäbischen Pietismus*, 1910; J.C.F. Burk, *J.A. Bengels Leben und Wirken*, etc., first ed. 1831; W. Claus, *Württembergische Väter*, vol. 1, 1887; J.P. Fresenius, *Zuverlässige Nachricht von dem Leben, Tod und Schriften des J.A. Bengel*, n.d.; Hermann von der Goltz, "Die theologische Bedeutung J.A. Bengels und seiner Schule," *Jahrbücher für deutsche Theologie*, vol. 6, 1861; K. Hermann, *Johann Albrecht Bengel, der Klosterpräzeptor von Denkendorf*, 1937; G. Mälzer, *Bengel und Zinzendorf*, 1968; E. Nestle, *Bengel als Gelehrter*, 1893; F. Nolte, *J.A. Bengel, ein Gelehrtenbild, aus der zeit des Pietismus*, 1913; *J.A. Bengel, Leben und Auswahl seiner Schriften*, 1868; O. Wächter, *J.A. Bengel. Lebensabriss, Charakter, Briefe und Aussprüche*, 1865. The standard biography is that of Hermann. For an excellent list of bibliographical material see pp. 458-460; also Mälzer, pp. 158-168, and p. 14f; for a list of many writings of Bengel in chronological order see E. Ludwig, "Schriftverständnis und Schriftauslegung bei Johann Albrecht Bengel," BwKG, 1952, Sonderheft 9, pp. 7-8. Unfortunately, no full list of Bengel's works is presently available. Of some help in interpreting him are, of course, the histories of German theology — Gass, vol. 3, and Hirsch, vol. 2, — as well as Hermelink, *op. cit.*, p. 208f.

early wanderings continued until at the age of 12 he came to Stuttgart where he then enrolled in the *Gymnasium*. Characteristically he sought comfort and strength during his later childhood in Arndt's *Wahres Christentum*, in Johann Gerhard's *Heilige Betrachtungen*, and in Immanuel Sonthom's *Golden Gem*.

Bengel knew nothing of any sudden conversion. He could remember no time, in fact, when he did not pray or find deep delight in the edificatory books which had been given him. Under the influence of his foster father personal religious devotion was as natural to him as the air he breathed. The result was that he was eminently prepared for what he found at Tübingen when he entered the *Stift* in 1703. The ongoing movement of religious renewal among students, and the warm religiosity of Reuchlin and Hochstetter, provided a completely congenial environment for his religious maturation. His intellectual interests were turned toward mathematics, philosophy, the classics, and, of course, theology. He graduated in 1707, briefly took a vicarage near Urach, and then spent five more years as tutor at Tübingen. In 1713 he became a teacher at the "cloyster school" of Denkendorf near Tübingen and pastor of the local congregation. In spite of an offer to join the faculty at Giessen he stayed in this position to the end of his life. His relatively humble career was interrupted only by the usual study trip during his first year at Denkendorf. It took him to the various intellectual center of Germany, including Halle. Here he not only met Francke, Anton, and Breithaupt, but he learned to appreciate their work. From Halle he wrote to a cousin that for the first time he was beginning to realize the need for fellowhsip.[1]

Theologically Bengel shared in general the convictions of the Spener-Halle Movement, the significant literature of which he had studied during his days at Tübingen. Yet, he put upon this Pietism the stamp of his own genius. Thus he shared Halle's concern about the new life, but he did not even care to suggest any particular road that leads to it. With the Spener-Halle tradition Bengel believed in the need for repentance, yet his writings yield no evidence of any exaggerated emphasis upon man's radical sinfulness or upon the need for a personal religious crisis. Like Halle he was apprehensive about the adverse effect of indifferent things (*adiaphora*) upon a person's religious maturation, yet he insisted that "in such things one should not immediately come along with rules."[2] With Spener and Halle Bengel shared a

[1] Wächter, *op. cit.*, p. 13.

[2] Quoted by Wächter, *op. cit.*, p. 423.

profoundly critical attitude toward the Lutheran Church of his day, yet he refrained from promulgating any program for its renewal. Halle's political approach to a projected reformation was, in fact, totally foreign to his thinking. The institution of conventicles, deemed necessary by most Pietists of his day, received only passive support from Bengel. On the other hand, while at Halle biblical interpretation was part of the total theological enterprise, at Denkendorf it became Bengel's exclusive concern. Where Francke and his followers exercised the greatest restraint with regard to their eschatological speculations, Bengel rushed into this area with all the intensity of his being.

As implied in what has been said Bengel made his contribution to Protestant theology chiefly at two points — biblical criticism (as well as the exegesis based upon it), and eschatology. Though in his own understanding of things the two are inseparable, each of these topics needs to be given some attention in this discussion.

Before we speak of Bengel's interest in biblical interpretation, however, reference should again be made to the relationship between Lutheran Pietism and the Reformed Tradition. Within historic Lutheranism a certain Melanchthonian tradition, which was open to Reformed influences, had always maintained itself.[1] Speaking broadly it may be said that these extraneous elements within Lutheranism grouped themselves around two foci : There were always Lutherans who put emphasis on the Christian life as over against the prevailing Lutheran emphasis upon the truth content of the Christian message; there were always Lutherans who put emphasis upon the primacy of the Bible itself as its own theological norm, over against the more typical Lutheran insistence on the authority of confessional symbols in the matter of biblical interpretation. During the seventeenth century it had been the Lutheran reform party which had made the attempt, unconscious as it may have been, to graft these Reformed elements upon contemporary Lutheranism, an attempt which was repeated later by the Spener-Halle movement.

This same process can be witnessed at Württemberg. It is well known, of course, that at the time of the Reformation it was only the determined effort of Luther's Swabian friend, Johannes Brenz, which finally erected the necessary dogmatic bulwarks against the Reformed theology of Württemberg's neighbors to the south and to the west.[2]

---

[1] See RI, p. 189.

[2] For the story of the Reformation in Württemberg see Hermelink, *op. cit.*, p. 5f.

Inspite of this, however, the Reformed elements referred to above gained entrance into Swabian Lutheranism. They were transmitted by men such as Andreä and Hochstetter. Jäger had unabashedly adopted the federalist theology of John Coccejus. Hedinger's annotated edition of the New Testament was being strenuously opposed by Orthodoxists for inserting Calvinistic "heresies" into the stream of "pure" Lutheran doctrine. And Andreas Adam Hochstetter had not only absorbed fully the Reformed elements in Spener's theology, but he was in close touch with Reformed theologians both in the Netherlands and in England. Under these circumstances the theological atmosphere which Bengel breathed at Tübingen was fraught with a certain amount of confessional ambiguity. The Tübingen faculty was consciously loyal to the Lutheran confessions. Unconsciously, however, and to the dismay of many Orthodoxists Tübingen, like Helmstädt, Rinteln, Giessen, and Göttingen, was open to transconfessional insights.

Bengel began his work on the Bible in this theological climate. Basic to his methodology is the work of Johann Coccejus, who had pioneered in altering completely the course of scriptural interpretation. For the scholastic approach to this theological discipline he had substituted the historical one. Coccejus' work had in turn been carried foreward by Campegius Vitringa (1659-1722), who with relative freedom in textual criticism had insisted upon basing all biblical exegesis upon a carefully applied critical apparatus. Joachim Lange of Halle had thereafter introduced the exegetical methodology of Vitringa into the stream of Lutheran Pietism. Bengel's contribution, therefore, to the field of textual criticism has nothing to do with breaking new ground. He simply applied models which had already been established. On the other hand, his significance lies in carrying forward the work of his predecessors and in applying their methodology with unprecedented thoroughness.

It seems that Bengel felt the need for critical study of biblical texts from the very beginning of his days at Tübingen. What troubled him were the various readings of the Greek text to which his studies referred him. He was agitated by the question of the relationship of these variants to the absolute religious authority of the Bible, which he regarded as an axiomatic presupposition for all earnest Christians. In the face of various readings of many biblical passages how can one regard the totality of such passages as the infallible Word of God? This was the problem which confronted him. The immediate occasion was the *Oxford Greek Testament*, of which he had secured a copy through the help of Francke. In it a number of variants of the Greek text were given without explanation as to which might be the better reading. The situation was not helped when the year after Bengel came to Tübingen Hedinger published his annotated New Testament, which purported to correct Luther's translation, and which, for that reason, became a source of great irritation to the Orthodoxists of the day. The subsequent rush of Bible editions in Württemberg aggravated the situation. Bengel's mounting interest in textual problems is attested by the fact that his esteemed teacher, Hochstetter, asked Bengel to proofread his own contribution to the *Biblia pauperum* of 1712. Thus it is quite understandable that by 1715 Bengel registered in his diary the decision to work on a critical edition of the New Testament.[1]

In order to be able to appreciate what Bengel attempted to do one must understand both his task as he saw it and the presuppositions with which he began.

Beginning with the latter it should be pointed out that Bengel's basic assumption with regard to his critical work was the following : "The Scriptures, therefore, of the Old and New Testaments, form a most sure and precious system of divine testimonies. For not only are the various writings, when considered separately, worthy of God, but also, when received as a whole, they exhibit one entire and perfect body, unencumbered by excess, unimpaired by defect. The Bible is, indeed, the true fountain of wisdom, which they, who have once actually tasted it, prefer to all mere compositions of men, however holy, however experienced, however devout, however wise."[2] Bengel thus assumed that there is an objective system of divinely revealed truth embodied in the original manuscripts which underlie later translations. He assumed, furthermore, that through all the periods of history out of which the biblical documents have come biblical language remained essentially unchanged.[3] It was not his contention, of course, that particular words have the same meaning in all contexts. What he meant in this connection was that the basic scriptural concepts are the same wherever they appear in the Bible. With Zwingli he assumed, furthermore, that in the original text God speaks with perfect clarity, though Bengel tempered the bold theological implications of such a view with Calvin's

---

1 Mälzer, *op. cit.*, p. 17.

2 Bengel, *Gnomon of the New Testament*, transl. by Bandinel and Fausset, 1860, vol. 1, author's preface, p. 7.

3 *Ibid.*, p. 45.

doctrine of divine condescension, i.e., God has adjusted the language of Scripture to man's level of apprehension. In spite of this, he felt, however, that even the external forms of biblical language manifest a certain aura of divine excellence never approached by subsequent Christian writers.[1]

Underlying Bengel's exegesis, which was based upon his critical work, were two further assumptions, which are always implicit even if not consciously set out. On the one hand there is the assumption of the same kind of an *analogia fidei*, inherent in the corporate religious experience of the regenerated community, which was discussed in reference to the theology of the Spener-Halle type of 18th century Protestantism.[2] Like his contemporaries at Halle Bengel was quite sure that the system of truth disclosed by God in the original manuscripts of the Bible is not equally available to all. It becomes amenable to full human understanding only upon the fulfilling of two conditions, namely, man's regeneration and his willingness to engage in "proper and careful research."[3] Added to this assumption is the other, namely, that to the people of God the Bible is meant to be more than a guide to salvation. In addition to being such a guide it is divinely intended to afford a breath-taking glimpse into the fullness of God's purposes to the final glorification of the entire natural order. This is what Bengel means when he tells us that the Bible is "an incomparable report about the divine economy regarding the human race, from the beginning to the end of all things."[4]

In the light of these presuppositions Bengel understood his task to be a twofold one. On the one hand, he felt providentially called[5] to restore to the Christian community a biblical text which is completely reliable, because it is as close as is humanly possible to the original documents. It was not his primary intention, therefore, to write a scholarly work, but to employ his skill for the purpose of giving concerned Christians new confidence in the scriptural foundation of their faith. Nor was he interested in constructing another theological system, but rather to point to the Bible, critically examined, as the end of any need for such

---

[1] "Even in their external form the Holy Scriptures have a peculiarity which manifests a select flavor — and this delicate flavor is impaired even by the most minute change." (Quoted from Bengel by Hermann, *op. cit.*, p. 370.)

[2] *Ante*, chap. 2, p. 48.

[3] Bengel, *Erklärte Offenbarung Johannis*, etc., 1834, p. XVIII.

[4] From Bengel's *Ordo Temporum* ed. by H. von der Goltz, *op. cit.*, p. 13.

[5] *Gnomon of the New Testament*, *op. cit.*, p. 8.

systems. Precisely this is the significance of the word *Gnomon* (pointer) which he used in the title of his famous work, and the use of which he explains as folllows : "I have long since given the name *Gnomon*, a modest, and, as I think appropriate title, to these *Exegetical Annotations*, which perform only the office of an index. — The *Gnomon* points the way with sufficient clearness. If you are wise, the text itself teaches you all things."[1]

The second, and equally important, aspect of his task, was that of applying his critical findings to the exegetical task in hand. Bengel chose to distinguish carefully between criticism and exegesis, feeling that the only justification for the former lies in the latter, and that the latter apart from the former is wholly unreliable. He was deeply exercised about the tendency of his day, found among Orthodoxists, enthusiasts, and Enlighteners alike, to read into Scripture their own notions, or to superimpose upon it their own systems. "Down to the present time —," he said, "there has not developed in the church either the experience or the insight with reference to Scripture, which is exhibited in Scripture itself. A proof of this we have in the luxurious growth of opposing opinions."[2] His avowed aim was, therefore, to circumvent the plurality of theological opinions of his day through exegetical pointers toward that which, in his opinion, the writers of the sacred books really meant. To this end he employed not only his massive linguistic gifts, but his capacity for extensive historical research. Rather naively, perhaps, Bengel believed that he could excise from the memory of the church the divisive theological excrescences of the centuries, and to repristinate in the mind of each sincere reader of the Bible the exact historical conditions necessary for its true understanding. In this way, he hoped, the truth of God would finally prevail in the land, and the loquacious stridency of theological controversy would at last perish in the net of its own contradictions.

In order to achieve this task Bengel perfected a set of rules for biblical criticism which long elicited the admiration of European scholarship.[3] The most frequently quoted of these is the following : "The more difficult reading is to be preferred over the easier one." In executing his critical and exegetical work he labored with a patience and dedica-

---

1 *Ibid.*, p. 9.

2 Quoted by Hermann, *op. cit.*, p. 390.

3 Many of them are found in the preface to his *Gnomon*. They are embodied, of course, in the critical apparatus to his *Novum Testamentum*. For an analysis of his critical method see Ludwig, *op. cit.*

tion which would be difficult to exaggerate. Thus he says in a letter to his brother-in-law C.F. Reuss : "Almost all of December I spent in examining the passage I John 5 : 7, and I now believe to have saved its genuineness. It was done in this way, however, that this verse is inserted after verse 8."[1] His labor involved the collection of manuscripts from all over Europe and the critical comparison of thirty of these. As a result of his dedication he was able to publish his *Novum Testamentum* in 1734. This he did in two parts, the first containing the received text with variant readings and the second containing the critical apparatus. The same year he published a small edition giving only the corrected Greek text together with marginal notes. The final result of all his critical labors he published in his massive *Gnomon Novi Testamenti* (1742).[2] It represents a distillation of 20 years of scholarly activity.

In Bengel's day there was considerable criticism of his critical-exegetical work, which forced him into writing several apologies. What must have hurt him more deeply than anything else was Halle's ambiguous response. Francke felt that the Oxford edition was sufficient to satisfy Protestantism's scholarly needs and that Bengel's work was, therefore, quite superfluous. In his quiet way Bengel responded as follows : "While these men continue to divide the streams of life — I look after the well-chambers (*Brunnenstuben*). This is a work about which many think little, though they, too, enjoy its results. They, in doing their work, are unknown to the wicked. Well, I have something which is unknown to the pious."[3] In time, however, the scholarly world reacted favorably. His critical-exegetical works were translated, published and republished for many years to come. Typical of the accolades heaped upon their author was John Wesley's reference to him as "that great light of the Christian world."[4] While Bengel did not reach his objective of giving Christendom an absolutely unassailable text he set the tone for all subsequent efforts in the area of text criticism. Above all, his accomplishments should lay to rest forever the astonishing claim that Pietism was intellectually unproductive.

In the area of eschatological speculation the movement of history in

---

[1] Quoted by Hermann, p. 384.

[2] The title is significant. In translation it is : *A Pointer for the New Testament in Which is Indicated, from the Original Meaning of the Words, the Simplicity, Depth, Unity, and Salutariness* (*salubritas*) *of the Heavenly Thoughts* (*sensuum*).

[3] J.C.F. Burk, *Dr. Johann Albrecht Bengel's literarischer Briefwechsel*, 1836, pp. 76-77.

[4] J. Wesley, *Explanatory Notes Upon the New Testament*, 10th ed., 1856, p. 4.

itself has placed a question mark behind the value of Bengel's equally conscientious efforts. The Parousia, which he so confidently expected in 1836, did not occur, and the exact date which he set for this event fills most modern readers with amazement at the boldness of such an undertaking. Nevertheless, Bengel was absolutely convinced that he was to be the divinely chosen instrument to make these disclosures. Whenever his contemporaries counseled caution he countered with a remark such as the following : "After the fair in autumn a number of attacks upon the *Erklärte Offenbarung* and the *Ordo Temporum* came to hand, which, of course, do not confuse me. Yet, they make me sad, because the world, and those who permit themselves to be respected as the eyes of the world, are so far from the truth, though it is spread before them."[1] With an astounding sense of charisma, therefore, this otherwise retiring and self-effacing scholar proceeded to tell the world of the details of its destiny. The blueprints for man's tomorrow, which he projected, are found in his *Erklärte Offenbarung* (1740), his *Ordo Temporum* (1741), his *Cyclus* (1745), and his *Weltalter* (1746).[2]

In writing these books Bengel sincerely believed that the entire progression of historical events was fully present in the mind of God before the world began. He further held, as has been mentioned above, that God in his love and mercy has purposed to let his own people in on the secrets of man's corporate destiny. Thus he regarded the apocalyptic passages of the Bible, and especially the Book of Revelation, as prefigured history. Yet, its unfolding remains a veiled secret to which God's Spirit himself must impart the key. This he will do for the Christian who in diligent research seeks to understand. Bengel thus claims no special revelation, and he specifically rejects all cabbalistic or astral sources.[3] Nevertheless, he proceeded to set out an exact chronology of the history of God's dealings with men, beginning at creation (3939 B.C.) and ending with the final judgment.[4]

It is difficult, indeed, to comment on the peculiarities in the belief-system of a man who appears to have been so sincerely wrong as Bengel. He grew up in an environment, of course, in which this kind of expectation was making itself widely felt within that whole segment of Protes-

---

[1] J.A. Bengel, *Erklärte Offenbarung Johannis oder vielmehr Jesu Christi*, ed. by Burk, 1834, p. 721 (In an appendix added by Burk).

[2] For the full title of these works see Mälzer, pp. 160-161.

[3] *Erklärte Offenbarung, op. cit.*, p. XVI.

[4] For details see Burk's summary in *Dr. Johann Albrecht Bengel's Leben und Wirken*, 1831, p. 273f.

tantism which was tired of the old wine skins of Orthodoxy. Spener had already stirred up controversy about his own insights into the course of future history, though he had never systematized his views. Halle had followed closely in his footsteps. Far more reckless had been the disciple of Philadelphianism, Johann Wilhelm Petersen, who had astonished his fellow Lutherans in 1692 with an apocalyptic alarm.[1] Among the separatists the otherwise mild, but very enthusiastic, wig maker Johann Tennhardt had thrown many Lutherans into an uproar when in 1718 he had forecast the imminent judgment of the Almighty upon an unrepentant church.[2] Furthermore, Bengel lived in an age in which one could see everywhere the signs of the breakup of traditional values and attitudes, a circumstance which has always made for apocalyptic speculation. Still, one cannot help but wish that he could have seen fit to be more restrained in the use of his predictive powers.

This is not to say, however, that Bengel's prophesies did not perform a service for a large segment of Protestantism during the decades to come. Amazingly enough, a great many predictions he had made subsequently appeared to come true.[3] The result was that in numerous pietistic circles Bengel's influence continued to grow, and this not only because of his exegetical helps, but precisely because of his predictions. Gradually a religiously awakened laity began to consider him an outstanding authority in the whole area of religiously inspired prognostication. His commentary on *Revelation*, therefore, served as a widely trusted guide to God's secrets in many homes, as well as a study book for the numerous conventicles which have since been part and parcel of Swabian Protestantism. By insisting, as he did, that all history is God's history, and that the times of men and nations are in the hands of a heavenly Father, who is both just and merciful, Bengel helped his countrymen to transcend the problems, ambiguities, and frustrations of human existence.

Yet, Bengel's very substantial influence upon clergy and laity alike was not merely the result of what he accomplished, but of what he was. Almost every testimony which comes to hand regarding his character is filled with unstinted praise and admiration. In the long history of Christianity Bengel belongs to that select group of men, whose memory

1 *Die Wahrheit des herrlichen Reiches Christi welches in der siebenten Posaune noch zu erwarten ist.*

2 *Nützliche und höchstnötige Warnung* etc.

3 For details see Hermelink, pp. 226-227.

is treated lovingly by even the most critical observers. In his autobiography he tells us : "My aim was never to have good, easy, pleasant days or hours, to amass or save worldly goods, or to capture positions of honor; my ambition was exclusively directed toward doing faithfully whatever was at hand, be it important or unimportant — according to the ability which God has given me."[1] In this self-estimate there is no over-statement. He was a dedicated, utterly meticulous, as well as courageous scholar, an effective and deeply esteemed teacher, a pastor beloved by hundreds of people beyond the limits of his congregation, and a preacher whose transparently sincere love for God and man seemed to make every sermon an event to his listeners. During a religiously intolerant age Bengel insisted upon the right of free religious expression; in the face of reckless religious enthusiasm he counseled balance and common sense; against the arrogant sophistication of many professional religionists he set a childlike religious faith in a Father who can be utterly trusted. "My entire Christianity," he says with that simplicity which was characteristic of him, "consists in this, that I belong to my Lord Jesus Christ, and that I count this as my only glory."[2] While he was entirely open toward the mystical approach to religion[3] he tried to check the rampant religious subjectivism of many of his contemporaries by establishing what he regarded as a solid foundation in Scripture. Toward the godless he advocated a confident "soft-sell."[4] He supported those who felt that they had a need for conventicles, but he did not regard the latter as an essential institution in the church.

The characteristics of Bengel's own religious life — warmth, simplicity, toleration, ethical sensitivity, a sense of balance — were communicated to much of the Pietistic Movement in Swabia. There are instances, of course, where religious emotion ran rampant, but generally speaking, the Pietism of Württemberg was like a leaven which slowly and unobtrusively leavened the whole lump of Lutheran thought and practice in that region.

Bengel's influence was disseminated throughout his native Württemberg, and territories contiguous to it, by a considerable group of able

---

[1] *Das Leben Johann Albrecht Bengels von ihm selbst beschrieben* etc., 1829, p. 15.

[2] *Ibid.*, p. 13.

[3] Claus, *op. cit.*, p. 24.

[4] "No one," he said, "is so coarse-haired, that he does not have a spot where he can be reached." *Ibid.*, p. 26.

followers.[1] These men produced an astounding amount of edificatory literature, mostly sermonic in form, of which it is possible to mention only the most important here. Among the highly prized books of sermons read in Swabian homes were those of I.G. Brastberger. His *Evangelische Zeugnisse der Wahrheit* (1758)[2] summed up the substance of Christianity as being a right attitude toward God, toward oneself, and toward one's neighbor.[3] Also very popular were G.C. Rieger's *Herzenpostillen*, a collection of down to earth sermons in two volumes, the aim of which was to promote godliness by informing the mind and by strengthening the will.[4] J.F. Reuss took the Pietism of Württemberg to Scandinavia, being court preacher in Denmark and later professor of theology at Copenhagen. The high seriousness of his preaching is evidenced in the questions he put to the Danish court : "Is everything in order? Is your heart free from the world? Are you cleansed of all sins— ? Are you made holy by the Spirit of God?"[5] The essence of Swabian Pietism was distilled into a series of brief meditations, two for every day of the week, and then published under the title *Hausbuch* by M.F. Roos.[6] The purpose of the book, as stated in the preface, was to stimulate personal devotion among Christians and to help them maintain it.[7] Its popularity attests the fact that the author accomplihsed what he had set out to do. Through the efforts of P.F. Hiller Swabian piety entered the hymnody of world Protestant-

[1] See R. Kübel's introduction to Bengel's *Gnomon*, 1891 ed., p. 17. Among Bengel's best known followers during the eighteenth century were : Georg Conrad Rieger (1687-1743), Philipp Friedrich Hiller (1699-1769), Jeremias Friedrich Reuss (1700-1777), Friedrich Christopher Steinhofer (1706-1776), Johann Christian Storr (1712-1773), Johann Friedrich Flattich (1713-1794), Philipp David Burk (1714-1770), Immanuel Gottlob Brastberger (1716-1764), Carl Heinrich Rieger (1726-1791), and Magnus Friedrich Roos (1727-1803), as well as the lawyer Johann Jakob Moser (1701-1785).

[2] For his other works see MI, vol. 1, p. 559.

[3] *Evangelische Zeugnisse der Wahrheit* etc., 1758, p. 131.

[4] *Herzens-Postille oder zur Fortpflanzung des wahren Christentums etc.*, 1742, preface, p. 11.

[5] *Zweite Sammlung heiliger Reden vor hoher Königlicher Dänischer Herrschaft* etc., 1748, p. 56.

[6] For a long list of his other works see J.J. Gradmann, *Das gelehrte Schwaben, oder Lexicon der jetzt lebenden schwäbischen Schriftsteller*, 1802, pp. 518-521.

[7] *Christliches Hausbuch welches Morgen und Abendandachten aufs ganze Jahr — enthält*, etc., 1783, vol. 1, preface, p. 12.

ism.[1] His *Liederkästlein*, first published in 1767, and containing 366 compositions, immediately won him a place in the heart of his countrymen. This place he maintained, so that in time his fame began to approach that of Paul Gerhard. When he said, "I believe, therefore I sing," he put his finger on the secret of his power. His hymns were a natural, untortured, yet highly lyrical, outflowing of his own religious life, which purposely omitted what he called, "exaggerated expressions of a high flying imagination."[2]

It is interesting to note, that in all of these men, most of whom had been associated with Bengel from their boyhood days at Denkendorf, we find only the best that was in their master — a sane, balanced emphasis upon love for God and man. In their thinking Bengel's eschatological speculations constituted an *addendum* to which they may have held privately, but which was, as Bengel undoubtedly wanted it to be, quite unobtrusive in their public utterances.

The most systematic statement of the theology of these men, and by implication, of the theological heritage of Bengel, is found in P.D. Burk's three volume *Rechtfertigung*.[3] In it, too, Bengel's eschatology is suppressed, while his insights into the nature of the Christian life constitute the substance of the discussion. The influence of Bengel upon the author is immediately apparent in the latter's avowed intention to do only two things, namely, to inform the reader about the teachings of the Bible and to help him to apply this information to his own situation. Methodologically Burk seems to go beyond his master, however, by a rather radical emphasis upon the principle of experiential verification of biblical insights. To be sure, he treats the biblical "ground of knowledge" in the first part. All the rest of the discussion, however, has to do with the application of these truths to Christian experience, and with their verification in that experience. It is quite apparent, therefore, that while the title of the book speaks of justi-

[1] For a good article on him see A. Leidhold, "Philipp Friedrich Hiller," BwKG, vol. 59, 1959, pp. 150-170. Among Hiller's most popular hymns are, "Mir ist Erbarmung widerfahren," and, "Jesus Christus herrscht als König." For a list of his many works see Leidhold, pp. 162-170; also BMC, vol. 103, column 1125.

[2] *Geistliches Liederkästlein zum Lobe Gottes* etc., first part, 1768, preface, p. 4.

[3] *Die Rechtfertigung und deren Versicherung im Herzen nach dem Worte Gottes betrachtet*, 1763-1765. This is a massive work in seven parts, the first two of which were published in 1757 under the title, *Theologia pastoralis practica*. Many other works by him are available at Tübingen, among them this multi-volume *Fingerzeig*, 1760-1766. As a young man Burk had spent long periods of time in the Bengel home and finally married one of his daughters. Bengel referred to him as his alter-ego.

fication, the real concern of the author was the personal religious certainty (*Versicherung*) which in the life of the Christian must follow upon God's justifying act. Such "joyous, happy, felt certainty,"[1] he insisted, is not the result of any intellectual pondering of Christian affirmations, but of the personal experience of their significance. Thus we find that in Burk and his friends there was the same shift of theological emphasis which had taken place at Halle. Orthodoxy's exclusive preoccupation with God's saving acts and their intellectual significance now became a secondary concern. In the foreground of theological interest was the question of their psychological and social significance.

Oetinger and the Theosophical Tradition

The second important personality in connection with the Pietism of Württemberg was Friedrich Christoph Oetinger (1702-1782).[2] By most estimates he was, in fact, the most original theologian of the eighteenth century in Württemberg, and perhaps in all of Germany. For that reason he needs to be given some attention here.

The outward circumstances of his life are uneventful and hence need not detain us.[3] More important is the story of his religious maturation. In his autobiography[4] he affords the reader an insight into that profound restlessness which made him above all else a religious seeker. Even during his boyhood days he was aware of the fact that he seemed

---

[1] *Die Rechtfertigung*, vol. 1, p. 12.

[2] The literature on Oetinger is extensive. See K.A. Auberlen, *Die Theosophie Oetingers*, 1847; M. Wieser, *Der sentimentale Mensch*, 1924; Elizabeth Zinn, *Die Theologie des Friedrich Christoph Oetinger*, 1932; F. Seebass, *Friedrich Christoph Oetinger, Denker und Seelsorger*, 1953; W.A. Hauck, *Das Geheimnis des Lebens. Naturforschung und Gottesauffassung Friedrich Christoph Oetingers*, 1947; J. Herzog, *Friedrich Christoph Oetinger*, 1962. Selections from his works are found in O. Herpel, *Friedrich Christoph Oetinger, die heilige Philosophie*, 1923, as well as in K.C.E. Ehmann, *Friedrich Christoph Oetingers Leben und Briefe*, etc., 1859. His works are available in various editions, among them *Sämmtliche Schriften*, ed. by K.C.E. Ehmann, 1858-1863, and *Sämmtliche Predigten*, 1852f.

[3] Oetinger was born at Göppingen, received his early training at Blaubeuren and Bebenhausen, and spent the years 1722-1727 at the *Stift* at Tübingen. After the usual study trip (1729f) he came to Tübingen once more, this time as tutor (1731-1738), his second stay at Tübingen being interrupted by another study trip. Upon completion of his education he held successive pastorates at Hirsau (1738-1743), Schnaitheim (1743-1746), and Walddorf (1746-1752), deanships at Weinsberg (1752-1759) and Herrenberg (1759-1766), and finally a prelacy at Murrhardt (1766f).

[4] *Selbstbiographie. Geneologie der reellen Gedanken eines Gottgelehrten*, ed. by J. Rössle, 1961. The title is significant.

to be divided against himself. For a time he had difficulty in deciding whether he should take up law or theology. Finally, after a conversion experience (1721), the question was resolved in favor of the latter. Accordingly he began his studies at Tübingen the following year. Deeply dissatisfied, however, with the answers which Orthodoxy gave to his questions he devoted himself to a thorough study of Leibnitz and Wolff. Yet, the more thoroughly he entered into their world of thought the more he became convinced that he had chanced upon another valley of dry bones.

At this juncture a happy circumstance occurred. In revealing his intellectual difficulties to the proprietor of the powder mill at Tübingen, Johann Kaspar Oberberger, the latter handed him the works of Jakob Boehme. Oetinger read them avidly, and presently found that they opened up to him vistas of insight of which he had been wholly unaware. Not even Bengel, who had hitherto been his religious mentor, had been able to do for him what Boehme promised to accomplish. Accordingly Oetinger drank deeply at the well of Boehmist speculation and was thus introduced into the world of theosophic thought. Boehme, however, did more for him than give him philosophical answers. He whetted the young man's appetite for yet other sources of religious insight. When the time came, therefore, he used his study trips to find these sources. Thus he went to Berleburg, where Johann Friedrich Rock espoused inspirationism, and where mystical Pietism was currently supplying the inspiration to publish the *Berleburger Bibel* in eight folio volumes (1726-1742). Via Halle and Jena he went to *Hernnhut* upon the invitation of Spangenberg. During his second trip, which had become possible because his parents had passed away, he seems to have made it a point to visit a whole variety of peculiar saints, both in Germany and in the Netherlands, including a circle of Jewish cabbalists at Frankfurt a.M. The latter acquainted him with Knorr von Rosenroth's commentary on the *Sohar* (his *Cabbala denudata*), as well as with the works of Jizchak Lorija, whose messianic cabbalism made a deep impression on him. Only upon the earnest urging of his friends not to become a complete "loner" did he finally return to his homeland and take up, in time, the duties of a pastorate.

Of the many streams of influence which converged upon the intellectual development of Oetinger the most revolutionary was undoubtedly that of the theosophical tradition eminating from Valentin Weigel (1533-1588) and Jakob Boehme (1575-1624). Throughout Germany the quietly pervasive influence of Böhme, the shoemaker of Görlitz, had made itself felt increasingly during the second part of the seventeenth century. To religiously sensitive people in all walks of life, at the court and in the farm houses, at the universities as well as in the studies of humble country pastors, Boehme seemed to answer many of the religious questions which Lutheran Orthodoxy did not even understand.

Boehme's thoughts were mediated to the generation under discussion by a deeply devoted and very vocal group of followers, whose radical critique of the church became a mounting source of irritation to all who regarded doctrinal stability and institutional tranquility as the great allies of religion.[1] Württemberg, too, came to hear the disturbing echoes of the voice of Görlitz. Thus pastor Ludwig Brunnquell of Grossbottwar found himself already dismissed from his post in 1679 for taking Boehme seriously. The same fate had befallen Johann Jacob Zimmermann of Bietigheim in 1681, and for the same reason. The edict of 1694, though it protected Spenerian Pietism, was specifically aimed at Boehmist "enthusiasm."[2] Established Lutheranism in Württemberg became especially alarmed about the activities of the famous spur-maker of Heilbronn, Johann Georg Rosenbach,[3] who seemed to be part of the Boehmist conspiracy to corrupt the faith. Generally speaking, however, repressive measures in Württemberg were mild, making it possible for people like the powder miller of Tübingen to attend the rather unexciting Lutheran worship service on Sunday morning and to discuss the more breath-taking revelations of Boehme with friends in the afternoon. In this way Oetinger found a congenial religious atmosphere in which his theosophical perspective could mature and bear fruit.

That Oetinger was profoundly influenced by Boehme he himself acknowledged repeatedly. How deeply he felt himself indebted to him is indicated by the fact that he wrote a tract in his mentor's defense,[4] as well as by the fact that he systematically tried to answer the questions arising out of Boehme's system.[5]

There were several insights in Boehme's writings which seemed to

---

[1] See section on radical Pietism, p. 169f.

[2] See Hermelink, *op. cit.*, p. 191f.

[3] See p. 206f.

[4] *Halatophili Irenai. Vorstellung wie viel Jacob Boehmes Schriften zur lebendigen Erkenntnis beitragen*, 1731. *Sämmtliche Schriften*, vol. 1, 1858, pp. 249-328.

[5] *Versuch einer Auflösung der 177 Fragen aus Jakob Boehme*, 1777, *Sämmtliche Schriften*, vol. 1, 1858, pp. 329-396. It is noteworthy to find that he wrote this work at the end of his career.

intrigue Oetinger especially. In an age in which the realms of spirit and of matter were being increasingly torn apart (Newton vs. Leibnitz and Wolff) he found in Boehme a conceptual scheme for keeping them together. This was the idea of evolution, of which the latter speaks at many points, By means of the seven fountain spirits (*Quellgeister*), or properties of all material and spiritual existences, the total process of becoming is described by Boehme as a movement toward ultimate harmony.[1] Related to this was the latter's understanding of God, which seemed especially impressive to Oetinger. To Boehme God was that Mystery which moves deliberately and constantly toward self-understanding through progressive self-actualization. Philosophy, therefore, as Boehme understood it, becomes basically the history of the ultimate Mystery striving to know itself.[2] In this process of becoming God unites in himself all opposites, both in the realm of matter and spirit. To Oetinger, who had hitherto thought of God statically, along the lines of Malebranche, this concept of deity as *actus purissimus* was especially revealing.[3] It promised to tie together, vitalistically and organismically, the entire cosmic process, the natural realm and the spiritual realm, and to do so objectively as well as in cognition. The fact that Boehme's system, furthermore, found ample room for God's love[4] made it doubly appealing to Oetinger. The seer of Görlitz truly seemed to have given his Swabian disciple the key to the secrets of nature and grace, good and evil, the present and the future. His whole thinking was changed. He now knew that in all and over all, behind all and before all, in the knower and in the known, is God — a God who must be understood paradoxically as both immanent and transcendent, vital force and heavenly Father, ever just and ever kind.

Besides this Oetinger adopted from Boehme the related idea that the natural realm, as well as Scripture, is a medium of divine revelation, and that therefore the study of one will yield at least some insight into the other. Of course, so Boehme taught him, it is not possible for man to think the full range of God's thoughts after him, unless the latter in

---

[1] See Boehme's *Von der Gnadenwahl* (1623), *Sämmtliche Schriften*, facsimile edition of 1957, vol. 6, p. 24f; also the *Aurora*, *ibid.*, vol. 1, beginning with chapter 8.

[2] Adopted from H.H. Brinton, *The Mystic Will*, 1930, p. 108.

[3] Ehmann, *op. cit.*, pp. 36-38.

[4] See Boehme's *Aurora*, *Sämmtliche Schriften*, facsimile ed. of 1955, vol. 1, p. 103f. Love is the fifth *Quellgeist* involved in the creative process.

his condescension opens himself the floodgates of understanding.[1] The reason is that human reason (*Vernunft*), which necessarily proceeds by bits and pieces, has access only to the most elementary knowledge. The deeper layers of divine self-disclosure must be apprehended through a divinely wrought *Verstand*,[2] which is associated with the new being in Christ, and which involves the whole of that new being. It is this *Verstand* which alone opens up to man the true vision into reality, thus permitting him to see the natural and the spiritual in right relation. Hence, Boehme taught, philosophy and theology cannot be separated, both being integral parts of the one *philosophia sacra*. Scientific study, too, has its motivational springs in personal religion, and religious study is experimentally augmented and corroborated. On this basis Life, which in so many people is fragmented, becomes whole again, its wholeness including that spiritual corporeality in which alone it can see God.[3]

To try to follow up the other wells of wisdom at which the young Oetinger tried to quench his intellectual thirst would be as difficult, as it would be futile. He always felt himself deeply indebted to Bengel and, as is apparent from the extant correspondence between them, continued to remain the older man's friend. There can be no doubt about the fact that in his understanding of the Christian life, as well as in many of his basic theological presuppositions the influence of Bengel remained strong — so strong, in fact, that he has frequently been considered as belonging to the Bengelian circle. On the other hand, his syncretistic temper lead him to sample every opinion which promised to shed some light upon the problems posed by his questing mind. Still it needs to be said that Oetinger digested well what he heard and read, and then made it thoroughly his own. The insights which he gained he wrote down in approximately one hundred works. Unfortunately for the people who would like to understand him he made little effort at a systematic presentation of his thoughts. The only real attempt in this direction is his *Theologia ex idea vitae deducta* (1765), which turned out to be his most significant work. The more practical aspects of his thought may be culled from his *Reden nach dem allgemeinen Wahrheitsgefühl* (1758), a book of sermons which gained considerable popularity.[4]

[1] Boehme felt that in fifteen minutes of special revelation, which he compared to a cloud-burst, all his essential insights had come to him. See W.E. Peuckert's introduction to the *Aurora*, *Sämmtliche Schriften*, facsimile ed. of 1958, vol. 1, p. 5f.

[2] See *Clavis*, *Sämmtliche Schriften*, vol. 9, pp. 104-105.

[3] See *Mysterium Magnum*, *Sämmtliche Schriften*, facsimile ed. of 1958, p. 70f.

[4] A rather full list of his works is available in MI, vol. 10, pp. 198-204.

In turning from the Pietists we have discussed thus far to Oetinger we find ourselves suddenly in a different intellectual climate. Instead of the antimetaphysical bias of the Halle men, or even of Bengel, Oetinger regarded his task as being in part at least that of finding an adequate philosophical undergirting of the pietistic theology. Being thoroughly aware of the shifting philosophical winds of his time, he saw quite clearly what was not seen at Halle, namely, that it was no longer possible for Protestants to seal off their religious affirmations from insights gained by means of other perspectives upon reality. Such insights, he felt, must either be refuted or else integrated into one's own understanding of the Christian message. Furthermore, the Protestant Christian's understanding of the Gospel must be part and parcel of a larger view, congenial with that Gospel, yet able to include all those elements of men's thoughts, which seem to be intrinsically true and right.

As has already been indicated Oetinger began his intellectual activity in a seriously apologetic mood. He was fearful, on the one hand, that Orthodoxy's way of presenting the Gospel to his generation could no longer elicit the respect, and hence the commitment, if intellectually sensitive people. The reason was, of course, that it was associated with, and buttressed by, a traditional dogmatic structure which took little account of the intellectual ferment of his day. On the other hand, Oetiger was equally afraid, however, of the philosophy of Leibnitz and Wolff, which, he felt, would substitute a series of rationally established moralisms, both insipid and lifeless, for the ancient Christian affirmations. Beyond this he was sure, that the static monadology of Leibnitz would make philosophically untenable many of the basic Christian doctrines, such as the doctrine of the trinity, of the incarnation, of inspiration, and of the church as the body of Christ. He was even more profoundly apprehensive of the psychology associated with the philosophical school, which tended to stress the primacy of reason as over against will (Leibnitz-Wolff), and mechanism over against freedom (Leibnitz-Newton). Oetinger's philosophical presuppositions, then, must be understood within this framework of religio-intellectual concern.

As implied in what has been said, the ontological structure of Oetinger's world view was closely patterned upon that of Boehme. "God," he says, "is that which is eternally one (*das ewige Eine*), without properties in itself, which is not moved by anything external to himself. He is purest activity, in which is that which acts, the activity itself, and that which is acted."[1] While he thus tries to get away from a static concept of God Oetinger speaks of him in Boehmist fashion as pure act. The word which he prefers when speaking of the innermost nature of God, however, is "life." God, he holds, is essentially Life.[2] He is "the insurpassable form of escalation and the mightiest manifestation of the life-principle."[3]

One of the greatest concerns of our author is that between God, conceived in the above mentioned way, and nature no gulf must be posited. God is that principle in everything which brings it into being, maintains it, and moves it toward its divinely appointed goal. Thus he is not beyond space, time, and history, but in them. While the universe is distinct from God, God is its vital center, as he is the vital center of every creature. On the Boehmist premise that spirit and body are two essential and inseparable aspects of Reality and all of its manifestations, Oetinger further insisted that the whole process of the self-actualization of the divine Life moves toward indestructible corporeality. Every form of life is oriented, therefore, toward the creation of a "spiritual body," i.e., a counterpart to its physical form in a kind of over-world of "spiritual" existences.[4] The totality of such spiritual forms will finally constitute God's body, which he must have in order to be "all in all."[5] This cosmic movement from God as pure act through physical to spiritual corporeality includes man, of course, whose promised immortality is here rooted in the very scheme of things. Or, perhaps, it should be said differently, Oetinger's vision of the scheme of things is, in the last analysis nothing else but his rationale for the biblical promise of man's immortality.

How did Oetinger come to know all of this? In trying to answer this question his basic reference would have been to Scripture. Like Bengel and the other Pietists of whom we spoke he regarded the Bible as God's authoritative revelation. Unlike them, however, he emphasized the

---

[1] *Versuch einer Auflösung der 177 Fragen aus Jakob Boehme* etc., 1777, *Sämmtliche Schriften*, vol. 1, 1858, p. 331.

[2] Note the title of his major work: *Theologia ex idea vitae deducta* etc. Also instructive in this connection is the following statement, "Denken ist nicht das Erste und Sein ist nicht das Erste sondern Leben und bewegen gehet beiden voraus." (Quoted by Hauck, *op. cit.*, p. 129).

[3] Hauck, *op. cit.*, p. 111.

[4] Oetinger states this quite uncompromisingly when he says, "Corporeal indestructibility is the end of God's works." (*Sämmtliche Predigten*, vol. 3, 1855, p. 27).

[5] *Die Theologie aus der Idee der Lebens abgeleitet*, ed. by J. Hamberger, 1852, p. 281.

notion that it is the key to all truth, not only in the realm of grace, but in the realm of nature as well. As such every aspect of it, its message and its form, constitutes "a complete symphony, in which everything is in tune."[1] To him who, with the aid of God's Spirit, opens himself to its insights the Bible imparts a comprehensive wisdom, which includes God, nature, man, earth, heaven, present and future. Of course, one must not become bogged down in literalisms. The truly enlightened person sees the whole of Scripture from its center, namely Christ, or more specifically, Christ's resurrection, through which he restored the possibility of man's indestructibility.[2] Such an interpreter will then proceed by means of certain basic concepts — life, light, glory, fire, water, blood, salt.[3] Interestingly enough, all of these, as he works out their presumed significance, are related to Oetinger's overriding interest, namely corporeality as the end of divine activity. Corporeality, therefore, becomes not only the *telos* of divine activity but the key to God's total revelation.

This revelation is not only given through the Bible, however. What we have in the Bible is only the record of a part of God's activity. In actuality God reveals himself to man throughout the whole, breathtaking range of his mysterious doings. For that reason scientific experiment, which was of great importance to Oetinger, is simply a way of thinking God's thoughts after him. Through it man gains insights not only into the relations of the natural order, but into the spiritual world as well. A case in point here is the significance he attached to his famous experiment with balm-mint leaves. If such a leaf is crushed, and if its juice is spread upon water, so he alleged to have found, it invariably forms itself into the pattern of the leaf from which it came. This he regarded as conclusive proof of the inter-connection of the natural and the spiritual orders, so that the former is not merely a symbol of the latter, but a direct means to a fuller understanding of the spiritual world. Little wonder that at the end of every scientific experiment Oetinger insisted upon reverend silence, since God was about to answer a question.

The God-given organ through which man apprehends all truth, whether it comes through Scripture or through God's cosmic activity, is the *sensus communis*. Here we come upon Oetinger's basic episte-

---

1 Quoted by Zinn, *op. cit.*, p. 87.

2 See *Die Theologie aus der Idee der Lebens abgeleitet*, p. 290f; also p. 253.

3 See especially Oetingers *Inquisitio in sensum communem et rationem*, 1753.

mological concept, which he promulgated first at Walddorf, and which thereafter became the cornerstone of his theory of knowledge.[1] He defines it as follows : "It is the feeling (*Empfindung*), which precedes investigation and piece-meal unfolding, and which brings with it certainty and assurance before one disentangles the distinguishing attributes."[2] Actually, however, Oetinger feels, it cannot be precisely defined because it is part of the unity between subjective and objective processes, and hence not subject to numerical division. It is, to use Hauck's words, the way to truth and wisdom "through immediate contact with the innermost center of man."[3] As such it is basic to any insight into nature, history (personal as well as social), ethics, and religion. It is related to God's image in man and hence the divinely intended possession of all men. Yet, it remains imperfect unless it is strengtened by divine power and informed by God's revelation.[4] What we have here, of course, is an initial acceptance of Boehme's distinction between *Vernunft* and *Verstand*, and then a more precise conceptualization of the latter until it becomes what Oetinger sometimes refers to as "inner experiences" in contradistinction to rational deduction. Its advantage over mere *Vernunft* is that, on the one hand, it involves the whole human being while, on the other, it intuitively penetrates to the actuality which is the center of things. Thus it proceeds toward truth and wisdom "generatively," refusing to impose artificial patterns upon the realms of both nature and grace.

The more traditional features of Oetinger's *philosophia sacra* tie in closely with his ontological and epistemological presuppositions, which have been outlined, as well as with his inherited set of Protestant doctrines. In the interest of preserving the proper balance in this essay they can only be mentioned summarily.

In line with Pietists in general, and in contradistinction to many of his "enlightened" contemporaries, Oetinger regarded with utmost seriousness the historicity of man's fall and of God's saving acts

---

[1] For his major discussions of this concept see his *Inquisitio, op. cit.*, as well as his *Die Wahrheit des sensus communis, oder des allgemeinen Sinnes in den nach dem Grundtext erklärten Sprüchen und Prediger Salomo*, also 1753. For his explanation of what he intended to do see his *Selbstbiographie, op. cit.*, p. 89.

[2] K.C.E. Ehmann, ed., *Friedrich Christoph Oetinger's Leben und Briefe, als urkundlicher Kommentar zu dessen Schriften*, 1859, p. 199.

[3] Hauck, *op. cit.*, p. 30.

[4] *Die Wahrheit des sensus communis* etc., 1754 ed., *Sämmtliche Schriften*, vol. 4, 1861, p. 42; also *Die Theologie* etc., p. 240.

recorded in the Bible. Nor did he ever doubt the objective nature of Christ's salvatory work, as one would expect of a man reared in the Lutheran Tradition. Yet, in pietistic fashion the emphasis in his theology was always on the subjective effects of the events of *Heilsgeschichte.* Thus the fall implies primarily the partial loss of the *sensus communis*, and hence man's loss of the full range of divinely intended insights into the mysteries of life.[1] Christ's work provides preeminently the basis for the restoration of these insights.[2] Religious faith is essentially the connection through which the lifestream coming from God can flow again into man's existence, thus moving him toward indestructible corporeality.[3] The essence of personal religion is the *cognitio centralis* which helps the Christian to see beyond the inevitable polarities of existence, so as to find peace and joy in the recognition of the divine intention of ultimate harmony. The Gospel is basically a message of hope, for Christians are above all else people who are sensitive to "the motivational causes of the world to come."[4]

In his understanding of the Christian life Oetinger differed little from his mentor, Bengel. Upon justification must follow rebirth, and upon imputed righteousness actual righteousness. Man must become a new creature, the newness manifesting itself in personal holiness. The latter, which is partly God's and partly man's doing, he defines as "the complete harmony of the *Verstand*, the will, and of one's desires or affections, with the instruction of the divine Law, as it is prescribed in the law of Moses," a condition which, however, cannot be fully attained in this life.[5] Specifically it must manifest itself in such virtues as righteousness, transparent truthfulness, love for the neighbor which is informed by the light of God, and a joyfulness oriented toward the invisible.[6] The daily life of the Christian must be motivated not merely by the death of Christ but more especially by the impulses of the world to come.[7] Nor must his religious efforts be directed only toward personal ends, but toward the good of the community, where the *sensus communis* becomes the communal conscience, which provides the basis for all satisfying togetherness.[8]

[1] *Die Theologie* etc., p. 215.

[2] *Ibid.*, p. 253.

[3] *Ibid.*, p. 295.

[4] *Sämmtliche Predigten, vol.* 1, p. 200f.

[5] *Die Theologie* etc., p. 318.

[6] *Sämmtliche Predigten*, vol. 5, p. 105; vol. 3, pp. 453, 540.

[7] *Ibid.*, vol. 1, p. 201.

[8] See Hauck, *op. cit.*, p. 43.

In studying Oetinger one becomes quickly aware of the fact that his contribution to Protestant thought has not been sufficiently valued. He was, of course, a child of his time. Much of what he wrote, therefore, had meaning only for his day — perhaps only for a select circle of his day. Yet, in reading him one has the curious feeling that his restless genius anticipated, however dimly, much of what was to come. In his passion for scientific verification, in his religious awe before the mysterious powers of the universe, in his effort to keep religion and science, Christianity and culture, intellectual curiosity and Protestant piety from flying apart he was one of the great pioneers of the century among theologians. His ecumenicity, his spirit of tolerance, his openness to truth from whatever source it may come, constitute an oasis during an age in which Protestantism was generally barren of such characteristics. His shift in the area of religious epistemology from the exclusive hegemony of doctrine to that of religious intuition bore fruit in later Protestant thought. His insistence upon a theology of hope, which rejoices in what God will do tomorrow while holding fast to what he did yesterday, held out the promise of an awakening social consciousness, which Continental Protestantism might have done well to heed more fully. In the face of these intellectual assets even the most conservative among his critics should find it possible to forgive him for some of his theological idiosyncrasies, such as his rampant chiliasm which surpassed even that of Bengel, and his somewhat reckless assertion of progressive revelation. Even his rather critical stance toward the ecclesiastical follies of his day should be balanced against his vision of a renewed church able to meet the needs of a new day, as should his insistence upon universal salvation.

Whatever may be Oetinger's significance for the development of Protestant thought, during his lifetime he was only modestly appreciated. As may be expected, the Orthodoxists of his time had vast reservations about the purity of his Lutheranism, and they were annoyed for not being able to meet him on his own ground, He, in turn, being far more fully aware of the current shifts in theological perspective than they, ignored them wherever he could. In this instance, many of the Pietists, too, shared the misgivings of Orthodoxists. While they approved fully of Oetinger's pietistic concerns, as well as of his more traditional theological presuppositions, they preferred to draw the line when it came to his theosophical speculations. It was even more difficult for him to convince the people of his congregations. They were often startled by his terminology, awe-struck by the range of his thought, and frightened by his efforts to press home to them the obligations of the Christian life as he understood it. At Weinsberg, especially, significant rapport between the congregation and its preacher seems to have been lacking. "A preacher of fables" some of his parishioners called him. It was in the face of this that he published his *Reden* (1758), as a kind of demonstration to himself that he was an solid ground.

While the situation improved when he left Weinsberg he could hardly be called a popular preacher. Nor was his public image improved when in 1763 he non-plussed his readers with a thoroughly cabbalistic piece,[1] and two years later with an equally mystifying discussion about Emmanuel Swedenborg's revelation concerning the world of spirits.[2] Quickly the rumors spread that the *Märleinprediger* had now become a *Geisterprediger*, and charges of heresy were brought against him. Oetinger was censured and the book on Swedenborg was forbidden. While he at first protested against the verdict, he gradually pulled away from the influence of Swedenborg. To the end, however, he retained a profound appreciation for the world of spirits, and thus helped along a developing cult[3] which emphasized communication of the living with the dead. When he died there were few intellectual currents of which he had not tasted. Oetinger was truly a man *zwischen den Zeiten.*

Among the immediate followers of Oetinger only two need to be mentioned, namely Johann Ludwig Fricker (1729-1766) and Philipp Matthäus Hahn (1739-1790).

The former[4] studied philosophy and theology at Tübingen during the days when Oetinger was pastor at the neighboring village of Walddorf. Having been previously inclined toward theosophy Oetinger quickly began to exert considerable influence upon him. Furthermore, Fricker shared with his spiritual adviser the same restless curiosity about the secrets of nature and the well-springs of the religious life. Hence he began to travel extensively, drinking in the wisdom of both

[1] *Die Lehrtafel der Prinzessin Antonia.*

[2] *Swedenborgs irdische und himmlische Philosophie.*

[3] For other instances of widespread interest in the world of spirits see p. 263.

[4] His works were edited by L.C. Hazelin under the title *Unvollständige jedoch brauchbare Überbleibsel aus den hinterlassenen Handschriften — Johann Ludwig Frickers*, 1775. Included is the oldest biographical sketch by the editor. They were reprinted several times. Frickers most important piece is his *Weisheit im Staube* etc., which was edited by J. Rössle and published separately in 1963 in vol. 5 of *Zeugnisse der Schwabenväter.*

John Wesley and George Whitfield in England and of the surviving Labadist circles in Holland. Along the lower Rhein he enjoyed the fellowship of the many groups who were given to the mystical piety of Tersteegen. His understanding of the Christian life is embodied especially in his *Weisheit im Staube.*

This little book quickly took its place in the edificatory literature produced by Swabian Pietism. Since it was intended as a devotional guide for the whole Pietistic Community its author kept his theosophical convictions in the background. Its content consists of practical suggestions regarding the practice of piety, such as six rules for gaining an adequate knowledge of God, six rules for listening to the Spirit etc. Included is a simple statement of the basic Christian affirmations. Fricker's chief emphasis seems to be contained in the following statement, in which one finds overtones of Tersteegen : "Learn diligently to differentiate between the voice of God and of your Savior in your heart and all other stirrings within you."[1] The Christian is advised, in fact, not to live by rules, but by being continually tuned to the voice of God.[2] In such unbroken fellowship with God lies the secret of life.

The other reasonably prominent disciple of Oetinger was P.M. Hahn.[3] He, too, studied at Tübingen, where he imbibed the pietistic influences which were found among some of the students of the *Stift.* Most decisive for his intellectual maturation seems to have been the thought of Boehme, Oetinger, and Bengel. Oetinger had inspired him with a profound appreciation of the realms of mathematics and physics. His chief fame rests, therefore, on his manufacturing of cylindrical clocks, and on his invention of usable calculating machines as well as other gadgets, which brought him to the attention of the Swabian court. This is true, though he himself felt that his mechanical accomplishments remained merely a sideline to support him and his eight children.[4] His theology is a combination of Bengel's eschatology and Oetinger's *philosophia sacra.* During the earlier part of his career he

---

1 *Weisheit im Staube,* ed. by J. Rössle, 1963, vol. 5, *Zeugnisse der Schwabenväter,* p. 42.

2 *Ibid.,* p. 37.

3 His writings were edited by C.U. Hahn under the title *Philipp Matthäus Hahns hinterlassene Schriften,* 1828. His best known book bears the title *Die gute Botschaft vom Königreich Gottes.* It was re-edited by J. Rössle and published in *Zeugnisse der Schwabenväter,* vol. 8, 1963. For other books by Hahn see Rössle's introduction. See also M. Brecht, "Philipp Matthäus Hahn in Onstmettingen," BwKG, vols. 60-61, 1960-1961, pp. 214-224.

4 See Hahn's autobiography in his *Hinterlassene Schriften, op. cit.,* p. 37.

followed the former so closely that he, too, expected the *Parousia* in 1836.[1] Subsequently Bengel's suggestions about the Kingdom of God were transformed by Hahn into his central theologial concern.[2] All of God's activity, both in the realms of nature and of grace, he held, is oriented toward the coming of this Kingdom. It is the great reality toward which all things move.[3] By faith in Christ man becomes part of that Kingdom; he governs himself by its laws and is motivated by its promise. It is, in fact, the final exhibition of God's glory in divinely wrought corporeality. Interestingly enough we have here the same joyful look to the future and concern for the neighbor which we find in his immediate theological predecessors,[4] and which are part of Swabian Pietism's chief legacy to Protestant thought. Little wonder that the poet C.F.D. Schubart said of Hahn, who himself was the best example of his theology of glory : "What I was looking for, that I found in him."[5]

Pietistic Fellowships

During the eighteenth century Protestantism in Württemberg gradually accepted conventicles as a legitimate way for earnest Christians to share their religious insights and concerns and to encourage one another in the difficult task of living the Christian life. Some of these conventicles, or *Stunden*, as they were generally called, existed apart from the fellowship of the Lutheran Church. In that case they were usually called into being and supervised by some temporary leader, whose charisma was somehow recognized by his followers. In such separatistic groups the influence of Boehme and of the leading separatists occasionally created a religious climate which was more or less critical of the Christianity practiced in the established churches. Most of the people who attended the *Stunden*, however, did so within the confines of their own parish. Very frequently their own pastor, or someone designated by him, supervised a particular meeting, which was usually arranged for Sunday afternoon. Thus the conventicle

---

[1] See Hahn's *Hauptsache der Offenbarung*, 1772.

[2] Note the title of his books : *Fingerzeig zum Verstand des Königreichs Gottes und Christi*, 1774; *Die heiligen Schriften der guten Botschaft vom verheissenen Königreich, oder das Neue Testament*, 1777; as well as his *Gute Botschaft*.

[3] *Die gute Botschaft*, 1963 ed., p. 142.

[4] *Ibid.*, pp. 63, 109.

[5] *Ibid.*, preface, p. 5.

became a device by which it became possible for a conscientious pastor, who had to function in the setting of an established church, to serve all three major segments of his congregation — those who would only call on him for baptisms, weddings, and burials, those who felt the Sunday morning sermon gave them enough religious stimulation, and that comparatively small group who felt they needed the more intimate religious fellowship of the conventicle.

An interesting phenomenon within this whole context of Swabian conventicle Protestantism was (is) the so called Hahnisch Fellowship (*Hahnische Gemeinschaft*). It came to be called a *Gemeinschaft* because it became a movement which reached into a great many communities. The rural sections especially were open to its message, so that in time few villages were untouched by its influence. At the same time, however, the members of the Hahnisch Fellowship followed meticulously the advice of their founder not to become a separatistic sect. They remained loyal members of their churches, seldom missed the Sunday morning service, and took perhaps more seriously than most other worshipers their pastor's admonitions. Yet, on Sunday afternoon they gathered at some home in order to sing the Hahnisch hymns, to drink at the fountain of Hahnisch spiritually, and to exhort one another to faithfulness in their religious calling.

The founder of the group was Johann Michael Hahn (1759-1819), a self-taught religious genius, the simplicity and beauty of whose life was certainly as much of an asset to his movement as anything he said or wrote.[1] He was born at Altdorf near Böblingen. As was the case with many other religious geniuses his sensitivity to matters of religion already manifested itself during his boyhood. Upon hearing one of the

---

[1] Hahn's works are available in a fifteen volume edition called *Johann Michael Hahn's Schriften*, 1819-1849. In his writing he was assisted by Anton Egeler, who together with Immanual Kolb had the editorial responsibility for Hahn's works. The most concise statement of his thought is found in the *System seiner Gedanken von der ersten Offenbarung Gottes bis ans Ziel aller Dinge* which is in vol. 15 of his *Schriften*. It consists of seventeen letters. The best discussion of his theology is that of J. Trautwein, *Die Theosophie Michael Hahns und ihre Quellen*, 1969, which constitutes vol. 2 of *Quellen und Forschungen zur württembergischen Kirchengeschichte*. Still helpful is W.F. Stroh's *Die Lehre des württembergischen Theosophen J.M. Hahn*, 1859, 1928, which is in the nature of an anthology. A history of the Hahnisch Fellowship, put out by this fellowship itself, is that of L. Widmann, *Die Hahnische Gemeinschaft, Ihre Entstehung und seitherige Entwickelung*, 1827. For helpful bibliographical suggestions see Trautwein, pp. 15-30 and Stroh, pp. 18-19. See also C. Palmer, *Die Gemeinschaften und Sekten Württembergs*, 1877.

popular hymns of his day[1] at the age of seventeen he was thrown into a state of deep depression which lasted approximately three years. The situation was aggravated by the totally unsympathetic attitude of his father, who had forced him into taking up the trade of a butcher. He finally came out of this mood of depression as a result of two very remarkable experiences. The first of these, lasting about three hours, occurred in 1777 while he was working in the fields. The second took place in 1780 and was extended over approximately seven weeks. Both of these experiences impressed him as having been visions into the very heart of Reality, or, from another point of view, gracious revelations of God who now answered all the questions which had troubled him. With reference to the second of these experiences, Hahn describes the effect of what took place as follows : "In this long vision from the center of things (*zentralischen Schau*), in this disclosure of innermost meanings, all possible secrets — questions which had to do with God, Christ, the Spirit of God, how, where, and who is the triune God, how everything comes from him and consists in him, and how it will be restored through him, of his plan, and intention, and other such matters — were suddenly answered, so that all previous doubts vanished."[2]

With these two visions the religious career of "Michele," as his friends affectionately began to call him, actually began. The seeker had become a finder, doubts had been replaced by certainties. Hahn the untutored rustic, the simple child of nature, was on his way to become one of Protestantisms influential lay theologians. He regarded himself as an instrument chosen by God to disclose to man those secrets which are necessary to his eternal well-being.[3] His message was the more effective because it was accompanied by a naturalness and simplicity, a dignity and devotion which to many of the religious seekers of his day seemed almost irresistible. Hahn himself manifested a lifelong sense of wonderment at the thought that he, of all people, should be chosen for this task. Because of his sense of mission he never married, spending his days in study, in writing, and in giving advice to the many people who sought it. For this purpose he lived in his modest little home together with several likeminded men — Martin Schäffer,

---

1 The hymn was, "Der am Kreuz ist meine Liebe."

2 Quoted by A. Köberle *Das Glaubensvermächtnis der schwäbischen Väter*, 1959, p. 26.

3 See his eighteenth letter, *Schriften*, vol. 3, second section, p. 89f.

Martin Mager, and later Anton Egeler. From here the Hahnisch fellowships were supplied with the writings of the founder, which increasingly consituted the cohesive center of the movement, as well as with the practical directions which were required by its continued expansion.

The question of Hahn's intellectual indebtedness remains a baffling one. He himself always insisted that his basic insights did not come from books. They were given to him directly by God during those weeks of religious enlightenment which have been described. Being such a transparently honest man, without artifice or undue ambition, it would be difficult for anyone who has read him not to take him seriously at this point. On the other hand, the basic structure of his thought, as well as his terminology, are so close to that of Boehme and his followers that originality can hardly be assumed. It would seem, then, that unconsciously Hahn absorbed the basic theosophical ideas of his day from the religious environment in which he grew up. Accordingly he thought of God and his relationship to the world in essentially theosophical terms. Furthermore, we find here once again the need of a *Zentralschau* in the realm of religious epistemology, the Sophia doctrine, the notion of androgynous man and its implication for God's salvatory work,[1] the understanding of man as a microcosm whose fall and restoration affect all of creation, the idea of a supra-historical fall, the importance of corporeality in the divine creative intention, and the hope of a universal restoration.[2] Whatever theological thinking Hahn did took place within this context.

That he made certain individualistic modifications must be expected. Thus he conceptualized God not so much as Life (Oetinger), but as Light, or Glory. Creation, therefore, is not out of nothing, but out of God's glory. In the trinity we do not have "persons," but "revelations" of the original, undifferentiated Glory.[3] Evil is the divinely permitted, temporary absence of light. The fall is essentially a matter of succumbing to darkness,[4] which becomes ever more dense as creatures are removed from the center of light. Salvation is the reimpartation of light through Christ. Scripture is essentially the authoritative source

---

[1] Thus Christ was male and female, and hence able to restore man to his intended condition. (*Schriften*, vol. 8, section 3, p. 360).

[2] *Schriften*, vol. 12, section 2, p. 164.

[3] See quotations by Stroh, *op. cit.*, p. 46.

[4] *Schriften*, vol. 8, section 1, p. 25.

of God's light for man.[1] The end of the whole process of becoming is a new creation, or the full blaze of God's glory in every creature.

On these theosophical foundations Hahn based the pietistic insistence upon radical rebirth and progressive moral renewal. It was his conviction that after a personal religious experience, with which a person's religious life must begin, the Christian is like a child. As such he must grow not only in religious insight, but in a progressive severance from all aspects of life which might tyrannize his spirit and thus impair his religious maturation. Through a mighty effort of the will, assisted by all of God's saving agencies, he must find the mastery "over all inclinations, lusts, and desires of the life of nature." In this Hahn included sexuality, though he did not single it out for special treatment. Though he himself remained unmarried, he taught that sex, like the other gifts of God, requires moderation, and under special circumstances, abstinence. The important thing is that the Christian becomes Christ-like in all of his doings.[2] Not infrequently this may include suffering, since suffering has a very special place in God's scheme to help man reach his high destiny.[3] Complete ethical perfection, however, is reached only after death.[4]

Even though Hahn was not satisfied with the state of the Lutheran church of his time, and said so upon occasion, he was not schismatic. For that reason the Hahnisch groups, which began to spread through Württemberg during the early forties, preserved the status within the church to which reference has been made. In that role they made a lasting contribution to the life of Swabian Protestantism down to the present time.

Somewhat more ambiguous is the history of another Swabian pietistic group, namely, the so called Pregizerians, remnants of which also maintained themselves into the twentieth century.

The founder of this pietistic fellowship was Christian Gottlob Pregizer (1751-1824).[5] In 1768 he matriculated at the *Stift* in Tübingen,

---

[1] See his hymn, "Das Heiligtum ist Gottes Wort," *Schriften*, vol. 1, p. 241.

[2] See quotations in Stroh, *op. cit.*, pp. 321, 322.

[3] *Ibid.*, p. 377.

[4] *Schriften*, vol. 1, section 1, p. 164.

[5] Until relatively recently Pregizer was almost unknown, and information regarding him was often unreliable. The study of his life by modern historians began with a dissertation written at Heidelberg University by F. Pfeil in 1939 which bears the title, *Christian Gottlob Pregizer und die Gemeinschaft der Pregizerianer*. As must be expected Pfeil's work contains a number of inaccuracies which were then corrected by Gotthold Müller. The latter wrote the most carefully documented study of Pregizer in 1962 under the title

where the pietistic influence, especially that of Bengel, had not yet been fully eclipsed by the rationalistic atmosphere of the age, and where Oetinger frequently joined the pietistic conventicle which was still held by a group of theological students. It seems likely that as a result of these associations he underwent the conversion experience which was more or less expected in this circle.[1] After several pastorates, during which he met J.J. Eytel and Johann Michael Hahn, and during which he not only studied Oetinger but also Boehme, he took up his very successful pastorate at Haiterbach (1795-1824).

More or less decisive for Pregizer's future work was a second religious crisis which he experienced in 1801. It was preceded by a period of great depression and self-doubt, which eventually made it necessary for him to hand over his preaching activity to a vicar. In this state of mind he discovered a copy of Praetorius' *Geistliche Schatzkammer*,[2] the content of which seemed to be tailor-made for his condition. Praetorius' emphasis upon a joyful Christian life, based on the certainty of the Christian's acceptance of God in baptism, became the balm that brought healing to his spirit. Presently he went home and announced to his wife that the time of his depression was over.[3] His vicar was dismissed and the rest of the story of his Haiterbach ministry is that of a very effective, much beloved Lutheran pastor, who was especially successful with the youth of his congregation. The message he preached carried conviction. Understandably it differed somewhat, in tone at least, from the more sombre notes of both orthodox and pietistic preaching in general. The result was a period of difficulty with the consistory which lasted about four years. The reservations of the latter were motivated by the fear that, while Pregizer's intentions were good, and his theology acceptable, the note of "enthusiasm" in his preaching might play into the hands of separatistic groups. Being essentially a responsible person, the concern of his superiors sobered Pregizer, and prompted him to speak in a lower key. As a result he was permitted to spend the last thirteen years of his pastorate in peace.

With the Pietists in general Pregizer insisted upon a conscious conversion experience, and the new state of being which must follow.[4]

Christian Gottlob Pregizer. Biographie und Nachlass. He not only lists all the known sources (p. 31f) but reproduces the ones which are available (p. 169f). This is of great value since most of Pregizer's works were not made commercially available to the public.

[1] Müller, *op. cit.*, p. 59.

[2] See RI, p. 193f.

[3] Pfeil, *op. cit.*, p. 28f.

[4] See "Erweckungslied," Müller, *op. cit.*, pp. 385-389.

From Bengel and his circle he had taken over a precise set of understandings regarding God's plan for the future.[1] From Oetinger and the theosophists he had adopted the theosophic understanding of the resurrection[2] as well as the idea of the restoration of all things, based on a consideration of God's love.[3] While his followers often manifested a certain antinomian tendency, which prompted Johann Michael Hahn to oppose the movement,[4] Pregizer did not support this understanding of the Christian life. In contradistinction to antinomian separatists he gave the following counsel : "As long, then, as we journey here below let us undertake our walk with fear, and follow sanctification, which consists preeminently in sobriety and chastity."[5]

The central emphasis of Pregizer, however, and the emphasis which gave a distinctive cast to the movement that took his name grew out of his own experience in 1801. Pietists, whether at Halle or at Württemberg, generally held that the new state of being must above all else eventuate in a new life. While Pregizer agreed with this he insisted with Praetorius that the "newness" of this life must express itself primarily in religiously motivated, almost uninterrupted joy. Over against the general pietistic emphasis upon a life lived under God's Law, Pregizer thus stressed an emotional state of constant elation based on the existential knowledge of divine forgiveness and mystical union in baptism. Documentation at this point is unnecessary since the religious doggerel which he wrote in abundance moves almost exclusively in this direction. This is the reason, too, why he insisted that he is not interested in *Pietismus* but in *Christianismus.* The joyful state into which the Christian supposedly enters immediately upon a genuine conversion experience was to Pregizer the very essence of personal Christianity. It truly seemed to him to have the promise of this life and the life to come. It was, in fact, an earnest of the life to come in the midst of the Christian's earthly existence. Over against it the Christian life as understood by men like Johann Michael Hahn seemed dour and legalistic.

It appears that Pregizer's advocacy of *Freudenschristentum* over

---

[1] See his tract *Schriftmässige Lehre von dem Himmel und von dem seligen Zustand derer, die im Himmel sind,* Müller, *op. cit.,* pp. 187-271.

[2] See his tract *Vom Zustande nach dem Tode,* Müller, *op. cit.,* pp. 275-310, especially p. 290f.

[3] See his tract *Fragen von der ewigen Liebe Gottes in Wiederbringung aller Dinge,* Müller, *op. cit.,* pp. 311-317.

[4] See Hahn's *Sendschreiben an Freunde der Wahrheit* etc., Müller, *op. cit.,* pp. 553-567.

[5] *Schriftmässige Lehre* etc., *op. cit.,* p. 233.

against *Gesetzeschristentum* had a popular appeal which could not be confined to his parish. Unfortunately the relation of this pastor of Haiterbach to the movement which took his name is at this time not at all clear.[1] Currently it is held, however, that a group of conventicle Christians who were inclined toward religious emotionalism began to look to Pregizer as their guide. The latter in turn accepted this responsibility so as to keep these people within the fold of the Lutheran church. On the model of Johann Jakob Eytel, and perhaps Johann Michael Hahn, he welded them together into a rather close fellowship, which was expected to function within the confines of the established church. Presently, however, Pregizer's grip upon the movement began to loosen, and his theological restraints were pushed into the background. In some of its conventicles at least emotionalism became rampant. Hymns were set to popular tunes and accompanied by zither music, Schwarzwald style. Meetings became religious "happenings," livened up by repeated calls of *Juchhei*. Thus Pregizerians were popularly referred to as *Juchheichristen* or "galloping Christians." Some of them insisted that they could not sin, or, at least, that for them sin is not sin in the sight of God; and all of them shifted the emphasis from ethical concern to the experience of blessedness both here and hereafter. Since the Lutheran pastors were often reserved toward this kind of Protestantism, a tendency toward separatism developed within some Pregizerian groups. As always, however, time slowly moderated excessive enthusiasm and Pregizerians took their place among the "Stillen im Lande" within the milieu of Swabian Protestantism.

During the eighteenth century other church-related pietistic groups could be found in certain sections of Württemberg. They were local in nature, and of relatively brief duration. Leadership was provided either by a pastor or a charismatic layman. Perhaps the most prominent of these was founded by Johann Jakob Eytel (1742-1788) of Neubulach at the northern end of the Schwarzwald. By sheer moral force this beloved pastor, who combined a deeply devotional spirit with remarkable organizing ability, founded a series of conventicles in the region in which he worked. After his untimely death the movement was headed by G.C.F. Härlin (d. 1818). Throughout its existence it was characterized by the sane, ethically sensitive approach to the Christian

[1] Müller gives a long series of Pregizer interpretations (*op. cit.*, pp. 22-29), all of which seem ultimately to involve the problem of the relation of Pregizer to the movement which bears his name.

life which was characteristic of the religious legacy of Bengel and the Tübingen circle of pietistic pastors.

An Over-view of Swabian Pietism

In conclusion a brief historical overview of Swabian Pietism during the period in question may be helpful. The most critical period of its history extends from 1694 to 1743. The question of pietistic conventicles and what to do about them came before the consistory at Stuttgart for the first time in 1692. It was the result of J.A. Hochstetter's suggestion that pastors might well institute religious conversations with their parishioners on Sunday afternoon. An extended discussion ensued, the main tenor of which was summed up by A. Bardili, a member of the consistory, as follows : "*Collegia pietatis* promise much good, as well as much abuse."[1] Upon this inconclusive result followed a period of watching and waiting on the part of the ecclesiastical authorities. It was the conventicle of 1703 at Tübingen[2] which forced the consistory to pay further attention to the development of pietistic circles. The question was whether preaching and the administration of the sacraments are sufficient for the nourishment of the religious life of people, or whether these may be supplemented by religious conversations. It was Johann Reinhard Hedinger who energetically supported the conventicle at the *Stift*, and thus by implication conventicles in general. Others were stoutly opposed to the idea that the means of grace, as historically defined, should be inadequate for the needs of the age.

In the meantime separatistic groups began to make their appearance. To them conventicles were not meant to supplement the traditional means of grace, but, in part at least, to supplant them. Under Boehmist influence they were sometimes very critical of the state church and its alleged inadequacy in dealing with the religious problems of the age. Their meetings, often under the supervision of laymen, seemed to countenance more or less unconventional conduct. The result was the Edict of 1703, which was meant to contain the "enthusiasm" engendered by people like Peter Poiret, Gottfried Arnold, and J.W. Petersen. Both Hochstetter and Hedinger strenuously opposed this edict on the ground that it tended to restrict the holding of religious conversations by concerned pastors. Consequently the repressive edict was modified

---

[1] Hermelink, *op. cit.*, p. 192.

[2] *Ante*, p. 92f.

by the General Rescript of 1704 which permitted such pastorally supervised conventicles within a given parish.

The question of conventicles now became a political issue between the Pietists and moderates, on the one hand, and the hard-line Orthodoxists, on the other. For almost a decade sentiment within the ecclesiastical power structure seemed to favor the orthodox party. This was aided especially by the separatistic "excesses" of 1710 at Stuttgart, where men and women were allegedly prone to remain in religious conversation until midnight.[1] During the same period, however, Pietism in Württemberg expanded rapidly. It was aided politically by the spirit of toleration which stems from the Enlightenment. Hence, the ecclesiastical regulations beginning with 1711 became ever more tolerant. While the decree of 1711 still purported to harry incorrigible separatists out of the land, the General Rescript of 1743 granted the right of private religious meetings to all who seemed qualified to hold them. It was to be understood, of course, that certain regulations had to be respected. Thus lay leaders were to be under the supervision of pastors, conventicles were not to be held during hours set aside for regular worship, objectionable books and offensive hymns were to be avoided etc. These regulations were so broadly interpreted, however, that punitive action became the exception rather than the rule. The result was that during most of the eighteenth century Swabian Pietism was free to develop according to its own genius.

Under these conditions Pietism in Württemberg manifested a remarkable vitality. While it may be said that in other sections of Germany it often appeared to attract especially the nobility, this was not the case here. In Swabia it became a genuine grass-roots movement, in which the butcher, the baker, and the candlestick-maker had a real stake. There were few villages and towns, indeed, in which one or more pietistic cells did not function either within or without the Lutheran church. Furthermore, Pietism in Swabia had been made intellectually respectable by the Tübingen-Bengel axis around which it revolved. For that reason it had laid hold upon a broad segment of the most able Lutheran churchmen. Hence the Enlightenment in the Lutheran church of Württemberg was long delayed in coming,[2] and

[1] For details see Hermelink, *op. cit.*, p. 183f.

[2] The first official signs of the spirit of the Enlightenment in Württemberg are found in the much opposed hymnal of 1791 and in the liturgy of 1809.

when it finally did arrive, it never had the impact upon Swabian Lutheranism which it had elsewhere. Even today the careful observer finds that Protestantism in Württemberg bears the hall-marks of its strongly pietistic heritage.

CHAPTER FOUR

ZINZENDORF AND THE RISE OF THE RENEWED MORAVIAN CHURCH

Eighteenth century German Pietism, as understood in this discussion, was a highly diversified movement of religious renewal. As such it included the development which stems from the work of Zinzendorf, and which eventuated in what came to be known as the Renewed Moravian Church.[1] Because of the wide influence exerted by Moravianism upon Protestant church life during the eighteenth century a discussion of it at this point is imperative.

In order to understand the early Moravian development, it is necessary, on the one hand, to take a careful look at the life and work of its founder. Even a casual reading of its history leads to the conclusion that the man and the movement must be seen together. It would, in fact, be impossible to understand the renewal of the Old Moravian Church apart from the genius of this remarkable man.

Nikolaus Ludwig, Count and Lord of Zinzendorf and Pottendorf, was born in the city of Dresden, Saxony, on May 26, 1700. The same year his father died. During the summer of 1703 his widowed mother, Charlotte Justine nee von Gerstorff, joined her own mother, whose

---

[1] The attempt of Moravian interpreters of Zinzendorf has traditionally been that of trying to maximize the difference between Zinzendorf and Pietism. This process began with B. Becker (*Zinzendorf im Verhältnis zu Phil. u. Kirchentum*, 1886, p. 103f) and culminated, perhaps, in W. Bettermann (*Theologie und Sprache bei Zinzendorf*, 1935, pp. 55, 114f). This attitude is understandable in so far as the writing of Continental church history has been more or less dominated by a generally antipietistic bias, which Moravian historians shared either consciously or unconsciously. For one who does not begin to study the history of Moravianism and the life of its founder on the basis of such presuppositions, however, this position is problematical indeed. Zinzendorf's indebtedness to and affinities with the Spener-Halle tradition, as well as his indebtedness to the spirit of radical Pietism, most especially of Philadelphianism, simply cannot be ignored. Unfortunately the subject is so complex as to need separate and extended treatment. In this discussion we can only take refuge in our general definition of Pietism, which finds the really distinguishing mark of the movement under discussion not in the *Busskampf*, or in a legalistic moralism, but in its emphasis upon a new state of being. On this basis it would be difficult, indeed, to distinguish between Zinzendorf and other eighteenth century representatives of the same religious emphasis who are discussed in this volume.

husband had also passed away, at the latter's estate of Grosshennersdorf, near Zittau. The following year Zinzendorf's mother married the Prussian field marshal Dubislav Gunomar von Natzmer, who hailed from the vicinity of Berlin. Four year old Nikolaus was now left in the care of his maternal grandmother, Henriette Catherine von Gerstorff. Only occasionally was he favored, henceforth, by visits from his mother, though the latter appears to have taken considerable interest in her son's development.

Henrietta von Gerstorff, who supervised Zinzendorf's development for the first decade of his life, was one of the very gifted women of her age.[1] The long tradition of nobility from which she had sprung was clearly evident in her bearing. "She was as much at home," says Renkewitz, "in the Latin expressions of dogmatic theology, as she was in the practical questions concerning her household. She painted, made music, and wrote poetry."[2] Intellectually she encompassed all the significant movements of the day. Her energy was given direction and focus by a profound desire to be of help to people, even people who did not share her interests or appreciate her way of life.

Under Henrietta's regime the castle of Grosshennersdorf became a center of the Spener-Halle type of Pietism. The latter had been part of the very atmosphere which she had breathed during her younger years. Spener had long been a welcome guest in the von Gerstorff household. Little wonder that he had been prevailed upon to become godfather to young Nikolaus. During the difficult days of Francke's early work at Halle Henrietta von Gerstorff had been one of his close collaborators and enthusiastic supporters. Her brothers-in-law, Baron von Canstein and Baron von Schweinitz, were pillars in the Halle undertaking. Thus we find that the best of Halle, namely, religious devotion without artifice or guile, concern for man's needs and problems, sensitivity to the conditions of one's divinely appointed vocation, a vivid sense of God's unfailing presence in all situations of life, a joyful acceptance of the ways of Providence, pervaded all phases of the von Gerstorff household.

In this home environment the young Zinzendorf was privileged to remain until at the age of ten he was ready to go to school. By a process of psychological osmosis he absorbed not only the refined tastes, the

---

1 For a section on her life and character see E.B. Beyreuther, *Der Junge Zinzendorf*, 1957, p. 44f.

2 H. Renkewitz, *Zinzendorf*, 1939, pp. 6-7.

self-assurance, the imperious temper, and the great variety of interests of the grandmother he both loved and admired, but the simplicity and depth of her religious devotion as well. Already at the age of four, he reminisces, he had been brought to a point where he had learned "to love the Savior dearly." Through the influence of his grandmother his religious devotion was nourished, so that he actually could remember no time when such love for God was not a basic element in his consciousness.[1] That this empirical fact influenced his theology profoundly will become clearer as we go along.

From a religious point of view, then, Zinzendorf's childhood was unusual. Few children at the age of six write love notes to the Savior, or find pleasure in conducting prayer meetings. Zinzendorf did both. In fact when he visited Grosshennersdorf in later life he could speak eloquently of the many nooks and crannys of the old castle which were hallowed places for him because of their association with specific religious experiences during his childhood. If religious devotion ever comes natural to a human being, therefore, it came that way to Zinzendorf. For the rest of his life the same affective response to an ever present, almost tangibly apprehensible, divine reality remained the basis of his personal religion. Seldom, since the days of St. Paul. could anyone in the Christian tradition say with more conviction and truthfulness "for me to live is Christ."

Under these circumstances it was almost inevitable for his grandmother, as well as his mother, to decide that the most perfectly suited educational institution for young Nikolaus was Halle. Accordingly he entered Francke's *Paedagogium regium* on August 16, 1710 and remained one of its students for the next six years.

In later life Zinzendorf looked back upon his days at Halle with mixed feelings. Upon his entry Francke had been informed of the boy's tendency toward arrogant self-assertion. In the hope of curbing such inclinations his tutors saw to it that young Nikolaus found himself frequently humiliated. Nor did his introspective temper and his strong drive toward recognition help him to gain the confidence of many fellow students and instructors. His status was not enhanced, furthermore, when he repeatedly took it upon himself to exhort his fellow students toward greater religious dedication and zeal. Somewhat naively his early biographer, admirer, and fellow worker, August

---

[1] He speaks of this ever and again in his *Reden an die Kinder*, ZE, vol. 6, second part. See for instance, p. 7.

Gottlieb Spangenberg, reports, "People who did not have Our Lord Jesus Christ and his discipline were angry at him, in so far as they knew that he was not of one mind with them."[1] The result was, as Spangenberg continues to report, that life in school was often "hard and bitter."

Under these circumstances young Zinzendorf found both solace and strength in a vividly experienced personal relationship with Christ. This expressed itself in considerable zeal to make converts among his fellow students. The result was that ever and again small groups of likeminded students formed around him, in whose friendship he found joy and encouragement.[2] It meant also that a number of faculty members, notably Anton, were well disposed toward him. While thus his years at Halle could hardly be described as having been "happy," they afforded him his first opportunity for religious leadership.

During his time at Halle the special gifts of Zinzendorf, his linguistic ability, his leadership qualities, his ability to conceive novel schemes, had become abundantly apparent to the responsible members of his family. So, too, had his enthusiasm for the religious life, his absorption in religiously meaningful activities, and his singular commitment to religious ends. Possibly in the hope of containing such unrestrained religiosity Zinzendorf's guardian, Count Otto Christian, was happy to have the young count transferred to Wittenberg for the purpose of studying law.

To move from Halle to Wittenberg was a rather traumatic experience for the highly sensitive Zinzendorf. Wittenberg, the bastion of Orthodoxy, the defender of the tried and true, the stronghold of tradition, the implacable enemy of all religious dynamism, at first threatened to crush his spirit. Looking back upon his initial year he confessed that it had turned out to be one of the worst of his life.[3] In typical fashion, however, he decided not to be conquered by his environment, but to master it. Through a rigid regime of religious exercises, consisting chiefly of Bible reading, prayer, and meditation, and through a spirited defense of Halle wherever he had an opportunity to do so, Zinzendorf now moved in the direction of a fuller theological self-understanding. Thus

---

[1] A.G. Spangenberg, *Leben des Herrn Nicolaus Ludwig Grafen und Herrn von Zinzendorf und Pottendorf* etc., 1772-1775, vol. 1, pp. 41-42.

[2] *Ibid.*, p. 46.

[3] *Ibid.*, p. 64.

he insisted later that it was at Wittenberg where he really became a strict Pietist. In time he even succeeded in establishing a certain rapport with Wittenberg's belligerent guardians of Orthodoxy, notably Gottlieb Wernsdorf.[1] True to form, he promptly conceived a scheme of reconciliation between Halle and Wittenberg, which eventuated in the conference of Merseburg between Francke and V.E. Löscher. Needless to say, this daring venture into the realm of theological dialogue was premature and hence bore no fruit. In the meantime Zinzendorf patiently sat out the rigidly prescribed scheme of alternating his studies with required practice in riding, dancing, and fencing. He worked hard at Latin, French, and Hebrew, and spent the time that remained in reading theology.

Early in 1719 it was decided that Zinzendorf should embark upon the usual study trip in order to supplement his legal training. By this time he had learned to appreciate Wittenberg and had found an opportunity to plan for his Order of the Grain of Mustard Seed, a kind of spiritual knighthood. Yet he obeyed the counsel of his family and proceeded to Utrecht by way of Dresden, Leipzig, Eisenach, Frankfurt on the Main, Mainz, and Düsseldorf. It was at the picture gallery of Düsseldorf where an *Ecce Homo* made a lasting impression upon him.[2] His trip to Holland helped him to widen his extensive system of important connections, gave him an opportunity to study English, but above all afforded him his first clear insight into the theology of the Reformed Church. Having visited various Reformed centers in Holland he proceeded to Paris, where he met some of the important Roman Catholic leaders, including Cardinal Noailles. These contacts were of inestimable importance to Zinzendorf, since they opened his eyes to the possibility of amicable, inter-religious dialogue.[3]

During the spring of 1720 Zinzendorf continued his travels via Strassburg and Basel to Castell, located between Bamberg and Würzburg. Having contracted a fever he remained at the castle of his paternal aunt, the Countess of Castell, for a protracted period of time. Up to

---

[1] It was in 1717 under Wernsdorf's influence that he decided in favor of a religious vocation. See *Naturelle Reflexiones*, in ZE, vol. 4, p. 173. (See note 2, p. 141 for meaning of symbol ZE).

[2] Spangenberg, *op. cit.*, vol. 1, p. 99.

[3] In reference to his conversations with Cardinal Noailles he reports, "We were together for half a year with divinely joyful hearts, without thinking anymore to which religion the one or the other belonged ! " *Naturelle Reflexiones*, ZE, vol. 4, p. 12. Though the ways of the two men parted later, their mutual appreciation persisted.

this time he had taken seriously the counsel of his grandmother not to become involved with "women-folk" during his trip. Here the charm of his cousins proved too much for the young man. He fell in love first with the older of his two cousins, Juliane. The latter, however, felt far greater affinity for Zinzindorf's stepbrother and hence rebuffed his offer of marriage. Zinzendorf's attentions were now turned toward his younger cousin, Theodore, whom he confidently expected to marry. In his ardour the young count was not immediately aware of the fact that Countess Theodore did not really return his affections. The gradual realization of this circumstance was a very sobering experience for him, which had profound implications for his religious development.[1] Being aware of a sense of guilt for such "excessive love"[2] he tried to atone by making a successful match between Theodore and his best friend, Count Henry XXIX Reuss. Though this experience initially was difficult, he learned to regard it as God's will which must prevail.[3]

In the meantime Zinzendorf had come of age. The responsibilities of life had to be shouldered. While he would have preferred to enter the Christian ministry his family insisted that he stay with the legal profession. Accordingly he took a position as legal counsel with the Saxon government at Dresden.[4] Toward the end of 1721 he bought the estate of Berthelsdorf in Oberlausitz near Grosshennersdorf. As pastor for the people on the estate he selected Johann Andreas Rothe, and as steward of the estate he installed Johann Georg Heitz, a man of the Reformed Faith.

After his experience with Theodore, Zinzendorf had grown wary of emotional attachments.[5] During the following year he arrived at his characteristic understanding of the meaning of marriage. He thought of it as a union which is primarily directed toward religious ends, "mere creature love" being consciously eliminated. It is a union, therefore, which may seem "indifferent" to outsiders, but which, nevertheless, is full of "joy." Into this kind of union he confidently expected Erd-

---

[1] See E.B. Beyreuther. *Der junge Zinzendorf*, 1957, p. 220.

[2] Spangenberg, *op. cit.*, vol. 1, p. 161.

[3] See various letters quoted by Spangenberg, *op. cit.*, vol. 1, p. 160f.

[4] See his letters to his grandmother, quoted in the introduction to his *Gegenwärtige Gestalt des Kreuzreichs Jesu in seiner Unschuld* etc., in ZE, vol. 5, n.p., especially his letter of October 1721.

[5] See his interesting letter written from Dresden on June 19, 1722, in the introduction to his *Kreuzreich*, ZE, vol. 5, n.p. See also E. Beyreuther, *Der junge Zinzendorf*, 1957, p. 221.

munthe Dorothea, the sister of his friend Reuss, to enter. In this he was not mistaken. On September 7, 1722, Count Nikolaus and Countess Erdmunthe were married with the mutual understanding that initially at least, no expressions of tenderness were to pass between them, that their honeymoon was to be devoted to a discussion of common goals, and that their marriage was to be purely a *Streiterehe* (a marriage of Christ's warriors).[1] Perhaps it should be said that this philosophy was found elsewhere within eighteenth century Pietism,[2] In part, however, it must be evaluated with reference to the singular religious dedication of the contracting parties.

The Establishment of Herrnhut

At this point the story of Zinzendorf's life needs to be interrupted in order to present a brief over-view of the origin of the community with which his life presently became entwined.

It is generally held that the roots of renewed Moravianism go back to John Huss (1369-1415). A branch of his followers were the so-called Calixstines. Sometime in 1457[3] a congregation of Calixstines settled at the village of Kunwald, near the castle of Lititz in Moravia. They began to refer to themselves as "The Brethren of the Law of Christ," and later as the *Unitas Fratrum*. In 1467 they took steps to separate themselves from the Calixstines. Three of their number were chosen by lot to be priests. They were ordained by Michael Bradacius, who had been given episcopal consecration by the Waldensian bishop Stephen. Inspite of severe persecution the Unity flourished. During the days of the Reformation it maintained fraternal relations with the major Protestant reformers. Under the intellectual leadership of the "incomparable" Bishop Johann Amos Comenius[4] it was given one of the earliest glimpses of an ecumenical vision in Christendom.

Through the efforts of Christian David, a carpenter from Senftleben

---

[1] E.B. Beyreuther, *Nikolaus Ludwig von Zinzendorf in Selbstzeugnissen und Bilddokumenten*, 1965, p. 58.

[2] See our discussion of Hochmann von Hochenau, p. 202f. For a discussion of Hochmann's influence upon Zinzendorf see E.B. Beyreuther, *Der junge Zinzendorf*, 1957, p. 277.

[3] The date of settlement is disputed by Moravian historians. It has been somewhat arbitrarily fixed for March 1, 1457. See J.E. Hutton, *A History of the Moravian Church*, 1909, footnote on p. 47. For a brief and lucid account of the pre-history of the Renewed Moravian Church see also A.J. Lewis, *Zinzendorf the Ecumenical Pioneer*, 1962, p. 34f.

[4] M. Spinka, *John Amos Comenius; That Incomparable Moravian*, 1943.

in Moravia, the way was prepared for the Brethren to find a new home on Zinzendorf's recently acquired estate at Berthelsdorf. Pastor Rothe had introduced David to the Count, who had responded immediately to the need of the Brethren by inviting them to settle at Berthelsdorf. On June 8, 1722 the first emigrees from Moravia arrived at Berthelsdorf under the leadership of Christian David. They were the Neisser brothers, Jakob and August, with their families, Michael Jaschke and Susanna Dorlich. Others quickly followed and, before Zinzendorf realized what was happening, the new settlement was on its way. In 1727 it already consisted of 200 Moravian emigrees as well as people who had come from elsewhere.

Because of the remnants of feudalistic thinking which prevailed, Zinzendorf felt himself responsible for both the material and religious well-being of the settlers. He therefore assumed the leadership of the colony to the extent to which his reponsibilities at Dresden permitted. Since his physical presence at Berthelsdorf was impossible, however, grave difficulties ensued in the little community of religious enthusiasts. There was serious contention between Johann Georg Heitz, a Swiss of Reformed persuasion, and the Lutheran pastor Johann Andreas Rothe[1] over the issue of free grace. Toward the end of 1724 Zinzendorf had to step in to restore harmony. Even more divisive was the influence of the able lawyer Johann Sigismund Krüger, whose mental reservations about the full humanity of Jesus Christ clashed with the theology of the Lutheran confessions, which had hitherto been assumed to be the doctrinal expression of the faith of the community.

In the face of these difficulties Zinzendorf resolved to take full charge of the settlement, which in the meantime had been called *Herrnhut*. Accordingly he took leave of Dresden early in 1727 to take up temporary residence in the newly built orphanage at *Herrnhut*. With great dedication he devoted himself to the task of building bridges of mutual understanding and affection. As a result the people of *Herrnhut* were ready to sign Zinzendorf's *Manorial Injunctions and Prohibitions*, which were meant to regulate the civil life at Herrnhut.[2] Shortly thereafter Zinzendorf asked all members of the community who wished to do so to sign a second document, the so called *Brotherly*

[1] For a helpful discussion of Rothe and his work see E. Teufel, "Johannes Andreas Rothe, 1688-1758," BbKG, vol. 30, 1917, pp. 1-69; vol. 31, 1918, pp. 1-111.

[2] For the full text see J.T. Müller, *Zinzendorf als Erneuerer der alten Brüderkirche*, 1900, appendix, pp. 106-110. All the inhabitants of Herrnhut signed the document on May 12, 1727. It was signed once more on June 15, 1727.

Union and Compact, which was to regulate the religious practices of *Herrnhut*.[1] Thus the count had now joined the company of those people of his day who meant to transform Spener's *ecclesiolae in ecclesia* into communal settlements, the whole life of which was dominated by a given religious ideal.[2] The fact that this newly constituted community was nominally Lutheran, and that many of its members had once belonged to the ancient Moravian Church, makes it an even more remarkable ecclesiological phenomenon.

In order that the newly promulgated statutes might be observed the community chose twelve "elders" who were to have spiritual oversight, four of these being designated by lot to be the chief elders. They were Georg and Melchior Nitschmann, Christoph Hoffmann, and Christian David. Some months before this, "bands" had been organized, which consisted of a small number of mutually congenial members of the community. The object of such "bands" (later called "classes" or "choirs") was that of promoting the devotional life of the members through prayer and religious conversation. Zinzendorf himself came to be referred to as *Vorsteher*, or *Ordinarius*, terms which in the mind of the people appear to have had not only a civil, but a religious connotation. The result of the religious emphasis which under the able and enthusiastic leadership of Zinzendorf began to dominate every phase of communal life was the memorable communion service of August 13, 1727. It has ever since been regarded by Renewed Moravianism as a kind of religious birthday.[3]

After the summer of 1727 *Herrnhut* became a unique religious community with its characteristic doctrinal, liturgical, and communal features. The machinery for administering its civil as well as its religious life continued to be perfected. The Sunday sermon, preached by Pastor Rothe at the Berthelsdorf church to which the Herrnhuters still belonged, was summarized and discussed at *Herrnhut* in the afternoon. Since the above mentioned August 13 experience of the community the lovefeast was observed.[4] In 1728 the monthly day of prayer was

---

[1] *Ibid.*, pp. 110-115. Only those people who expected to join the *Verein* were asked to sign the 42 statutes of this religious compact.

[2] The immediate model for *Herrnhut* seems to have been the community at Ebersdorf in Thüringia on the estate of his wife's parents (Müller, *op. cit.*, p. 11f). Visiting Ebersdorf in 1721 Zinzendorf realized for the first time that Christians of differing theological persuasions can live together in close religious fellowship.

[3] For eye-witness descriptions of what happened see Spangenberg, *op. cit.*, vol. 3, p. 436f.

[4] *Ibid.*, pp. 446-447.

instituted. The same year the daily texts, or *Losungen*, and the frequent use of the lot as an instrument for decision-making, came into existence. In 1731 the Lord's Supper was celebrated monthly, in 1732 followed the Easter sunrise service and in 1733 the watchnight service. Preaching by Zinzendorf and other members of the community was frequent; and great emphasis was put upon singing. In 1728 twenty-six young men banded together under the leadership of Christian David and Melchior Nitschmann to form a common household, single women following suit in 1730. The intention here was that of subordinating all of life's interests to a religious ideal. In time these beginnings issued in the so-called "choir system," under which the community was organized in various groups, each with common housing and common activities.

Beginning in 1727 various members of the community at *Herrnhut*. including Zinzendorf, began undertaking evangelistic tours to many parts of Europe. Out of such evangelistic activity came the establishment of Moravian settlements in places other than *Herrnhut*. The first of these was *Pilgerruh* in Schleswig, which came into being in 1737. Upon Zinzendorf's visit to Copenhagen in 1731 began *Herrnhut's* tremendous concern for foreign missions, with the Moravian missionary enterprise getting under way the following year. Especially momentous from an ecclesiological point of view was David Nitschmann's consecration as bishop by Daniel Ernst Jablonski, the latter representing the episcopacy of the *Unitas Fratrum*. This took place in 1735. Two years later Zinzendorf himself was consecrated bishop by Jablonski and Nitschmann. Little wonder that the connection between *Herrnhut* and the Lutheran congregation at Berthelsdorf was eventually severed (1756) and that relations with the Lutheran Communion became strained. Renewed Moravianism was now on its way as a separate Protestant enterprise.

An Interpretation of Zinzendorf

In so far as the religious thinking of early Renewed Moravianism was heavily dependent upon Zinzendorf's theological development an analysis of his intellectual maturation and of his major doctrinal emphases would seem to be necessary at this point. It should be remembered, of course, that while his theological influence upon his people was of central importance, Zinzendorf was a manyfaceted genius.[1] For that reason the present attempt to focus mainly upon his

[1] Pointing to Zinzendorf's amazing variety of gifts H. Renkewitz rightly observes :

theology is merely an attempt to keep this discussion within the available limits of space.

The serious student of Zinzendorf's thought finds himself immediately confronted by a number of vexing problems. Not the least of these is a result of the fact that the Count was not, and did not mean to be, a systematic theologian. His theological insights must, therefore, largely be culled from speeches and homilies of which he produced many thousands during his lifetime. A large number of these he purposely refrained from publishing,[1] while some of them were pirated and published without his consent. In the face of these difficulties the American student of early Moravianism finds himself largely dependent upon the *Hauptschriften* and the *Ergänzungsbände* which have lately been made available.[2]

A related difficulty has to do with his choice of words. Zinzendorf did not use precise theological language. He delighted, in fact, in giving his exceedingly fertile imagination free linguistic reign. Words to him were not primarily a medium of rational expression, but a means of communicating religious feeling.[3] This implies, and quite correctly, that in his understanding of the meaning of the Christian faith the latter took precedent.

Here as in so many areas of the history of Christianity the most disconcerting problem, of course, has to do with the plenitude of interpreters and interpretations to which one can only hope to add one more. Nor is this problem relieved by the fact that Zinzendorf was one of the most controversial figures of his age.

The self-interpretation of Renewed Moravianism begins about the

---

"Er war zugleich Staatsmann, Standesherr, Unternehmer, Jurist, Organisator, Diplomat, Dichter, und es ist wohl noch niemand gelungen, diese Persönlichkeit so nachzuzeichnen, dass die lebendige Feinheit aller dieser sehr beschiedenen Gaben voller Lebenswirklichkeit vor uns stünde." (See "Zinzendorf als Theologe," *Zinzendorf Gedenkbuch*, Benz and Renkewitz, eds., 1951, p. 80).

[1] E. Beyreuther and G. Meyer, eds., *Nikolaus Ludwig von Zinzendorf, Hauptschriften in sechs Bänden*, vol. 1. preface, p. vi.

[2] The full titles of these two sets are the one just mentioned, published 1962-1963, and by the same editors *Nikolaus Ludwig von Zinzendorf. Ergänzungsbände*, 9 vols., 1964-1966. These sets will be referred to in this chapter as ZH and ZE respectively. The fact that H. Nielsen (*Intoleranz und Toleranz bei Zinzendorf*, 3 vols., 1952, 1956, 1960), who claims to have worked with unprinted sources, comes up with nothing substantially new would seem to indicate that the printed sources here collected are quite reliable.

[3] For a helpful discussion of Zinzendorf's use of words see W. Bettermann. *Theologie und Sprache bei Zinzendorf*, 1935, p. 95f.

middle of the eighteenth century with A.G. Spangenberg. His 8 volume *Leben* was understandably apologetic in nature.[1] The same is true of the work of David Cranz, which, like Spangenberg's, originated in a context of distrust and frequent misrepresentation. With L.C. von Schrautenbach and his successors — B. Plitt, B. Becker, J.T. Müller, W.L. Kölbing, G. Reichel, and the American J. Weinlick — Moravian self-interpretation dares to move toward a more critical stance.

It was Albrecht Ritschl's famous account of the whole Pietistic Movement (1886) which first brought into focus the entire problem of Zinzendorf interpretation. Having applied his well known thesis concerning the nature of Pietism to the theology of the Count, Ritschl's position was critically examined by B. Becker. Henceforth the question was whether the founder of Moravianism was basically a disciple of Luther or of the Christian mystics. The Lutheranizing interpreters, on the one hand (B. Becker, W. Bettermann, S. Eberhard, H. Renkewitz, E. Beyreuther, as well as L. Bergmann), have generally attempted to legitimize Zinzendorf's theology by drawing it into the orb of Wittenberg. The line originally taken by Ritschl, on the other hand, was continued by O. Uttendörfer, G. Hök, and L. Aalen. The impressive volume by the latter on the theology of the young Zinsendorf should perhaps be regarded at this moment as a kind of summation of the Scandinavian approach,[2] while Beyreuther may be regarded as the spokesman for the Lutheranizing group.[3]

In this brief study it would obviously be impossible to say anything meaningful on the question of whether Zinzendorf was essentially a Lutheran or a mystic. The very fact, however, that this discussion has arisen would seem to indicate that in his theology elements of each of these traditions are unquestionably present. In the present context, therefore, it may be best to remain as uncommitted as possible to a particular line of interpretation and to follow an approach which recognizes both the mystical and the Lutheran elements in his theology. It is a matter of record that beginning about 1730 the Count began to have serious mental reservations about the teaching of the mystics. Furthermore, as time went on his conscious attitude toward them

---

[1] See A.G. Spangenberg, *Leben des Herrn Nicolaus Ludwig — von Zinzendorf* etc., 1772-1775, vol. 1, preface.

[2] L. Aalen, *Die Theologie des jungen Zinzendorf* in *Arbeiten zur Geschichte und Theologie des Luthertums*, 1966, vol. 16. This book was first published in Swedish in 1952.

[3] See especially E. Beyreuther, *Der junge Zinzendorf*, 1957; *Studien zur Theologie Zinzendorfs*, 1962; as well as "*Zinzendorf und Luther*," *Luther Jahrbuch*, vol. 28, 1961.

became ever more negative. This does not prove, however, that unconsciously he did not remain closer to mystical forms of religious apprehension than his Lutheranizing interpreters are willing to admit.[1] While it is true, for instance, that in 1747 he could severely censure the mystics for opening the way to religious presumptuousness,[2] he nevertheless continued to give priority to what he calls "heart religion."[3] By this he means the individual's immediate contact with God in a relationship of unreserved love. This is, of course, a recurrent theme in western mysticism.

The world in which Zinzendorf attained religious maturity was in the grip of tremendous intellectual ferment. In Lutheran circles, and to some extent in the Reformed churches, Orthodoxy was fighting a rear-guard action. Because of the change of intellectual climate it was unable to command the loyalty of the rising generation. On the one hand, it was threatened by the rationalistic impulses which had long since made themselves felt in England, and which were now beginning to be felt on the Continent. On the other hand, in Germany the first harbingers of the spirit of what toward the middle of the eighteenth century became the *Sturm und Drang* movement were beginning to be noticeable.[4]

In Zinzendorf this incipient *Sturm und Drang* approach to religious reality was already manifesting itself. For that reason he looked with disdain upon the scholastics and their systems, for, he said, "As soon as truth becomes a system, one does not possess it."[5] This was undoubtedly the reason also for his unqualified fondness for the writings of Pierre Bayle (1647-1706), which mystified many of his contemporaries. What Zinzendorf appreciated in Bayle was his ruthless attack upon both Orthodoxy and rationalism in order to make room for an understanding of personal religion, which is based upon the total experience of the individual.[6] It was this spirit, then, which helped him to recognize the importance of experience in the realm of religious epistemology, and

[1] For more detailed interpretative suggestions see especially Aalen, *op. cit.*, pp. 11-14. It should also be mentioned in this connection, as will be pointed out later, that during the last few decades a whole group of special studies related to some phase of Zinzendorf's life or thought have come into existence.

[2] *Gemeinreden* II. ZH, vol. 4, p. 278.

[3] *Londoner Reden*, first sermon, 1753, ZH, vol. 5, p. 154f.

[4] This movement will be discussed more fully in the last chapter.

[5] Quoted by G. Meyer in his preface to vol. 3 of ZH, p. XV.

[6] For an excellent discussion of the relationship of Zinzendorf to Bayle see E. Beyreuther, *Studien zur Theologie Zinzendorfs*, 1962, pp. 202-234.

the importance of the poetic imagination, rather than reasoned argument, in the attainment of meaning.

Coupled with Zinzendorf's sensitivity to the spirit of the times was his amazing ability to see through a problem or an issue, to evaluate it from its core, and to do so without an excessive amount of investigation. It is not surprising to find, therefore, that, maturing in the intellectual climate indicated above, his theology revolves around the words *Empfindung* (feeling) or *Gemüt* (not translatable).[1] Personal religion, he held, is a matter of feeling, not of reasoning. Its locus is not the head, but the "heart." It has nothing to do with theoretical judgments, but with a mode of religious apprehension which involves the whole man, and preeminently his affective nature. It is, therefore, not thinking about God, but "experiencing" God. This is an understanding of the nature of personal religion quite different from that of the scholastics, who tended to understand it preeminently as assent to theological propositions. It differs also from the basic stance of the Enlighteners, who wanted to reduce religion to that which they understood to be reasonable. It differed, finally, from the more representative Pietists, who tended to put the emphasis upon a once-for-all experience of personal religious renewal, which must manifest itself henceforth in a life of love and service according to the ethical standard which is thought to prevail in the New Testament. Over against these contemporary approaches Zinzendorf made the continual affective response to the revelation of God in Christ the core of personal religion.

Not only did he help to thrust upon his age a new understanding of the nature of religion, but a new understanding of religious apprehension. The only valid road to personally meaningful religious reality is here considered to be "feeling." The meaning of religious affirmations is to be found basically in the way in which they meet the religious needs of the believer.[2] How does a religious statement affect my experience of religious reality? is the question which is of paramount importance to the *Ordinarius*. It was the empirical effect, then, not the theoretical truthfulness of biblical revelation, to which both theology and preaching had to address themselves. The theology of Zinzendorf,

---

[1] In English religious discourse the meaning of *Gemüth* is perhaps best conveyed by the word "heart" in such expressions as "head and heart."

[2] See his sermon on the topic "How the One True Religion Actually Begins in the Heart," *Gemeinreden* I. ZH, vol. 4., p. 259f. For a fuller discussion of Zinzendorf's understanding of the nature of personal religion see O. Uttendörfer, *Zinzendorfs religiöse Grundgedanken*, 1935, p. 12f.

therefore, projected for itself a new task. It was no longer Orthodoxy's attempt to systematize the faith by the use of logically consistent propositions; nor was it the attempt of the Enlighteners to conform it to contemporary notions of reasonableness and value, or mainstream Pietism's attempt to make it the rationale for a new life. The task of theology now was thought to be that of conceptualizing and formulating the affirmations of the biblical revelation in a way which would evoke a continuing and authentic experience of God's love.[1]

Having pointed out that Zinzendorf made feeling the organ of religious apprehension it should also be emphasized, however, that he did not, by the same token, make it the final criterion of religious truth. He was too deeply rooted in the Lutheran Tradition to come to such a conclusion. With Luther he regarded God's self-disclosure in Jesus Christ, and most especially in the suffering and death of Christ, as ultimately and incontrovertibly normative for religious faith and life. Thus, throughout his writings, the objective basis of religious authority is a literal, natural, pre-critical interpretation of the Bible. Bettermann is quite right, therefore, when he states that in Zinzendorf faith (as regards its content) is not based upon feeling, but feeling upon faith.[2] The biblical revelation, understood through the suffering and death of Christ, was regarded by Zinzendorf to be as firm as the Rock of Gibraltar, its content being fixed and immoveable. At the same time, however, he would wish to understand it relative to its effect on religious experience, and the preacher must communicate it so as to evoke that experience. For Zinzendorf, therefore, meaningful religious faith was trust in God as revealed in Christ, based upon the testimony of Scripture, authenticated in personal religious experience,[3] and productive of an affective identification with Christ which is clearly felt.

In speaking about the major aspects of Zinzendorf's theology itself we must begin with the God of the Judaeo-Christian tradition. Throughout his writings the Count assumes the existence of God as a living reality, on whose revelation in Jesus Christ man's religious welfare is wholly dependent. Nowhere, however, does he presume to penetrate rationally the problem of God's being. In fact, he repeatedly emphasizes that this cannot be done. Such an attempt could be compared, he states, with the effort of a mouse in the basement of a castle to reason

[1] *Berliner Reden*, ZH, vol. 1, p. 80f.

[2] Bettermann, *op. cit.*, p. 175.

[3] Especially important here are his *Berlinische Reden* I, 1758, ZH, vol. 1, which are meant to set forth his *credo*.

with another mouse about the architecture of such a structure.[1] The being of God, Zinzendorf insisted, is wrapped up in inscrutable mystery, which can be approached by man only with a sense of profound awe. What has been said about God's being applies equally to the Christian doctrine of God's triunity. It is, he held, essentially a statement of faith, for which there is support in the New Testament, as well as in the Lutheran confessions, but which is philosophically impenetrable.[2] If, therefore, theologians begin to speculate about intertrinitarian relationships they are engaging in mental activity which is essentially pagan. No amount of reasoning can take man to the living God. A religiously meaningful understanding of deity is dependent entirely upon God's self-revelation.[3] Such a revelation has been given man in Christ.

At this point it becomes necessary to introduce Zinzendorf's Christology, which constitutes a startlingly novel chapter in the history of Christian thought. Nowhere else is the originality and theological daring of the *Ordinarius* more in evidence. As a result of his Lutheran heritage Zinzendorf developed a christocentric understanding of God, which, however, went far beyong Luther. It was centered in the idea of Christ as *Spezial-Gott,* or God's total revelation.[4] Zinzendorf did not think of God in trinitarian terms which are familiar to students of historic Christianity. He insisted, rather, that those aspects of God's nature which are amenable to human understanding became such only in Christ. "The Savior is our God," he says. "Through him we know the Father and the Holy Spirit. If, however, we call the Savior God, we do not speak of the depth of his divinity, for this we do not understand. Rather, the Savior is the *Amtsgott* (God revealed in his offices) through whom everything was made, by whom it is sustained and through whom it will be restored."[5]

Christ, then, is not merely the revelation of God; he is the known God in his totality. Christ is God the Creator and Sustainer of the universe, God the Lord of history, as well as God the Redeemer. Only

---

1 Quoted by O. Uttendörfer, *op. cit.*, in his *Textbeilagen*, pp. 199-200, from a sermon preached Nov. 3, 1750.

2 *Sieben Letzte Reden*, sermon 1, 1741, ZH, vol. 2, pp. 5-6.

3 *Homilien Über die Wundenlitanei*, sermon 2, ZH, vol. 3, p. 16f.

4 This idea is developed especially in the *Sieben Letzte Reden*. See ZH, vol. 2, pp. 3-128, notably p. 11.

5 Quoted from O. Uttendörfer, *Zinzendorf und die Mystik*, 1952, p. 167.

temporarily, during the days of his flesh, did his divinity lie relatively dormant, while he delegated dominion of the universe to the Father. At the end of history, however, it is he who will reign forever and ever, for he is "the Lord within deity,"[1] the *causa prima* and *ens entium* of all things.[2]

Under the impact of such a Christology Zinzendorf was forced to find a new way of conceptualizing God's triunity. This became especially imperative when he found himself accused of being anti-trinitarian in his preaching. Accordingly he replaced the classical explanatory apparatus borrowed from Greek philosophy with one taken from man's historical life, namely, the model of the family. Shocking though it was to his contemporaries, he proceeded to speak of the divine Father, Mother, and Son. He used these terms symbolically, of course, but he did so at a time when the analogical nature of religious language was not generally understood. For that reason both orthodox and pietistic theologians were profoundly upset by what to them seemed to be wholly unjustifiable, if not downright dangerous, theological novelties.[3]

The difficult question is, of course, What did Zinzendorf mean when he applied such language to God? The answer to that question is obviously related to the basic orientation of his religious epistemology. As has been said, the *Ordinarius* was only minimally interested in gaining any knowledge about God as he is in himself. He neither expected revelation nor philosophical speculation to yield such knowledge. His over-riding concern was with that which God wants to be and do *for man*. When he read the Bible this is what Zinzendorf meant to be instructed in. In this context he understood biblical names applied to God and biblical statements made about God. They were essentially analogs for God's gracious and undeserved movement toward man.

When the Count spoke about the "Son," therefore, he meant God manifesting his love in both creation and redemption. The Son, he held, is God speaking creation into existence and crowning it with a creature which bears his image. The Son is God humbling himself in the incarnation and in suffering for man the agonies of the cross.[4] The Son is God going all the way in order to make it possible for man to find

---

1 *Sieben Letzte Reden*, ZH, vol. 2, p. 33.

2 *Ibid.*, p. 14.

3 See the prince of pietistic interpreters, Johann Albrecht Bengel's *Abriss der so genannten Brüdergemeine* etc., 1751, p. 528f.

4 See *Homilien über die Wundenlitanei*, ZH, vol. 3, p. 6f.

his true destiny. The Son is the divinely provided point of redemptive contact between God and man, and therefore man's true spiritual refuge.[1] The Son, furthermore is God giving himself in the most intimate union to man, so as to lay the foundation for a salvatory relationship of fervent mutual love between God and man, a relationship in which such terms of endearment as "bride-groom," or "little Jesus" (*Jesulein*), can be applied to Christ in worship.[2]

Zinzendorf's pronounced distaste for metaphysical language, as well as his essentially functional understanding of trinitarian language, is equally apparent in the way he thinks of the Father. Continuing to apply the model of the human family to God's triunity, the Father was not considered to be the fountainhead of deity as in many of the older formulations. He was thought to be God the provider, God the protector, and God the ruler of his people. Zinzendorf thus tended to restrict the concept of divine fatherhood to the relation between God and the church, i.e. to God's concern for the welfare, both temporal and spiritual, of his family.[3] The Father was thus emphatically regarded to be not the Father of all men, but God in a fatherly relation to those to whom Christ through his redemptive work has become their Brother and to whom the Spirit has become their Mother. All men outside of this fellowship of the church were thought to be exclusively the concern of Christ.[4] In fact, in reaction against the rising tide of natural theology, and in reaction against notions of emanatinal descent, Zinzendorf explicitly explains that "the Father of our Lord Jesus Christ is not directly our Father;" he becomes our Father only in a secondary sense, namely, through Christ who created and redeemed us.[5]

Most offensive, perhaps, to the ears of the theological establishment of his day were Zinzendorf's references to the Holy Spirit as Mother, which he began to make quite frequently by 1741. Becker speculates that he may have been driven to this by the thought of having to present the Christian message to the uncultured minds of the American

---

[1] The idea of refuge was especially in the foreground during the so-called "sifting-time," during which the cult of the *Seitenhölchen* became intolerably sentimental. See especially the *Wundenlitanei, op. cit.*

[2] Note the language of the sermons on the *Wundenlitanei, op. cit.*

[3] *Sieben Letzte Reden,* ZH, vol. 2, pp. 35, 39. See also Spangenbergs *Apologetische Erklärung,* ZE, vol. 5, pp. 46, 48.

[4] G. Spangenberg's *Apologetische Schlussschrift,* p. 488.

[5] Quoted by B. Becker, *Zinzendorf im Verhältnis zu Philosophie und Kirchentum,* 1886, p. 397.

Indians.[1] It is more likely, however, that this was a natural development from the familial model which he had earlier applied to the Father and the Son. Interestingly enough, in 1747 he gave credit for his insight into the motherhood of the Spirit to A.H. Francke,[2] though Francke would hardly have been happy with the use which the Count made of his suggestion.

In speaking of the Spirit as Mother Zinzendorf makes the interesting observation that he is not responsible for the fact that Christians talk about a trinity. Since this is their way of speaking about God, however, they must demonstrate that such language makes sense.[3] In order to make sense of trinitarian language with reference to the Spirit, therefore, the *Ordinarius* continued to use the familial model. Furthermore, he continued to ignore Christianity's historic interest in metaphysical concepts and to get at the meaning of the designation "Spirit" functionally. For that purpose he connected Is. 16 : 13 and Jo. 14 : 26 and came up with the assertion that when Christians speak of the Spirit they really mean God comforting, teaching, and inspiring his people, i.e., they mean God in the office of a mother within a human family unit.[4] Every Christian, therefore, is thus encouraged continuously to remain in the same relationship to God the Spirit in which a child stands to its natural mother.

In this rather novel approach to the Christian understanding of God one becomes aware of Zinzendorf's marked originality, his innovative spirit, but most of all of his daring, almost defiant insistence, upon being unfettered by traditional theological explanations. In his straining for theological freedom he was thus thoroughly a child of his time, though amazingly enough, he was as anxious to be free from the prevailing intellectual party-lines of his own day, as he was to be unhampered by theological tradition. In deepest essence he was a rather rare religious genius who was bent upon using every aspect of his environment and history to serve the religious ends to which he had dedicated himself.

These same characteristics are also apparent in Zinzendorf's religious anthropology, i.e., his understanding of man's need for God, his understanding of the way to God, and his understanding of man's life with

---

[1] *Ibid.* pp. 400-401.

[2] The reference is to Francke's *Gnade und Wahrheit*, chapter 13, par. 8. See *Special-Historie* etc., ZE, vol. 4, p. 50.

[3] *Oeffentliche Gemein-Reden*, part 2, ZH, p. 249f.

[4] *Ibid.*, p. 262f; also part 1, p. 368f, and p. 381f.

God. In speaking of these matters next we come to the very core of the Count's religious interest. In a sense, he regarded everything else which is usually discussed under the heading of theology as either preface or postscript.

In his understanding of man's sinfulness Zinzendorf remained thoroughly Lutheran. "Not to believe in Christ," he says in his *Berlin Discourses*, "is sin,"[1] while the rest of the passage implies that man's unfaith must be regarded in the context of an objective power of evil. Yet while man is subject to dark powers and principalities, he is also drawn, and profoundly so, by God's love manifest in Christ. Being free to accept God's grace[2] he will find in Christ the kind of abundant life God intended for him. On these premises it is important for Zinzendorf, on the one hand, to bring people into a religiously meaningful relation to Christ and, on the other hand, to point out in detail that life with Christ promises the complete fulfillment which every man naturally craves.

Zinzendorf's conceptualization of the way to Christ gives evidence of thought forms which stem from both Lutheran Pietism and mysticism. Thus while Aalen does not want to reckon the Count among the mystics he notes that his *ordo salutis* does have affinities with the general notion of mystical ascent.[3] At the same time, it would be difficult not to see a connection with the Spener-Halle Tradition in his insistence upon conscious conversion and the sharp difference between the old state and the new state made by such an experience of conversion. As in the Spener-Halle Tradition, furthermore, the means toward such an experience is the divine gift of trust, rather than the contemplative approach of the mystic. On the other hand, Zinzendorf declared himself repeatedly against Halle's *Busskampf*, insisting that the new life with all of its joys and blessedness is God's instantaneous gift.[4] Furthermore, he pressed for a complete psychological identification with the image of the suffering Savior which was foreign to Halle as well as to the Lutheran Tradition in general. In this sensualism, in fact, the new empirisist impulses of his day are perhaps most in evidence in his theology.

Whatever may have been said to the contrary there is a marked

---

[1] ZH, vol. 1., p. 27.

[2] *Büdingische Sammlung*, part 1, ZE, vol. 7, p. 92.

[3] Aalen, *Die Theologie des jungen Zinzendorf*, in *Arbeiten zur Geschichte und Theologie des Luthertums*, vol. 16, 1966, p. 251.

[4] See his sermon *Von dem Busskampfe*, *Sieben Letzte Reden*, ZH, vol. 2, p. 108f.

divergence between Zinzendorf's presuppositions regarding the meaning of salvation and those of historic Lutheranism, as well as those of Pietism in most of its manifestations outside of *Herrnhut.*

W. Bettermann, and the Lutheranizing interpreters of Zinzendorf in general, tend to emphasize the Count's affinity with Luther with respect to the *theologia crucis* which they note in both men.[1] They insist quite rightly that to Zinzendorf it was only God's love manifest in Christ's death upon the cross, which can bridge the gulf between God and man.[2] At the same time it should be pointed out, however, that the two men were very different in the way they expected the individual believer to appropriate the benefits of this saving act of God. To Luther salvation was the result of a firm trust in the sufficiency of the salvatory work of Christ on the cross. Zinzendorf, on the other hand, while affirming the Lutheran understanding of the meaning of Christ's victory over sin and death, put the emphasis upon man's psychological identification with the suffering Christ. In the one case, therefore, saving faith is faith in the facticity of an event, and faith in the divinely intended meaning of that event for the believer. In the other case, faith becomes preeminently a willed repristination in the individual's imagination of an historic event and its meaning for the believer.

It is on this basis alone that we can explain the generally offensive blood-and-wounds cult, which for a season (1743-1750) threatened to cut Moravians off from most other Christians, and which on the basis of Luther's understanding of faith is simply unthinkable. In essence this cult was based on the presupposition that through willed psychological identification with another, in this case the man Jesus, one can experience his suffering (and his ecstasy) vicariously, and that in this way one appropriates the divinely intended benefits of such vicarious suffering, namely, the new state in Christ. What we are dealing with here, are essentially mystical thought-forms reminiscent of St. Francis of Assisi.[3]

---

[1] W. Bettermann, *op. cit.*, p. 47f. Along the same line moves S. Eberhard's *Kreuzes-Theologie. Das reformatorische Anliegen in Zinzendorfs Verkündigung*, 1937. See also H. Ruh, "Die christologische Begründung des ersten Artikels bei Zinzendorf," *Basler Studien zur historischen und systematischen Theologie*, vol. 7, 1967.

[2] What Zinzendorf felt to be God's condescension in Christ for the purpose of providing the pre-conditions for man's way back to God are stated especially forcefully in the *Berliner Reden*, ZH, vol. 1. See particularly his summary statement, p. 97 f.

[3] For the literature coming out of this period see especially ZH, vols. 3 and 4. See also the many hymns which he wrote during this time.

There is no doubt about the fact, of course that after 1750 Zinzendorf modified the element of psychological identification in his presentation of the way of salvation. At the same time, however, a feeling of intimacy with the Savior remained the most important aspect of his piety.

In this connection one must speak of his concept of *Ehe Religion* which is another characteristic feature of his theology. It is a concept which, as Beyreuther indicates, he never relinquished,[1] which according to L. Aalen grew out of the mystical soil prepared by Jacob Boehme, Fenelon, and Madam Guyon,[2] and which found a congenial soil in Zinzendorf's predilection toward empiricism. To understand it one must keep in mind Zinzendorf's conscious attempt to explain religious realities analogically.

Zinzendorf chose to understand the relationship between the awakened Christian and Christ on the model of bride and groom, and he freely used the language of sentimental poetry to describe it.[3] Thus individual Christians, as well as the church, were advised to regard themselves as the bride of Christ, the latter being the true man. The Christian's, as well as the church's most profound joy and most intense delight is, therefore, that of being in the most intimate union of mutual love with Christ. The erotic language used to describe this relationship tends to strike the modern ear as offensive.[4] It should be pointed out, however, that the nobility of Zinzendorf's time was hardened to such linguistic sentimentalities. Furthermore, the *Ordinarius* always remains aware of the qualitative difference between the human bride and her heavenly groom, as well as of the fact that the bride is essentially related to a dying groom. For these reasons the language of easy familiarity with the divine, found in older forms of mysticism which is associated with the language of the *Songs* of *Songs*, is generally avoided. In fact, the abundance of symbols which refer to suffering and dying, to external pain and internal agony, lend a rather sombre tone to Zinzendorf's language of devotion.

---

[1] E. Beyreuther, *Studien zur Theologie Zinzendorfs*, p. 35f.

[2] Aalen, *op. cit.*, p. 253. Needless to say, analysts like O. K. Pfister (*Die Frömmigkeit des Grafen Ludwig von Zinzendorf*, 1910) regard this aspect of his theology as a gold mine for gaining psycho-analytical insight into Zinzendorf's personality.

[3] See especially his *In Zeyst — gehaltene Reden* etc., ZH, vol. 3.

[4] Under these circumstances we are not surprised to find an interest of psychologists in Zinzendorf. Like other geniuses he provides fascinating insights into human personality. See the exchange between O.K. Pfister and G. Reichel, 1910, 1911.

Related to what has just been said is the fact that to the Count love between a man and a woman is essentially a shadow of, or an arrow pointing towards, the love between a believing Christian and Christ. As long as it is understood as such it is good. In fact, a marriage in which sexuality is regarded in this light is a sacrament, and deserves the Christian community's full support. Even the sexual act is treated as holy by the *Vorsteher*, in so far as in Christian marriage it is essentially an outward representation of the underlying mystery of Christ.[1] The pleasure associated with it is hallowed by the fact that it points to the delights of the Christian's attachment to Christ. Lust, on the other hand, which is an end in itself, is reprehensible and must not be found in Christian family life. Thus in reference to the right and wrong attitude toward sexuality Zinzendorf wanted his followers to distinguish between ordinary marriages and *Streiterehen.*[2] In the latter all relationships are ultimately motivated by the love which is the inner nature of the divine Family — Father, Mother, and Son.

There can hardly be any doubt about the fact that Zinzendorf's understanding of sexuality and marriage must be considered an outstanding contribution to Christian thought. Yet, it would be a mistake to consider it in isolation. To Zinzendorf Christian marriage was, in fact, a symbol of the Christian life in general.[3] As in a marriage in which Christ is the motivational center, everything finds meaning ultimately in God's love alone, so it must be in the life of every individual Christian, as well as in the life of the Christian community. In contradistinction to many other Pietists Zinzendorf was not primarily interested in what Christians ought to do, or not do. True to his Lutheran heritage he profoundly disliked any legalistic approach to the understanding of the Christian life. Not that he did not expect his followers to govern themselves in general by the ethic he read out of the New Testament. What he insisted on was that the heart of Christian piety must not be considered a set of regulations but a joyful, affective, unutterably satisfying, personal relationship with "the Savior." This is what he meant by the phrase "connection with the Savior," or the expression "heart-religion," both of which he used quite frequently in his *London Sermons*,[4] To produce such heart-religion was the aim of all

[1] *Büdingische Sammlung*, part 1, in ZE, vol. 7, p. 328f.

[2] *Zurückgelassenes Eventual-Testament* etc., *Büdingische Sammlung*, ZE, vol. 8. p. 256.

[3] *In Zeyst — gehaltene Reden* etc., ZH, vol. 3. pp. 207-208.

[4] *Londoner Predigten*, ZH, vol. 5.

of his preaching and writing. It was the purpose, also, of the tremendous amount of religious poetry which he produced; the latter in the belief that the language of poetry lends itself far more perfectly to this end than the language of reason.

Zinzendorf taught that once a person has come into such a "connection with Christ," and thus knows the secret of "heart-religion," he has found the happiness and peace which God has intended for him.[1] Beyond this, he has now been eminently sensitized to the meaning of God's will in every situation of life.[2] Even the most prosaic decisions of everyday existence are made "with Christ."[3] On this basis the Christian really understands what it means to be concerned about the neighbor, for it is the love of Christ which motivates him to do so.[4]

In this connection it should be pointed out that while Zinzendorf expected his followers to be sensitive to the ethical claims which he found in the New Testament the emphasis relative to the Christian life was not upon the *praxis pietatis* of the Spener-Halle tradition, but upon the aim of *Glückseligkeit*.[5] As Bettermann points out Zinzendorf's most frequent advice to his followers was, "One must become a sinner, then one is given grace, and with that everything has been accomplished."[6] As Luther before him, Zinzendorf was the inveterate enemy of all legalism. What he expected of his followers was the doing of that which comes natural in a continuously experienced joyful relationship to Christ. The Christian life is thus essentially a matter of living through every moment of time, of meeting every challenge and trial in happy contemplation of the crucified Lord, and of his gift of salvation.

With such an understanding of the Christian life one is not surprised to find that among the early Moravians the difference between piety and worship becomes minimal. All of life's tasks and challenges become occasions for worship and are in turn transformed into acts of religiously motivated service. A kind of celestial light is, in fact, cast upon all

---

1 *Berliner Reden*, ZH, vol. 1, p. 85.

2 *Ibid.*, p. 62.

3 He speaks of going to the toilet in the name of Christ. *Zurückgelassenes Eventual-Testament* etc., *op. cit.*, p. 257.

4 *Pennsylvanische Reden*, part 1, ZH, vol. 2, p. 121.

5 This word is not really translatable. It expresses a religious state of utterly joyful satisfaction and peace, a state which the English word "blessedness" only approximates. Zinzendorf used it frequently throughout his active career.

6 Bettermann, *op. cit.*, p. 21.

facets of human experience. In the deepest sense the life of the believer, both in its individual and its corporate aspects, takes on a certain provisional nature, in so-far as every conscious segment of it points beyond itself to the happy state of divinely intended fulfillment.

Closely related to what has been said is the frequent use of the lot by the early followers of Zinzendorf, which appears to have taken rise during the late 20's.[1] The Count himself was convinced of the legitimacy of this practice. "For me," he says, "the lot and the will of the Savior will be one and the same until I gain more wisdom. I am not yet wise enough to find the Lord's will in my own ideas. An innocent little piece of paper for me is more reliable than my own feeling."[2] On the basis of this conviction the lot was used in a two-fold way. On the one hand, Moravians used it, and still do, to find the right Scripture verse for a particular day or occasion.[3] Quite frequently however, it was also used for decision-making, both in personal life and in the life of the church. The presupposition was, of course, that the believer's life is lived in the immediate, conscious presence of Christ, and that through the lot the latter expresses his will among his people. It should be mentioned, however, that Zinzendorf did not recommend this somewhat questionable practice to all Christians, holding that God has various ways of dealing with different kinds of people.

Mention has been made above of the Zinzendorfian transformation of human experiences by placing them into a context of religious devotion. This is nowhere more evident than in the attitude of the *Ordinarius* and his early followers toward death, an aspect of human existence with which all religions concern themselves in one way or another. Perhaps it is not too much to say that no group of religious people anywhere have succeeded more completely in taking the sting out of the sombre and frightening experience of dying than did the eighteenth century Moravians. They regarded death as "going home," but chose to understand those words with a literalness seldom found among other Christian groups. "We are happy," said the *Ordinarius* in one of his *Berlin Discourses*, "wherever we find ourselves, whether we sit or lie

---

[1] For a detailed account of the Moravian use of the lot see E. Beyreuther, *Studien zur Theologie Zinzendorfs*, 1962, p. 109f.

[2] Quoted by F.W. Kantzenbach, *Orthodoxie und Pietismus*, 1966, p. 202, in *Evangelische Enzyklopädie*, vols. 11, 12.

[3] Out of this came the widely appreciated *Daily Texts*, which originated in 1728 and have been published on a yearly basis since 1731.

down, wake or sleep, conquer or suffer, die or live."[1] Not infrequently one finds references to a "happy death" or to the blessed experience of going "up yonder." An early Moravian's dying, as well as his living, was done *sub specie aeternitatis*. It became a ritual, as it were, for joining the happy throng of 'God's people' who had gone before, and whose bliss was now uninterrupted by the vicissitudes of an earthly existence. Little wonder that the Easter sunrise service early became an institution among them.

Zinzendorf's ecclesiological insights closely follow the lines of thought which have already been pointed out. The church consists essentially of all created beings who love Christ. Some of these, the blessed dead, and other heavenly beings, are already gathered before God's throne,[2] and thus constitute the heavenly fellowship, to the blessed state of which the church on earth looks with joyful anticipation. The latter consists of all men and women, wherever, and under whatsoever circumstances they exist, who are experientially and affectively united with Christ. All existing ecclesiastical groupings Zinzendorf called by various names, such as religions, or *tropi*.

Among these the word *tropus* (from *tropoi peideias*, ways or methods of training) is most apt, since it expresses Zinzendorf's basic ecclesiastical point of view. He regarded each ecclesiastical grouping of his day — Lutheran, Reformed, Anglican, Catholic, etc. — as a particular school by means of which God meant to impart saving knowledge to his people.[3] Each had its contribution to make and was, therefore, important in God's economy to the extent to which it met its divinely appointed task. All were regarded as temporary however; i.e., as mere shadows of the church come to full reality in Christ and constituting the body of Christ.

Under the impact of such ecclesiological presuppositions Zinzendorf had no sympathy for the separatistic tendencies inherent in certain

---

[1] *Berlinische Reden*, part 1, ZH, vol. 1, p. 176.

[2] *Londoner Predigten*, ZH, vol. 5, p. 113.

[3] For a succinct statement of the *tropus* idea as found among Moravians in 1757 see the so called *Zeremonienbüchlein*, p. 19, ZE, vol. 6. According to Beyreuther's introduction the author of it is probably the early Moravian historian David Cranz (p. XVI, footnote), who here rather adequately sums up the Count's teaching. For Zinzendorf's general attitude toward what he called *Religionen* (denominations) see especially his *Sammlung öffentlicher Reden — in dem nördlichen Teil von America* etc. (usually called his *Pennsylvanische Reden*), ZH, vol. 2. In this connection K. Schuster's discussion ("Gruppe, Gemeinschaft, Kirche : Gruppenbildung bei Zinzendorf," in *Theologische Existenz Heute*, vol. 85, 1960) is also helpful.

other forms of Pietism. At the beginning of his career he ardently hoped to be able to carry on Spener's *ecclesiolae in ecclesia* idea within the Evangelical Lutheran Church, whose traditions continued to be profoundly meaningful to him. When he finally found himself forced out of that communion he sought refuge in the Moravian Church, regarding it as a temporary "guest-house" of the family of the Savior.[1] He maintained these connections with historic Christian traditions deliberately, and in the belief that the time for the independent establishment of the "true church" on earth was not yet ripe. If we thus find him vigorously defending the Moravian Church, as he did upon occasion,[2] he did so not because he regarded the Renewed Moravian Church as the one true church on earth. He *did* so, rather, in the belief that in the Renewed Moravian Church the "true church" is, perhaps, somewhat more fully prefigured than in other Christian traditions.

Still there appears to have been latent in the Count's mind the hope that as a result of his own labors the "true church" might become an ever more visible reality on earth. Only on this basis can we explain his strong advocacy in the American colonies of what he called a "Fellowship of God in the Spirit."[3] The ecumenical significance of such thinking is obvious, and has been pointed out at length. On the other hand, it is not too difficult to see that Zinzendorf's attempt to support the visible ecclesiastical entity of the Renewed Moravian Church in one sermon, and his advocacy of a "Fellowship of God in the Spirit" in another sermon was confusing to many of his North American hearers. Hence many of them did not fully trust his intentions, and did not finally accept his ecumenical leadership. The result was that in the end Zinzendorf had to settle for what he did not want at the beginning, namely, another religious group, the Renewed Moravian Church, as the chief bearer of his religious insights.

Implied in what has been said above is the fact that Zinzendorf was not impressed by the doctrinal definitions *per se* of the older confessional

---

1 Quoted by J.T. Müller, *Zinzendorf als Erneuerer der Brüderkirche*, 1900, p. 99.

2 See his farewell speech to his workers in Pennsylvania, ZE, vol. 9, p. 204. The whole address is most instructive from an ecclesiological point of view.

3 The expression which Zinzendorf used in his American discourses was *Gemeine Gottes im Geist* (See *Sammlung öffentlicher Reden — in dem nördlichen Teil von Amerika* etc., ZH, vol. 2, p. 314). In so far as he did not think of a local congregation, however, but rather of a felllowship including believers in all *tropi* the word *Gemeine* should here be translated as "fellowship," or possibly as "community," but never as "congregation." It would seem that the translation "Congregation of God in the Spirit" often used in the past (See A.J. Lewis, *Zinzendorf the Ecumenical Pioneer*, 1962, p. 14), is quite misleading.

groups, any more than by the lack of such definitions among some of the sectarians. He regarded all as acceptable as long as they helped people into the religious experience which he regarded as the core of personal religion. What he was preeminently interested in was the full meaning of the existential possession of the Christian faith — love for Christ and the attendant certainty, power and joy. It is for this reason that he abjured all theological controversy, though he continued to hold privately that the Lutheran confessions as he chose to interpret them, embodied the most authentic interpretation of God's revelation.

In the light of what has been said it is hardly necessary to point out that there was a certain eschatological element which ran through much of Zinzendorf's thought. Understandably it penetrated not only his insight into the nature of the church but also his concept of worship. For the *Ordinarius* worship was the way in which the church below comes into blessed union with the church above through the medium of vivid imagination.[1] Even the efficacy of the sacraments was understood with reference to this eschatological tension. Above all else they were regarded to be divinely appointed means by which the worshiper comes into psychological union with the body of Christ as delineated above.[2]

Under these circumstances Christian worship, both private and public, was to Zinzendorf preeminently a joyful occasion. This is the reason for the well known Moravian emphasis upon the singing of hymns, as well as the composition of hymns and hymn tunes. "Hymns and music," says A.J. Lewis, "were poured out and sung on every possible occasion, on land and sea, throughout the far stretches of the Moravian enterprise. No opportunity for singing was lost : even the harvesters had their own hymns and the night watchmen sang on their rounds. — In particular Zinzendorf loved the famous *Singstunde* or songservice which he himself had founded in *Herrnhut*. Many complete hymns were sung at such a service, and single stanzas were then chosen to continue a spontaneous theme as the evening advanced. Hymn-singing from memory was cultivated because only in this way,

1 See *Einundzwanzig Diskurse* etc., p. 324f, ZH, vol. 6. For the earliest official regulation, for both family and public worship, see the so called *Zeremonienbüchlein*, probably written by David Cranz, and published in 1757, p. 35f, ZE, vol. 6.

2 This does not exhaust Zinzendorf's theology of the sacraments, of course. In line with his Lutheran background he did seem to give them some objective validity. For a careful treatment of his sacramental teaching see G. Hök, *Zinzendorf's Begriff der Religion*, 1948, p. 69f.

Zinzendorf argued, could the verses most effectively express the individual's experience."[1]

Early Moravian piety, as initiated by Zinzendorf, was thus essentially a joyful, emotional, perhaps basically romantic, attachment of the individual Christian to the "Savior," whose will regarding all the prosaic duties of everyday existence was thought to be apprehended most fully within a fellowhip of likeminded people. The most immediate result was that religion to these people became a most profoundly satisfying reality at the very center of their personal existence. A further result was that they had an extremely vivid sense of religious fellowship which helped them to transcend radically life's ambiguities and difficulties.

Renewed Moravianism on its way

Returning now to the story of the Renewed Moravian Church, it hardly needs to be emphasized that its members not only had a message in which they believed wholeheartedly, but a mission to which they dedicated themselves enthusiastically. Under the inspiration of Zinzendorf's genius they conceived this mission in utterly realistic terms. In the sermons of the *Ordinarius* and in early Moravian hymnody there are no triumphalist schemes for bringing the nations to Christ, no grandiose notions about establishing some utopian kingdom, and no hidden schemes for church extension, and nothing, of course, about making this a better world by imposing western culture upon the "heathen." Instead, Zinzendorf and his people contended themselves with showing to all who would listen that the happiness which had come to them as a result of their attachment to Christ was available to everyone at home and abroad, black or white. To that end they took their primary religious obligation to be that of "preaching the crucified Savior" into men's hearts.[2]

---

[1] A.J. Lewis, *op. cit.*, p. 164. It is interesting to note in this connection that the irenical and meticulously conscientious J.A. Bengel accuses the early Moravians of putting the authority of their own hymnody, based chiefly on Zinzendorf's often novel theological interpretations, above the authority of Scripture. (J.A. Bengel, *Abriss der so genannten Brüdergemeine* etc., 1751, p. 34).

[2] *Berlinische Reden*, part 1, p. 62, ZH, vol. 1. See also K. Müller, *200 Jahre Brüdermission. Das erste Missionsjahrhundert*, 1931, p. 267. For Zinzendorf's philosophy applying to foreign missions see his *Zeyster Reden*, p. 186f, ZH, vol. 3. Rather than following the Halle pattern of concentrating on one area the Count was interested in planting small cells in as many parts of the world as possible.

In the area of foreign missions, however, this way of understanding their task did not militate against a basic human concern which the early Moravian missionaries quickly manifested for all of man's needs. Hence they soon began to dispense medical aid, agricultural and commercial know-how, and instruction in various industrial skills. Often supporting themselves by following a trade they worked with extraordinary dedication. The result was the world-wide impact of Renewed Moravianism which has been widely recognized and which was entirely disproportionate to the size of the home community. To follow the far flung enterprise of eighteenth century Moravian missions would be impossible in the space of this chapter.[1]

More important at this point is some reference to the so called *Diaspora*, which grew out of Zinzendorf's ecclesiology. On the one hand he gave support to the Renewed Moravian Church, which he regarded as a *tropus*, and which, therefore developed into a regularly organized and administered Protestant denomination. Basically, however, Zinzendorf was not interested in such a denominational development, hoping at one point, it seems, that within fifty years the Renewed Moravian Church might yield up its existence to the projected Fellowship of God in the Spirit. This being the case, the *Ordinarius* put great emphasis upon the *Diaspora*, which was no less important to him than foreign missions. In fact, in the *Juengerhaus Diarium* he stated, "I would rather be a *Diaspora* peasant than a messenger to the heathen."[2]

The *Diaspora* consisted of people who had been religiously awakened according to the pattern advocated by Zinzendorf, but who kept their church membership in their respective communions (*tropi*). They were thus united not by a common confession, ecclesiastical tradition, or organization but by "heart-religion" alone. The *Diaspora* might be represented in a village or town by only one family, though more often by a small circle of people, who would meet together for mutual edification. The term itself came into local use during the thirties and was first applied officially to this phase of Moravian work at a synod held in London in 1749. The *Diaspora* idea as such is undoubtedly related to the Philadelphic Movement, which had many adherents among Continental separatists at this time.[3] As always, however, Zinzendorf

---

[1] The best discussion of it is that of Müller, *op. cit.*

[2] Quoted by J.R. Weinlick, "The Moravian Diaspora," *Transactions of the Moravian Historical Society*, vol. 17, 1959, part 1, p. 20.

[3] *Infra*, p. 208f.

stamped his own genius upon the prevailing philadelphic concept. From it he took over his conviction that God's rule over men's hearts and consciences must be extended quietly, on the principle of the leaven, not by means of mass meetings or all manner of religious commotion. On the other hand, the Count completely rejected the separatistic tendency which, he felt, was generally associated with Philadelphianism.

The relatively rapid extension of the Moravian *Diaspora* was carried on by a growing group of tavelling lay evangelists. It was not deemed necessary at first that these *Diaspora* workers needed any formal training for the task. The only requirements were a liberal supply of "heart-religion," a willingness to be sent, and the approbation of a regularly constituted congregation of the Renewed Moravian Church.[1] The lot was used to determine a particular field of labor. At the beginning *Diaspora* workers were not even given formal instructions beyond a letter of personal advice by Zinzendorf. They worked at a trade and, during the years of inception, itinerated as much as circumstances would permit. As various societies were established they were able to take residence in a given location.

The *Diaspora* societies kept in close touch with their home congregation through voluminous correspondence in which significant events were carefully reported. The members met regularly for fellowship and mutual exhortation and usually in private homes. Upon these occasions the people present were encouraged not to study the Bible directly, but to read the sermons of the *Ordinarius*, or the memos of other respected members of the fellowship. The reason for this was the need to discourage separatistic tendencies through exaggerated individualism in the area of biblical interpretation. There were also prayers, religious testimonials, and above all, the singing of the much loved hymnody which had come out of the life of the Moravian fellowship. As a result of these measures, of course, the religious ethos of Renewed Moravianism was carefully preserved throughout the far-flung reaches of its work.

---

[1] In this connection one should keep in mind Zinzendorf's interesting distinction between a pastor (*Pfarrer*) and a witness (*Zeuge*). The former needs to be respected because he is an agent of the state and carries out certain civil responsibilities though he may not have the kind of religious experience which makes possible a meaningful Christian witness. The latter, on the other hand, is called by God himself to give such a witness. Therefore he needs neither the training nor the position of the former (*Berliner Reden*, discourse 31, ZH, p. 277f). The affinity between this and the whole Pietistic Movement of Zinzendorf's day is obvious.

The spirit of eighteenth century Moravian *Diaspora* work can best be gathered from a letter of instruction written by Zinzendorf in 1727. In it he says to two prospective evangelists : "Since the dear *Herrnhut* congregation has found it desirable that you go out to preach the merits of Him who has called you, so go forth in the peace of the Lord. The Lord be with you everywhere in blessing. May he break forth ahead of you and let you break through. Freely have you received; freely give. Do not go only to one place, but openly in the day wander along the streets called righteousness. Acknowledge your King freely and courageously. About us and the blessing among us speak in accord with your convictions, but meekly. — Listen to what each has to say. — Seek everywhere only those in all churches who after Luke 6 have dug deeply and found Jesus to be the only one. Do not be satisfied with proud words, but seek after power. Next I bury you in the heart of the love of Jesus and am eternally your fellow fighter Zinzendorf."[1]

During the eighteenth century the Moravian approach to religious reality, like that of other pietistic groups on the Continent, struck a responsive chord in the lives of many people. The result was that the Moravian *Diaspora* found entrance into most of the sections of Germany. Beyond its borders Moravians were found in the surrounding countries including Russia, England, as well as North America.[2]

It was partly because of the very success of the Moravian enterprise that opposition developed in many sections of Germany. Added to this were the excesses of the "sifting-time," which threatened to drown the whole Moravian Community in a morass of religious sentimentalism. Not to be underestimated in this connection is the fear which was

---

1 Translated by J.R. Weinlick from O. Steinecke's *Die Diaspora der Brüdergemeine in Deutschland*, 1905, 1911, vol. 1, p. 44. (Weinlick, *op. cit.*, p. 29).

2 The story of the Moravian *Diaspora* during the eighteenth century has by no means been written up fully. In addition to the works of Steinecke and Weinlick many references to the Moravian *Diaspora* work are available in local histories and historical journals. Among these are : F. Brehm, "Bischof Sailors Freund J.B. von Ruoesch und die Brüder-Gemeinde," ZbKG, vol. 27, 1958, pp. 75-81; K. Schornbaum, "Herrnhuter im Markgrafentum Brandenburg-Beyreuth," ZbKG, vol. 22, pp. 199-216; *ibid.*, "Herrnhuter in Franken," BbKG, vol. 26, 1920, pp. 13-17; M. Witten, "Die Geschichte der Brüdergemeinde in Schleswig-Holstein," SVshKG, vol. 4, numbers 1-5, 1906-1909, pp. 271-414; T. Wotschke, "Die Herrnhuter in Neuwied," MrKG, vol. 26, 1932-1933, pp. 193-207; *ibid.*, "Pastor Johann Gaugolf Wilhelm Forstmann in Solingen," MrKG, vol. 21, 1927, pp. 225-243; and another article on the same man, pp. 257-287; L. Koehling, "Minden-Ravensburg und die Herrnhuter Brüdergemeinde," JVwKG, vols. 53-54, 1960-1961, pp. 94-109; and vols. 55-56, 1962-1963, pp. 69-103.

engendered in many quarters of the religious establishment by the strange militancy which Zinzendorf inspired among his followers. It was the militancy of the meek, who are nevertheless bent upon inheriting the earth.[1]

The opposition which was engendered sometimes came from the orthodox camp, sometimes from other Pietists and more rarely from the side of the Enlighteners. Occasionally, it took the form of fines or imprisonment, but more often that of literary attack or criticism. An example of an orthodox attack is that of Pastor Georg Ludwig Oder who wrote a missive with the enlightening title, *The Well-Meant Warning of the Servants of the Church in Feuchtwangen — On How to Keep from Being Infected by the Herrnhutian Epidemic*, etc.[2] Other critics — Carl Gottlob Hofmann, Johann Hermann Bemer, Alexander Volk, Johann Leonard Froreisen — added their voices. Perhaps the most vociferous opponent of Zinzendorf in the orthodox camp was Johann Philipp Fresenius (1705-1761), whose *Tried and True Reports of Things Herrnhuttian* came out from 1747-1751.[3]

In the meantime an anti-Zinzendorfian party was formed within the major camps of Lutheran Pietism throughout Germany. This was true of Halle, to which Zinzendorf was most deeply indebted.[4] The major voice here was that of Joachim Lange, of course, whose *Fatherly Admonition*, given to the theological students of Halle, more or less sums up Hallensian misgivings about the theological novelties of the *Ordinarius*.[5] The faculty of the University of Giessen, otherwise friendly toward Pietism, was equally wary of the Count's theological influence upon Lutheran church circles.[6] Even the Württemberg Fathers, whose

---

[1] This attitude is tellingly revealed in his farewell speech at Herrendyk on August 16, 1741, in which he defines a prophet as a man who tells God's truth as it is, and who in the process of doing so forgets himself and how he fares. (*Pennsylvanische Reden*, part 1, p. 2, ZH, vol. 2).

[2] Mentioned by K. Schornbaum, "Religiöse Bewegungen im Markgrafentum Brandenburg-Ansbach" etc., BbKG, vol. 16, 1910.

[3] The German title is *Bewährte Nachrichten von Herrnhutischen Sachen* etc. Fresenius had studied theology at Strassburg. In 1742 he had been called to St. Peter's Church in Frankfurt a.M., where in time he had become senior of the consistory.

[4] See G. Reichel, "Die Entstehung einer Zinzendorf feindlichen Partei in Halle und Wernigerode," ZKG, vol. 23, 1902, pp. 549-592.

[5] The German title is *Väterliche Warnung an die der Theologie ergebene studierende Jugend vor der Herrnhutischen Kirchenreform und dem damit verbundenen Missionswerk* etc.

[6] See I.W. Baumann, *Der Kampf der Giessener Theologischen Fakultät gegen Zinzendorf und die Brüdergemeine*, 1740-1750.

generally irenical temper made for a minimum of theological polemic, felt uncomfortable in the presence of the Brethren's religious enthusiasm.[1]

Perhaps the most effective criticism of Renewed Moravianism during the 18th century came from the pen of the kindly Johann Albrecht Bengel, who finally took up the cudgels against Zinzendorf in a major work, which was the fruit of eighteen years of study of the Count's writings.[2] Early in the thirties Bengel had stated that the Count was an enigma to him, but that he believed Zinzendorf to have an "honest heart."[3] He seems to have preserved this opinion of the *Ordinarius* and, therefore, censures his person mainly for having assumed an improper amount of apostolic authority,[4] an authority for which he had neither the theological know-how nor the religious maturity. Zinzendorf's theology came in for criticism at several points — its hermeneutical freedom (p. 1), its understanding of the trinity (p. 41f), its "blood and-wounds" emphasis (p. 81f), its improper language (p. 146f), and its philadelphic eschatology (p. 204f). That the great linguistic scholar finds Zinzendorf's attempt to translate the New Testament somewhat inadequate (p. 181f) is understandable. He also disliked the Count's idea of *tropi* and his subjectivism as evident in the frequently used expression, *Es ist mir so.*

In general Bengel's criticism was sincere, moderate, to the point, and rather effective. Because of the immense respect which Pietists of every description had for the person and scholarship of the teacher of Denkendorf his criticism was undoubtedly a major factor in checking the progress of the Moravian *Diaspora*,[5] at least in some sections of Germany.

---

1 R. Geiges, "Herrnhut und Württemberg. Die Verhandlungen zwischen Zinzendorf und der württembergischen Kirche. 1745-1750," BwKG, 1938, pp, 28-88, and "Die Auseinandersetzung zwischen Christian Friedrich Oetinger und Zinzendorf," BwKG, 1935, pp. 131-148; and 1936, pp. 107-135.

2 His work, which had been preceded by shorter pieces, was the afore-mentioned *Abriss der so genannten Brüdergemeine* etc., 1751. For a minute study of the relation of Bengel and Zinzendorf see G. Mälzer, *Bengel und Zinzendorf; zur Biographie und Theologie Johann Albrecht Bengels*, 1968, in *Arbeiten zur Geschichte des Pietismus*, vol. 3, edited by K. Aaland, E. Peschke, and M. Schmidt.

3 J.C.F. Burk, ed., *Dr. Johann Albrecht Bengels literarischer Briefwechsel*, 1836, p. 136.

4 *Abriss*, p. 280f.

5 R. Geiges, "Württemberg und Herrnhut im 18. Jahrhundert, Johann Albrecht Bengels Abwehr und der Rückgang des Brüdereinflusses in Württemberg," BwKG, 1938., pp. 28-88.

Because of a rising crescendo of criticism, and because they themselves were becoming uneasy in the presence of Zinzendorf's "sifting time" excesses a number of his leading men — the Neissers, Christian and David, A.G. Spangenberg and others — began to urge upon the Count a certain measure of restraint. Presently the latter began to see the religious and moral perils involved in his "blood-and-wounds" theology and began to apply the brakes to the flood of religious sentimentalism which threatened to bring his entire movement into general disrepute.

In the meantime, however, the mantle of theological leadership was beginning to fall increasingly upon the very able, and very sober August Gottlieb Spangenberg (1764-1792).[1] During the second half of the eighteenth century his steadying hand upon the life of the Moravian Church was felt not only in Germany but in England and America as well. Presently he emerged as the most incisive apologist of the Moravian understanding of Christianity.[2] In the process of defending it, however, he toned down, or even eliminated what he regarded to be the Count's more startling theological aberrations and antinomian sentimentalities. This process of domesticating and legitimizing Renewed Moravianism among the family of Protestant churches was completed upon publication of his *Brief Idea of Christian Doctrine in 1779.*[3] Spangenberg had now succeeded in bringing the Zinzendorfian movement back under the roof of an essentially pietistic understanding of the Lutheran confessions. By the same token, however, some of the early dynamic had gone out of the movement, so that in terms of numerical expansion its successes henceforth remained modest.

---

[1] The following are the major biographies of Spangenberg : J. Risler, *Das Lebeu August Gottlieb Spangenbergs, Bischofs der evangelischen Brüderkirche*, 1794; G. Reichel, *August Gottlieb Spangenberg, Bischof der Brüderkirche*, 1906. His significance for Moravian missions was written up by T. Bechler, *August Gottlieb Spangenberg und die Mission*, 1933. Unfortunately a definitive work on Spangenberg, which would especially take up his theological contribution to Moravianism, has not been written. In this chapter it is impossible even to begin to speak of Spangenberg's decisive significance for the theology, life, and mission of the Moravian enterprise.

[2] Notably in his *Declaration über die seither gegen uns ausgegangenen Beschuldigungen* etc., 1751; his *Darlegung richtiger Antworten auf mehr als dreihundert Beschuldigungen gegen den Ordinarius Fratum* etc., 1751; and his *Apologetische Schlussschrift, vorin über tausend Beschuldigungen gegen die Brüdergemeinen — beantwortet werden* etc., 1752.

[3] *Idea fidei Fratrum, oder kurzer Begriff der christlichen Lehre in der evangelischen Brüdergemeine.* An English translation of it was published in 1784 under the title, *An Exposition of Christian Doctrine, as Taught in the Protestant Church of the United Brethren* etc.

The Increasing Appreciation of Zinzendorf

Among church historians, and other people who are knowledgeable with respect to the history of Protestant Christianity, the twentieth century has witnessed an ever increasing appreciation of Zinsendorf's contribution to the ongoing stream of Protestant thought and life.[1] On the one hand, his influence merged with that of Pietism in general to bring about a certain revitalization of European church life, the latter having fallen victim first to the cold theologisms of Orthodoxy and then to the airid moralisms of the Wolffian Enlighteners. In addition to this the Moravian *Diaspora* became as it were, a gadfly to large numbers of pastors in the religious establishment of the day, who had to compete for men's religious loyalty with the contagious enthusiasm of the Brethren.[2] Such competition became ever more serious when, as a result of the Enlightenment, it became increasingly difficult for these pastors to evoke from the civil authorities repressive measures against heterodoxy in thought and practice.

That the *Ordinarius*' influence upon the Renewed Moravian Church was decisive is acknowledged by all of its historians. This is true, though among the Moravians, as in other religious communities, later developments introduced various modifications of the founder's original religious insights.

The impact of Zinzendorf's life and work, however, reached far beyond his own day, and far beyond the religious community which he founded. His place, for instance, in the saga of Protestant missions has long been recognized and needs no documentation; neither does his place in the development of Protestant hymnody.

During our own century his pioneer efforts in the direction of

---

[1] This was true even of Karl Barth, who otherwise consistently chose to subjectivize Pietism by making the spiritualistic element within the movement, typified by Tersteegen, the pietistic norm (See his *Die Protestantische Theologie im 19. Jahrhundert*, pp. 93-94). This understanding of Pietism fitted in with Barth's thesis, of course, but it tends to do violence to the historian's sense of *was wirklich geschehen ist*. Unfortunately from our point of view Barth's estimate of Zinzendorf, though favorable, is equally problematical, for here he objectivizes the Count's blood-and-wounds theology in a way which seems totally insupportable. This leaves F. Gärtner's study open to question as well ("Karl Barth und Zinzendorf; die bleibende Bedeutung Zinzendorfs auf Grund der Beurteilung des Pietismus durch Karl Barth," *Theologische Existenz Heute*, N.F. vol. 40, 1953).

[2] For an early recognition of Zinzendorf's influence upon the Evangelical Lutheran Church see O. Steinecke, *Zinzendorfs Bedeutung für die evangelische Kirche*, 1900. See also G. Gloege, *Zinzendorf und das Luthertum*, 1950.

ecumenical thought and practice have been given increasing recognition. In the light of this fact it is interesting to find that in 1902 O. Steinecke still found it necessary to write a defense of Zinzendorf against Ritschl's charge that he had been influenced too much by Roman Catholics.[1] That in praying for French Catholics during the Jansenist difficulties he came close to being unique among eighteenth century Protestant leaders hardly needs to be pointed out to anyone acquainted with the religiously inspired animosities of the age. In fact, much of the opposition which he encountered was the result of his trans-confessional sympathies. Beginning in the forties of our own century, however, the latter began to be more positively evaluated, until he gradually came to be appreciated as one of the great early ecumenists.[2]

Zinzendorf's influence upon pedagogical practice also has come to be rather widely recognized since Uttendörfer and Seefeldt began to point it out in 1912.[3] Early in our century R. Meyer called attention to the Count's influence upon Schleiermacher, and hence upon the subsequent development of Protestantism, a fact which has since been generally accepted by historians of Protestant thought.[4] Within an even broader perspective Peter Baumgarten makes a fairly convincing case for the Count's impact upon the rise of historicism in western thought.[5]

In general it may be said, then, that Zinzendorf was one of the truly great men in the history of Protestantism. His impact upon the religious life and thought of a substantial number of people during his own age is beyond question, while the larger implications of his contribution to man's total history will be a subject of discussion for a long time to come.

---

[1] O. Steinecke, *Zinzendorf und der Katholizismus*, 1902.

[2] See H. Motel, *Zinzendorf als ökumenischer Theologe*, 1942; F. Blanke, *Zinzendorf und die Einheit der Kinder Gottes*, 1950; E. Benz, *Zinzendorfs ökumenische Bedeutung* in E. Benz and H. Renkewitz, eds., *Zinzendorf-Gedenkbuch*, 1951, pp. 118-139; S. Nielsen. *Intoleranz und Toleranz bei Zinzendorf*, vols. 1-3, 1952, 1956, 1960; and Lewis, *op. cit.*

[3] O. Uttendörfer, *Das Erziehungswesen Zinzendorfs und der Brüdergemeine in seinen Anfängen*, 1912; P. Seefeldt, *Zinzendorf als Pädagoge*, 1912. See also Ruth Ranft, *Das Pädagogische im Leben und Werk des Grafen Ludwig von Zinzendorf* in *Göttinger Studien zur Pädagogik*, 1958; and Mabel Haller's painstaking investigation of *Early Moravian Education in Pennsylvania*, 1953.

[4] R. Meyer, *Schleiermachers und C.G. Brinkmanns Gang durch die Brüdergemeine*, 1905; G.W. Wehrung, *Schleiermacher in der Zeit seines Werdens*, 1916, p. 16. Hök wrote *Zinzendorfs Begriff der Religion*, 1948, partly in order to make clear the intellectual connection between Zinzendorf and Schleiermacher.

[5] P. Baumgarten, *Zinzendorf als Wegbereiter historischen Denkens*, 1960.

CHAPTER FIVE

RADICAL PIETISM

"No, my dear Fritz," wrote Jakob Boehme to an obscure Silesian Orthodoxist in 1621, "opinions will not suffice, but rather the living Word, through which the heart experiences certainty. Out of the Spirit of Christ I received insight into the great mystery."[1] This sentiment, oft repeated by Boehme, and the theological presuppositions on which it is based, continued to agitate the guardians of theological normalcy throughout the seventeenth century. At first they tried to ridicule the prophet of Görlitz. When they found that this was to no avail they attacked him bitterly. Inspite of it all, however, the influence of the humble cobbler continued to grow. The result was that at the end of the seventeenth century, Boehmism, together with other spiritualistic traditions, constituted a considerable challenge to established Lutheranism and its commonly accepted theological formulations.

There were three streams of mystical piety, really, which converged at this time, and which, therefore, form the background for what may be called radical Pietism.[2] The one came down from Johann Arndt and

---

[1] *Die erste Schutz-Schrift wieder Balthasar Tilken*, pars. 306, 301, in *Jacob Boehme; Sämmtliche Schriften*, 1730, facsimile reprint edited by Will-Erich Peuckert, vol. 5, 1960.

[2] There is still some hesitancy on the part of certain historians as to whether or not the development covered in this chapter should be discussed under the category of "Pietism." Such reluctance seems to grow out of a desire to legitimize the phenomenon of Pietism by restricting the name to intra-confessional developments. In that case 'spiritualists," "mystics," or "enthusiasts" are terms applied to the people with whom we are here concerned, all of whom are more or less indifferent toward traditional standards of theological or ecclesiological normalcy. We do not share this hesitancy for two reasons. For one thing, in the modern world in which confessional standards of normalcy within Protestantism have become very problematical such attempts at legitimizing a particular movement within historic Christianity have become quite unnecessary. The present account, at any rate, is based upon broader criteria. Secondly, the people discussed in this chapter had in common with church-related Pietists an overriding interest in the kind of Christian piety which concerned itself with practical, everyday matters, and which was based on a more or less literal interpretation of the New Testament ethic. It is utterly arbitrary to think of them, as some church historians have done, as being primarily interested in mystical union. Their mystical-spiritualistic theo-

his circle of followers within the Lutheran Tradition. Since it has been discussed elsewhere little needs to be said about it here.[1]

A second such stream was the Boehmist theosophy which has been alluded to in our discussion of Oetinger. Its main strength, however, is not to be found in bequeathing its insights upon a segment of eighteenth century Lutheran theology, but rather in helping to lay the foundations for a certain critical attitude toward accepted theological and ecclesiological norms. For that reason we need to speak once more of the Boehmist movement prior to the period with which we are here concerned. In this context we must restrict ourselves, of course, to a summation of those facets of that movement which helped to prepare the ground for the rise of radical Pietism.[2]

Perhaps Boehme's utterly reckless genius becomes most clearly visible in his ability and willingness to distinguish between religious insights and their intellectual formulations in an age in which such an attempt still seemed little short of preposterous. Dissatisfied with Lutheran Orthodoxy and its bias toward *ex opere operato* interpretations of the efficacy of Word and Sacraments,[3] yet bent upon re-vitalizing the Christian enterprise, he embarked upon the well known venture of creating his own theological concepts and language. He did this not primarily because he meant to be rebellious, but because he was profoundly convinced that in his day the traditional conceptualizations of the Christian faith were largely obscuring the Christian message.

Boehme wanted to proclaim the existence of a living God, not a God hedged in or dehydrated by dogmatic propositions and theological systemics. He wanted to tell the world that God is Love, not the cruel deity, which, inadvertently at least, he had often been made out to be.

---

logy was merely their rationale for such piety. For these reasons the term "Pietism," would seem to be as applicable to this phase of eighteenth century religious striving as it is to the movements associated with the names of Francke, Bengel, or Zinzendorf.

[1] See RI, p. 202f. Its influence upon eighteenth century Lutheranism has been alluded to in our present volume at various points.

[2] The subject of mystical piety within seventeenth century Protestantism on the European Continent needs further investigation. It would seem, however, that by focussing almost exclusively upon Boehmism E. Hirsch tends to over-state the Boehmist influence (*Geschichte der neuen evangelischen Theologie im Zusammenhang mit den allgemeinen Bewegungen des europäischen Denkens*, 1949-1954, vol. 2, p. 208f). The evidence for his contention that Hohburg, for instance, was dominantly under Boehmist influence is slim (239f). Theologically, at least, Hohburg seems to have been in the orb of Caspar Schwenckfeld and Johann Arndt, rather than that of Weigel and Boehme. Still, Boehmism is an important element in the soil out of which radical Pietism came.

[3] *Weg zu Christo*, p. 135f, in *Jacob Boehme*; *Sämmtliche Schriften, op. cit.*, vol. 4,

He wanted his contemporaries to know that the essence of biblical faith is love for God as revealed in Christ, not confidence in the workings of a given *ordo salutis*. He wanted all men to know that a Christian is essentially a new being in Christ, in whom love has found its home in Love, not the same old sinner to whom God has imputed some one else's righteousness by an incomprehensible, perhaps even immoral, system of heavenly book-keeping. He wanted to tell his generation that God's saving love, supremely visible in Christ, goes out to all men, and that it takes only a resolute act of man's will to unite himself with that love.[1] Above all he wanted to get across the message that a religiously meaningful knowledge of God, and all he means to be to man, is not the result of a formal study of Christian theology. It is the result, rather, of opening oneself in humble resignation to the wisdom which is the gift of God's Spirit. In short, to Boehme the essence of a personally meaningful Christian faith was an affectively accomplished, existential union with God,[2] and, secondarily, the life of piety which may be expected to result from such union. "Let everyone simply practice," he writes, "how he might once again enter into the love of God and of his brother."[3]

The impact of Boehme's thought upon his age was neither immediate nor overwhelming. It was too radical, perhaps even too profound, for that. Gradually, however, this very remarkable cobbler made his influence felt, both within the Lutheran Communion and beyond its confines. Perhaps the most direct and important result of his speculations was the rise of a profoundly critical spirit within traditional Protestantism. It was the malcontents and rebels within the established churches, who looked to Boehme for inspiration, and who, once having absorbed his attitude, often went beyond him in their rebellion. Not infrequently they left the church either voluntarily or under duress.

It was Boehme's attitude toward the external church, then, and that of his immediate followers, which tended to supply the motivation for ecclesiastical separatism. He made a distinction between the

---

[1] *Ibid.*, p. 125.

[2] Throughout the course of this discussion we accept as valid and helpful Walther Köhler's distinction between substantial and existential union (*Dogmengeschichte als Geschichte des christlichen Selbstbewusstseins*, sec. ed., 1943, p. 286). The latter involves neither objective identification, nor merely conceptual identification. It is a matter of experiencing God through an affective response to him. Hence we use interchangeably the terms existential union, experiential (not experimental) union, and affective union.

[3] *Ibid.*, p. 140.

Church of Cain and the Church of Abel, the former referring to the church visible in history, the latter to all who are experientially, affectively, united with God, be they living or "dead." To the ecclesiastically disaffected groups of the day this distinction made a great deal of sense. Hence they gleefully took up Boehme's rather heavy polemic against the "stone churches" and their unregenerate pastors. The latter were considered to be servants of Babel, who found themselves in sacred office purely by the will of man, not by the will of God.

During the seventeenth century this critical attitude, nourished originally by the Arndtian tradition, and having come increasingly under the aegis of Boehme's genius, was fostered by a whole group of religious writers. Prominent among these were Joachim Betkius (1601-1663), and his spiritual guide Ludwig Friedrich Gifftheil (d. 1661),[1] Christian Hohburg (1607-1675), the emotionally unstable Quirinius Kuhlmann (1651-1689),[2] Friedrich Breckling (1629-1711),[3] and Johann Georg Gichtel (1638-1710).[4] While in both Betkius and Hohburg Arndtian thought forms still predominated, Boehmist influence was noticeably strong in Breckling[5] and Gichtel. All of them went beyond their spiritual mentors, however, in their condemnation of established Lutheranism, and all but Betkius eventually ended up as confirmed separatists.

The third stream of seventeenth century mystical spirituality, which blended with the other two to form the background for eighteenth century radical Pietism, was the Quietism of men like Miguel de Molinos (1640-1697). Even at Halle his *Guida spirituale* was frequently read, while the separatists, particularly in Reformed territories, considered

---

[1] T. Wotschke, "Zwei Schwärmer am Niederrhein," MrKG, vol. 27, 1933, pp. 144-178.

[2] AGLF-III, columns 960-961.

[3] T. Wotschke, "Friedrich Brecklings niederrheinischer Freundeskreis," MrKG, vol. 21, 1927, pp. 3-21.

[4] For Gichtel see E. Seeberg, *Gottfried Arnold*, 1923, 1964, p. 364f. For others in this group see G. Arnold, *Unparteiische Kirchen- und Ketzerhistorie*, 1741 ed., vol. 2, p. 406f.

[5] Breckling's influence has not been fully recognized. Wotschke has established the fact that there were many circles of spirituals who looked to him for inspiration, his writings being read in Moscow, Sweden, Denmark, Hungary, Syria, and the East Indies ("Friedrich Brecklings niederrheinischer Freundeskreis," MrKG, vol. 21, 1927, pp. 3-21). Considerable attention is given to Breckling also by G. Arnold, *op. cit.*, vol. 2, p. 917f. Having been forced out of the pastorate his home in the Netherlands seems to have been a center of Boehmist influence and a stop-over for Continental Philadelphians on their way to visit Jane Leade.

it one of the major sources of religious inspiration.[1] The fact that within the Roman Catholic Church Quietists were severely persecuted at this time tended to recommend their beliefs to those Protestants who resented both the Catholic and the Protestant religious establishments.

Apart from Molinos himself the spirituality of the older mystics (Theresa of Jesus, St. John of the Cross) had, on the one hand, been transmitted to representatives of eighteenth century radical Pietism by two of the very remarkable women mystics of the seventeenth century, namely, Antoinette Bourignon (1616-1680) and Madame de la Mothe Guyon (1648-1717). The former, who began as a Roman Catholic, but later abjured all "sects," had absorbed both Quietism and Boehmism, and had poured out a veritable stream of mystical literature.[2] She had made disciples among Protestants in many places, the most famous of them being the Reformed pastor Pierre Poiret (1646-1719), her friend, biographer, and the indefatigable editor of her writings.

Quite as remarkable as Antoinette was Madame Guyon,[3] one of the Lord's peculiar saints if there ever was one. The history of her calamities, if we may borrow a famous title, contains the material for a stirring novel about a religious rebel and her sufferings at the hands of the defenders of the tried and true. She, too, had her religious origins in Roman Catholicism, had taken as her spiritual guides St. John of the Cross, Jean de Bernieres-Louvigny (1602-1659), and Abbé Bertot (d. 1681), and had subsequently left that communion.[4] Again through the efforts of Pierre Poiret who wrote her biography, edited some of her works, and finally inspired Tersteegen to edit and publicize her writings, she came to be widely read among the separatistic Protestants.

The man in whom the above mentioned three streams of mystical

---

[1] For a conventient summary of the *Guida* see H. Heppe, *Geschichte der quietischen Mystik in der katholischen Kirche*, 1875, p. 113f.

[2] For her life and work see A.R. Maceven, *Antionette Bourignon, Pietist*, 1910; also A. von der Linde, *Antoinette Bourignon, das Licht der Welt*, 1895. The latter of these highly laudatory accounts contains a list of her writings (p. 286f).

[3] For her life and work see L. Guerrier, *Madame Guyon; sa vie, sa doctrine, et son influence*, 1881, which is the best discussion. Helpful for an insight into her relation with her friend Fenelon is D.F. Ribadeau, *Fénelon et les saintes folies de Madame Guyon*, 1968; E.A. Seillière, *Mme. Guyon et Fénelon, precurseurs de Rosseau*, 1918; Viscount St. Cyres, *Francois de Fénelon*, 1901; and M. de la Bedoyere, *The Archbishop and the Lady*, 1956. H. Heppe's *Geschichte*, *op. cit.*, deals largely with her.

[4] For an introduction to the spirituality which forms the background to that of Madame Guyon see especially P. Pourrat, *Christian Spirituality*, transl. by D. Attwater, 1953-1955, vols. 3 and 4.

spirituality converged, and who appears to have been most fully responsible for channeling them into eighteenth century Protestantism was Pierre Poiret, whose work has already been alluded to. It is he, therefore, who above all others, should be considered the spiritual ancestor of eighteenth century radical Pietism, with its characteristically mystical approach to religious reality, its pronounced spirit of independence in reference to ecclesiastical institutions, and its philosophy of history based on a profound belief in the sevenfold periodisation of divine activity.[1]

Poiret was born at Metz, and in time became pastor of the French Reformed congregation at Anweiler in the Palatinate. He had early read Tauler and Thomas à Kempis, and in time not only read, but translated, the *German Theology* into French. With Boehme's works he had a passing acquaintance. It was Antoinette Bourignon, however, whose mystical spirituality seemed to touch the deepest springs of his being. Somehow her insights appeared to afford him a look into Reality itself, while his religious life had hitherto been dependent upon words and concepts. Little wonder that he attached himself to Antoinette in spiritual friendship until the latter's death. In time he took Madame Guyon as his religious guide, so that in his later works her influence can definitely be traced. According to all the sources he lived an exemplary life, which prompted even the critical Johann Georg Walch to assure his readers that Poiret had a "pure" heart and lived a "godly" life.[2]

Beginning in 1677 Poiret published an abundance of edificatory religious literature, which found its way into all Protestant territories.[3] Among the best known of his writings were his *L'oeconomie divine* etc. (1687),[4] his *La théologie du cœur*, etc. (1690), and his *La théologie réelle* etc. (1700). On the basis of these works one must conclude that he was thoroughly dissatisfied with Christianity as he found it, whether among

---

[1] Poiret is presently not generally seen in this light. His influence has, in fact, been widely ignored and needs to be investigated from the point of view here presented. The best discussion of his life and work is that of M. Wieser, *Peter Poiret : Der Vater der romantischen Mystik in Deutschland*, 1932; also by the same author *Der sentimentale Mensch, gesehen aus der Welt holländischer und deutscher Mystiker im 18. Jahrhundert*, 1924.

[2] J.G. Walch, *Historische und theologische Einleitung in die vornehmsten Religionsstreitigkeiten. Aus Herrn Johann Francisci Buddei Collegio herausgegeben*, 1728, p. 626.

[3] For a list of his many writings see M. Wieser *Peter Poiret* etc., *op. cit.*, pp. 330-342.

[4] It is available in English under the double title *The Oeconomy of Sin* etc. and *The Oeconomy of Universal Providence* etc., 1713. Attached to it in the copy which came to hand is *The Principles of Real and Internal Religion Asserted and Vindicated*, etc., 1713.

the Reformed, the Lutherans, or the Roman Catholics. Though Roman Catholicism seemed to him to be generally more hospitable toward true spirituality than Protestantism, he was severely critical of all three traditions. The endless religious controversy which they had fostered, their misuse of reason for polemical purposes, their bureaucratic ecclesiastical machinery, as well as their endless theological hairsplitting struck him as utterly distasteful and out of keeping with the Gospel of Christ. In place of this he advocated, naively perhaps, the preaching of a simple Gospel, with which even laymen should have no difficulty. The Gospel he believed in was essentially a call to men to turn from self-love to a genuine love of God, who himself is Love and the source of all other love.[1] The heart of Christianity, therefore, as in both Arndt and Boehme, is thought to be man's affective response to God, coupled with the life of piety which results therefrom. All other aspects of Christian theology must be supportive of this central religious insight, or else they are false.[2] Theology, in fact, is a legitimate enterprise only for those people whose insight into Scripture is given by the Holy Spirit. Unfortunately the "sects"[3] and their theologians, he felt, are not fully aware of this. That being the case, they often spent their energies upon matters which are either meaningless or positively harmful.

Poiret's influence resulted not so much from any original contribution which he made himself. As previously indicated, his rather considerable impact upon eighteenth century Pietism, both within and without established Protestantism, stems from the fact that he invested much of his time in making mystical tracts available to his contemporaries in translation. In this way the writings of Antoinette Bourignon, Madame Guyon and many others, became accessible to the Protestant laity. As a result he helped materially to prepare the religious climate in which separatistic Pietism, with its characteristic dependence on mystical spirituality, could flourish.

According to Hirsch[4] it was Boehme's influence which eventually made itself felt in a gradual softening of Lutheranism's dogmatic

---

[1] See his long prayer at the end of his *Oeconomia*, Engl. transl. of 1713, p. 246f.

[2] In his *Oeconomia* he strongly attacks the Reformed doctrine of predestination on this basis.

[3] Since radical Pietists tended to regard their loosely knit religious fellowship as the "true" church, they frequently referred to the established communions such as the Catholic, the Lutheran, and the Reformed as "sects."

[4] Hirsch, *op. cit.*, vol. 2, p. 225f.

stance; in a more liberal attitude toward the authority of its symbols; in a new approach to hermeneutics, asserting that only the Spirit-filled person can interpret Scripture in a religiously meaningful way; in severing saving knowledge from strictly historical knowledge, in substituting the emphasis upon the new birth for the traditional Lutheran emphasis upon justification; and in restricting, or even explaining away, the traditional Christian doctrine of eternal damnation.[1]

There can be no doubt about the fact that the theological transformation of which Hirsch speaks had been at least partially accomplished by the end of the seventeenth century. It had made itself felt, in fact, not only within the Lutheran Communion, but within Continental Protestantism as a whole. Yet, it hardly seems justifiable to attribute this change almost entirely to Jacob Boehme, his remarkable religious genius notwithstanding. Many factors had actually contributed to such a change. Even if we look at it from a purely religious point of view the fact seems to be that Boehme's influence was mingled with that of Arndtian and quietistic spirituality, as we attempted to outline above. In this way the kind of religious environment was gradually produced in which the radical Pietism of the eighteenth century could arise.

The heterogeneity of the movement to be discussed in this chapter is obvious and poses a certain problem of organization. So as to avoid confusion, therefore, the attempt will be made to deal at some length with the most representative radicals among the Pietists, to mention more or less briefly others who contributed to the total phenomenon, and to conclude the chapter with a section on German Philadelphianism and its concrete expression at Wittgenstein. A certain amount of insight into the Philadelphian Movement would seem to have special significance for the understanding of early American Pietism, especially as it was found in the Middle Colonies.

Major Voices

Perhaps the most widely known among the radical Pietists of the eighteenth century was Gottfried Arnold (1666-1714),[2] whose *Unpartei-*

[1] Hirsch's implication that Boehme moved toward the doctrine of the restoration of all creatures is problematical. The passage on which he bases his assertion (vol. 2, p. 232) should be read in the light of such passages as the following: *Von den drei Prinzipien. Anhang*, par. 10, in *Jacob Boehme*; *Sämmtliche Schriften*: vol. 2, p. 486.

[2] The definitive work on Arnold was done by E. Seeberg (*Gottfried Arnold. Die Wissenschaft und die Mystik seiner Zeit*, 1923, 1964, which contains a list of his works, pp. 56-62;

ische Kirchen- und Ketzerhistorie (1699) has generally been considered a mile-stone in the writing of the history of Christianity. The theological storm which some of his writings precipitated can be at least dimly imagined if one reads the epitaph which was suggested for him by one of his opponents : "Here lies Gottfried Arnold," wrote the well-intentioned Orthodoxist J.C.C. Colerus in 1718, "not so much a theologian, as the bitterest enemy of orthodox theologians; the persistent defender of heretics, the stupid repristinator of mystical theology, — perhaps the first of all distorters of church history. — He had a mixed religion, or, none at all. Henceforth he is commended to God's jusdgement. — Wanderer, go hence !"[1] Who, then, was this man, so deeply disliked by some, and yet so profoundly loved by others, and all for the sake of Christ ?

Gottfried Arnold was born at Annaberg in the Erzgebirge. He studied at the citadel of orthodox Lutheranism, Wittenberg, and then spent some time at Dresden. Here he came under the influence of Spener. Presently he began to react against his Wittenberg training and, as a consequence, began to absorb a liberal measure of the mystical spirituality which has been described. The result was that he developed a profoundly critical attitude toward the established churches. He came to a point, in fact, where he felt that he could not accept in good conscience a pastoral appointment in his own communion. Being in circumstances which afforded him sufficient income he decided to devote all of his energies to writing.

Out of this second period of his life came some of his best known works, as well as the inspiration for others. It was his *Erste Liebe der Gemeinen Jesu Christi* etc. (1696) which first brought him to the attention of his generation. As a result he was given the position of professor of history at Giessen (1697), a post which he felt impelled to vacate, however, in the course of the very first year. During the following years he embarked upon a remakably active literary career, turning out over twenty works. Some of these were quite extensive, and among them was his *History of Heresy*, which has been cited. All of

---

also his *Gottfried Arnold in Auswahl herausgegeben*, 1934). Very helpful, too, is the published doctoral dissertation by T. Stähelin, *Gottfried Arnolds geistliche Dichtung*, 1966. Excellent bibliographical suggestions are found on pp. 139-147. H. Dörris' *Geist und Geschichte bei Gottfried Arnold*, 1963, constitutes a good introduction to Arnold as an historian. See also the monograph by F. Dibelius, *Gottfried Arnold*, 1873.

[1] Quoted in Albert Knapp's preface to the 1862 ed. of Arnold's *Wahrer Christenspiegel*, p. XXXIV.

these works indicate that he had become very critical of all organized "sects" and much of what they stood for. His over-riding religious concern now was that of living a life of simple piety, consisting essentially in love for God and man.

Presently Arnold fell in love with Anna Sprögel, daughter of the court preacher in whose home he had stayed, and who had performed the wedding ceremony for August Hermann Francke. With the blessing of Spener he married Anna in 1701, an event which marks the beginning of the third period of his life. Having spoken favorably of the single state in his *Geheimnis der göttlichen Sophia* (1700), his spiritualist friends had confidently expected him to follow the party line and to devote all of his ardor to *Sophia* alone. When he married they still had contined to hope that it would be a "pure" marriage. Their consternation was complete when the birth of their first child proved otherwise. His friend, Johann Georg Gichtel (1638-1710), complained that he had now "even fallen into having children." Nevertheless, his wife's quiet strength stabilized his restless genius, so that in time he accepted a Lutheran pastorate and finally ended up as superintendent.

While it can hardly be asserted that he changed his fundamental theological stance, his attitude toward established Protestantism henceforth became a great deal milder and his criticisms more responsible. At the same time, however, his movement back into the church brought him both new friends and new enemies. Above all, it made it difficult for many of his contemporaries to know exactly how to evaluate him, a circumstance which was exacerbated by the general religious intolerance of the age. Even Spener, who had always regretted Arnold's separatistic leanings, continued to regard him with some reserve, though his judgement upon the man remained characteristically mild.

From the point of view of his theological contribution to western Christianity Arnold should not be considered an innovator so much, as a man who clarified, sharpened up, and popularized certain basic ideas which were held in common by the adherents of radical Pietism within late seventeenth century Continental Protestantism. His theological models had essentially been Johann Arndt and Jacob Boehme. The latter, it would seem, was understood by him basically as he was understood by the English Philadelphians and their Continental counter-parts, Gichtel and Breckling.

While traces of Boehme's theosophical mysticism are unmistakably present in Arnold's thought[1] the latter's aim is different. Boehme's major task was that of revising the orthodox conceptualization of the Christian message. Arnold, on the other hand, concentrated upon the pragmatic attempt of reforming the Christian life. With him even the writing of the history of Christianity moved chiefly toward one end, namely, that of justifying to the intellectual community the *praxis pietatis* which had become accepted by large groups of Christians, both within and without established Protestantism.[2] His over-all aim, then, was not the reformation of theology, nor mystical union, but the amendment of life, both corporate and private. It is for this reason, of course, that he and others like him are included here among the company of radical eighteenth century Pietists.

For Arnold all theology can be divided into two major types. There is the Aristotelian approach, which has its locus in reason and deals with logically coherent propositions about religious reality. It is the approach which to the great church historian appears to be an abomination before the Lord, for, on the one hand, it does not yield religiously meaningful knowledge, while, on the other hand, it is largely responsible for the multitude of divisions and controversies in the history of Christianity. In Arnold's understanding of things Luther had rejected Aristotelian theologizing, but unfortunately Melanchthon reintroduced it into Lutheranism,[3] and this injected the spirit of dissension and quarrelsomeness into that communion from the beginning.

The other approach to religious reality Arnold calls "mystical theology," which, however, is not what it appears to be on the surface. As Seeberg has pointed out, what is actually meant here is experiential theology.[4] In fact, it is not theology in the traditional sense at all, but the wisdom which comes to the religiously regenerate and committed person as a divine gift.[5] In this sense every awakened Christian is a theologian and compares quite favorably with the "school-theologians," who waste much of their time in harmful controversy. The precondition for theological expertise, therefore, is not the study of formally prescribed theological disciplines, but openness to God's truth as it

---

1 See especially his *Geheimnis der göttlichen Sophia* etc., 1700.

2 See the introduction to his *Kirchen- und Ketzerhistorie*, 1740, vol. 1, par. 37.

3 *Ibid.*, vol. 1, p. 702.

4 E. Seeberg, *Gottfried Arnold. Die Wissenschaft und die Mystik seiner Zeit*, 1964, p. 212.

5 Arnold defines it carefully in his *Beschreibung der mystischen Theologie* etc., 1703, chapts. 1 and 2.

comes to man through the Bible and through the examples of God's people.

On the basis of these premises it must be expected that "true Christianity" to Arnold involved a radical experience of re-birth. In such an expectation the reader is not disappointed. Here Arnold remained one with the Spener-Halle tradition, insisting on a "violent break-through," a "painful birth," and a "thorough cleansing of the heart."[1] While such an experience is regarded to be made possible by God's grace, the initiation of it also requires an act of man's will.

The result of such experience is twofold. On the one hand, it brings about an affective union with Christ, or *Sophia*, which must henceforth be nourished through appropriate religious exercises. For Arnold the normal expression of man's affection for God was so intense that he could only describe it in terminology borrowed from the realm of human sexuality. Thus his otherwise highly lyrical and movingly poetic hymns strike the modern reader often as offensively erotic.[2] Nor can this love for God be partial. It must be all-embracing and all-consuming. Our author's aim here is nothing short of perfection. "A perfect servant of Christ," he insists, "possesses nothing but Christ, and if he does possess anything other than Christ, he is not perfect."[3] He thus consciously set perfection in love in opposition to the orthodox understanding of perfection, which relied on divine imputation and an *ex opere operato* efficacy of the means of grace. While Arnold would not have disputed God's redemptive activity in the ontological realm he felt that it was a mystery we can say little about. What he was really interested in, therefore, was God's work in man's psyche. To that end he regarded the cross as being significant primarily because it calls to religious commitment, and because it symbolizes the inner meaning of the new life of faith.

The second result of a break-through, such as Arnold prescribed, is the new life of faith. The essential difference between the old life and the new life is, he taught, that the latter is wholly motivated by love for God and other men, while the former is essentially motivated by self-love. This new love, though divinely inspired, must be consciously and constantly nourished by the doing of appropriate deeds. "No one,"

---

[1] See his *Wahrer Christenspiegel,* ed. by Albert Knapp, 1862, p. 142. (This is an abbreviation of his *Erste Liebe, oder wahre Abbildung* etc., 1696).

[2] See his *Poetische Lob- und Liebessprüche von der ewigen Weisheit nach Anleitung des Hohenlieds Salomonis* etc., 1700.

[3] *Wahrer Christenspiegel, op. cit,* p. 146.

he insists, "can attain to life through hearing alone, and apart from labor."[1] Yet, it must not be regarded as merely a human achievement, for it is possible only to the soul which has been "penetrated" and "vivified" by Christ.[2] Such a soul abides by God's eternal Law, though not because it fears the Law, but because it loves the Giver of the Law.[3] Still, to live by God's Law in a wicked world frequently necessitates a course of action opposed to that of the world, and hence necessarily involves the bearing of the cross. Such being the circumstances under which the Christian lives out his life true Christianity has little to do with a set of rationally approved dogmatic propositions. It is basically a way of life, or, more accurately, a way of dying to that which is not life while one is in the midst of life.

On the basis of these theological presuppositions it is not difficult to imagine how our author regarded organized Christianity in general and Lutheranism in particular. As has been pointed out previously, during the second part of his active career at least, his attitude was very negative. Having been attacked by Ernst Salomo Cyprian[4] for writing his *History of Heresy* he answered with an explicit statement of his estimate of the external church.[5] Speaking of Lutheran churches as he saw them he says, "The horror of devestation is everywhere so great and undeniable, that even a natural man who is honest, must be ashamed of it and must wish, that none but the blind, the deaf, the dumb, and the lame might enter the Lutheran churches, so that they might not be induced to witness it all."[6] In defense of his position he cites the long history of Lutheran self-criticism, treating it as corroborative evidence for his uncomplimentary estimate of the general state of decay which had come over his communion.

In this criticism he singled out Heinrich Müller's four Lutheran idols — confessional chair, altar, baptismal font, and pulpit — for special censure.[7] Basically, however, his ire was directed, on the one

---

[1] *Ibid.*, p. 8.

[2] *Geistliche Erfahrungslehre; Oder Erkenntnis und Erfahrung von den vornehmsten Stücken des lebendigen Christentums,* 1735, part 2, p. 201. This massive volume of sermons was posthumously published by his wife in 1714. Seeberg dates it 1715.

[3] *Ibid.*, part 1, p. 183f.

[4] *Allgemeine Anmerkungen über Gottfried Arnolds Kirchen- und Ketzerhistorie* etc., third ed., 1701.

[5] *Vom gemeinen Sektenwesen, Kirchen- und Abendmahlgehen* etc., 1700.

[6] E. Seeberg, *Gottfried Arnold in Auswahl herausgegeben,* 1934, p. 150. Seeberg's selections from Arnold's writings are most happily chosen.

[7] *Ibid.*, p. 136.

hand, against Orthodoxy's *ex opere operato* understanding of the religious activities associated with these alleged idols, which, he felt, render the church's preaching and sacramental action not only meaningless to the contemporary generation of believers, but downright harmful. The reason is, he thought, that such an understanding conveniently transfers the change which must take place in the human psyche to the problematical realm of religious magic. His other outstanding criticism of contemporary Lutheranism had to do with the contentiousness of its theologians. Along with other Pietists he attributed this to their notion that religion consists in the intellectual acceptance of propositions, rather than in the "inner," or affective, identification with Christ.

In all of this Arnold felt that his attitude toward the external church differed only in degree from that of both the Spener-Halle Tradition and of Swabian Pietism. This is borne out by the fact that he was always aware of a certain basic affinity between himself and these church-related Pietists. It is corroborated also by his pointed reference to himself as a Lutheren in his defense against Cyprian. At the same time, however, his inner state of division, during part of his active career at least, is indicated by his statement that he is indeed *in territorio* of the Lutherans, but not *de territorio illorum.*[1] Later in life he modified this stand to the point of being willing to reform the Lutheran Church from within, thus espousing more unambiguously the ideals held in common by all Lutheran Pietists.[2]

Much could be said about Arnold's energetic defense of the principle of religious freedom at a time in history when intolerance was still the order of the day, though this would transcend the limits of this study. This is true also of his contribution to the field of historiography in general, and religious historiography in particular. As was previously mentioned, he used the writing of Christian history as a tool with which to substantiate his own theological position. He cannot be credited, therefore, with the attempt to write unbiased history, but he did succeed in opening the eyes of Protestant Christians to the fact that their history can be seen from more than one interpretative stance. Furthermore, his vast knowledge of historical data, and his will to use such data to substantiate his own understanding of the meaning

[1] *Ibid.*, p. 148.

[2] For an analysis of his reasons for accepting ecclesiastical office see H. Dörris, *Geist und Geschichte bei Gottfried Arnold*, 1963, p. 84f.

of Christianity, helped greatly to make the pietistic cause intellectually respectable during the first half of the eighteenth century.

Perhaps the most controversial personality of his day, and a man whose contribution to the development of Prostestant thought has never been fully recognized was Johann Konrad Dippel (1673-1734).[1] His works are a unique mixture of Christian spirituality and abrasive vituperation.[2] His penetrating thrusts at the most cherished theological convictions of his day, his fearless exposure of the ecclesiastical shortcomings and of the foibles of his contemporaries, his reckless repudiation of authorities hitherto deemed venerable, and his corresponding knack for stirring up religious and political controversy whithersoever his restless spirit took him seems to have linked his name proverbially to the emotion of exasperation. "Du dummer Dippel," a Swabian father will still say to his son when he becomes sufficiently aggravated with the child's deviation from accepted norms of behavior or rationality.

Dippel was born as the third son of a Lutheran pastor at the castle

---

[1] A very reliable discussion of Dippel is still that of W. Bender, *Johann Konrad Dippel, der Freigeist des Pietismus*, 1882, though E. Hirsch questions the validity of his presentation because of an allegedly insufficient knowledge of Boehme (*op. cit.*, vol. 2, footnote on p. 277). It would seem, however, that Hirsch's excessive preoccupation with Boehme's influence biased his judgment. (To be noted here also are Dippel's reservations about Boehmism in his *Christian Democritus, ein aufrichtiger Protestant* etc. in *Eröffneter Weg*, vol. 3, p. 399f, where he says that in Boehme one finds "dross" and "absurdities," p. 403. It may well be that for this reason he generally refused to use Boehme's vocabulary.) The whole subject needs investigation. A more superficial discussion of Dippel is that of J.C.G. Ackermann, *Das Leben Johann Conrad Dippels*, 1781. Especially helpful is K.L. Voss, *Christianus Democritus. Das Menschenbild bei Johann Conrad Dippel.* in *Beihefte der Zeitschrift für Religions- und Geistesgeschichte*, vol. 12, 1970. Voss gives excellent bibliographical suggestions, p. 114f. See also W. Diehl, "Neue Beiträge zur Geschichte Johann Konrad Dippels in der theologischen Periode seines Lebens," in *Beiträge zur Hessischen Kirchengeschichte*, Neue Folge, Ergänzungsband 3, 1908, pp. 135-184; W. Rustmeier, "Johann Conrad Dippel in Schleswig-Holstein," SVshKG, second series, vol. 14, 1956, pp. 36-50; vol. 15, 1957, pp. 91-116; vol. 16, 1958, pp. 147-169: vol. 17, 1959-1960, pp. 69-76; H. Pleijel, *Der schwedische Pietismus in seinen Beziehungen zu Deutschland*, 1935, pp. 170-199; GBL, vol. 3, pp. 166-193; E. Hirsch, *op. cit.*, vol. 2, pp. 277-298; T. Wotschke, "Pietistisches aus Ostfriesland und Niedersachsen," ZGnKG, vol. 39, 1934, pp. 151-195.

[2] They are available in *Eröffneter Weg zum Frieden mit Gott und allen Kreaturen durch die Publikation der sämmtlichen Schriften Christiani Democriti* etc., 1747. This edition is an elaboration of the 1709 edition and was made available in three volumes. Appended to it is a *vita*, vol. 3, p. 743f. An autobiography of Dippel is found in vol. 1, pp. 379-396. From the point of view of his theological contribution his most important work was his enormously controversial *Vera demonstratio evangelica, das ist, ein — Beweis der Lehre und des Mittleramts Jesu Christi* etc., 1729.

of Frankenstein on the mountain road above Darmstadt. According to his autobiography one is lead to believe that he was an extremely precocious child,[1] who at an early age elicited both the envy and admiration of teachers and fellow students alike. As a lad of 16 he matriculated at the University of Giessen to study theology and medicine. Here he promptly resolved to remain orthodox and to use the theological tools made available to him by his studies against the Pietists. This resolve came to an end, however, in 1697. In that year Dippel, now under the influence of Gottfried Arnold, experienced the kind of radical religious conversion which the latter was advocating. Henceforth Dippel profoundly respected his spiritual father and decided to put his intellectual gifts to use in the promotion of *unparteiisches Christentum*, which was so dear to the heart of Arnold.

Under the impact of this resolve Dippel embarked upon what turned out to be a very rough road indeed. Soon after his conversion his rapier-like pen was turned against Orthodoxy in a whole series of controversial writings. He was not so much interested in attacking particular dogmas as he was in undermining the whole orthodox methodology. This attempt is already noticeable in his *Papismus protestantium vapulans* etc. (1698), which contains all of his later theological thrusts in embryonic form. Upon the publication of this work he quickly became *persona non grata* in official Lutheran circles. Recognizing the meaning of this for his career he now began to channel his seemingly boundless energy into the study of medicine and alchemy, achieving in time a very considerable reputation in both of those fields. His medical knowledge, furthermore, made it possible for him to go wherever he listed. This complete freedom of movement was facilitated by the fact that under the influence of Gichtelian spirituality he had renounced all thoughts of marriage.

While doctoring hither and yon, however, and usually in circles which could afford to reward him generously for his medical ministrations, he continued to involve himself vigorously in theological controversy. This was an avocation which brought him much unpleasantness and even imprisonment. The longest of his incarcerations was on the island of Bornholm, where he found himself inured for seven years. Harsh though such punishment may seem it was not sufficient to stop Dippel from saying what he thought ought to be said. Not very long after he was freed from Bornholm he turned to Sweden and promptly threw

---

[1] *Eröffneter Weg*, vol. 1, p. 380.

Swedisch Lutheranism into an uproar. As a result he found himself banned from that country. Similar activities in various parts of Germany raised the bitterest possible clerical opposition against both his person and his books. This opposition took on formidable proportions when, in utter disregard of his own welfare, he not only polemicised against all "sects," but against all major theological camps as well. Orthodoxists, church related Pietists, Zinzendorf, and even the rising school of Wolffians found themselves attacked in places where it hurt the most. As if that were not enough he took on the philosophers as well. Little wonder that he quickly wore out his welcome in territory after territory. At last, in 1729 the kind-hearted Count Kasimir of Wittgenstein-Berleburg brought him to Berleburg, where the "world famous Dr. Dippelius," now highly esteemed by the more humble members of that strange community, lived out the rest of his years in relative peace.

The reason for Dippel's stormy career is not to be found merely in the kinds of enemies he chose to make. In part his very personality, and the style in which he wrote, are to blame. He appears to have been the kind of person who is utterly unhappy in the presence of any established order or norm. If pastors, for instance, prayed for the three estates, as they normally would and as they were expected to do, Dippel advised them to pray for the coming of the Kingdom only. If Frederick I wanted church union, Dippel insisted upon saying out loud that the king wanted it for the wrong reasons; if people in general held university faculties in high esteem, he preferred to refer to them as "learned plebeians;" and if Protestants regarded the Reformation as a divine gift, Dippel chose to speak of it as the event which divided Babylon into three "sects."

Quite as disconcerting as his other doings was the fact that neither friend nor foe was ever sure whether his arguments were sincere or derisive. There was common agreement only upon the effectiveness of his merciless polemic. People read Dippel as much for entertainment as for intellectual profit. He knew how to use irony, satire, invective, irrefutable logic, or *argumentum ad hominem*, whichever would be the most devastating under the circumstances. At the same time he was utterly dedicated to the cause he felt he represented, caring little for fame or infamy which might result from his actions. He was essentially an ideological visionary, who really hoped to accomplish in one life-time the kind of religious revolution which took more than a century. Under the circumstances his *modus operandi* necessarily had to be more negative than positive, though, in contrast to rebels of other ages, he did seem to know exactly the end he had in mind.

Dippel's aim was twofold and was closely connected with his understanding of meaningful Christianity. On the one hand, he meant to restore the visible church to the pristine innocence, purity, and power, which he attributed to the apostolic community.[1] In this he was not much different from his teacher Arnold and the mystical tradition which has been discussed, except, perhaps, in the vehemence with which he pursued his goal. In espousing this aim he, too, used frequently the word *unparteiisch*. By using it he meant to emphasize, as did Arnold, that he had no preference for any of the existing "sects," but that he wrote from the point of view of the ideal church, which once was, from which historical Christianity departed during the second century,[2] and which he and his followers meant to re-establish as an historical entity.

This could be accomplished, he felt, if the clergy were willing to discard their wrong-headed preoccupation with Word, Sacrament, and Orthodoxy as ends in themselves and to begin to emphasize the new life in Christ, adorned by the fruit of the spirit.[3] Christian love, he insisted, not rote knowledge of the Bible and of the catechism, is the mark of true Christianity and must, therefore, be the goal of Christian worship. Not that theology has no place in the church, but it must be made to serve the end in view. Above all else there must be intellectual freedom supplanting once for all the present orthodox attempt at 'ox-and-ass unanimity' in theological opinion.[4] Unfortunately, Dippel opined, such a new church, which must be gathered out of all "sects," and of which the marks are love and freedom, will not be brought about unless the clerical and theological leadership is changed. For that reason he suggested that the secular prince exercise the *jus episcopale* conscientiously in appointing only such men as pastors and

---

[1] His major tract related to this aim was his *Ein Hirt und eine Herde : Oder unfehlbare Methode — alle Sekten und Religionen zur einigen wahren Kirche und Religion zu bringen* etc., 1706, in *Eröffneter Weg*, vol. 1, p. 1062f. In the preface he says that he is here expressing more clearly what he tried to say in two previous tracts, namely, *Anfang, Mittel und Ende der Ortho- und Heterodoxie* etc., 1699, and *Wegweiser zum verlorenen Licht und Recht* etc., 1705.

[2] *Ein Hirt*, p. 1080.

[3] *Ibid.*, p. 1074f.

[4] *Ibid.*, p. 1089.

teachers who are "in fact committed to true regilion."[1] It goes without saying, of course, that "true religion" here is Dippel's.

He was equally concerned about theological reform. In fact, in his own mind the two were closely related, since, as he saw it, the church's plight was preeminently the result of its theological misadventure, while the latter was the consequence of an unregenerate clergy, including the "school foxes" on the various theological faculties who extract the theological venom from the "whore breasts" of Orthodoxy. Under the circumstances Dippel addressed himself to a re-statement of theology in the hope of conforming theological concepts and language to what he conceived to be "true religion."[2] In doing so he was heir to Arnold and the mystical spirituality which has been discussed earlier. What he added to it was a logical consistency, an incisiveness of expression, and an element of linguistic shock-treatment which makes everything he wrote typically Dippelian.

Reminiscient of the Arndtian, Boehmist, and quietist traditions the anchor of Dippel's theology, as Hirsch points out,[3] was in his steadfast belief that God is essentially Love. "This description of the being of God (namely of God as Love)," Dippel says, "is according to our understanding the most complete (*wesentlich*) and the most perfect which is found in Holy Scripture, in which come together as in their center all other attributes of the Being of beings."[4] A necessary corollary of this is man's freedom.[5] His argument in the *Fatum Fatuum* for such freedom goes as follows : God is Love, but in his absolute freedom he could have been satisfied with self-love. Instead he chose to create beings as the objects of his love. Being Love himself he bestowed on these beings the highest gift, namely his own image. Thus they, too, are free either to love themselves or their Creator. In the one case they find their highest fulfilment, in the other their deepest hell.

Dippel's whole system of theological thought, then, turns about these twin assertions of God's unconditional love and man's freedom to love God or himself. While these insights were not new in his day he followed them with a ruthless consistency which made much of what

[1] Ibid., p. 1097. W. Rustmeier says succinctly that what Dippel wanted was "wesentliches Christentum ethisch-religiöser Prägung," *op. cit.*, vol. 14, 1956, p. 42.

[2] Especially important here is his *Vera* mentioned above.

[3] *Op. cit.*, vol. 2, p. 284.

[4] *Fatum Fatuum* etc. in *Eröffneter Weg*, vol. 2, p. 6.

[5] His whole *Fa.um Fatuum* was written to show the necessary connection between God's love and man's freedom.

he wrote appear utterly heterodox, as well as deeply threatening, to the ecclesiastical establishment of his generation.

The representatives of Lutheran Orthodoxy, and of church-related Pietism, were especially disturbed to find that their hitherto unimpeachable religious authority, namely Scripture as interpreted by the Augsburg Confession, no longer meant anything to Dippel. He treated it as cavalierly as he did the theologumena which they had drawn from that source, in that way rendering their polemic against him singularly archaeistic and hence ineffective. Sneering at the traditional hermeneutic of what he called "ox-headed theologians," he ventured to make Scripture interpreted *im Lichte Gottes*[1] his norm. Thus he had moved far beyond the Halle-Bengel Pietists, and even beyond Zinzendorf. While they held that only the regenerated Christian can interpret Scripture and the Lutheran symbols correctly, Dippel taught that the Spirit-wrought, inner light of the person who through conversion has come into harmony with the whole sweep of God's activity takes precedence over both. Thus the *unpartheiisch* principle was now fully recognized, not only in the interpretation of Christian history, but in the realm of prolegomena to Protestant theology as well. The content of Christian theology was now to be deduced from what were held to be self-evident principles, to which the witness of Scripture was thought to conform. Needless to say, there is but an hair's breadth between Dippel's understanding of religious authority and that of the *Aufklärung*.

On the basis of his newly gained theological vantage point Dippel now asserted with radical abandon what the mystical spirituality of the previous age had whispered more softly into the ears of those who were attuned to its message. With regard to man and his destiny our author insisted that man is indeed sinful as long as his will is set upon his own advantage, but that God in his love gives him freedom to seek the highest Good, and hence the highest happiness. The choice is strictly man's. The fall is indeed an historic fact in the sense that the first transgression established an environment in which man is prone to indulge his self-will. This must not be regarded as a divine punishment, however, but as a loving God's reminder that every man's happiness lies in him alone.[2] Similarly, if man chooses to make his way in this

---

[1] *Ein Hirt,* p. 1067. See also his tract *Etwas Neues, oder Retirade der lutherischen Orthodoxie* etc. in *Eröffneter Weg,* vol. 3, p. 288f.

[2] See especially his *Grundriss zu einem solchen Syztemate Theologico* etc. in *Eröffneter Weg,* vol. 2, p. 581f.

fallen condition the resultant misery must not be attributed to God's retributive judgment, but to the fact that in the world as it came from God's hand all sinful action generates its own punishment.[1] What is needed, if man would escape from his misery, is a resolute act of the will to become affectively united with God. Religious faith, therefore, is resolute and continued commitment to God, rather than mere confidence in the efficacy of Christ's vicarious suffering and death.[2]

The life which results from such religious commitment is essentially one of love for God and man. On the one hand it is full of self-denial and cross-bearing, and of all the sufferings which attended the life of Christ in the midst of a wicked world. Still, it brings the greatest fulfillment, since it is open to all the blessed influences of God's unfathomable love.[3] Nor can the Christian possibly be satisfied with an imputed righteousness while he continues in sin. His goal must be perfection in love, a state to which all creatures who were created by God to know him, will finally attain, though some of them will do so only after much tribulation, both in this life and in the life to come. The joys of heaven and the pains of hell are thus determined by man's separation from, or union with, Eternal Love.[4] Through such union with God man becomes clothed with a spiritual body in which he dwells forever.

Disconcerting as much of this was to his religiously conservative contemporaries, Dippel's understanding of God and of his redemptive activity was even more so. They were immensely troubled, for instance, by his complete indifference toward the traditional Christian understanding of the trinity. Veering at this point in the direction of Boehme he, like Zinzendorf, decided to interpret biblical language about God's mysterious triunity functionally.[5] They were troubled, furthermore, by the implications of his insistence, based on Rom. 11 : 36, that the world was originally not created out of nothing, but out of God's nature, and that the world as it now is is a second creation. Nor were they happy with his understanding of Christ as being found in both a heavenly and a fleshly humanity.[6]

---

[1] *Ibid.*, p. 584f.

[2] *Ibid.*, p. 593f.

[3] *Ibid.*, p. 596.

[4] *Ibid.*, pp. 580, 587.

[5] *Glaubensbekenntnis* etc. in *Eröffneter Weg*, vol. 1, p. 492f; also *Unparteiische Gedanken* etc., *ibid.*, p. 1228f.

[6] *Entdecktes, falsches Mass der Prüfung* etc., *Eröffneter Weg*, *op. cit.*, vol. 1, p. 720f.

By far the most upsetting facet of his purported theological reform, however, was his interpretation of Christ's redemptive work. It was in 1729 when he decided to thrust his most mature thoughts on the subject upon an already disturbed Continent in his *Vera demonstratio evangelica* etc. It speedily became one of the most controversial religious tracts in Protestant history. For years to come preachers felt upon themselves the obligation to preach against it, and religious polemicists took up their cudgels against it. Among his most immediate detractors were the Orthodoxist Erdmann Neumeister of Hamburg and Halle's polemicist Joachim Lange, against both of whom he wrote his most intemperate *Verteidigung*.[1] No less important is the lengthy refutation of Dippelian soteriology published in 1731 under the name of Christophilus Wohlgemuth.[2] One of the most elaborate and systematic refutations was Friedrich Wagner's *Widerlegung*,[3] which, together with its *Continuation* and *Addenda* runs to over twelve hundred pages. On the other hand, in many regions of Germany and of Sweden growing groups of separatists treated Dippel's *Vera demonstratio evangelica* as their basic theological text. Thus they made it possible for his heterodoxy to gain a broad foot-hold within many Lutheran territories of Europe.

The reason for the many and often virulent attacks upon Dippel's *Vera* is to be found in the fact that in it he dared to give a thoroughly unlutheran interpretation of the redemptive work of Christ, and to do this in Lutheran lands. In the most radical re-conceptualization possible, and in the most uncompromising language possible, he substituted the "Christ in us" for the "Christ for us." *Ipso facto* such an attempt became more than a revision of traditional Lutheran soteriology. It became, rather, an attack upon the Lutheran self-understanding at its very core.

In doing this Dippel began with a model which one might expect of an eminently successful and self-assured physician, namely with the idea that man is sick, that his loving heavenly Father wants him well, and that in the divine intention the cure is to be accomplished through

---

1 *Verteidigung seines Traktats vera demonstratio evangelica* etc., in *Eröffneter Weg*, vol. 2, p. 931f.

2 *Entdeckung des Systemmatis Christianis Democriti* etc., against which Dippel wrote his *Entdeckung der gewissenlosen Verdrehung* etc. *Eröffneter Weg*, vol. 3, p. 1f. He says (p. 13) that Wohlgemuth is really Dr. Christian Weissmann.

3 *Christian Democritus Autocatacritus, das ist : Der sich selbst verurteilende Democritus, oder, schrift- und vernunftmässige Widerlegung* etc., 1732.

Christ the great Physician.[1] This is not a new model in the history of Christian interpretation, of course, but Dippel used it with a polemical vigor which was calculated to make all orthodox conceptualizations related to this doctrinal theme seem absurd. Using Scripture and the "true" Christian's restored sense of the rightness of things as the dual principle of religious authority, he attempted to expose all "sectarian" explanations as thoroughly wrong-headed. Can a physician take the patient's medicine and cure him by imputation? he asks pointedly.[2] If the doctrines of merit and satisfaction were really essential to man's salvation, could it be that Christ never mentioned them? he wants to know.[3] Is it really possible that God, the highest Good, gives us medicines (in his Law) which no one can use? he prods.[4]

The point of all 153 questions, of which the tract is composed, is to drive home Dippel's central religious insight into the Christian understanding of salvation, namely, that the obstacle to salvation is not in God, but in man's love of himself in place of God. Hence to be reconciled man must repent of his self-love and imitate Christ by embarking with him on the way of the cross. In doing so man, like Christ before him, will find spiritual healing and hence the divinely intended perfection of his humanity.

While Dippel pursues this major argument, however, he manages to give expression in the same tract to all of his other concerns. Thus his references to the *ex opere operato* understanding of Word and Sacrament among "sectarian" Protestants, and to Lutheranism's deference to its historic symbols are always caustic. So are his allusions to the traditional Protestant doctrine of biblical inspiration, which does not, he contends, distinguish between Scripture and the Word of God. Established Protestantism's imperious way of using the power of the state for its own ends is pointed up as one of the chief reasons for the prevailing religious lethargy. On the positive side, Dippel continues to point here, as he did in previous writings, to the need for visible piety, making, in fact, moral sensitivity rather than correct belief the mark of the "true" church, in the service of which he writes. In all of this he keeps before him the ideal of a humane religion, motivated solely

---

1 *Vera* in *Eröffneter Weg*, vol. 2, p. 661f.

2 *Ibid.*, p. 677.

3 *Ibid.*, p. 666.

4 *Ibid.*, p. 679.

by love for God and his creatures, which will increasingly be espoused by God's people.

The result of all of this was that Dippel's *Vera* became a kind of handbook of ecclesiastical criticism. Christians who for one reason or another were at odds with established Protestantism, as well as with Roman Catholicism, could and did use it with telling effect to support their own opinions and those of their fellow-believers and, by the same token, to confound their opponents.

It would be difficult indeed to evaluate precisely Dippel's influence. Among all the men and women who have come within the purview of this study none have been as radically free from accepted theological norms as was Dippel. Neither was there among them anyone so utterly uncompromising, and so deliberately offensive, as he in stating publicly such heterodox convictions. Whether he should be regarded, however, as being simply a milestone on the road to the Enlightenment, as Bender does, presents a problem. It would seem that besides being such a milestone he also helped considerably in shaping the Protestant piety of his day. The fact is that in trying to make "love" the heart of religious relevance, and the mind of Christ in re-born men the ultimate criterion of religious knowledge and value, he felt impelled to oppose the Enlighteners of his age as passionately as he opposed the Orthodoxists. His goal was the transformation of the Christian life, both individual and corporate. His way of doing this was that of keeping those among his contemporaries who did not wish to be so transformed as uncomfortable as possible, and all of this in the hope of providing the conditions by which others would be moved in the right direction. In pursuing this goal Dippel became one of Protestantisms' most single-minded zealots, whose all encompassing aim in life was to promote among men God's enterprise, as he understood that enterprise. If in the process of being himself, and of saying what he felt he must say, he further prepared his age for the spread of Enlightenment sentiments this would seem to have been quite unintentional indeed.

A very different person was the third man in the trio which needs to be given special attention in this chapter. This is Gerhard Tersteegen (1697-1769), the saintly citizen of a higher world, perhaps the best loved spiritual adviser of his day, the writer of some of the most treasured hymns in Protestantism, and the author of edificatory books which have held their own inspite of the shifting moods of the modern intellectual climate. To turn from Dippel to Tersteegen is like shifting one's attention from a riot scene on a hot city street to the whispy clouds which move tranquilly overhead. If it can be said of anyone that he was in the world but not of it, this can be said about Tersteegen. The reason was not insensitivity to the world's problems. It was, rather, his amazing success in creating his own world of peace, and freedom, and universal good-will out of an inner life which was totally integrated with what he regarded as the will of a loving God.

Tersteegen's spirit is remarkably well expressed in a prayer which is part of the preface to his *Selected Biographies of Saintly Souls*: "In the spirit of humility, and with childlike trust I hereby ascribe to You what is wholly Yours, namely the examples and testimonies of Your saints. Everything they are, they are through You and for the praise of Your abundant loving-kindness. You have united Yourself with them. You have lived in them and through them. If I praise them, I praise only Your gifts. — I have found these precious jewels, and I have loved them, and I acknowledge both as evidence of Your extraordinary graciousness, and for both I offer You publicly my gratitude."[1] While Arnold may be presented as a critic of the church, and Dippel as a theological gad-fly, Tersteegen, if he is to be understood, must be presented basically as a lover of God and a friend of men. Characteristically he had severe mental reservations about the religious usefulness of the kind of theological learning which prevailed in his day.[2] For that reason he spent a minimum of time upon intellectual clarification. His contribution was made through the writing of religious lyrics and of books of devotion. The result is, of course, that his theological presuppositions are often hazy and his language correspondingly ambiguous. This must not be regarded to mean, however, that his works are shallow, or that his language is lacking in beauty and power. Quite to the contrary. In Tersteegen's writings there is a richness and a religious profundity which has perhaps never been equalled by other mystically inclined Protestants. In his religious lyrics, furthermore, there is a certain timeless appeal, which for the modern reader is marred only by a recurrent note of excessive sweetness.

Tersteegen lived a relatively uneventful existence. Hence the facts of his life need to be given attention only in so far as they shed light upon the kind of person he was and the influence he exerted within the pietistic circles of his day.[3] He was born at Moers and attended the

---

[1] *Auserlesene Lebensbeschreibungen heiliger Seelen* etc. 1784 ed., preface.

[2] See *Geistliche und erbauliche Briefe* in *Gesammelte Schriften*, 1844-1845, vol. 8, p. 130.

[3] The literature on Tersteegen is growing steadily. Perhaps the best biography on him is C.P. van Andel's *Gerhard Tersteegen*, 1961, which contains excellent bibliographical

local Latin school. At the age of fifteen he became a business apprentice in the home of Matthias Brink at Mühlheim a.d. Ruhr. Already during the second year of his apprenticeship the pietistic atmosphere which had lingered on at Mühlheim since the days of Untereyck began to have its effect upon his religious sensibilities. The result was the kind of personal religious break-through advocated by most Pietists of his day. Henceforth Tersteegen took the opportunity to drink deeply at the well of quietistic literature, which abounded among the Reformed Pietists of that region.

Having served his customary four year apprenticeship Tersteegen began a business of his own. He quickly found, however, that the responsibilities thus incurred afforded him little time for meditation. Hence he gave up his business in 1719 and learned the trade of weaving silk ribbons. He worked at this during the day, with some time out for the contemplation of matters of religious import. His evenings were devoted to reading and meditation, as well as to the needs of the poor, whom he visited diligently and helped with his own funds. The more he read and pondered, however, the greater became his religious difficulties. Somehow he did not seem to be able to measure up to the ideal set before him by his spiritual guides.[1] Presently he experienced a period of what in quietistic literature is often referred to as "dryness," though Tersteegen preferred to use the descriptive symbol of "darkness." He was filled with religious apprehensions so profound, that he often doubted the very existence of God. An austere program of ascetic living did not bring any relief.

This characteristically quietistic period of struggle and doubt ended abruptly in 1724. On Maundy Thursday of that year he wrote the following and oft quoted covenant in his own blood : "To my Jesus! I pledge myself to You, my only Savior and Groom, Christ Jesus, to be completely and eternally Your own. From this evening on I gladly

---

suggestions, pp. 204-207. Unfortunately for many Americans this book is presently available only in Dutch. M. Schmidt in the third ed. of the RGG, vol. 6, column 698, also gives bibliographical suggestions. Specially helpful books in German are A. Löschhorn's *Gerhard Tersteegen*, 1946; J. Rössle's *Leben und Werk des Gerhard* Tersteegen, 1948; W. Blankennagel's *Tersteegen als religiöser Erzieher*, 1934; and G. Wolter's *Gerhard Tersteegens geistliche Lyrik*, 1929. In English H.E. Govan's *Life of Gerhard Tersteegen*, 1902, is useful as a general introduction. The periodic literature on Tersteegen is considerable. Foremost here among his interpreters is H. Forsthoff, whose many articles on our author, however, tend to be heavily biased against the mystical piety represented by him.

[1] See RI, p. 169f.

deny all right and power over myself, which Satan may wrongfully have given to me. — From this evening on my heart and my entire love shall eternally and out of due gratitude be devoted to You and sacrificed. Not mine but Your will be done from now on and to all eternity! May Your Spirit seal what has been written in humility."[1] The following year Tersteegen ended his hermit-like existence by taking into his home his friend Heinrich Sommer. The latter had a certain liberalizing effect on him, so that he now modified his austere life, occasionally even allowing himself the luxury of a cup of coffee. During this period began in earnest his literary career, which gradually spread his fame and his religious influence throughout Europe. As a result of the revival which spread through the section around Mühlheim during the years 1725-27 Tersteegen was prevailed upon by Wilhelm Hoffmann, its moving spirit, to help him in the ever more burdensome task of holding conventicles. In time (1730) Tersteegen's religious responsibilities forced him to give up his trade and to live upon the support of his friends. He now spent all of his time as spiritual adviser to an ever increasing circle of followers, as well as in the writing, translating and editing of devotional books. During this period he also made various trips to the Netherlands, thus establishing connections with a considerable group of like-minded friends, who had been "awakened" by Poiret. Through an extensive correspondence he kept in touch with others throughout Germany, Holland, and Sweden.

At Mühlheim, which continued to be home-base for Tersteegen, the orthodox party in the meantime gained the upper hand. The result was that the holding of conventicles was forbidden by law between 1740 and 1750. Tersteegen now spent all of his time in writing, religious counseling, and in the dispensing of medicines. He had taken up the latter activity out of concern for the physical as well as religious welfare of his friends and neighbors. Because of a profound sense of dedication he achieved considerable success as a physician, though he was determined to use simple herb remedies, and not to become ensnared in the labyrinth of alchemy and the lure of making gold. After 1750 he was able once again to hold conventicles and did so with great success. His home had now become a haven for an endless stream of religious pilgrims, who coveted not merely his words of religious counsel, but who felt encouraged, and were sent upon their way rejoicing, by his very presence. With his death passed away one of the choicest souls in

[1] Quoted from van Andel, *op. cit.*, p. 27.

Christendom, free from pretension, and endowed with a majestic simplicity, which lent both authenticity and power to all he said and did.

While Arnold and Dippel had been dominantly influenced by Arndtian and Boehmist spirituality Tersteegen had been open especially to the appeal of quietistic mysticism.[1] Both his works[2] and his life breathe the quietistic spirit with its resolute supplimation of the desires and ambitions which normally motivate human behavior. The question is, therefore, how the tradition of mystical Quietism first gained its foothold in the life and thought of Tersteegen.

In a series of carefully researched articles H. Forsthoff seems to have provided the answer to this question.[3] In these articles he points to Wilhelm Hoffmann as the spiritual father of Tersteegen, an assertion which is supported by F. Winter,[4] and which seems to have the weight of historical evidence behind it. Hoffmann, having attended the University of Duisburg (matriculated in 1694), had been won for the pietistic approach to religious reality by Hochmann von Hochenau (1670-1721). He had come to Mühlheim a.d. Ruhr and had found a

---

[1] Though toward the end of his life Dippel, too, veered in a quietistic direction.

[2] Van Andel discusses the various source materials which are available (pp. 14-19). M. Goebel's discussion of Tersteegen as author is still helpful (GBL, vol. 3, pp. 316-337). Most of his works are conveniently available in a set of eight volumes called *Gesammelte Schriften* etc., 1844-1845, though a new and critical edition is urgently needed. His most frequently quoted book is probably his *Geistliches Blumengärtlein inniger Seelen*, which was first published in 1727 and which is usually appended to his *Der Frommen Lotterie*. This volume was reprinted in Pennsylvania in 1747 and was one of the most popular books of devotion among the Germans of Colonial Pennsylvania. Walter Nigg (*Grosse Heilige*, 1946, 1955) thinks that his most important book was his *Auserlesene Lebensbeschreibungen heiliger Seelen*, 1733-1753, while M. Goebel tends to down-grade it as the least sound of all his works. Other tracts by him which were popular were his *Weg der Wahrheit* etc., 1752, and his *Geistliche Brosamen* etc., 1769-1773. His various translations of mystical writers gained considerable prominence for them among the Protestants of his day. Especially important here is his translation of Jean de Bernieres-Louvigny (1603-1659) under the title *Das verborgene Leben mit Gott* etc., 1727.

[3] H. Forsthoff, "Theodor Under Eyck in Mühlheim an der Ruhr, 1660-1668," MrKG, vol. 10, 1916, pp. 33-76; "Wilhelm Hoffmann, der geistliche Vater Tersteegens," MrKG, vol. 11, 1917, pp. 97-123; "Tersteegens Mystik," MrKG, 1918, vol. 12, pp. 129-191, 193-201; "Die Mystik in Tersteegens Liedern," MrKG, vol. 12, 1918, pp. 202-246; "Der religiöse Grundcharakter Tersteegens," MrKG, vol. 22, 1928, pp. 1-22; "Von Tersteegen zum Methodismus," MrKG, vol. 10, 1916, pp. 321-329.

[4] F. Winter, "Die Frömmigkeit Gerhard Tersteegens in ihrem Verhältnis zur französisch-quietistischen Mystik," *Theologische Arbeiten aus dem wissenschaftlichen Prediger-Verein*, vol. 23, 1927, pp. 3-165.

religiously congenial environment among the Reformed people of that city, in which pietistically inclined ministers had functioned continuously since the days of Untereyck (1660-1668). When finally the pietistic ministry of the Reformed congregation of Mühlheim ceased in 1708 many of the members found themselves forced into separatism. From these groups Wilhelm Hoffmann had recruited his followers and among them he gradually assumed religious leadership. And within the fellowship of this pietistic circle the young Tersteegen found a spiritual home during the days of his apprenticeship with Matthias Brink, assuming gradually the mantel of leadership which was hitherto worn by his friend and mentor Hoffmann.

If we may assume this spiritual succession to be an historically established fact Forsthoff's article on Hoffmann's religious development gains added significance. It seems that Hoffmann began his religious pilgrimage with a typically pietistic religious experience and then moved slowly in the direction of Quietism, as did many other earnest Protestants in his day. This is evident in the difference between his *Short Instruction for Little Children*[1] and his later *Interior Practice of Faith and Love.*[2] While the mystical element in the former is negligible the latter is permeated by the mysticism of Poiret, Madam Guyon, and Bernieres-Louvigny. It may safely be assumed, therefore, that under the spiritual leadership of Hoffmann the community of separatistic Pietists in and around Mühlheim opened litself increasingly to the influences of Quietism. Tersteegen, a committed member of that community, was no exception.

This leads us directly into the problematic which has surrounded the interpretation of Tersteegen during the past few decades. His older interpreters, notably Max Goebel[3] and G. Kerlen,[4] being great admirers of Tersteegen, gave more or less uncritical accounts of his life and work. Here, too, Ritschl sounded the first discordant note, when he insisted that Tersteegen is really a Quietist, and hence denied him status as an evangelical Christian. The Ritschlian thesis has since been perpetuated by Forsthoff, who asserts, "Tersteegen's religion is that of pagan mysticism, (neo-platonism) not that of the Christian

---

1 *Kurze Unterweisung für kleine Kinder* etc. (Date of first printing uncertain).

2 *Inwendige Glaubens- und Liebesübung einer Seele gegen Gott und dessen Gegenwart* etc., 1720.

3 GBL, *op. cit.*

4 *Gerhard Tersteegen,* 1851.

revelation."[1] Subsequently the Ritschl-Forsthoff thesis has come under critical review by many others.[2] The extensive debate which ensued may safely be detoured in this study. The reason is that it is centered in the question whether or not mysticism is a legitimate expression of the spirit of Christianity, or whether a truly Christian approach to God must be limited to some mysterious element called "evangelical."[3] From our point of view this question has lost its significance with the passing of the rigid confessionalism of a bygone era. Tersteegen was Christian, and mystical, and "evangelical," all at the same time, if we define these terms historically rather than dogmatically.

It is not even necessary to debate the related question as to whether Tersteegen should be regarded as a mystic or a Pietist. On the basis of his writings one must conclude that he was obviously both, as were many other radical separatists in his day.[4] What appears to have happened was that soon after his characteristic pietistic experience of conversion he began to steep himself in the mystical literature which was available to him. He thus read Boehme and rejected him. Thirsty for religious guidance he turned to other sources. Under the influence of Hoffmann, he found that the Quietism of Molinos, as mediated by Poiret, Madam Guyon, and Bernieres-Louvigny touched the deepest springs of his being. Hence he combined the insights of Reformed Pietism with those of French Quietism, and came out both as a mystic and a Pietist, depending on what aspect of his theology one wishes to emphasize. For Tersteegen then, as for Arnold and Dippel, the essence of personal religion was love for God, reflected in the Christian's relation to his neighbor. All other matters which may come under the heading

---

[1] "Tersteegens Mystik," etc., *op. cit.*, p. 165.

[2] See W. Nelle, *G. Tersteegens geistliche Lieder mit einer Lebensgeschichte*, 1897; O. Söhngen, "Gerhard Tersteegen und die Gemeindefrömmigkeit," MrKG, vol. 20, 1926, pp. 119-137; F. Winter's article quoted above as well as his "Zur Frömmigkeit Tersteegens und zum Problem der Mystik," MrKG, vol. 22, 1928, pp. 129-143. See also W. Rotscheid, "Was versteht Tersteegen unter Mystik?" MrKG, vol. 20, 1926, pp. 279-289; and J. Moltmann, "Grundzüge mystischer Theologie bei Gerhard Tersteegen," EvTH, vol. 16, 1956, p. 208f.

[3] See especially Winter's "Zur Frömmigkeit."

[4] It is interesting to find here that H. Forsthoff makes out Tersteegen as simply an echo of Quietist Bernieres-Louvigny ("Die Mystik — Liedern", p. 203) and denies him all originality, while F. Winter ("Die Frömmigkeit," p. 59) and O. Söhngen see him as essentially part of the Reformed Tradition. The latter denies outright that Tersteegen was a genuine mystic (p. 127).

of religion were regarded as distinctly secondary. There were many differences between them, of course, in the way each would have wished to implement this over-riding religious concern. While Arnold sat in judgment especially upon the practices of the established church, and while Dippel meant above all else to revamp the conceptual structure of the Protestant faith, Tersteegen put relatively little stock in criticism or theological reconstruction. It was his desire to move his fellow men toward the desired goal through the writing of religious lyrics and of edificatory literature in general. This does not mean, of course, that he was any less out of tune than they with both the Orthodoxists and the Enlighteners of his day, or that he was not critical of many of the practices of the Reformed Protestantism out of which he had come. To him, as to them, much of what was going on in the organized church seemed meaningless and hence harmful by default. Still, his *modus operandi* was essentially that of religious exhortation addressed to individuals, rather than that of criticism of the institution. He thus chose to rely on the principle of the leaven, confident that in God's time the lump would be as thoroughly leavened as any human institution can be expected to be.

As has been said above, to enter into the details of the debate about the nature of Tersteegen's spirituality is neither necessary nor possible in this context. At the same time, however, it is possible to characterize his approach to religious reality by pointing up certain distinctions between him and the Quietists who had influenced him so profoundly. One quite obvious difference between his theology and theirs is to be found in his pronounced emphasis upon a personal experience of religious conversion as the *sine qua non* of the religious life. To the saint of Mühlheim the religious quest did not begin with a search for mystical insights resulting from the willful suppression of man's normal avenues of contact with the world surrounding him. In typical pietistic fashion he insisted, rather, that man must go through a conscious inner renewal in which man the sinner experiences God's forgiveness and regenerating power. So great was this emphasis that Söhngen felt justified in including in his discussion a section on Tersteegen as the preacher of conversion.[1]

Not only was Tersteegen at home in the pietistic, rather than the quietistic, tradition with regard to his witness to the primacy of a

---

1 See also his *Geistliche Brosamen von des Herrn Tisch*, first Am. ed., 1807, vol. 1, part 2, p. 316f.

personal religious conversion experience. With the Pietists he also concurred fully in their theological presuppositions about the objective validity of Christ's saving work as a necessary precondition for such an experience, a theologumenon not emphasized to the same degree by the Quietists. This "evangelical" aspect of his understanding of Christianity is the reason for his counsel to his unregenerate hearers to offer the following prayer : "O Lord Jesus — let my sin be blotted out through Your blood, o let me find grace in Your blood."[1] The fact is that the emphasis of both the Lutheran and the Reformed communions upon God's initiative in the matter of forgiveness and religious renewal of the individual was as strong in Tersteegen as it was in any of the church-related Pietists. To deny him status as a Christian, or as a Protestant, therefore, is to do violence to what was really the case.

In contrast to the Quietists, furthermore, and in line with the Pietistic Tradition, Tersteegen meant to be thoroughly biblical in his theology. His final criterion of the religious life was not a particular psychological process calculated to lead to mystical insight but a simple, unsophisticated reading of the Bible. As Löschhorn points out, his biblicism was concentrated especially upon the suffering and death of Christ, which he understood along with most Pietists of his day, as the objective basis for man's reconciliation with God.[2] "In Jesus alone," he insisted, "there is salvation, power, and life."[3] At the same time, of course, he regarded the life of Christ, his compassion for men, his suffering and death, as the supreme pattern of Christian piety. With St.Paul he felt that man must die to the "world" so as to find his true freedom, joy, and destiny in God alone.

All of this is obviously quite pietistic. There is actually little difference in what has been said so far between Halle, Swabian Pietism, Zinzendorf, and Tersteegen, a fact which is attested by the great esteem which Pietists in general had for him and his writings. At the same time, however, Tersteegen's writings, especially his lyrics, are pervaded by a profoundly mystical tone. The typically quietistic vocabulary is in evidence everywhere. Words like *Stille*, *Einkehr*, and *Gelassenheit* abound. It is this vocabulary which has prompted some of his interpreters to treat him as a mystic and to deny him status as a Protestant

---

[1] *Ibid.*, p. 252. See also his *Erklärung* etc., written shortly before his death and found in his *Gesammelte Schriften*, *op. cit.*, vols. 1-2, pp. 541-542.

[2] A. Löschhorn, *op. cit.*, p. 18f.

[3] *Geistliche und erbauliche Briefe* in *Gesammelte Schriften*, vol. 8, p. 112.

or even as a Christian. As Winter has pointed out, however, this is a serious mistake, in so far as the quietistic element in Tersteegen must be understood within the context of Protestant, and specifically Reformed, theology.[1] This changes rather radically the whole nature of his Quietism, a point which Forsthoff unfortunately missed when he denied Tersteegen any originality and called him simply an interpreter of Bernieres-Louvigny.[2] His originality consists precisely in the fact that he succeeded in combining pietistic and quietistic insights in a way this was not accomplished by anyone else.

A few comparisons should point this out quite clearly. While Tersteegen accepted the validity of the mystic way it was to him not man's self-appointed and self-executed way into God's presence. It was rather, the earnest attempt of the person who has already been regenerated by divine grace to integrate his own will with that of God. Thus the mystic way in Tersteegen must be understood against the background of the Reformed doctrine of religious growth, which was present in that tradition from the days of Calvin. Again, what the bard of Mühlheim understood by union was a progressive, affective identification with the person, the will, and the purposes of God on the part of an individual who, before he makes any such effort, believes himself to be a new creature in Christ. Furthermore, the goal of the Christian life in Tersteegen was not mystical union with God in isolation from the world and its problems. It was rather, the gift and the achievement of harmony with the will of God, and hence with God's entire creation, which unifies man's energies and empowers him for the kind of service God demands. Finally, the way of the cross to Tersteegen was not a scheme for self-mortification in the hope of a mystical break-through, but a way of demonstrating in one's own life God's love for all of his creatures.[3] "You are acceptable to God," he advises in his letters, "when you suffer for his sake," thus making suffering a token of love for God and his creatures rather than a means to propel oneself into his presence.[4]

Tersteegen's major concern, therefore, was that of the Christian life — a life of love for God and man. Still it must be granted that he understood the Christian life in essentially passive terms. Arnold's

---

[1] Winter, *op. cit.* This is a most discerning comparison.

[2] Forsthoff, "Die Mystik in Tersteegens Liedern," *op. cit.*, p. 203.

[3] *Geistliche Brosamen*, part 1, in *Gesammelte Schriften*, vol. 3, p. 203.

[4] *Geistliche und erbauliche Briefe*, *op. cit.*, p. 105.

apologetic concern for the suffering of religious minorities, and Dippel's passion for ecclesiological and theological reform are nowhere to be found in his writings. To Tersteegen's way of thinking man's religious needs are primarily met in the sanctuary, not in the social arena, through the writing and reading of edificatory books rather than through controversy. His lyrics are an attempt to call Christians away from the ambitions and pursuits which tend to tyrranize them and to offer themselves at the altar of complete religious dedication. His concern was strictly for the little flock of religiously sensitive people to whom alone, he felt, the Kingdom was promised. He was sure that the secret of the religious life was not that of straining for something, or of doing something, but of simply permitting oneself to be caught up in the flood-tide of divine love, and thus to be carried in the direction of fulfilling God's purposes among men. The perfection which he counseled, therefore, was not at all the perfection of accomplishment, but rather the perfection of absolute surrender to God's redemptive activity. This was a kind of Quietism, to be sure, though a Quiestism manifesting itself in a new theological context.

During his lifetime Tersteegen caused no sensation and he successfully avoided the religious controversy of his day. His aim was to make God a reality in the lives of his contemporaries by insisting that his presence can actually be felt. Among Protestants, therefore, he became the poet laureate of the interior life, the high priest at the altar of personal religious devotion. Inspite of their occasional sensualistic note, his religious lyrics remained popular as aids to worship down to the present day. Attempting to account for this wide acclaim Martin Schmidt calls him the greatest, theologically the most profound evangelical mystic, and the one who manifested the greatest wealth of thought.[1] It is difficult to know just how great his influence has been. Certain it is, however, that by interiorizing Christianity he helped his age to transcend the religious divisions and controversies which continued to agitate it, and that by singing of love, and acting accordingly, he was the herald of a new day.

Little wonder that in the region around Mühlheim the followers of Tersteegen were numerous and the burdens of spiritual leadership which this imposed on him were heavy. Amongst the best known of his followers were Engelbert Evertson (1722-1807) the wealthy owner of a ribbon factory who, together with other people of means, amply

---

[1] M. Schmidt, *op. cit.*, column 697.

supported Tersteegen in his many charitable endeavors.[1] Important among his followers for different reasons was Johann Christoph Zollinger (1733-1800), who left a diary of some 2,000 pages giving an excellent insight into the kind of piety which Tersteegen had engendered among his followers.[2] Mention should also be made of Wilhelm Weck (b. 1688), friend of both Tersteegen and Zollinger, who collected an extensive series of letters from and to Tersteegen under the title *Geistliches Blumenfeld*, which give insight into the spirituality found in these circles.

With Tersteegen's emphasis upon the cultivation of the interior religious life the development of a number of hermitages as centers of Tersteegian spirituality was just about inevitable. The best known of these was the so called *Otterbeck*, sometimes called *Pilgerhütte*, and located between Mühlheim and Elberfeld. It was a religious community which had been founded by Hoffmann in 1727 and consisted of about eight brethren who meant to live together in solitude. They made their living through weaving, lived under a rule given to them by Tersteegen,[3] and acknowledged the latter as their religious adviser. The community disbanded after the death of Zollinger, who had joined it after the demise of Tersteegen, and had become its spiritual head. At least two other such communities of Tersteegians existed, one at Mühlheim and one in the home of Evertson. The cloyster at Ephrata in Pennsylvania is historically tied to these hermitages, as well as to Wittgenstein.

Other Radicals

At this point it becomes necessary to call attention to at least three other men whose activities and writings brought comfort to the growing circle of radical Pietists and exasperation to the defenders of theological normalcy and ecclesiastical stability. Like Arnold, Dippel, and Tersteegen they had imbibed the heady wine of mystical spirituality, they had little esteem for organized Christianity and external forms of worship, they were more or less critical of the Lutheran, Reformed, and Catholic "sects," and they looked for a new day when their own religious vision would triumph in the land.

The first to be mentioned of this trio was Ernst Christoph Hochmann

---

[1] For details see GBL, vol. 3, p. 396f. See also van Andel, *op. cit.*, p. 46f.

[2] See the excellent article by Hollweg, "Der Mystiker Johann Christoph Zollinger," MrKG, vol. 15, 1921, pp. 113-156.

[3] The rule is found in GBL, vol. 3, p. 440f.

von Hochenau (1670-1721) to whom reference has been made at various points.[1] Von Hochenau was undoubtedly the most successful evangelist of his day, and is, therefore, important not so much from the point of view of what he wrote but from the point of view of his success as a preacher. He had studied law at Halle, and had been converted under Francke. He had continued his legal studies at Leipzig and Jena. At the same time, however, he had drunk deeply at the well of mystical-pietistic spirituality and in 1697 went to Giessen where he befriended Gottfried Arnold. The result was that he decided to embark upon a career of religious witness, which began with the publication in 1699 of his well meant *Exhortation to the Jews* to come to Christ. Making Wittgenstein his home base he spent most of the rest of his life on evangelistic tours. Because of the determined opposition of the Orthodoxists of his day he met with the usual trials, including a banishment from Wittgenstein as a result of the interference of the fanatically orthodox Count Rudolf, and an imprisonment at Lippe-Dortmund in 1702.

Von Hochenau's theology had been formed under the influence of both the church-related Pietists and the representatives of mystical spirituality. As a result he combined the dislike of men like Arnold, Dippel, and Petersen for the externals of religion with many of the characteristic insights of Spener and of the Halle theologians. He was critical of the way Lutheranism understood its mission and message, feeling that these were distorted by the orthodox interpretation of the Lutheran symbols, whose message, after all, must be regarded as historically conditioned. He was especially critical of the way Lutheranism used the power of the state in order to enforce theological and ecclesiastical compliance. Thus in writing to the Landgrave of Hesse-Darmstadt and to the Council of Frankfurt he took a position on religious liberty which was a century in advance of his day. At the same time, however, von Hochenau remained mild in his criticism, revealing always his desire to make peace rather than to stir up controversy.

As an evangelist he was a fit counterpart to his younger contemporaries George Whitefield and John Wesley. His preaching was simple and

[1] The AGLF-II, column 2030 gives the titles of five pieces by him. Among these are his *Ermahnungsschreiben an die Juden* (1699) and his *Glaubensbekenntnis*, which he was forced to write while in prison at Lippe-Detmold. F. Auge has published "Acht Briefe des E. Chr. Hochmann von Hochenau," MrKG, vol. 19, pp. 133-154. See also H. Renkewitz, "Hochmann von Hochenau — Quellenstudien zur Geschichte des Pietismus," *Breslauer Studien zur Theologie und Religionsgeschichte*, vol. 2, 1935 (second ed., 1969).

direct, without any artifice or straining for effect. Jung-Stilling characterized it as follows : "Hochmann had received a special gift from God in so far as he was a Spirit-filled man and a genius in the matter of eloquence. — An old Pietist told me once that Hochmann preached on a large meadow near Elberfeld, and he did so with a plenitude of spiritual power which moved the many hundreds of listeners to believe that the dawn of eternity had come."[1] Testimonies of this kind abound. When von Hochenau spoke his listeners forgot all about time, giving him their wrapt attention for the space of two hours and then going away with the feeling that the Almighty had moved perceptibly in their very midst. His message was re-enforced by a life of singular and unselfish devotion which spoke almost as eloquently as his words. The result was, of course. that great numbers of people were won for his understanding of Christianity, including the wife of Zinzendorf, the Countess Hedwig Sophie von Wittgestein, on whose estate later stood his little home *Friedensburg*, as well as Wilhelm Hoffmann, the spiritual mentor of Tersteegen. The testimonies of his friends, as well as his own letters quoted by Auge, indicate that he was a separatist because his enemies had forced him into that position. What really interested him, however, was not the destruction of the church, or even its reform, but the amendment of the individual life. To that end he hoped a Church of the Spirit might some day replace the quarrelsome and religiously ineffective "sects."

Similar in point of view, though a very different person, was Dr. Heinrich Horch (or Horche),[2] whose life and activity was alluded to elsewhere.[3] Horch (1652-1729) was one of the restless ideologoues of his day with a predilection toward abrasive criticism of contemporary institutions, notably the institutions of the church. He appears to have gone through several stages of religious development, beginning as a Reformed Pietist according to the pattern of Untereyck. Under the influence of one of the local radical Pietists, namely Balthasar Christoph

---

[1] Quoted by J. Schmitt, *Die Gnade bricht durch*, 1958, pp. 100-101.

[2] For the life and activity of Horch see GBL, vol. 2, pp. 741-751; H. Heppe, *Kirchengeschichte beider Hessen*, vol. 2, pp. 318-325. The most extensive treatment of Horch is that of C.W.H. Hochuth, *Heinrich Horch und die philadelphischen Gemeinden in Hessen*, 1876. Unfortunately Hochuth's account is marred by a somewhat negative bias. See also W. Zeller, "Heinrich Horch in Kirchheim," *Jahrbuch der hessischen kirchengeschichtlichen Vereinigung*, vol. 11, 1960. The titles of his works are given in the AGLF-II, columns 2139-2141. For bibliographical suggestions see also Hochuth, pp. 157-164.

[3] See RI, pp. 175-176.

Klopfer, he gradually moved toward separatism. Soon he found himself captivated by the ever more popular apocalypticism, which had been generated among a group of English Puritans, and which was being popularized especially by Thomas Beverley.[1] Because of his heterodox opinions he presently found himself relieved of his offices of pastor and professor of theology, and even imprisoned. In time he allegedly made his peace with the Reformed Communion, and attested it with open letters to the secular authorities, as well as by receiving the Lord's Supper. Just how meaningful this act of submission to authority was, however, remains a question. While Horch moderated his language he never ceased to be critical of the church as an institution. Nor did he actively engage in its ministry. He and his large family were supported, rather, by the largesse of Landgrave Carl of Cassel who appears to have acted out of pity rather than out of agreement with Horch's doings.

During the last two decades of his life Horch became ever more interested in the Philadelphic Movement, which also came from England, and which will be covered more fully at the end of this chapter. The reason was that he had become disillusioned with his earlier notion of reforming the church. His hope now was placed in an ever enlarging fellowship of mystical Pietists, who will in time constitute the "true church," while the institutionalized church will gradually wither away.[2] Such a fellowship seemed to him to be advocated by the Philadelphians which was his reason for actively engaging in the establishment of philadelphic societies. In time, however, he seems to have become critical of some aspects of Philadelphianism, too, in so far as in 1718 he took issue with Petersen's notion of the restoration of all things.[3]

Horch, like the rest of the brotherhood of mystical Pietists, put the emphasis upon a person's immediate relation to God. Such affective identification with God as revealed in Christ seemed to him to be the only essential and valid religious requirement. This being the case,

---

[1] In 1689 Beverley had published his *History of the Reformation, or, the Reformation to be Reformed in that Great Reformation that is to be 1697*. Horch quotes Beverley in the preface to his *Das A und das O, oder Zeitrechnung der ganzen heiligen Schrift* (1697) and even accepts the general time scheme advocated by Beverly (see pp. 221-222), though he does grant the Almighty a little leeway regarding the critical year 1697.

[2] See his *Mystische und prophetische Bibel, d.i., die ganze heilige Schrift aufs neue nach dem Grund verbessert*, 1712, and his *Filadelfia*, d.i., *Bruderliebe, dem hl. Abendmahl, der Gnadenwahl*, 1712.

[3] See his *Der Unter dem Zeugnis Jesu verstellete Weissagungsgeist*, 1718.

he regarded the characteristic teachings of the various commuions as unnecessarily divisive, substituting the "spiritual" interpretation of Scripture for that based upon confessional formulas. In the interest of such a new hermeneutic he, together with some of his friends, brought out his *Mystical and Prophetic Bible,* usually referred to as the *Marburg Bible.*

While the influence of Horch was especially strong in Hesse-Nassau that of Johann Georg Rosenbach (1678-1747) was most noticeable in lower Württemberg, in the vicinity of Heilbronn a. N., and in the Franconian section of Bavaria.[1] In contradistinction to both von Hochenau and Horch, Rosenbach was an utterly self-taught man, having had next to no formal education. His father had been a spurrier at Heidelberg and later moved to Heilbronn. As expected, the son learned the father's trade, but in a fit of anger at his father left home at the age of 19. While soldiering he came under the influence of a Pietist by the name of Johann Adam Raab, who was a notary public at Erlangen. Raab was an advocate of a radical conversion experience which must follow a more or less violent *Busskampf.*[2] Under the tutelage of his spiritual adviser Rosenbach presently had such an experience, and, as a result, left military service. Upon a visit by God the Father himself he decided to devote himself wholly to the spreading of his religious ideas after the pattern of other radical Pietists.

It seems, furthermore, that Raab introduced his spiritual fledgeling to the whole milieu of pietistic and mystical spirituality. Accordingly Rosenbach immersed himself not only in the writings of Arndt, Spener, and Sonthom, but in those of Sebastian Frank, Breckling, Boehme, Dippel, Arnold, Robert Barclay, and the Philadelphians. The result was that he soon shared the attitude toward the "sects" which was typical of radical Pietism in general. He spread these views not only through incessant travel but through a number of writings.[3] The

[1] For information on Rosenbach, as well as other Pietists in Bavaria, see especially D.F. Fritz, "Johann Georg Rosenbach," ZbKG, vol. 18, 1949, pp. 21-59; T. Wotschke, "Neue Urkunden zur Geschichte des Pietismus in Bayern", ZbKG, vol. 6, 1931, pp. 38-44, 97-108, 234-251; vol. 7, 1932, pp. 44-55, 102-113, 181-187; vol. 8, 1933, pp. 173-185, 241-247; vol. 9, 1934, pp. 112-123, 173-178, 236-251; vol. 10, 1935, pp. 165-177; vol. 11, 1936, pp. 228-233; vol. 12, 1937, pp. 49-59, 176-179. A volume of writings by and about Rosenbach is available at the library of the University of Tübingen.

[2] See his *Der wahre und gewisse Weg durch die enge Kreuzespforte,* 1701. For a list of Raab's other publications see RTL, vol. 2, footnote on p. 342.

[3] For a list of his works and those of his opponents see footnote in Fritz, *op. cit.,* pp. 21-22.

remarkable thing about Rosenbach is not the rather considerable influence he appears to have had on his religiously like-minded contemporaries, but the stir this humble spurrier seems to have caused in the learned circle of theological watchdogs. As a result of their implacable opposition his days were liberally interspersed with banishments and imprisonments, before he ended his work among the Moravians.

Rosenbach's most determined enemy was pastor Johann Philipp Storr of Heilbronn, the father of the Swabian Pietist and student of Bengel Johann Christian Storr. It was the elder Storr who in 1703 addressed himself to a refutation of Rosenbach's confession of faith, and did so mostly through the ruthless employment of *argumentum ad hominem*.[1] According to Rosenbach's account, furthermore, Storr stirred up the city of Heilbronn to such a degree that Rosenbach actually feared for his life,[2] and was finally banished. Not only did he find himself persecuted, but some of the pastors in the vicinity of Heilbronn who had befriended him also felt the lash of Orthodoxy's righteous anger. Among these was pastor Christoph Mayer of Grossgartach, and pastor Eberhard Ludwig Gruber of Grossbottwar, both of whom lost their pastorates. When Rosenbach moved on into Bavaria Storr complained about his heresy to the theological faculty at Altdorf, where his defense by H.D. Lange and the favorable opinions rendered by some of the faculty members appear to have caused considerable internal strain.

In reading the highly biased accounts of the day one finds it difficult to know how to assess a life such as that of Rosenbach. That in his preaching and writing he often used intemperate language regarding the Lutheran Church and its pastors is obvious. Even Francke complained that during a visit at Halle his guest had called him a Pharisee.[3] Still he was not a rabble rouser or a willful controversialist like Dippel. What he wanted was simply the freedom of religious worship and witness, without interference by the church or the secular government. In insisting on this right he incurred the wrath of the religious establishment. This was especially true because he was a layman who was not supposed to understand matters of high theology and who was expected to treat with respect those who felt they did.[4] In resolutely ignoring

[1] See Storr's *Kurze und gründliche Abfertigung* etc. in the volume mentioned above, pp. 8-10.

[2] *Wunder- und Gnadenvolle Führung* etc. in the volume mentioned above, p. 143.

[3] Fritz, *op. cit.*, p. 55.

[4] Storr in his previously mentioned *Abfertigung* repeatedly refers to Rosenbach's lack of theological equipment and his duty as a layman to believe what he is told.

this attitude, whatever the cost, Rosenbach and other religious radicals bequeathed to succeeding generations a legacy of personal freedom which must not be ignored.

At least briefly mentioned among these radical Pietists with their mystical spirituality and their poor opinion of organized Christianity should be Johann Heinrich Reitz (1655-1720)[1] who, like Horch, was moved by Balthasar Christoph Klopfer to substitute for the Pietism of Joachim Neander and Theodor Untereyck that of the mystical separatists. Together with his like-minded contemporaries he was dissatisfied with Luther's translation of the New Testament and tried to improve on it (1703), though his chief contribution was his *History of the Re-Born* (1717), which went through many editions. It was not a history at all, of course, but, like Tersteegen's *Lebensbeschreibungen*, it was meant to use biography for edificatory purposes. Of a very similar frame of mind was Johann Tennhardt (1661-1720),[2] the wig-maker of Nürenberg, who heard the angels speak, and whose grandiose plans to reform the entire world threw southern Germany and Switzerland into considerable turmoil. The situation was aggravated by Tobias Eisler's (1683-1753)[3] spirited and repeated defense of Tennhardt. Eisler had studied law at Altdorf and Halle, but he spent most of his time in the cause of spreading radical Pietism. The last of these pietistic fire-brands to be mentioned was Samuel König (1670-1750),[4] who had been banned from his native Berne because of his religious enthusiasm. Accordingly he spent most of his active life in Germany, causing headaches for responsible ecclesiastics in the vicinity of Hesse-Cassel and Wittgenstein.

German Philadelphianism

In conclusion it is necessary to give at least a general introduction to the Philadelphic Movement which was making itself felt on the Continent during the early eighteenth century, and which could hardly

[1] See GBL, vol. 2, pp. 751-753; ADB, vol. 28, pp. 170-172; L.Köchlin, "Die Separatisten in Freudenberg," JVwKG, vols. 49-50, 1956-1957, pp. 101-123.

[2] For the most concise description of his life see P. Wernle, *Der schweizerische Protestantismus im 18, Jahrhundert*, vol. 1, 1923-1925, p. 180f. His works are mentioned in ADB, vol. 37, pp. 570-571.

[3] AGLF-II, columns 859-861; RTL, vol. 2, pp. 341-342. His works are listed in MI, 1804, vol. 3, pp. 83-87,

[4] For a helpful reference to his life and activity see Wernle, *op. cit.*, pp. 282-286. W. Hadorn in his *Geschichte des Pietismus in den schweizerischen Reformierten Kirchen*, 1901, speaks of him often in various connections.

be separated from the general phenomenon of radical Pietism. The idea seems to go back to Jane Leade (1623-1704) and her important English disciples John Pordage (1608-1688) and Thomas Bromley (1629-1729). Mrs. Leade[1] had had visions and dreamed dreams from childhood. Presently she came under the spell of Jacob Boehme, whose writings were beginning to be translated into English in 1645. In time she went beyond Boehme, however, combining her mentor's criticism of established Christianity with the apocalypticism which had found its way into the Puritan Tradition. The result was her philadelphic understanding of history, which was first clearly set forth in her *Heavenly Cloud Now Breaking* (1681). According to this understanding of things religious and secular, which took its cue from Revelation 3 : 1-13, God's dealings with men move through seven stages. The sixth, or sardic, dispension, in which true Christians are persecuted by the forces of Babylon (the representatives of organized Christianity) is about to come to an end. The reason is that God has abandoned Babylon and will thus permit it to be destroyed by the demonic forces which are already rampant within it. Out of its ruins will come the Church of Philadelphia, the spiritual church made up of re-born Christians, which will spread its message of love to all peoples. Under the impact of a rising humanitarianism and a wide-spread disgust with ecclesiastically inspired religious intolerance Mrs. Leade and her circle even went so far as to emphasize that divine love must ultimately reach all men. Hence they adopted the ancient doctrine of universal restoration.

Not satisfied, however, with merely holding such beliefs the English Philadelphians meant to do something about them. The result was that they began to organize philadelphic communities, into which they invited all who were in sympathy with their views. In this way the established churches were to be gradually depopulated and depotentialized, while the Philadelphic Movement was expected to grow in vigor and influence. Nor did its adherents think of themselves as separatists. They were profoundly convinced that they were the "true" church, and that, in fact, the Anglican, the Catholic, the Lutheran, and the Reformed communions are merely "sects." Thus they regarded the dogmatic and ecclesiastical intolerance, as well as the ecclesiastically inspired persecution of religious dissenters, as the outgrowths of a sectarian

---

[1] For a concise article on her, which also mentions her writings, see the *Dictionary of National Biography*, vol. 32, pp. 312-313. The best discussion of her life and work is N. Thune's *The Behmenists and the Philadelphians*, 1948.

mentality and a clear indication that the organized churches are largely ruled by the devil.

Mrs. Leade's writings, which provided the theoretical basis for Philadelphianism, were beginning to be translated into Dutch in 1693 and soon thereafter into German. Their message was presently taken up by the Lutheran pastor and superintendent Johann W. Petersen (1649-1727) and his illustrious wife Johanna Eleanore of the house of Merlau. In two early works[1] Eleonora set forth the philadelphic concept in German to be supplemented by a kind of symposium on the matter put out by her husband.[2] Dr. Petersen having been dismissed from ecclesiastical office because of his views, he and his wife spent all of their time in the promotion of Philadelphianism, and became, for that reason, the leaders of the movement in German speaking territories. Together they helped to create the extensive literature thrown up by German Philadelphianism[3] and established innumerable contacts with disaffected Protestants everywhere.

In the task of promoting Philadelphianism the Petersens were assisted by a group of rather able men who had pinned their hopes for the future of Christianity upon this movement. Among them was Dr. Horch, who was mentioned above. Equally gifted was the prominent physician, Dr. Johann Samuel Carl (1675-1757), who not only lent a great deal of prestige to the movement, but who entered actively into the creation of the literature mentioned above.[4] In 1730 he began to edit the *Geistliche Fama*, which was quickly recognized as the most influential organ of German Philadelphianism.[5] Not far behind him in influence was Johann Friedrich Haug (d. 1753) who edited the most monumental literary work of German Philadelphianism, namely, the so called *Berleburger Bibel*.[6] Others in this group were Victor Christoph

[1] *Anleitung zum gründlichen Verständnis der Offenbarung Christi*, 1696 and *Der geistliche Kampf der berufenen, auserwählten, und gläubigen Ueberwinder*, 1698.

[2] *Des Geheimnis der Wiederbringung aller Dinge* etc., 1700. (The full title would fill half of a page).

[3] In Petersen's autobiography (*Das Leben Johann Wilhelm Petersen* etc., 1717) 106 pieces are listed, pp. 368-394. In the volume which came to my attention a life of Mrs. Petersen, printed in 1718, was appended.

[4] GBL, vol. 3, pp. 93f, 106f, 116f; RTL, vol. 2, p. 353.

[5] The *Geistliche Fama, mitbringend verschiedene Nachrichten* etc. came out from 1730-1744 and consisted of 30 pieces, the first 20 of which were collected and edited by Dr. Carl. His successor was Johann Christian Edelmann.

[6] For its full title see footnote in GBL, vol. 3, p. 104. It was meant to be an exact translation of the original text, interpreted in the philadelphic spirit through a liberal supply of glosses. The reason for the re-translation was the general dissatisfaction with

Tuchtfeld, Johann Dithmar, Johann Kaspar von Hachenberg,[1] Dr. Johann Kaiser, who wrote under the pseudonym of Timotheus Philadelphus[2], Christian F. Knorr, who wrote under the pseudonym of Nathanael Philadelphus,[3] and possibly Conrad Brüske,[4] who in 1696 opened the radical pietistic circles in Germany to the influence of Beverley.

Under the rising tide of philadelphian sentiment the temptation to organize became great. In time, therefore, a whole series of philadelphic societies came into being, all of them patterned upon the London society, which had been established by Mrs. Leade and her circle during the years 1694-1697. Many of these were either established or dominated by women. Thus we read of societies established in Hesse by a Frau Gebhard and a Frau Wetzel.[5] There were various societies in the Hart region, shepherded especially by Tuchtfeld.[6] Widely known are the rather infamous philadelphic experiments at Bordelum,[7] Elberfeld, and Ronsdorf,[8] and most especially at Allendorf in Hesse, where the notorious Eva von Buttlar and her friends committed their immoralities in the name of religion.[9] While some of these societies were characterized by a spirit of sobriety and religious candor, others became centers of religious fanaticism, emotional excesses, and moral decay. As has been

---

Luther's translation which Philadelphians shared. The Bible came out in eight volumes between 1728 and 1742. Haug's collaborators were Ludwig Christoph Schefer, Christoph Seebach, and Johann Christian Edelmann. For an analysis of its content see M. Hofmann, "Theologie und Exegese der Berleburger Bibel," *Beiträge zur Förderung christlicher Theologie*, vol. 39, Heft 2, 1937.

1 For further information on Dittmar (or Dithmar) and Hachenberg see T. Wotschke, "Der Philadelphier Johann Dithmar in Neuwied," MrKG, vol. 28, 1934, pp. 33-57.

2 For his works see AGLF-III, column 40.

3 See R. Steinmetz, "Die Generalsuperintendenten von Grubenhagen und auf dem Harz," ZGnKG, vol. 41, 1936, pp. 79-175.

4 GBL, vol. 3, p. 80f.

5 See C.W.H. Hochuth, *Heinrich Horch und die philadelphischen Gemeinden in Hessen*, 1876.

6 See K. Kayser, "Hannoverische Enthusiasten des siebzehnten Jahrhunderts," ZGnKG, vol. 10, 1905, pp. 1-72. R. Ruprecht (*Der Pietismus des 18. Jahrhunderts in den Hannoverschen Stammländern*, 1919) feels that Hochuth's sources are not entirely reliable.

7 See R. Matthiesen, "Erweckung und Separation in Nordfriesland (Bordelumer Rotte)," SVshKG, 1927, p. 16f.

8 GBL, vol. 3, p. 448f. See also T. Wotschke, "Der Ronsdorfer Ellerianer Beschuldigungen wider Daniel Schleiermacher," MrKG, vol. 33, 1939, pp. 225-231; E. Strutz, "Elias Eller, der Gründer der Stadt Ronsdorf," *Rheinische Lebensbilder*, vol. 1, 1961, pp. 102-120. To this article is appended a bibliography of Elias Eller.

9 GBL, vol. 3, p. 778f.

the case so often in the history of Christianity what began in the spirit ended up in the flesh. This should not be too surprising in so far as it is undoubtedly true that Philadelphianism, in the very nature of the case, tended to attract not only some of the most able prophets of the day, but the most unstable, unrealistic, and irresponsible religious visionaries as well.

Many of these philadelphic societies which sprang up in various parts of Germany acknowledged the spiritual primacy of Mrs. Leade, an honor which the latter was perfectly happy to accept. In fact, with native English segacity she seems to have hoped that the whole Philadelphic Movement could be tied together, at least minimally, in a central organization with a common set of rules and a common statement of beliefs.[1] In this way the predilection toward local excesses could have been minimized. It was Dithmar who was to win the German Philadelphians for such a scheme. Unfortunately, however, Mrs. Leade's vision of visible unity among Philadelphians did not appeal to the more impractical teutonic temper, which preferred to keep the emphasis on theory. Hence the German Philadelphians objected to the scheme on the ground that it would lead to another "sect." When efforts were made to collect funds in Germany for English Philadelphians, thus furthering the spirit of unity, the Germans who were again fearful of organizational unity, sabotaged the effort with the excuse that there is quite as much need for charitable funds in Germany. The result was that Philadelphianism in Germany remained badly fractured and suffered all the handicaps of a movement which is long on theory but short on wise and practical leadership.

The center of German Philadelphianism was located at the southern tip of Westphalia in the counties of Sayn-Wittgenstein-Wittgenstein and Sayn-Wittgenstein-Berleburg.[2] The ruling families of the two counties, which had been separated from each other since 1605, continued to maintain friendly relations with each other. The region had officially accepted the Reformed Faith under Dr. Caspar Olevianus, but the counties of Wittgenstein had maintained a tradition of being hospitable toward religious refugees. Many of these had come in under Louis XIV, and more came when at the beginning of the eighteenth century religious persecution was rife in various Protestant territories

---

[1] Thune, *op. cit.*, p. 115f.

[2] For a detailed account of the Wittgenstein phenomenon see GBL, vol. 2, pp. 698f; GBL, vol. 3, p. 71f; H. Heppe, *Geschichte der quietistischen Mystik* etc., 1875, p. 506f.

of Germany. Presently two thriving communities came into being, made up largely of religious rebels, recluses, and self-appointed religious reformers, namely Schwarzenau and Berleburg. They were protected by the benevolent policies of the ruling aristocracy, notably those of Countess Hedwig Sophie of Berleburg, and of her son, Count Kasimir of Wittgenstein-Berleburg (1687-1741). After the latter's death a radical change in governmental policy put an end to this haven of religious non-conformity.

It seems that before 1724 the center of religious activity was Schwarzenau, while after that a change in political philosophy at Schwarzenau made Berleburg the citadel of radical Pietism. In these communities was assembled what was probably the most unusual conglomeration of religious individualists in Protestant history. Very active among them was von Hochenau, who has been mentioned elsewhere. So was Samuel König, the Bernese separatist. Toward the end of his life the much controverted and persecuted Dr. Dippel had found asylum here. At Schwarzenau, too, lived the saintly Charles Hector, Marquis St. George de Marsay (1688-1753)[1] with his "sister through marriage," the former Clara Elizabeth von Callenberg. Here we also find the peripatetic enthusiast Victor Christoph Tuchtfeld (d. ca. 1741),[2] who seems to have remained long enough to be court preacher to Countess Hedwig Sophie, and religious counselor to her son Kasimir.

It is hardly necessary to point out that among these people, and many other inhabitants of the counties of Wittgestein, whose opinions and exploits must be passed over in silence, there was great heterogeneity of religious sentiment and theological conviction. Many of them lived here because they had been persecuted for clinging stubbornly to religious affirmations which were unpopular elsewhere. For this reason they often held, with what to the outside world appeared to be unreasonable tenacity, to some novel religious insight, which they claimed to have received from God himself.[3] Nevertheless, as time went on a certain sub-stratum of theological agreement seems to have emerged. It consisted essentially of the philadelphic understanding of Christianity which has been discussed. Indeed, the philadelphic self-understanding was so pronounced that Zinzendorf was unsuccessful when in 1730 he

---

[1] *Idem.*, pp. 506-512.

[2] A brief synopsis of his life and a list of his works are found in ADB, vol. 38, pp. 772-774. See also K. Kayser, *op. cit.*, p. 69f.

[3] Witness, for instance, Marsay's complete horror of any normal expression of human sexuality.

attempted to bring Wittgenstein under the aegis of *Herrnhut*. Berleburg's reigning theology of Philadelphianism is attested also, of course, by the editing of the *Fama* and of the *Berleburger Bibel*, which have been previously mentioned.

At least tangentially related to Berleburg's Philadelphianism were two other groups of separatists, which had also found their way into Wittgenstein. One was headed by Alexander Mack (1679-1735), who is considered the founder of the so called *Dunkers* or the German Baptist Brethren.[1] Mack rather fully agreed with von Hochenau's confession of faith at first, but later seems to have had a falling out with him over the question of church government and the meaning of the ordinances. When Schwarzenau became inhospitable he and his followers moved on into the lower Rhine country and finally to Pennsylvania.

Not only did Anabaptism find its way into Wittgenstein, but Inspirationism as well. The latter took rise originally in France under the heavily repressive measures of Louis XIV, appeared in England about 1705, and in Germany at the beginning of the second decade of the eighteenth century. Here its leaders became Johann Friedrich Rock (1687-1749), Eberhard Ludwig Gruber (1665-1728), and for a season at least, the above mentioned Dr. Carl. All three of these men lived at Wittgenstein and stoutly defended the gift of glossalalia found in various inspirationist centers against the skeptics both within and without its borders.[2] Fortunately for the peace of the community all of the inspirationists but Rock gradually lost their prophetic gifts, and with Rock's death prophetic ejaculations ceased altogether until this form of religious enthusiasm was resurrected once more during the religious revival a century later.

Radical Pietism as described in this chapter was a religious movement of considerable scope in Germany, only a fraction of which was concentrated in the counties of Wittgenstein. In contradistinction to the Spener-Halle Movement it tended to attract the peasants more than the nobility, and the laity more than the clergy. To follow its expansion in detail would necessitate an extended treatment, for which the preliminary studies of individual localities are gradually becoming available.[3]

---

[1] Their history has been written up repeatedly. For literature on this group see the lists at the end of each chapter in H.A. Kent, *250 Years — Conquering Frontiers*, 1958.

[2] Among its chief detractors was Dippel, who in 1731 wrote but did not publish *Ein theologisch-medizinisches Bedenken über heutige mit extraordinären Concussionen, oder Bewegungen, des Leibes verknüpfte Inspirationswerk* (Published 1737).

[3] Some of these not mentioned elsewhere are: K. Schornbaum, "Religiöse Bewegungen

Among other things it should be evident from the foregoing discussion that inspite of many and obvious individual differences there was among radical Pietists an amazing unanimity of religious sentiment. They generally insisted on a thorough experience of religious conversion, on affective union with God, on love as the inner meaning of the Christian Gospel, on a life of piety as read out of the New Testament, on separation from the "world," as well as separation from the external church, and on freedom from theological, ecclesiastical, and political restraint. More often than not they espoused the doctrine of the restoration of all things, and many of them regarded human sexuality as the chief enemy of spiritual growth. They were thus not only unorthodox, but consciously and stubbornly so, and usually ready to suffer the consequences of religious and political dissent.[1]

In evaluating their contribution, therefore, it is undoubtedly true that from the point of view of the representatives of order and conformity, both in church and state, the radical Pietists presented a serious problem indeed. Their unwillingness to conform to accepted patterns of religious interpretation threatened to open the pandoras box of pluralism in the realm of religious authority, an ordeal for which the eighteenth century was not yet ready. In the matter of Christian belief it was simply unthinkable for most people to have individuals set aside the venerable authority of the church's doctrinal system as interpreted by duly constituted theological faculties. Because of the concept of religious establishment it was even more unthinkable for most people to

im Markgrafentum Brandenburg-Ansbach im 18. Jahrhundert," BbKG, vol. 16, 1910, pp. 145-168; "Separatisten in Fürth," BbKG, vol. 17, 1911, pp. 1-27: "Separatisten im Bibertgrund," ZbKG, vol. 18, 1948, pp. 176-196; "Zur Geschichte des Separatismus im Beyreuther Unterland," ZbKG, vol. 16, 1941, pp. 209-229; *ibid.* in ZbKG, vol. 23, 1954, pp. 10-16; F.P. Schaudig, *Der Pietismus und Separatismus im Aischgrunde*, 1925; T. Meister, "Separatisten in Beyreuth," BbKG, vol. 10, 1904, pp. 211-217; W. Sauerländer, "Pietismus und Rationalismus im märkischen Sauerland," JVwKG, vol. 44, 1951, pp. 165-189; W. Horstmann, "Anna Dorothea Wuppermann," MrKG, 1939, pp. 257-273; H.W. Zur Nieden, *Die religiösen Bewegungen im 18. Jahrhundert — in Westfalen und am Niederrhein*, 1910.

[1] It seems to have been this suspicion of sexuality and its supposed negative effects on the religious life which led Gichtel to form the loose association of *Engelsbrüder*, which is difficult to distinguish from Philadelphianism. On the basis of Matth. 22 : 30 it required celibacy of all of its adherents. Among its chief promoters during the period with which we are concerned seems to have been Johann Otto Glüsing (d. 1727) and Christian Anton Römeling. (For information on the former see H. Haupt, "der Altoner Sektierer Johann Otto Glüsing" etc., SVshKG, vol. 11, 1952, pp. 136-163, and for information on the latter see RTL, vol. 2, p. 346f.)

have individuals, other than Jews, to declare themselves free from that large body of written and unwritten laws which were expected to regulate both the religious and the secular aspects of the life of the community. Radical Pietists, therefore, were widely regarded as enemies of both church and state, as disrupters of the ordered life of the community, as stiff-necked rebels who must be disciplined for the good of the community at large. As a consequence few of them escaped severe persecution and some of them felt repeatedly the cruel lash of governmental sanctions. Nor can there be any doubt about the fact that their willful non-conformity seriously hurt the organized religious bodies of their day. What they said and did helped to increase the ever-widening skepticism regarding the church's message, as it helped to break down the values traditionally supported by the pulpit. On the other hand, it also helped to lay the groundwork for a new day in which theological conformity was to be replaced by freedom of conscience, religious and political autocracy by increasing tolerance, and religious exclusivism by the first rays of the ecumenical vision.

CHAPTER SIX

GERMAN REFORMED PIETISM AND PROMINENT NEO-PIETISTS

Inspite of the Huguenot migration into various German territories during the late seventeenth century[1] northwest Germany and the Rhine region remained the most dynamic center of Reformed Protestantism in Germany. The reason for it was that the close ecclesiastical and intellectual ties, which had been established earlier,[2] continued to unite these territories with one another and with the Reformed Church of the Netherlands throughout the eighteenth century. Under these circumstances it is possible to limit the present account of Reformed Pietism largely to these territories.

The growth of pietistic sentiment among the Reformed Protestants of these lands cannot easily be dissociated from the socio-political situation which obtained. The politics which are relevant to this study revolved around the stated policies of the two competing constellations of political power which vied for the allegiance of the Reformed territories in Germany throughout the eighteenth century. On the one side were the rulers of the Palatinate, who continued to be deeply devoted to the Roman Catholic Church and its claim to complete hegemony over the religious life of all subjects of a Catholic state.[3] On the other side was the House of Hohenzollern, Reformed in faith, and bent upon hitching its star to a certain ideological liberalism and progressivism unknown elsewhere among European royalty at this time.[4]

---

[1] As a result of the Edict of Revocation, issued by Louis XIV on October 22, 1685, approximately half of a million Reformed Protestants, the so called Huguenots, were forced out of France. A considerable number of these found refuge in territories under the control of Elector Frederick of Brandenburg.

[2] See RI, p. 109f.

[3] The reigns of Philip Wilhelm, 1685-1690, and especially of his son, Johann Wilhelm, 1690-1716, as well as of Carl Philip, 1716-1742, all of them of the House of Neuburg, were felt by Reformed Protestants under their jurisdiction to be disconcertingly oppressive. Even Carl Theodore, 1742-1799, of the Sulzbach line, though personally given to the new spirit of tolerance, permitted his ecclesiastical administrators to continue the old repressive policies.

[4] See p. 39f.

For both philosophical and political reasons the rulers of the ascending Prussian state, therefore, consistently championed the cause of religious minorities within their sphere of influence. They were not averse, of course, to use the principle of toleration for the purpose of steadily expanding their own power in European affairs.

James I. Good in his somewhat tendentious *History of the Reformed Church of Germany, 1620-1890* began with the assumption that Pietism is intrinsic to the life and history of the Reformed faith.[1] On that basis he made it appear as if Pietism became the important force within the German Reformed churches which it actually was during the eighteenth century without any really determined opposition by Reformed Orthodoxists. This is hardly the case, however. Human nature being the same everywhere it is not likely that the orthodox temper among the Reformed differed very much from that found among the Lutherans of the day. That this assumption is justifiable would seem to be borne out by the rather virulent controversy occasioned in the Netherlands by the writings of Wilhelmus Schortinghuis (1700-1750)[2] as well as by the difficulties experienced in Germany by early Reformed Pietists like Theodor Untereyck (1635-1693). Even Lampe during the eighteenth century had some hard things to say against the "unfaithful teachers" in his own communion.[3]

In German Reformed territories two circumstances combined, however, to soften the official attitude of the Reformed ecclesiastical power structure toward the growing inroads of pietistic influences. On the one hand it is true, though it may have been over-stated by Good, that by the very nature of its historical emphasis upon the Christian life the Reformed Tradition was historically more amenable to pietistic emphases than the Lutheran Tradition. Yet, quite as important as such an historical tendency was the fact that in German Reformed territories Orthodoxy simply could not count upon the support of the secular governments in any contest with Pietism. Cleve, part of Geldern, Moers, Mark, Ravensberg, Minden, and Tecklenburg were under Prussian sovereignty, and it was the inflexible policy of the Hohenzollern rulers to support the opponents of Orthodoxy, be they Pietists, Separatists, or Neologists. In Reformed territories this policy was the

---

[1] Published 1894. See p. 307f.

[2] HPE, p. 421f.

[3] Note his polemic in his *Grosse Vorrechte des unglücklichen Apostels Judas Ischariot* etc., 1713.

more effective in so far as the Hohenzollerns were themselves Reformed and could, therefore, enforce their will upon the ecclesiastical leadership which owed them many favors. Sponheim, Jülich, and Berg, on the other hand, were under Palatine sovereignty, which, as has been said, was exercised by Roman Catholic rulers. That the latter were less than enthusiastic about stifling pietistic dissent from Reformed Orthodoxy is quite understandable.

Under these circumstances whatever opposition there was among local pastors to pietistic preaching and practice, notably the holding of conventicles, did not reach beyond the level of the local classis. Because of the theological and political considerations mentioned above the Reformed synods generally deemed it wise to take an essentially tolerant, though moderately critical, attitude toward Pietism. Being in the Calvinistic Tradition as modified by the Heidelberg catechism they could hardly be against a mode of life which in that tradition had long since been regarded as "biblical piety." By the same token, and under the watchful eyes of the Prussian government, they had to be circumspect in not opposing any ecclesiastical institution, including conventicles,[1] which would foster such piety. The attitude of the General Synod of Cleve, therefore, became more or less typical for all Reformed territories. In paragraph 61 of the minutes of the year 1674 it stipulated that the practice of piety is to be supported in the local congregations, that ministers must permit conventicles, and that individuals may invite their immediate neighbors into their houses for the purpose of reading the Bible, singing, praying, and repeating the morning sermon. On the other hand, more widely attended conventicles may not be held without the presence of the pastor. "In fact, all private conventicles must be conducted in a way which will not hinder public worship or bring it into disrepute. Furthermore, ministers and consistories shall have freedom to forbid anything which in their particular circumstances is not helpful or is dangerous, though it is otherwise permitted."[2]

The result of this rather tolerant official policy made it possible for any energetic and able pastor with pietistic inclinations to have his way. This was true even in territories under Palatine control, since the

[1] These came into being in German Reformed congregations ca. 1660. See E. Dresbach, *Pragmatische Kirchengeschichte der preussischen Provinzen Rheinland und Westfalen*, 1931, p. 586. At first they seem to have been gatherings in private homes under lay leadership. About the middle of that decade such conventicles were held under the supervision of Untereyck at Mühlheim a.R.

[2] Quoted by Dresbach, pp. 587-588.

Prussian government made use of every opportunity to improve its own image by interceding for what appeared to be oppressed religious minorities. Pietism being thus relatively free to develop in German Reformed territories it became a much stronger force within that communion during the early eighteenth century than has commonly been recognized.[1] Ever and again throughout the first part of that century Reformed synods were called upon to mediate between pietistic enthusiasm and the fears engendered by it among representatives of the established order. Such mediation was called for especially since the historic openness of Reformed Pietism to quietistic mysticism frequently took it to the very brink of separatism.

Indeed not a few people of considerable ability and popular appeal either had stepped across that brink, or were about to do so, during the early decades of the century under discussion. They had thus brought into existence separatistic movements which must always be kept in mind in a study of Reformed Pietism. The reason is, that the ex-Reformed separatists, on the one hand, had considerable influence upon Pietism within the Reformed congregations, and that, on the other hand, they magnified the apprehensions of the people committed to the ecclesiastical, theological, and ideological *status quo* within those congregations.

The oldest of these movements was Labadism, which has been covered elsewhere.[2] It still had not been forgotten in German Reformed territories, however, during the early eighteenth century, though it now seems to have played more the role of a spectre to be feared than that of a positive force for Christian piety. By this time the word "Labadism" had become a term which the more conservative Reformed Christians applied to their enemies very much the way they applied the terms "Arianism" and "Pelagianism."

More vital at this time was the separatistic movement in the Netherlands which arose early in the eighteenth century as a result of the coalescing of the followers of Jacob Verschuir (1680-1737) and of Pontian van Hattem (1641-1706).[3] Verschuir's faction was originally known as Verschuirists or Hebrews, the latter because their leader

---

[1] The whole subject needs extensive investigation.

[2] RI, p. 162f.

[3] See HPE, p. 375f; vol. 1, p. 324f; L. Knappert, *Geschiedenis der nederlandsche hervormde kerk gedurende de 18e en 19e eeuw*, 1912, pp. 28-31; A. Ypeij and J.J. Dermout, *Geschiedenis der nederlandsche hervormde kerk*, 1824, vol. 2, pp. 115-128. Ritschl refers to Jacob Verschuir as Johannes Verschuir, RTL, vol. 1, p. 324.

deemed a knowledge of Hebrew essential for the Christian life. Hattem's followers were originally known as Hattemists. Later the designations became fluid. The movement spawned considerable religious controversy which in time involved the whole Reformed Church of the Netherlands. Indeed it was considered so totally inimical to the interests of the ecclesiastical establishment that J. Roggeveen's edition of Hattem's works[1] was suppressed in Holland in 1732. Verschuir's works, too, made for incessant controversy, especially his *Truth in the Inward Parts or Experiential Theology*,[2] which came to be widely circulated and highly respected among "awakened" Protestants, both in the Netherlands and in the Reformed regions of Germany.

The primary reason for the strenuous opposition which Verschuir encountered in the Netherlands was the antinomian tendency implicit in his belief-system.[3] The latter was based upon the presupposition of absolute determinism. Not even God's will is free, he insisted. It is determined, rather, by his nature, which must be considered good. Because of such absolute necessity there can be no evil and no sin, since everything necessarily comes to be in a given way. Feelings of sinfulness or guilt on man's part, therefore, are simply an indication of a lack of faith in the absolute goodness of things. Christ's death, too, is essentially a demonstration of God's love for man, rather than the result of his displeasure over man's sinfulness. The controversy which resulted from the enthusiastic proclamation of these religious convictions, and which has been referred to above, gradually compacted the theology of the movement. As a result the Hattemists, as they were generally called during the early eighteenth century, came to be widely credited with three basic religious assertions : Firstly, they were said to believe that saving faith manifests itself in a religious trust so absolute that it admits of no doubts; secondly, that the elect have been justified in Christ before they have saving faith; and thirdly, that the elect person must leave everything to God, his own efforts in any direction being really quite meaningless.[4]

The appeal which Verschuir had for his contemporaries was related

---

1 *Den val van 's werelds Afgod ofte het geloove der heyligen, zegepralende over de Leere van eygen geregtigheid* etc., part 1, 1718; parts 2 and 3, 1719; part 4, 1727.

2 *Waerheydt in het Binnenste of bevindelijke godtgeledrtheit* etc., 1736. This was reprinted repeatedly during the eighteenth century and translated into German by J. Fehr in 1743.

3 Ypeij and Dermout, *op. cit.*, p. 121f.

4 HPE, p. 378f.

to his further insistence that the religiously concerned group of conventicle Protestants are God's chosen people from eternity. They know this to be true since they *experience* God's redemptive activity, while Orthodoxists know it only rationally. It is this experience which carries with it absolute trust in, and surrender to, the ways of Providence, and hence makes for the kind of release from all psychological tension which Hattemists claimed to have found. That such a mixture of Reformed theology, Pietism, and Spinozistic mysticism,[1] would seem very attractive in the unstable intellectual and social milieu of the eighteenth century is quite understandable. This it did; and not only to religious separatists, but to many members of the Reformed churches in the Netherlands and in Germany.

A third such separatistic movement which came out of Reformed Protestantism is connected with the name of Gerhard Tersteegen. Since it developed on German soil his particular fusion of Quietism and Pietism has been discussed elsewhere and need not detain us here.[2]

It is necessary, however, to call attention, at least, to one other movement, again within the Reformed churches of the Netherlands, which provided a certain background for the Pietism found among Reformed Protestants in Germany. It stemmed from Wilhelmus Schortinghuis (1700-1750),[3] whose *Inward Christianity*[4] became one of the most highly appreciated edificatory works in Reformed circles throughout the eighteenth century. As was so often the case, the same book was profoundly disturbing to many other members of his communion and therefore became the occasion for considerable controversy. Indeed, to the fathers of Utrecht Schortinghuis' literary adventures seemed so subversive of the Reformed position that they branded his beliefs as heretical and enjoined upon him perpetual silence, a command which they could hardly hope to be obeyed. On the other hand, a group of prominent preachers at Emden in Germany defended him. The result was an intellectual atmosphere which was theologically charged to a degree which forced all the Reformed authors of the day, including Lampe, to react to the issues in one way or another.

---

[1] See J. Serrijn, *Spinoza en de gereformeerde theologie zijner dagen*, 1919, p. 191f. According to Serrijn Willem Deurhoff (1650-1717) and Frederick van Leenhof (1647-1712) belonged to the same group.

[2] See p. 191f.

[3] HPE, pp. 421-464; Knappert, *op. cit.*, pp. 31-36.

[4] *Het innige Christendom, tot overtuiginge van onbsgnadigte, bestieringe en opwekkinge van begenadigte Zielen* etc., first published in 1740 and reprinted as late as 1858. For a good summary of the work see HPE, pp. 434-446.

One of the basic difficulties had to do with Schortinghuis' uncompromising experientialism. In this connection he had latched on to Verschuir and van Hattem, though in other respects his theology differed considerably from theirs. Making a radical distinction between literal[1] and experiential[2] knowledge of God he raised the spectre of complete religious subjectivism in the mind of his opponents. Thus in the varied attacks which were made upon him he was always accused of substituting the authority of his own feelings for that of the Bible. He, on the other hand, insisted, as he does in his preface, that the experience he is speaking of is merely the experience of the truth of God's Word, without which one is not a Christian. The second major emphasis for which he was profoundly censured was upon man's utter nothingness. God is all and man is nothing in the sense that the latter is totally dependent upon God in every aspect of his being and endeavor.[3] Thus Schortinghuis, too, came out where Verschuir had come out, namely, with the insistence that the Christian must surrender completely and joyfully to God's will. Christian experience, then, and an absolutely trustful acceptence of God's ways, was the twin axis around which his understanding of the meaning of personal Christianity revolved.

The story of Reformed Pietism in Germany as such begins with Theodor Untereyck of Bremen and Joachim Neander, one of the foremost hymn-writers of Protestantism. Since the life of both of them falls within the seventeenth century their contribution was discussed in a previous volume.[4] As a result of their labors the city of Bremen became one of the centers of Reformed Pietism in Germany and continued in that role during the first part of the eighteenth century. Other beginnings had also been made, however. Thus in the county of Moers Samuel Nethenus (1628-1700)[5] had represented the spirit of Willem Teellinck and Jadocus van Lodenstein,[6] attempting, with a certain amount of rashness, perhaps, what he hoped would be a new reformation. His influence, though more or less localized, had blended in with

---

1 *Het innige Christendom* etc., 4th ed., 1752, p. 11f. The term he uses is *letterlyk*.

2 *Ibid.*, p. 23f. The term he opposes to *letterlyk* is *bevindelik*.

3 *Ibid.*, p. 293, par. 4.

4 RI, pp. 169-174.

5 See HPE, pp. 466-469; J.I. Good, *History of the Reformed Church of Germany, 1620-1890*, 1894, pp. 333-338; GBL, vol. 2, pp. 367-397. His rather intemperate *Seufzendes Turteltäublein und Zions Tränenklage* etc., 1676, lists his indictments, and those of many others, of the evils which he felt were rampant in his communion.

6 RI, p. 127f and 141f.

many other efforts at a pietistic reformation of the Reformed churches in Germany. Within the territory of the synod of Mark County Wilhelm Dieterici (d. 1690) had worked with great devotion toward a definition of Reformed Christianity which is again reminiscent of Teellinck, Amesius, and other Puritans of an earlier day.[1] In the city of Emden, which for members of the Reformed churches was hallowed by memories of having been a place of refuge in great need, Ernst Wilhelm Buchfelder (1645-1711) had worked earnestly for the pietistic understanding of Reformed Protestantism as president of the Coetus, as had John Alardin (1639-1707) before him.[2]

The result of the efforts of these men, and of others of like spirit, was that at the beginning of the eighteenth century Pietism had made heavy inroads upon the Reformed churches of Germany as well as of Switzerland. As has been pointed out, synods approved the holding of conventicles as long as they became no occasion for separatistic activity. They enjoined upon their preachers the duty to catechize diligently, putting emphasis upon the practice of piety. The effort was made to make the Lord's Supper as meaningful as possible through adequate preparation of the communicants. Preachers were reminded to make the amendment of life, rather than theological polemics, the aim of their endeavor. Parents were made aware of their moral and religious responsibilities toward their children. And wherever possible the representatives of local government were expected to exemplify the pietistic ethic. In general, therefore, the message of Reformed Protestantism in Germany had become ethicized to an extent to which this had not yet happened in the Lutheran Communion. This state of affairs continued until the Enlightenment created the Neo-Pietism which needs to be discussed later.

Lampe, Mel, and Hottinger

The outstanding theological exponent of Reformed Pietism in Germany, and one of the foremost Reformed theologians of all times, was Friedrich Adolph Lampe (1683-1729).[3] He was born in the city of

[1] His *Klare und gründliche Abbildung eines rechtschaffenen Christen* etc. (vol. 1, 1680, vol. 2, 1690), which was approved by the theological faculty of Herborn, reached a considerable audience.

[2] For all of these see also RI, p. 174f.

[3] The fullest account of his life is found in O. Thelemann, *Friedrich Adolf Lampe. Sein Leben und seine Theologie*, 1868, pp. 3-149. See also GBL, vol. 2, pp. 398-435; RTL, vol. 1, pp. 427-454.

Detmold. Much of his early childhood was spent in the home of his maternal grandfather, who had experienced a religious conversion under Jadocus van Lodensteyn.[1] Thus the pietistic understanding of Reformed Protestantism was as natural to him as the air he breathed. Having lost both father and grandfather before he was ten years of age it was his uncle who took charge of his education. At the age of fifteen he was given the opportunity to attend the Reformed academy at Bremen. Here he decided to concentrate upon theology, in so far as the kind of pietistic theology which was taught at Bremen seemed to hold a certain promise for him. It was the same promise which drew him to Franeker in 1702, for here a similar intellectual atmosphere prevailed.

At Franeker Lampe went through a profound experience of conversion at the age of nineteen. In order to preserve its meaning for himself and for posterity he described it in a poem of 36 stanzas, which gives an excellent insight into the psychological processes which were at work.[2] His active career began the following year when he was made minister of a little congregation at Weeze near Cleve, an appointment which afforded him continued opportunity for study. After a relatively brief stay at Weeze and at Duisburg he accepted a pastorate at St. Stephen's Church in Bremen in 1709. From 1720 to 1727 he was active as professor of dogmatics and church history at Utrecht. Thereafter he returned to Bremen as pastor of St. Ansgar's Church and teacher at the academy.

Were we to write up the career of Lampe in detail it would be necessary to do so under the headings of preacher, teacher, and hymn-writer, for he made a notable contribution to Protestant history in all of these areas. As preacher he was eminently successful and greatly esteemed by the various congregations he served. His hymnody enriched Protestant worship in northwest Germany for decades to come.[3] As previously indicated historians of the German Reformed Church regard him as one of the greatest theologians produced by that tradition. His massive *Geheimnis des Gnadenbundes*[4] in six volumes, was

[1] RI, p. 141f.

[2] Most of the poem is reproduced by Thelemann, *op. cit.*, pp. 10-13.

[3] The most popular one of his hymns was translated into English by H. Mills. It begins, "My life is but a pilgrim-stand." A small volume of his hymns was published in 1726, and an expanded edition in 1731.

[4] *Geheimnis des Gnadenbunds, dem grossen Gott zu Ehren*, etc., 1712-1719. This work was reprinted many times.

used not only as a text book in various universities and theological academies, but as a favorite book of religious instruction in local congregations and in the homes of the laity. His *Milch der Wahrheit*[1] dominated catechetical instruction in German Reformed congregations for about a century. His extensive *Delineatio*[2] was a major attempt to fuse Coccejan federalism and biblicism with the ethical concerns of Pietism. In addition he produced historical, exegetical, controversial, and edificatory works in considerable number.[3] Perhaps the most influential of these was his *Brautschmuck*[4], a volume of sermons to be read in preparation for Holy Communion.

In so far as in Lampe Reformed Pietism reached its zenith of theological development in Germany it is a discussion of his theology, or rather a discussion of certain pertinent aspects of his theology, which are of major interest in this connection. To do this, however, it is necessary to throw at least a fleeting glimpse at the state of Reformed theology immediately prior to his productive years.

At the beginning of the eighteenth century the long and difficult controversy between the federal theology of Coccejus and the rejuvinated orthodoxy of Voetius[5] began to subside. The issues were being resolved in favor of the Coccejan approach. This was the case in the schools, at any rate, though in the local classes the situation was still fluid. At Utrecht, however, as at Leyden, Franeker, and in the Reformed academies of northwestern Germany, Orthodoxy was in full retreat, while Coccejan thought-forms were beginning to dominate the theological enterprise. There were two branches of Coccejan theology, however, which had evolved by this time. The one, represented chiefly at Leyden, tended to exhaust its energies in formal discussions of biblical and theological themes. As has so often been the case in theology, it had essentially become a game played by professional theologians having only minimal contact with the life of the ongoing Christian

---

[1] *Milch der Wahrheit, nach Anleitung des heidelbergischen Katechismus* etc., 1718. It, too, as well as his other primers for catechetical instruction, were reprinted many times.

[2] *Delineatio theologiae activae* etc., 1727. It also, together with Lampe's own German edition of 1728 (*Grundriss der tätlichen Gottesgelehrtheit*), was reprinted often. It was even translated into Dutch.

[3] For a list of his works, see AGLF-III, columns 1117-1119.

[4] *Der heilige Brautschmuck der Hochzeitsgäste des Lammes,* of which the 1741 ed. was available to me.

[5] RI, p. 113f.

community. The other line of development, represented in the schools which Lampe chose to attend (Bremen, Franeker), attempted to keep Coccejan theology oriented toward the vital concerns of the church by fusing it with Pietism.

The person who had already commenced upon such a fusion during the previous generation was the aforementioned Theodor Untereyck.[1] He had first come under the influence of Jadocus van Lodensteyn, the Pietist, and Voetius, the famed Reformed theologian who had tried to make Orthodoxy relevant to his age by incorporating pietistic precicianism in his system. Untereyck had then moved on, however, to study under Coccejan teachers at Duisburg, and ultimately under Coccejus himself at Leyden. When he was finally called to Bremen, therefore, he brought with him the settled conviction that the pietistic concerns of his earlier teachers and the Coccejan methodology make for the most satisfying theological combination. He saw to it, furthermore, that this theological point of view found entrance into the Reformed academy at Bremen through his friend Cornelius de Hase.

It was this theological atmosphere, then, in which Lampe achieved intellectual maturation. Accordingly he looked for his pietistic models to such men as William Teellinck, Lodensteyn, William à Brakel, and especially Untereyck,[2] whose successor he became at Bremen. For his theological frame-work, on the other hand, he looked to Coccejanism as transmitted to him by the mediating theologian Hermann Witsius (1636-1708), by Untereyck, and by his teachers at Bremen and Franeker, notably Johannes van der Waeyen (1676-1719) and Campegius Vitringa. The latter was the outstanding theological light at Franeker, in whose biblical exposition the older Reformed emphasis on practical piety and Coccejanism had been indissolubly welded together.

Accordingly, Lampe's basic theological methodology was thoroughly Coccejan. Because his Coccejanism was joined to Pietism, however, it gave him a base from which he could oppose both Orthodoxy, on the one hand, and the equally sterile kind of intellectual exercise sometimes referred to in his day as "pure" Coccejanism, on the other. From the Pietistic Tradition Lampe had inherited his over-riding concern for the religious welfare of the individual, which, on the model of the older Pietists in the Reformed Tradition, made his theology essentially a

---

1 RI, p. 169f.

2 His references to Untereyck always betray profound respect. See, for instance, the footnote in his *Geheimnis des Gnadenbunds*, 1751, vol. 1, p. 20.

rationale for the Christian life. For this concern he found a great deal of support in the Coccejan theology as well.[1] From the Pietists, too, he had received the initial impetus for biblical rather than dogmatic theology. Coccejan theology not only supported him in this, but in its system, based on the covenants, it gave him the key for what he took to be meaningful biblical interpretation. To Coccejus Lampe was especially indebted for his profound appreciation of the concept of development, which the latter applied in modified form to biblical revelation, to the history of the church, to history in general, as well as to the personal history of each individual. In applying the Coccejan methodology to the individual Christian life he was able to present with renewed vigor the emphasis of Zwingli and Calvin upon religious growth, which in the grip of Orthodoxy had always been in danger of being merely a theologumenon in the tomes on Reformed theology. Last but not least, in the concept of contracts implicit in Coccejan federalism man is truly given an opportunity to be captain of his ship. In this Lampe found theological justification for coming down hard upon man's ability and responsibility to practice piety and so to gain the rewards held in store for him by a gracious God.

The most readily apparent characteristic of the more formal aspects of Lampe's theological endeavor is his deliberate effort to suit the form of his theology to its content. Hence, while the content of it is strictly oriented toward the Christian life the form cannot be such as to suit only the tastes of the professional theologians. On the basis of this consideration he meant to continue the tradition of Reformed Pietists, which was perhaps most fully developed in William à Brakel's *True Service of God*, of writing theology in language which the layman can understand. He thus tried earnestly to avoid all technical terms and to put even the most profound concepts into a linguistic form which would be meaningful in the local churches. Because of this Lampe was never given the credit which he deserves by professionals in the field. On the other hand, this is also the reason why Lampe's influence has been so amazingly pervasive within the Reformed Tradition.

In speaking of the content of his theology it is not possible within the limits of this study to cover the whole range of his thought. For this a major effort would be required.[2] Our interest is confined to a concise

---

[1] See the very fine thesis done at Yale by C.S. McCoy, *The Covenant Theology of Johannes Coccejus*, 1956, p. 301.

[2] Such an effort should be made in so far as Thelemann's work does not constitute a critical study.

discussion of those aspects of his theology only which relate to the study in hand. In the nature of the case of course, such an approach does go to what is undoubtedly the center of his theological perspective. By common consent of his interpreters this is contained in the first volume of his previously mentioned *Secret of the Covenant of Grace.*

The volume in question consists of fourteen chapters, the first six of which deal with the more general problems related to a federal approach to Christian theology. Immediately relevant to our endeavor are chapters seven to fourteen, which speak of matters which are directly related to the religious experience of the individual. In chapter seven he thus takes up the question of election, and more importantly, the subject of "effective election." This he defines as "that work of God and of his Spirit through which the elect sinner is not only invited and convinced by means of the Word, but also rationally and effectively motivated to think earnestly about the alteration of his condition" (232-233). The "effectiveness" of such election comes about in five steps, namely : The external use of the means of grace, notably the reading or hearing of the Word (239-240); man's heed of the World (241-242); conviction wrought by the Spirit with reference to the Word and human experience (242-243); enlightenment of man's reason (244-246); and finally the inclination of the will not to spurn God's offered grace, an act which follows naturally from the enlightenment mentioned (247f). In all of this, of course, there is the tension between the gracious offer of a sovereign God and man's response, which one finds in all Reformed Pietism, and which found support of Coccejan theology. At the same time, however, the chapter is pervaded by a strongly hortatory note to the effect that the sinner must make every effort not to thwart the divinely wrought impulse within him (264). His eternal welfare really depends upon his response.

The same hortatory tone pervades the eighth chapter, which is on saving faith. The latter is defined as "that gracious work of God and of his Spirit through which the divinely elected sinner is rationally and effectively inclined to accept Christ only and wholly as a perfect Savior, according to the testimony of the Gospel" (273). The word "acceptance" here is no accident, of course. Lampe uses it after a lengthy discussion of various kinds of faith and then dilates on its meaning (280f). He uses it, on the one hand, because he feels that it is a biblical term (280f), and secondly, because it expresses most fully the biblical meaning of saving faith. According to the biblical witness, he believes, such faith is nothing else but the hand by which man grasps

Christ and all his salvatory meaning (287). The very decided effort which such a response requires is detailed in the rest of the chapter. It calls for a willingness of letting go of everything else, of concentrating all of one's desires upon Christ, of self-denial, and of earnest prayer.

The result of it all is the elect sinner's re-birth, which is covered in chapter nine. Lampe's rigidly developmental, or progressivist, understanding of man's relation to God is especially in evidence here, though it intrudes upon every aspect of his theology. Accordingly the thinks of the term "conversion" as covering the whole process of progressive religious maturation which is experienced by the individual Christian. Of this process the word "re-birth" designates the beginning, while the term "sanctification" stands for its continuance. In this context re-birth is defined as "that gracious work of God and of his Spirit, through which the elect sinner is effectively, wholly, and instantaneously changed toward the good (*zum Guten verändert*) and is really brought from the state of corruption into the state of grace" (360). Again, however, while God is thought of as giving the initial impulse and supplying the power our author's emphasis is on what man must do to turn from sin and toward God. Hence the chapter concludes with a discussion of the means that are necessary to effect the required change in a person's motivational center, which is part of the new birth (416f).

Quite as important as re-birth is the continuance of the process of religious maturation, which is discussed in chapter eleven under "sanctification."[1] The latter is conceived as "consisting in nothing else but in the continuation of that change which was begun in re-birth, or, in the growth of the new life" (485). Here the Calvinistic principle of religious growth is set forth as the only proper motivational spring for religious living, in so far as such is the will of God. This growth proceeds in three stages, the first being marked by the kind of incessant struggle which is best described in martial terms (491f). Presently the Christian comes to the second stage, namely that of a new obedience (507f), in which he is not free from temptation, but in which he does have the equipment to practice the Christian virtues, and notably that of love for the brother. How seriously Lampe took life in this stage, in which most Christians remain, is evidenced by the fact that for such people he wrote his *Delineation of Active Theology*, which is in essence a lengthy, often astute, and eminently practical discussion of the traditional New Testament virtues as they apply to the conditions of

[1] Chapter 10 is on justification and is, therefore, only indirectly related to our subject.

life which the individual encounters. The highest stage is the experiential aspect of what he calls "evangelical perfection" (531f) which, he says, he has difficulty in describing because he himself has not reached it. It seems to be a condition, achieved by relatively few people in this life, in which their whole existence is completely conformed to God's will. For all Christians, however, this stage posits an ideal to which they must constantly aspire.

Chapters 12 and 13 properly deal with the rewards which the Christian can expect for all of his vigilance and effort. In the former Lampe discusses the sense of perfect security, based on God's promise, which the Christian may have as he faces the ambiguities of human existence, as well as God's expectation of human perfection. This he does under the traditional Reformed concept of "sealing." In chapter 13 he describes, again as best he can, the state of ultimate bliss, which is God's highest gift to all of his elect.

Even this final reward, however, our author envisions in stages — a foretaste on earth, the beginnings of its fullness in death, the complete realization of it after the resurrection (646). Chapter 14 is essentially a resume of what has been said and an application made in the earnest hope of motivating the sinner to respond to God's grace extended to him in the second covenent.[1]

The remaining aspects of Lampe's theology, which are significant in this context, are logically related to what has been said. For that reason they may he summarized briefly. Thus he began his ministry with an ecclesiology based on the model of the primitive church, which made it possible for him to be immensely critical of his own communion as he found it in his day.[2] In fact, in counseling earnest Christians to stay away from the Lord's Supper, if the latter is administered by pastors who are "the brothers of Judas," he came close to separatism. Fortunately for the Reformed Church, however, the radical idealism of his youth was gradually tempered until it was possible for him to find many "precious items" in the life of the external church.[3] Still his interest in the reformation of the Reformed Church, as he knew it both in the

---

[1] In the remaining volumes of his *Geheimnis* etc. Lampe attempts to flesh out his theological system by taking up in more detail certain pragmatically important theological themes. Thus in vol. 3, p. 266f, he discusses the typological importance of certain events in the history of ancient Israel, while in vol. 6, p. 987f, he gives a lengthy exposition of the teaching of Jesus Christ and its contemporary significance.

[2] See his *Grosse Vorrechte des unglückseligen Apostels Judas Ischariot* etc., 1713.

[3] See his *Geheimnis*, *op. cit.*, vol. 2, p. 74f.

Netherlands and in Germany, never abated. It was always his concern that in its life and in its witness the church must provide the kind of creative fellowship in which the religious maturation of the inidvidual Christian can best take place. In the interest of such a goal he opposed, furthermore, Orthodoxy's continued preoccupation with "purity of doctrine" based on an exclusivistic interpretation of the accepted confessions. It was the same aim which caused him to brave the ire of both Reformed and Lutheran Orthodoxists by supporting unionistic efforts between the two communions.

Reference should be made here also to the fact that Lampe shared the chiliastic hopes which were present in the theologies of Spener and Bengel, as well in the thinking of many separatists and Neo-Pietists, and which found support in Coccejanism.[1] The external causes of this must undoubtedly be sought in the relatively rapid socio-cultural changes which are characteristic of the age, and which, on the one hand, caused great anxiety and frustration, while, on the other, they held out the promise of new hopes and expectations. Sensitive to the need for a philosophy of history which could afford his contemporaries comfort and hope in difficult days Lampe, like many of the Pietists of his day, seized upon Coccejus' sevenfold scheme of dividing the history of the Christian enterprise. The sixth dispensation, which according to our author began at the time of the Reformation and which was about to come to an end in his own day, was, of course, full of suffering and tribulation for God's people, and especially for the Reformed segment of that people. Such trials will continue he believed, into the seventh age which is about to begin.[2] In God's time, however, the church will reap all the fruits of the promised millenium before another period of trial begins and history is finally consummated. The redeeming feature in all of this speculation is, however, that Lampe never permitted it to become an end in itself. All of it is written essentially from the point of view implicit in the Apocalypse of St. John. It is meant in other words, to be a book of inspiration and an exhortation to faithfulness, rather than a basis for fanciful projections about the meaning of contemporary events. That is why the author ends his discussion with a universal call to watchfulness and prayer.[3]

---

1 In his *Geheimnis*, vol. 5, p. 860f he gives a full treatment of his understanding of history.

2 *Ibid.*, p. 819f.

3 *Ibid.*, pp. 875-877.

More or less inadvertently Lampe was drawn into the quarrel occasioned by the intemperate criticisms hurled at the Reformed Church by Peter Friedrich Detry. The latter was suspected of being a disciple of the separatist Christian Anton Römeling, whom the Lutherans had deprived of his pastoral office at Hamburg in 1710. Lampe had to fend off, furthermore, occasional accusations of heterodoxy. By some of his peers he was especially suspected of being too close to his teacher Hermann Alexander Roëll (1653-1718), who attempted to combine Cartesian philosophy and Coccejan theology, and who in doing so came up with a rather novel interpretation of the eternal generation of the Son. In general, however, our author was successful in avoiding controversy and in investing his energies positively.

Long before his day William Perkins had insisted that "theology is the science (*scientia*) of living blessedly forever," and Amesius had said, *Theologia est doctrina Deo vivendi*.[1] Through Lampe this understanding of the theological task, wedded now to the Coccejan methodology, was fostered within the Reformed territories of Germany. Thus it helped materially to deal the final blow to an expiring Orthodoxy. Because of its strongly ethical orientation, furthermore, our author's theology stood out in stark relief against the antinomian influences of the Hattem-Verschuir movement, while its rigidly biblical orientation helped the German Reformed churches to fend off the subjectivistic tendencies emanating from Schortinghuis. Supported by a life of transparent piety and of singular concern for the welfare of all men Lampe's approach to Protestant theology came to be widely regarded as the norm in German Reformed circles. No less popular were his major treatises in certain sections of Switzerland,[2] while his work at Utrecht was intrumental in projecting his influence into the Netherlands as well.[3]

Representing essentially the same theological point of view as Lampe was Conrad Mel (1666-1733) who locally, at least, achieved a certain eminence in a number of roles and whose edificatory books were widely read in German Reformed circles.[4] He was born at Gudensberg

---

[1] RI, pp. 53, 134.

[2] P. Wernle, *Der schweizerische Protestantismus im XVIII Jahrhundert*, 1923-1925, vol. 1, pp. 444-445.

[3] Even Knappert, who erroniously treats him as preeminently a mystic, and whose rigidly confessional approach is, therefore, quite unfriendly, cannot ignore him (*op. cit.*, pp. 22-27).

[4] For a list of his works see AGLF-IV, columns 1354-1358.

in lower Hesse and studied at Bremen and Groningen. At Bremen he, like Lampe, had come under the influence of Untereyck, whose disciple he remained for the rest of his life. After several pastorates, as well as a temporary lectureship at the University of Königsberg, he came to Hersfeld in Hesse, where he remained from 1704 to the end of his life. He was inspector of the diocese and rector of the local academy, and became presently regarded as eminently successful in both capacities. Indeed, under his leadership the Reformed academy at Hersfeld became so popular that for a season it overshadowed the reputation of the University of Marburg. Students came not only to study theology under him, but scientific disciplines as well (notably physics and mechanics). Because of his tremendous interest in foreign missions he was made a member of the Society for the Propagation of the Gospel in Foreign Parts in 1706. In turn he attempted to promote the missionary enterprise through his own writings.[1] On the model of Halle, furthermore, he established an orphanage with the blessing of Countess Marie Amalie von Cassel, whose name it bore.

Mel wielded his greatest influence, however, through the writing of edificatory literature. Not aspiring to being a professional theologian he decided to invest his literary gifts in this way. The result was a number of books of sermons which went through several editions.[2] On the basis of his Coccejan assumptions he enjoyed especially to give typological explanations of Old Testament passages. Typical here is his explanation of the meaning of the Solomonic Temple with its furnishings.[3] In order to promote a piety which was both theologically and scientifically informed he wrote on ethics as well as on physics. By far his most widely read book, however, was his *Delight of the Saints in Jehovah.*[4] It was a book of prayers which first came out in 1715, and which had gone through sixteen or more editions by 1783. Many of the prayers are oriented toward man's difficult and anxiety producing situations. Thus there is a prayer of a soldier (122f), a prayer of a pregnant woman (103f), and a prayer for a blessed end (350f). The whole book is an eloquent testimony to the warm, humane, and transparently sincere piety of the author. Though the prayers recognize

[1] See his *Missionarius evangelicus* etc., 1711.

[2] One of the best loved of these was his *Posaune der Ewigkeit, oder Predigten vom Tode* etc., 1697, which was available for study in the Dutch edition of 1752.

[3] *Salems Tempel, oder Beschreibung des herrlichen Tempels Salomonis* etc., 1724.

[4] *Die Lust der Heiligen an Jehovah* etc., 1715. Available to the author in the Dutch edition of 1743.

life's ambiguities they are calculated to inspire cheerful confidence in a wise and loving God who supplies the strength to will and to do what is ultimately best. Little wonder the work came to be referred to affectionately as simply the *Mellenbuch*.

In speaking of Reformed Pietists in Germany during the early part of the eighteenth century the name of Johann Heinrich Hottinger (1681-1750) should not be omitted.[1] While his work as a scholar was concentrated upon the study of Hebrew he did manage to write a whole series of edificatory works which had some circulation in Reformed pietistic circles. He was born at Zürich, studied at Geneva and Amsterdam, and began his teaching career at Marburg. In the meantime he had come under the influence of inspirationism. As a result he became embroiled in a controversy concerning the authority of biblical vs. subjective revelations. Though he held that personal revelations have validity only with regard to matters on which Scripture is not clear his explanation was not sufficient for the authorities. For that reason he was dismissed in 1717, became pastor of a Reformed congregation at Frankenthal in the Palatinate, and in 1721 professor at Heidelberg. His sympathies were thoroughly pietistic as is evidenced among other things, by the fact that at Marburg he had opened an orphan school after the pattern of Halle. With reference to this endeavor he wrote his tract on *Christian Mercy*,[2] in which he advocated the position that active love is necessary for salvation. Of some importance, too, is his *Christian Manual*[3] which was republished several times. In it he follows the older Reformed Pietists in giving instructions as to how the practice of piety is to be carried throughout every day. Compared to Lampe, or even Mel, however, his contribution to Reformed Pietism seems to have been limited.

The Pietism of men like Untereyck, Neander, Lampe, and Mel reached its high water mark within the Reformed territories of Germany during the first few decades of the eighteenth century and remained a recognizable element within that segment of German Protestantism throughout the rest of the century. The pietistic literature which had

---

[1] For references to his life and work see H. Heppe, *Kirchengeschichte beider Hessen*, 1876, vol. 2, pp. 335-337; AGLF-II, columns 2157-2160. A list of his works is found in columns 2158-2160.

[2] *Christliche Barmherzigkeit, oder ausführliche Verhandlung von der zum geistlichen und ewigen Leben nötigen Pflicht der wahren und tätigen Liebe*, etc., 1715.

[3] *Christliches Manual, oder Anleitung wie ein Christ den ganzen Tag vor Gott wandeln soll* etc., 1724.

been produced in Reformed circles — theological treatises, biblical expositions, prayer books, hymns, and guides for religious living — continued to be a source of inspiration to ministers and laymen alike. Often the use which was made of this edificatory literature by the laity was indiscriminate, so that works by Lampe and Teerstegen, Untereyck and Schortinghuis, Mel and Horch were put side by side upon the shelf and valued equally.

Theological Transition

As the century progressed a new understanding of Pietism began to make itself felt both within the Reformed and the Lutheran communions. It is sufficiently different from what has hitherto been described to warrent the term "Neo-Pietism." In conclusion, therefore, it is necessary to give some attention to this new phenomenon.

In the background here is that immensely complex movement in western culture which is known as the Enlightenment. It resulted from a widely diffused intellectual ferment during the late 17th century caused by the relatively rapid expansion of western man's horizons in every direction — scientific, geographical, political, as well as economic. In an attempt to understand himself and his role vis-a-vis the forces that seemed to shape his destiny he found himself thrown back upon his own resources. Among these it seemed to be his rationality which contained the greatest promise, not only to comprehend, but also to direct the historic process of which he knew himself to be a part. The result was rationalism, or the belief in reason as the most reliable means for solving man's varied dilemmas. Characteristically, then, this movement addressed itself not to the theoretical problems which were of interest chiefly to professional philosophers, but to burning issues relative to man's own individual or corporate existence in the world in which he found himself. This is true whether we think of Sir Isaac Newton's *Principia Mathematica* (1687), or John Locke's *Letters on Toleration* (1689) or later Lord Shaftesbury's *Characteristics of Men, Manners, Opinions, and Times* (1711).

That man's religious endeavors could not be exempted from the spirit of the times is to be expected. To make sure that this would not be the case John Locke wrote his *Reasonableness of Christianity* in 1695, to be followed by John Toland's *Christianity not Mysterious* (1696). Though in what was regarded as a manifestation of righteous anger the Irish House of Commons consigned Toland's work to the flames the tide could not be stopped. Deism with its naive trust in "reason," or in that which seemed reasonable at the time, spread through England and her North American colonies and became ever more radically atheistic. It spread, furthermore into France, where it issued in the natural religion of Jean Jacques Rousseau's *Emile* and the violently anti-Christian attitude of Voltaire's *Dictionaire Philosophique.* Toward the end of the century it helped to bring about that ideological holocaust known as the French Revolution.

In Germany, on the other hand, the Enlightenment took a different turn. In its religious phase especially, with which we are mainly concerned here, it remained far more conservative. The first prominent impulses toward a new understanding of Christianity in central Europe came from the philosopher Christian Wolff (1679-1754). He was a close student of Leibnitz. Yet, he went beyond his master in working out the implications of the Leibnitzian philosophy, and in doing so introduced considerable clarity and preciseness. While Wolff was appreciative, furthermore, of the rationalistic developments in England and France, he deliberately maintained a positive attitude toward the historic Christian faith. Accordingly he set himself the task of showing that what he regarded as the revealed insights of the Bible and the claims of reason, as understood by his progressive contemporaries, were really the same. This is the intent of his *Rational Thoughts of God, the World, and the Soul of Man,*[1] and later more fully of his *Natural Theology.*[2]

With Leibnitz, and in conscious opposition to Descartes, Wolff assumed that the cosmic process is thoroughly teleological. It moves according to an order predetermined by God and toward the divinely ordained end of his own glory. The world in which we find ourselves is, moreover, the best of worlds, in so far as it is the world which is being created by a good God out of an infinite number of possibilities. Evil, therefore, is a metaphysical necessity, it being simply that state of imperfection in any given segment of the total process which must necessarily obtain before the ultimate goal is reached. Man's spirit, too, has God for its Creator. For that reason it finds its greatest happiness if it willingly identifies itself with the natural law which is apparent to it in the whole realm of God's creative activity. Essentially, therefore, piety consists in acting rationally, i.e., in harmony with the nature

---

[1] *Vernünftige Gedanken von Gott, der Welt, und der Seele des Menschen,* 1720.

[2] *Theologia naturalis methodo scientifica pertractata,* 1739.

of things, while sin consists in acting contrary to that which seems right under the same set of assumptions. Since God is the author of both reason and revelation the two cannot contradict each other. The truths established by reason and supported by revelation, if heeded by man, will afford him that happiness which the Creator has intended for him. Man's goal, therefore, is happiness, and the way to it is a life of rational conformity with the law of nature.

It is not difficult to see that during an incipiently humanistic age this was an understanding of the Christian message which was felt to have a great deal to commend it. It made it possible for theologians, pastors, and laity alike to regard themselves as being faithful to the Christian tradition, on the one hand, while on the other they could pride themselves upon being utterly relevant to the new age that was dawning. Accordingly sincere and earnest men, such as G.B. Bilfinger (1693-1750)[1] and I.G. Canz (1690-1753)[2] at Tübingen, took it up enthusiastically and recommended it to their contemporaries with much success. Associated with these men was a whole group of so called transitional theologians[3] who, each according to his own gifts and interests, had set for himself essentially the same theological task. Many of these were men who had studied at Halle and had absorbed the bridge building attitude of Johann Franz Buddeus (1667-1729). Prominent among them were J.G. Reinbeck, (1683-1741), whose multi-volume *Considerations*[4] more or less dominated the religious scene in Berlin, and most especially S.J. Baumgarten (1706-1757), who took over the duties of director of the theological seminary at Halle upon Lange's death (1744).[5]

The transitional theologians who recommended Wolff to their generation did not realize, or wish to realize, the possibilities of radical change in theological method which were implicit in the Wolffian system. Wolff had indeed succeeded in reconciling faith and reason

[1] See his *Dilucidationes philosophicae de Deo, anima humana, mundo et generalibus rerum affectionibus*, 1725, a work which was even read in France and Italy and which was put on the papal index in 1734.

[2] See his *Philosophiae Leibnitianae et Wolfianae usus in Theologia*, 1728, in which he insists that revelation is *supra rationem*, never *contra rationem*. A natural sequence was his *Disciplinae morales omnes*, 1739, in which he attempted to harmonize a revealed and natural ethic.

[3] Later this theological stance comes to be referred to as "rational orthodoxy."

[4] *Betrachtungen über die in der Augsburgischen Confession enthaltenen göttlichen Wahrheiten*, 1731-1741.

[5] We might also mention J.E. Carpov (1699-1768) and J.D. Michaelis (1717-1791).

for his generation and in making traditional Christian insights relevant once more. At the same time, however, he had shifted the ultimate criterion of the validity of religious insights from revelation to reason; he had substituted a natural ethic for a revealed ethic; and he had virtually transformed man's interest in eternal salvation into mere desire for temporal happiness. Theology had, in fact, become anthropology, and in the process whole areas covered by traditional Christian theology had been set aside as irrelevant and meaningless for modern man. In the course of German theological development it was the so called Neologists who adopted this radical alternative, disseminating their theological reductionism from lecture halls and pulpits alike.

One of the major representatives of Neology was Johann Joachim Spalding (1714-1804),[1] whose little book *Meditation Concerning Man's Destiny*[2] may be considered the classic expression of the kind of piety advocated by the Neologists. It bespeaks the cosmopolitan urbanity of its author, who was as much at home in translating Shaftesbury as he was in entertaining the Swiss Pietists Lavater, Hess, and Füssli. In it he first dismisses the claims of the senses (*Sinnlichkeit*)[3] and praises the joys of the spirit (18f). The energies of the latter must, he feels, be concentrated preeminently upon the gaining of virtue (19f). Such a quest is the essence of true religion (24f) and is sure of its eternal reward (27f). The heart of his faith and piety is expressed in the following passages : "My worth and my happiness shall consist only in this, that the highest claims of truth, unsullied by the tumult of the passions and by selfish desires, shall alone guide my actions; that a pure sense (*Empfindung*) of that which is seemly may truly constitute my highest obligation, and that thus I may generally, and in every moment of my life, be that which is determined by my own nature and by the general nature of things" (23). "I confidently await, therefore, a still distant series of times, which will constitute the full harvest of that

---

[1] Others were : J.G. Töllner (1724-1774), G.S. Steinbart (1738-1800), W.A. Teller (1734-1804), and J.C. Söderlin (1734-1807). The two best discussions of Spalding's theology are H. Nordmann's *Die Theologie Johann Joachim Spaldings*, 1929, and J. Schollmeier's *Johann Joachim Spalding. Ein Beitrag zur Theologie der Aufklärung*, 1967. For literature on him see also A. Uckley's "Johann Joachim Spalding, 1714-1804," in *Pommerische Lebensbilder*, ed. by W. Menn, vol. 5, 1966, pp. 110-122.

[2] *Betrachtung über die Bestimmung des Menschen*, 1748. The book became very popular, going through thirteen editions and catapulting its author into national prominence. It was so highly appreciated at the Prussian court that Queen Elizabeth Christine, wife of Frederick the Great, translated it into French in 1776.

[3] *Ibid.*, 1908 ed. by Horst Stephan, p. 16f.

which is presently sown, and which, by means of a general and true recompense, will justify the wisdom which supervises the whole" (28). Christian piety had thus become a confident and complete adjustment to a stoic understanding of the general rightness of things, which in this life and the next will necessarily bring the happiness for which man was created.[1] It was based on an utterly optimistic faith which simply averted its gaze from the darker aspect of human existence and made man alone the captain of his ship.

Following hard upon the heels of the Wolffian Enlightenment in Germany were the beginnings of what is generally spoken of as German Idealism. The latter manifested itself first in a literary movement usually referred to as *Sturm und Drang*, then moved on to the classicism of Goethe and Schiller, and, toward the end of the century to the early romanticism of Schlegel, Tieck, Novalis, and Schleiermacher. In the area of philosophy the more developed stages of the same movement manifested themselves in the critical approach of Kant, and later in the speculative idealism of Fichte, Schelling, and Hegel.

From the point of view of this discussion it is especially the *Sturm und Drang* phase of the movement which is of significance. Though much discussed in literary journals the genius of the *Sturm und Drang* period is difficult to delineate. It was in essence a protest of the younger generation against the hegemony of the prevailing rationalism. The emphasis was upon man's inner experience, upon the legitimacy and significance of feeling, upon the freedom of the individual to express himself vis-a-vis accepted artistic, attitudinal, intellectual, or behavioral norms. It made room for the irrational aspects of man's experience and for his elemental needs. The movement raised its voice for the first time in Friedrich Gottlieb Klopstock's *Messiah* (in process of publication from 1748-1773), in which traditional materials are freely handled to express the fullness of the poet's own experience of God. On the level of traditional Christian theology it issued in the works of Johann Georg Hamann (1730-1788), who made his radical conversion experience of 1758 the basis for his irrational biblical realism. The *Sturm und Drang* movement reached its final religious development in the student of Hamann and admirer of Klopstock, Johann Gottfried Herder (1744-1803), who utterly eschewed the idea of an extra-mundane God, prefer-

[1] For a full elaboration of these themes see his lengthy volume of *Predigten,* third ed., 1775.

ring to concentrate upon divine activity in the process of historical evolution. In that spirit he wrote : "All meaningless fear vanishes when hope, cheerful and clearheaded, becomes completely aware of a creation, in the minutest segment of which, all of God is present with his wisdom and goodness, and works with his undivided and indivisible divine power according to the nature of this segment of creation."[1]

The Neo-Pietists, who need to be discussed presently, grew up and lived in an intellectual atmosphere in which there was a lively dialogue between the representatives of traditional concepts, attitudes, and values and the devotees of the rationalistic and empiricist cults which have been mentioned. The result was that they became aware of both new enemies and new friends. Amazing as this may seem, therefore, the old enemy of Pietism, namely Orthodoxy in both the Lutheran and the Reformed communions, now became more nearly an ally than an opponent. Both Pietism and the older Orthodoxy, in so far as the latter persisted,[2] saw in the rise of Neology a common threat to the traditional understanding of the nature and message of Christianity to which they both meant to adhere. In the *Sturm und Drang* spirit of the day Pietism, on the other hand, had unexpectedly found support for its central thrust. After all, both movements were empiricist in nature, though in different senses, of course. What happened, therefore, was that Pietists during the second part of the 18th century found themselves forced to reject rationalism because of its shift from revelation to reason as the principle of ultimate religious and moral authority. In doing so they found an ally in the popular empiricism, though in the last analysis, they had to reject many aspects of this empiricism as well, because of its ever more blatant anchorage in human experience alone. This they did reluctantly, however, always regarding Neology as the chief enemy.[3]

Neo-Pietism, then, as understood in this discussion is that segment of

---

[1] Quoted by Baron von Brockdorf, *Die deutsche Aufklärungsphilosophie*, 1926, p. 78.

[2] Orthodoxy during the latter part of the eighteenth century was represented especially by J.B.E. Carpzov (1720-1803), J.M. Gooze (b. 1717), and in more latidutinarian form by J.F.S. Seiler (1733-1807).

[3] Originally Pietists were thoroughly antagonistic toward Wolff. This is illustrated by the controversy with him of the Halle theologians, notably Lange and Breithaupt, a quarrel into which even the irenical J.F. Buddeus (1667-1729) of Jena was drawn, and which finally led to the ouster of Wolff from Halle in 1723. Wolff's return to Halle in 1740, on the other hand, illustrates the change which had come over Pietism. At this time opposition at Halle and elsewhere was no longer directed at Wolff himself, many of whose insights now seemed acceptable, but at his radical followers, the so called Neologists.

the Pietistic Tradition which during the second part of the eighteenth century was, on the one hand, in reaction against the Enlightenment, while, on the other hand, it accommodated itself to the spirit of the new age. Its leaders, supported by the remaining Orthodoxists, now stood resolutely against the autonomy of the human spirit and for biblical revelation as final authority for faith and life; against a natural ethic and for a revealed ethic; against the reduction of Christian theology to reasonable principles of human conduct and for the biblical affirmations about God's redemptive activity; against the trend of positing a wholly immanent deity and for belief in a living God who transcends his creation. It stood, furthermore, against the prevailing optimism regarding man's nature and for the need of radical change at the very center of his being; as well as against the shallow eudaemonism which had begun to dominate western man's private and corporate life and for the reality of the eschatological dimension of human existence, which makes happiness the ultimate, not the immediate, goal of the salvatory process.

At the same time, however, Neo-Pietism manifested a new openness toward the world in which it was called upon to witness. It took seriously the whole range of human needs — intellectual, esthetic, emotional, social. Its representatives were sensitive to the impulses which came from contemporary literature. They felt a deep affinity with the spirit of Goethe and immersed themselves in Kant in the hope of being able to defend their religious perspective more successfully. They were impatient with denominational and political boundaries, looking to other Christian communions and other cultures for new insights. They thrilled at the newly gained insights into the immensity of the universe, while they bowed with profound reverence before its Creator. With religious awe they recognized the mysteries of the physical world, while they rejoiced about man's increasing skill in penetrating those mysteries. They enjoyed the singing of the birds, the beauty of the landscape, and the exhileration that comes from human love and friendship. Some of them even shared the concerns of the contemporary theatre. They, too, were optimistic regarding the future. It was an optimism, however, based upon faith in the greatness and goodness of a living God who is active in history, rather than in man's ability to master his destiny. It was an optimism, furthermore, which sought the cause of a better tomorrow in the religious renewal of individuals, rather than in the myth of man's innate goodness.

Early Representatives

As has been indicated, the seeds of the new Pietism were already noticeable in the theology of men like Dippel and Zinzendorf. They were present, too, in Oetinger, who, in conscious opposition to the Enlightenment, hoped to develop a total worldview which would be congenial to his age and yet based on biblical revelation alone. They became much more explicit, however, in the physician Samuel Collenbusch (1724-1803) and his extensive circle of friends. Collenbusch, together with his contemporary Urlsperger, may be considered the bridge between the old and the new Pietism in Germany. As such they differed from the earlier Pietism by reacting dominantly against the Enlightenment, while borrowing their apologetic tools, in part at least, from the people against whom they preached and wrote. They differed from the later Neo-Pietists, on the other hand, in so far as the latter were far more indebted to the *Sturm und Drang* spirit than either Collenbusch or Urlsperger.

Collenbusch was born at Wichlinghausen near Barmen, went through an experience of religious conversion in his eighteenth year, and studied medicine at Duisburg and Strassburg. At the completion of his studies he took up the practice of medicine, first at Duisburg, and after 1784 at Barmen. Like his older contemporary Dippel, however, his real interest was in theology.[1] In his middle thirties he came in contact with the Pietists of Württemberg, notably Bengel, Oetinger, and Johann Ludwig Fricker. As a result, his theology was thoroughly re-oriented in his 36th year. Henceforth he became an enthusiastic, dedicated, and very successful advocate of the pietistic approach to the Christian Gospel. Though his religious background was Lutheran he was especially influential among the Reformed Protestants of the lower Rhine region. His two most outstanding friends, who rather closely shared his theological perspective, were Johann Gerhard Hasenkamp (1736-1777)[2] and

[1] For an extensive discussion of it see F.W. Krug, *Die Lehre des Doktor Collenbusch*, 1846. An excellent article on Collenbusch is found in RE, vol. 4, pp. 233-241. Ritschl's discussion of him is marred by his heavy bias (RTL, vol. 1, pp. 565-582). His best known theological work is his *Erklärung biblischer Wahrheiten*, which was published posthumously in nine sections, 1807f.

[2] He studied at the academy of Lingen, but was largely selftaught. In 1766 he became rector of the Reformed academy at Duisburg. During his early days he was under the influence of Tersteegen, but later became a disciple of Collenbusch. Because of his opposition to the doctrine of predestination, and his friendly attitude toward the Lutherans (the Hasenkamps being Reformed) he became involved in severe controversy with

Gottfried Menken (1768-1831).[1] By the latter the impulses of Collenbusch's Pietism were mediated to the so called Revival Movement (*Erweckungsbewegung*) of the early nineteenth century.

Like most church-related Pietists Collenbusch was given to a strict biblicism. On the basis of such a biblicism he began with the assumption that by comparing passage with passage it is possible to come up with an internally consistent theology.[2] In his case, however, such a "theology" was conceived in the broadest possible terms. What he really meant by it was a total world-view, which in contradistinction to that of the Enlighteners was thought to be based on revelation rather than reason, and which, therefore, had divine sanction. Central to that world-view was the belief that God who created the world governs it in proportionately expressed love (*proportionierliche Güte*)[3] another name for which is righteousness. All of God's dealings with men are governed by this righteousness.[4] Because of God's righteousness man was created in the image of God, because of it Adam was tested, because of it God offers his redemption in Christ, because of it every man is tested, and because of it those who are faithful receive their reward. Furthermore, righteousness is what God expects of man, both in his individual and corporate life. In short righteousness is that in which all divine activity coheres as well as the goal toward which it moves. Hence the achievement of it is man's highest religious obligation.

In the spirit of his age Collenbusch viewed man with a certain optimism, though it is a more restrained optimism than that of the Neologists. The Fall, he held, has weakened man's spirit so as to make him more prone to temptation. With the theosophical school, notably

---

his synod. An article on him is found in RE, vol. 7, pp. 461-463. See also H.W. zur Nieden, *Die religiösen Bewegungen im 18. Jahrhundert und die evangelische Kirche in Westfalen und am Niederrhein*, 1910, pp. 114-122. His two brothers, Friedrich Arnold (1747-1795) and Johann Heinrich (1750-1814), were essentially of the same mind. In one of his letters the latter speaks of Collenbusch's influence on his life (E. Thiemann, "Aus Briefen des Dahler Pfarrers Johann Heinrich Hasenkamp," JVwKG, vols. 53-54, 1960-1961, pp. 110-116).

[1] See E.H. Gildemeister, *Leben und Wirken des D. Gottfried Menken*, 2 vols., 1860. *Menkens Schriften* were published posthumously (1858). See also the excellent article on him in RE, vol. 12, pp. 581-586. For his influence upon the next century see F.W. Krummacher, *Gottfried Daniel Krummacher und die niederrheinische Erweckungsbewegung zu Anfang des 19. Jahrhunderts*, 1935, p. 52f.

[2] *Erklärung biblischer Wahrheiten*, vol. 1, p. 73f.

[3] *Ibid.*, vol. 3, p. 215.

[4] *Ibid.*, p. 208f.

Oetinger, he also taught that the Fall has negatively affected man's corporeality, so that both body and spirit are in need of divine redemption. Collenbusch's understanding of the latter manifests especially his accommodation to his time. Flouting the norms of traditional Protestant Orthodoxy he knows of no original guilt, no original sin in the Augustinian sense, no imputation of either guilt of righteousness, no penal suffering expressing either God's anger or his righteousness, and no reconciliation of God to man. From the day of his theological enlightenment at the age of 36 he spoke as exclusively as Dippel before him of Christ's redemptive activity in man. Man's preeminently important religious motivation must be that of coming to know ever more fully "the secret of Christ within us."[1] In this knowledge lies the key to man's inner renewal and the motivation to move on toward the divinely intended perfection. To lead men to this end Christ became truly man (radical kenosis) so that under fully human conditions he could show man the way to his divinely intended destiny.[2] Thus Christ became in every way the counter-part of Adam who, facing the same conditions, fell and dragged mankind after him.

Related to what has been said are certain other beliefs which Collenbusch held. Understandably he was profoundly opposed to the Reformed doctrine of a particularized predestination,[3] which, he felt, does not give man the freedom to work out his religious destiny. In tension with this, however, he held to the belief that all history is God's history, thus moving in the direction in which God's righteousness will take it. Accordingly he could look forward with Spener to better times for God's people, though he always applied this hope conservatively and without resort to undue speculation, as he did his belief in the second coming of Christ. With Swedenborg and the theosophical school of Württemberg he manifested a great curiosity for the after-life, thus promoting unwittingly the expanding spiritualist cult of his day. His interest in the occult was fed by the visions of Dorothea Wuppermann, a young lady with whom he was acquainted. In contradistinction to Tersteegen, who worked in the same vicinity, Collenbusch advocated an active piety,[4] which must express itself under whatever conditions life may impose. Like Tersteegen, on the other hand, he

[1] *Ibid.*, p. 199f.

[2] *Ibid.*, pp. 206-207.

[3] *Ibid.*, vol. 1, p. 11.

[4] *Ibid.*, p. 68f.

did not wish to be confined by denominational boundaries, though he did remain within the Lutheran communion.

Perhaps the claims for Collenbusch's influence have been exaggerated. His interest in Protestant missions did ultimately eventuate in the missionary efforts associated with Barmen. Whether or not the theology of Gottfried Thomasius (1802-1875) and of J.C.K. Hofmann (1810-1877) is indebted to him[1] is a question which would require careful investigation. From many scattered references to him one would infer that his influence and that of his circle was chiefly local. In his immediate locality Collenbusch constituted a bridge between the old Pietism and the new. With the fathers he took his stand on the biblical revelation and oriented his theology toward fervent concern for the amendment of life in terms of an ethic read out of the Bible. In the spirit of his age, on the other hand, he took an optimistic view of man, sat lightly on inherited dogmas and on the confessional symbols of his communion, and gave to the salvatory work of God in Christ a strictly immanental interpretation. At the same time he polemicized against what he called the "unfaith" of the Neologists and the moral laxity which seemed to accompany it.

A contemporary of Collenbusch, and a fellow Lutheran, was the second man to be discussed in this context, namely, Johann August Urlsperger (1728-1806).[2] In his life and work he symbolizes perhaps more fully than anyone else the high aspirations, the accomplishments, as well as the failures of late eighteenth century Pietism. Johann was the son of Samuel Urlsperger, the latter being one of the most sincere, earnest and busy representatives of Halle Pietism in South Germany. Upon the advice of his father he matriculated at Tübingen University in 1747. Here he studied under Bilfinger, Canz, and Pfaff, all of whom,

---

[1] RE, vol. 4, p. 241.

[2] By far the most thorough research on Urlsperger has been undertaken by Horst Weigelt. Unfortunately his doctoral dissertation (*Johann August Urlsperger. Ein Theologe zwischen Pietismus und Aufklärung*, 1961) has not been published. His studies have been summed up, however, in a carefully done article by the same title in ZbKG, vol. 33, 1964, pp. 67-105, as well as in a section of his *Pietismus-Studien, I Teil. Der spener-hallesche Pietismus*, 1965, pp. 90-140. For an enthusiastic endorsement of Weigelt's research on Urlsperger see P. Schattenmann, "Zur theologischen Bedeutung von D. Johann August Urlsperger," ZbKG, vol. 33, 1964, pp. 106-108. See also W. Zorn, "Samuel und Johann Urlsperger," in *Lebensbilder aus dem bayerischen Schwaben*, ed. by Freiherr von Pölnitz, vol. 1, 1952, pp. 322-342; H. Schobert, *Der pietische Einfluss Urlspergers auf das Bildungswesen Augsburgs*, 1940; and the SPCK's *Henry Newman's Salzburger Letterbooks*, U. of Georgia Press, 1966.

as previously indicated, had come under the influence of Wolff, though the latter was closer to Pietism than to the Enlightenment, while both Bilfinger and Canz were of what we called the transitional school of theology (often referred to as rational orthodoxy). Wanting to go to a pietistic school, possibly out of a profound respect for his paternal heritage, he went to Halle (1751) and registered as a student of theology. Here, too, he found, however, that Wolff's influence was of major importance, not only because Wolff himself taught there, but because of the influence of the previously mentioned S.J. Baumgarten, who was, perhaps, the most universally respected representative of transitional theology of his time.

In 1754 Urlsperger left Halle deeply troubled. Already he had come under the sway of what became well-nigh an obsession with him, namely, that the traditional understanding of Christianity needed to be defended against the inroads of Neology, and that he was the divinely appointed man to do it. To his chagrin S.J. Baumgarten had forced him to re-write his dissertation, which was too directly critical of Wolff's position, who was still on the faculty.[1] To the utterly self-assured, eager young Urlsperger this should have been a warning, perhaps, of the difficulties which might lie astride his chosen path. If he recognized it as such, however, he did not heed it. After a lengthy study trip, the first abortive effort to form a society for the defense of Christian truth, and a number of minor pastoral assignments, he finally took over his father's manifold duties at Augsburg in 1765. In the meantime he had already been made a corresponding member of the Society for the Propagation of Christian Knowledge.

Urlsperger was a successful and very much appreciated pastor. With the model of his father before him, however, his restless spirit projected its ambitions far beyond the confines of his local parishes. Possessed of a profound sense of mission he looked upon his ministry in the widest possible terms. From the point of view of his vocation he was certain, as has already been indicated, that to him the first and foremost commandment was that of being an apologist for the faith of the fathers, and the second, which was like unto the first, was that of being active in the promotion of *Gottseligkeit*. Under the pressure of this twin ideal, then, of engaging in apologetics and spreading godliness he became

---

[1] *Kurzgefasstes System seines Vortrages von Gottes Dreieinigkeit. Es erteilt den einigen wahren Schlüssel zu schriftmässiger Auflösung solches grossen Geheimnisses* etc., 1777, preface, p. XI.

wholly absorbed in a number of ventures which ultimately failed. In that sense he represents one of the most tragic figures of his age. At the same time, however there was no one during his time who was quite as influential while in the process of failing as was Urlsperger.

In pursuit of the first of the two goals Urlsperger had already entered anonymously into the Supper controversy which had been called into being by Christian Heumann's assertion that the Lutheran teaching regarding the Lord's Supper was contrary to both Scripture and reason. His major literary activity in defense of the biblical faith, however, began in 1769. During that year he had printed, at his own expense, the first volume of his *Versuch*,[1] to be followed by three other volumes in 1770, 1771, and 1774.[2] This was succeeded by two other tracts the year after.[3] His final effort in this direction was his *Kurzgefasstes System* of 1777, in which he summed up once more his previously stated insights. The burden of our author's apologetic was to try to put an end to Neology's cavalier dismissal of such Christian doctrines as that of the trinity and of traditionally understood Christology.[4] This he meant to do by establishing what he felt was a valid philosophical foundation which would rationally undergirt these doctrines, thus demonstrating their absolute necessity. In the process of writing these books he had convinced himself that he had been privileged to discover the innermost secrets of the divine order of things which must necessarily be convincing to every philosopher and theologian who honestly seeks for the truth.[5]

Unfortunately for the self-esteem of Urlsperger, and from his point of view, unfortunately for the world, neither the philosophers, nor the theologians of his day took him as seriously as he took himself. Only the first volume of his *Attempt* caused some ripples in the learned journals, though by no means as many as Urlsperger had hoped for. Instead of

---

[1] *Versuch in freundschaftlichen Briefen einer genaueren Bestimmung des Geheimnisses Gottes* etc.

[2] For Urlsperger's own account of these successive efforts see *Kurzgefasstes System*, *op. cit.*, preface, p. XXf.

[3] *Was die Heilige Schrift von dem dem Menschen anerschaffenen göttlichen Ebenbilde lehrt* etc., as well as *Mein Bekenntnis von der Lehre der heiligen Dreieinigkeit.*

[4] In W.A. Teller's *Lehrbuch des christlichen Glaubens*, 1764, the doctrines of the trinity and of the two natures in Christ had simply been omitted.

[5] This is the burden of much of what he says in his *Zeugnisse der Wahrheit*, 1786. Thus on p. 73 he speaks of the insights given to the world in his philosophical discussions as the key which is necessary to unlock the "Zusammenhang göttlich geoffenbahrter und natürlicher Wahrheit." See also his *Kurzgefasstes System*, p. 47f.

convincing the world of the inescapable truth of his thesis, however, it involved him in considerable controversy. The rest of his apologetic writings were largely ignored. His oblique invitation to Immanuel Kant to respond to his philosophical discovery remained unanswered.[1] Somewhat unkindly Friedrich Nicolai, one of the Berlin Neologists and opponents of Urlsperger, summed up the feelings of many of his learned contemporaries when he wrote : "Mr. Urlsperger is a very well-meaning man but of very modest learning and intellectual powers — (his theology) is neither orthodox nor heterodox, only indefinite and unclear."[2]

Before we comment on the statement of Nicolai at least a brief indication of the nature of Urlsperger's supposed philosophical discovery would seem to be in order.[3] It had become his settled belief that the Christian doctrine of the trinity, if rightly interpreted, is the key to all of God's dealings in the realms of nature, history, and grace.[4] Without explicitly saying so Urlsperger had chanced upon such a "right" interpretation of this doctrine by absorbing the speculations of the theosophical tradition coming down from Boehme and channeled into church-related Pietism notably by Oetinger and his followers in Württemberg. Thus he asserted that there is a distinction between a trinity of being (*Wesen*) and a trinity of revelation,[5] an assertion which was quite typical of the theosophists. On the level of being, God, the infinite Spirit, consists of three "subjects" which are formally equal, so that in no sense one has priority over the other.[6] With respect to their attributes and their internal structure, however, each has its own characteristic spiritual nature.[7] Upon a mutual compact the three "subjects" go forth in a genetic process which makes it possible for them to assume the functions attributed to them in the Christian revelation as Father, Son, and Spirit. Thus the Father generates. The Son, because in his being he is the same as the Father but in his function he is subordinate, is the great point of connection between God and

---

1 *Ibid.*, p. 65.

2 Quoted by H. Weigelt, *Pietismus Studien, op. cit.*, p. 103. For Urlsperger's reaction to it see *Zeugnisse der Wahrheit*, p. 107f.

3 Because of its relative ineffectiveness a detailed account of it would seem to be irrelevant to this discussion. For such an account the reader is referred to Weigelt's works. Our analysis is based on his *Kurzgefasstes System*, 1777, and his *Zeugnisse*, 1786.

4 *Kurzgefasstes System*, p. 224.

5 *Ibid.*, pp. 106f, 167.

6 *Ibid.*, p. 214.

7 *Ibid.*, p. 169.

the world,[1] while the Spirit is the life-giving power which sustains the Whole. On these premises the Christian doctrines of the trinity and of Christology are, Urlsperger felt, indispensable to an understanding, not only of the Christian message, but to the innermost secrets of the world.[2] For this reason his apologetic works were largely concentrated upon the philosophical explication and defense of these doctrines.

Even this brief outline of Urlsperger's prolegomena to Christian theology would seem to indicate why many of his contemporaries had difficulties with his message. Perhaps the reason for this was not so much his lack of erudition or intellectual acumen for which he was censored by Nicolai. Most of the difficulties were implicit in the spirit of the times. Neologists regarded all ontological speculations as fanciful superfluities which were not worth one's time or effort. Old line Orthodoxy looked upon theosophical excursions as *ipso facto* heretical, while the rational Orthodoxy of the day viewed it with almost equal suspicion.[3] Old line Pietists, on the other hand, shared the attitude of Orthodoxy in this instance, and Neo-Pietists were too busy with more pratical concerns to devote their time to intra-trinitarian problems. In fine, Urlsperger's ineffectiveness on the theological level simply underscores the fact that, after the intellectual re-orientation of Halle, Pietism had lost its theological leadership to Neology, on the one hand, and to rational Orthodoxy on the other. Perhaps this was inevitable, in so far as a movement which was oriented toward the promotion of piety could hardly be expected to generate the intellectual vigor and the necessary imaginativeness to deal with the massive challenges presented to Christian theology by man's rapidly expanding consciousness during the eighteenth century.

By 1777 Urlsperger had come to suspect strongly that in theological circles his voice was that of a prophet crying in the wilderness where no one was willing to pause long enough to hear it. With characteristic tenacity, therefore, he cast about for a means of reaching the general religious public. The result was his effort to bring into being a society the purpose of which would essentially coincide with his sense of mission. That same year, therefore, he brought his initial suggestions

---

[1] *Ibid.*, p. 139f.

[2] *Ibid.*, pp. 223-224. See also *Zeugnisse*, p. 66f.

[3] This was the reason, no doubt, why in his *Mein Bekenntnis von der Lehre von der heiligen Derieinigkeit*, 1775, which was written for the largely neo-orthodox faculty of Tübingen, he omitted all theosophical speculation.

before the public in a printed piece.[1] From that time on he spent much of his time and effort in promoting this scheme through travel and the use of the printed page. By 1779 a definite plan for the society was ready for the printer.[2] Its purpose was to be that of "opposing by example, teaching, and active efforts, and on the basis of Scripture, that which cannot stand in the presence of the foundation established in the doctrine preached by Christ and the apostles."[3] Its name was to be German Society of Active Promotors of Pure Doctrine and True Godliness.[4] Upon further travel, however, and especially upon contact with the London Society for the Promotion of Christian Knowledge Urlsperger envisioned the possibility of giving the society an international, as well as an ecumenical, character. It was to include Anglicans, eastern Orthodox, and Roman Catholic Christians, as well as Protestants, and all of them irrespective of geographical or national boundaries. Hence he published a revised plan in 1781.[5] Actually his ambition seems to have been to make this society a kind of umbrella for the various local pietistic societies which had come into existence at places like Berlin, Hamburg, Magdeburg, Stuttgart, Wernigerode, Minden, Frankfurt a.M., Stendal, Nürnberg, as well as Sweden and Basel in Switzerland.

It is understandable that Urlsperger's scheme quickly began to involve him in considerable controversy. Criticism was directed, on the one hand, at its inter-confessional character, especially his tolerant attitude toward Roman Catholics. Many representatives of Orthodoxy saw it, in fact, as another Jesuit plot to take over Protestantism. The Neologists, on the other hand, were unhappy with the fact that it provided for Urlsperger's opinions a sounding board which the independent publication of his polemical tracts had not afforded him. To defend himself he published his often mentioned and insufferably disorganized *Zeugnisse* in 1776. It reiterates once more what he had been saying for almost two decades, namely, that he and his society stand for intellectual insights which all philosophers and theologians would have to acknowledge if they were honest and diligent enough to try. Unfortunately for Urlsperger, however, many of the members of

---

[1] *An das Publikum* etc., appended to his *Kurzgefasstes System.*

[2] *Zeugnisse*, p. 6.

[3] *Ibid.*, p. 5.

[4] *Deutsche Gesellschaft tätiger Beförderer reiner Lehre und wahrer Gottseligkeit.*

[5] The title of his publication was *Beschaffenheit und Zweck einer zu errichtenden deutschen Gesellschaft tätiger Beförderer reiner Lehre und wahrer Gottseligkeit.*

his own society now began to question his intellectual leadership. Others were simply not interested in its apologetic stance. When, therefore, the local society of Basel, which had gained a position of special eminence, communicated to other local societies its decision to give up all apologetic efforts (1785) Urlsperger's over-riding purpose had, to all intents and purposes, been defeated. Henceforth the society in question moved progressively in the direction of disseminating the older pietistic literature, notably of Halle vintage, and of engaging in purely charitable and missionary efforts. After an equally unsuccessful, though very determined, effort to found a new theological school Urlsperger restricted his activities largely to the needs of the Salzburgers in Georgia. He had long been interested in the Ebenezer Colony brought into existence by the efforts of his father, Samuel. After the retirement of the latter it was the son who represented its interests in England and on the Continent.

During much of his later life Urlsperger was plagued by ill health, a circumstance which forced him to give up his pastoral ministry in 1775. The result was that his financial situation became ever more perilous, making him increasingly dependent upon the generous gifts of his friends. During the last years of his life he lived in quiet retirement, a man, all of whose major ambitions had been tragically thwarted and who was now largely forgotten by his contemporaries. At the same time, however, the society which he had founded, and in the promotion of which he spent his energy and probably ruined his health, undoubtedly constituted a major bulwark against the spread of rationalism in religious circles. Furthermore, it must be regarded as having contributed materially to the rise of various missionary societies on the Continent during the early decades of the 19th century.

In passing, at least, a number of other men should be mentioned whose theology, like that of Urlsperger and Collenbusch, represents a cross between the older Pietism and the spirit of the new age. Many of them were graduates of Halle after that institution had come under the influence of Wolff. A veritable center for this kind of theological perspective was the section around Königsberg in East Prussia, where it had been introduced by the very able F.A. Schultz.[1] As a result of Schultz's influence Daniel Heinrich Arnold (1706-1773), S.F. Trescho (1733-1804), and T.C. Lilienthal (1717-1782)[2] combined Halle's original

---

1 *Ante*, p. 76.

2 See W. Wendland, "Ludwig Ernst von Borowski" etc., SSoKG, vol. 9, pp. 26-31.

concern for a biblically based theology and ethic with the Wolffian emphasis upon the rational support of such a faith and the well-founded, happy life on earth which results from it. Of similar spirit was Georg Adam Michel (1708-1780) in Bavaria, together with many of his fellow members of the Augsburg Society for the Promotion of Active Christianity.[1] H. Ernst gives a whole list of pastors, almost all of whom had studied at Halle, and who carried this same spirit into Eastern Frisia.[2] In Württemberg, which had developed its own brand of Pietism, the same spirit was represented by men like Jeremias Flatt (1744-1822).[3]

Jung-Stilling

In Germany Neo-Pietism reached the zenith of its development in Jung-Stilling. Before we discuss him, however, it is necessary to mention at least briefly Johann Caspar Lavater (1741-1801),[4] who represents essentially the same point of view. The latter was born in Zurich, spent most of his time in Switzerland and hence is not properly a part of this study. At the same time, however, Lavater was strongly influenced by the intellectual atmosphere of eighteenth century Germany and, in turn, was highly esteemed and widely read among many pietistic groups in that country.

In his extensive discussion of Lavater, which is both affectionate and critical, Paul Wernle makes the observation that the former remained a child all of his life.[5] This is true in the sense in which all the representatives of the *Sturm und Drang* movement retained an essentially adolescent outlook upon the world and its problems. Like the members of that movement Lavater subscribed to a certain superficial idealism which simply refused to take seriously the massive evidences of man's

---

[1] See P. Schattenmann, *Georg Adam Michel, Generalsuperintendent in Oettingen, und sein gelehrter Briefwechsel*, 1962; also his "Untersuchungen und Beiträge zur Kirchengeschichte der Grafschaft Oettingen im 17. und 18. Jahrhundert," ZbKG, vol. 28, 1959, pp. 97-118.

[2] H. Ernst, "Studien über die Einflüsse der Aufklärung auf die lutherische Kirche Ostfrieslands," ZGnKG, vol. 37, 1932, pp. 5-54.

[3] See his *Philosophisch-exegetische Untersuchungen über die Lehre von der Versöhnung des Menschen mit Gott*, 1797. For others associated with him see H. Lehmann, *Pietismus und weltliche Ordnung in Württemberg*, 1969, p. 166.

[4] The literature on Lavater is very extensive. For an excellent introduction to his life, work, and significance see P. Wernle, *Der schweizerische Pietismus im XVIII. Jahrhundert*, 1923-1925, vol. 3, pp. 221-284.

[5] *Ibid.*, p. 281.

cussedness in history, as well as the frightening recalcitrancy with which the natural order frequently seems to thwart utterly man's most desparate needs. Like the youthful dreamers of the *Sturm und Drang* group, furthermore, he subordinated reason to emotion as a guiding principle, and he regarded the demands of friendship as having priority over more objective or universalized criteria of truth and value.

While Lavater grew up within the pietistic circle of Zürich his mind was wide open to the highly pluralistic intellectual environment of his day. In his early twenties he undertook a trip to Germany and presently found himself almost overwhelmed by the influences which proceeded from men like Klopstock and Herder. Of the latter he wrote to his friend Zimmermann on May 4, 1773 : "Have you read Herder on language? If not, go and sell all your books and buy this valuable work. — A work like this has never before been seen in Germany."[1] Much of his poetry he wrote in imitation of Klopstock. Goethe collaborated with him in the writing of his important work on physiognomy (publ. 1772). From Boehme and the theosophical tradition he gained the insights into the close relation between body and spirit which resulted in his life-long interest in physiognomy. The spirit of Neology he absorbed from Spalding with whom he stayed over a long period of time.[2] His interest in individuality and perfection was stimulated by the philosophy of Leibnitz.

Lavater was great enough, however, to bent all of these influences to his own genius, and intellectually latitudinarian enough not to be troubled by the inner contradictions of such a feat. Apparently he felt no strain, for instance, in the attempt to reconcile the insights of the older Pietism with those of Herder and Goethe, though both of these men later felt constrained to put considerable distance between themselves and Lavater. Nor did he feel the tension between his own biblicism and the rationalistic moralism of Spalding. Perhaps the best way to put it is to say that his theology was essentially visceral. He regarded as right or wrong, intellectually acceptable or not acceptable, whatever his conscience felt to be attractive or repulsive in the immediate existential situation; and, as has been indicated, his conscience was informed by the older Pietistic Tradition as well as the moralistic

---

[1] J.C. Lavater, *Secret Journal of Self-Observer; or Confessions and Familiar Letters* etc., ed. by P. Will, 1775, vol. 2, p. 327.

[2] See his ode to Spalding in *Johann Caspar Lavaters Ausgewählte Werke*, ed. by. E. Staehelin, 1943, vol. 1, pp. 41-44.

idealism of the Enlighteners and the romantic empiricism of the *Sturm und Drang* group.

Under the circumstances his understanding of Christianity, together with that of Jung-Stilling, became the epitome of what we have called Neo-Pietism. On the one hand he accepted the moralistic concerns of Neology, as well as the individualism of the *Sturm und Drang* set. His understanding of the nature of man and of the course of history was influenced by the popular optimism of his day. The toleration of Leibnitz was part and parcel of his concern for his fellows. The love of Christ and the love of life were inextricably woven together in his creed. What ecstacy he knew he found in human friendship, not in visions of the divine. The life to come was cherished because of what the anticipation of it can do for man now. The older Pietists found themselves censured because of the narrowness of their allegedly other-worldly faith, the Orthodoxists because of their concentration upon doctrine rather than the concrete problems of life. On the other hand, Lavater was profoundly troubled by the rationalistic trend of the Enlightenment, which late in the century issued in attacks upon the biblical faith by Lessing and Reimarus, and beyond the borders of Germany in the French Revolution. Over against the philosophical idealism of his day, which at best threatened to fashion God into a rational construct, he chose to live moment by moment by child-like trust in the God of the Bible, the living God revealed in Christ. Personal Christianity, he felt, is a matter of following the teachings of Christ, which have the promise of this life and the life to come. Those who walk in the way of Christ are undergirded by God's power, a power which becomes especially explicit in concrete answers to prayer.[1] Like most Pietists of his age he adhered to a well-developed eschatology, which looked upon his own time as the end of the current dispensation. Contrary to many of his peers, however, he did not regard the pope as anti-christ, but reserved this dubious honor for the Enlighteners of his day,[2] who, he thought, were subverting the Gospel and invoking God's displeasure.

In the service of this religious perspective Lavater labored and wrote.

---

[1] In his *Aussichten in die Ewigkeit*, in *Briefe an J.G. Zimmermann, 1768-1773*, vol. 1, pp. 285-286 he says : "If anything is clear in the divine writings, — it is the doctrine of the almighty power of faith and prayer, and especially faith in Christ, and in prayer offered in his name." Even fellow Pietists, such as Urlsperger, had mental reservations about Lavater's faith in explicit answers to prayer.

[2] *Jesus Messias, oder die Zukunft des Herrn*, 1780, in *Werke, op. cit.*, vol. 3, p. 52f.

His literary output was prodigious, running according to Thirsch, to well over a hundred volumes.[1] His influence, especially in the Reformed sections of Germany, was considerable. Inspite of some of the peculiarities of his later belief system — Mesmerian magnetism, transmigration of souls, the continued earthly existence of St. John — his works were considered a source of religious inspiration in an age which was plagued by religious doubt and uncertainty. His advocacy of complete commitment to Christ, of absolute trust in God's loving concern, of unhesitating confidence in the power of prayer, and his faith in the practical benefits of godliness, were regarded by many as welcome relief from the insipid moralism of Neology, as well as the stoic devotion to duty which was increasingly being advocated by the Kantians.

The counter-part to Lavater among the German Neo-Pietists was Johann Heinrich Jung-Stilling (1740-1817).[2] Both of them were animated by essentially the same spirit, though certain theological differences between them were not lacking. Jung-Stilling was born in the village of Grund, near Hilchenbach in Westphalia, as the son of Wilhelm Jung. The latter was a thoroughly pious but melancholy man, who could barely earn his living as village taylor and later as village school master. His mother, a sensitive, dreamy, and deeply religious young woman, died when her son was but two years old. Her death sent the boy's father into a profound mood of depression, which hung like a pall over the early years of Heinrich. Any joyful exercise seemed incongruous in the tomb-like atmosphere which prevailed in the home. Throughout the day his every action was regulated by the severest discipline, interspersed with Bible reading, prayer, and admonition, and all of it designed to make him a model of Christian virtue. Almost

---

[1] H.W.J. Thirsch, *Lavatar*; *Ein Vortrag*, 1881, p. 25. For extensive bibliographical suggestions see Mary Lavater-Showmann's *Genie des Herzens*, 1939, pp. 456-460; also the references given in Wernle.

[2] The literature on Jung-Stilling is most extensive. He played many roles, a circumstance which has invited treatment from various points of view. Perhaps the most complete list of books and other materials about him is found in M. Geiger, *Aufklärung und Erweckung. Beiträge zur Erforschung Johann Heinrich Jung-Stillings und der Erweckungstheologie* in *Basler Studien zur historischen und systematischen Theologie*, vol. 1, 1963, pp. 38-46. Especially helpful toward an understanding of the man himself is H.R.G. Günther's *Jung-Stilling. Ein Beitrag zur Psychologie des Pietismus*, 1948. The best book on his literary activity is still G. Stecher's *Jung-Stilling als Schriftsteller*, 1913. A helpful insight into his Marburg period is provided by E. Benz, *Jung-Stilling in Marburg*, 1949. A comprehensive study of his life and work is that by R. Morax, *Le Docteur H. Stilling, sa vie et ses ouvres*, 1914.

daily the lad was chastised with the rod, in order that his flesh might be properly mortified.[1] With characteristic kindness Jung-Stilling later reflected that these frequent chastisements may have been his father's way of attempting to crucify his own love for his son. Not only did his father punish severely every infraction of household rules, but he kept him away from all company with other children so as to prevent him from picking up their bad habits. He was not even permitted to go to church, but was encouraged to worship God in solitude or in company with his father. The result was that Heinrich, precocious as he was, fashioned his own interior world out of the materials at hand. He did this by letting his imagination roam over the romantic country-side in which he lived. Being able to read with remarkable fluency at the age of eight he was aided in this exercise by the books he was permitted to read.[2]

In time his father's mental condition improved. Having reached his tenth year, Heinrich was permitted to go to Latin school at Hilchenbach. It was a festive occasion for him and the end of a period of unreasonable repression. Through diligent study and omniverous reading his intellectual skills expanded so rapidly that he was given his first teaching position at the age of fifteen. As a result of his own prodigious efforts and the help of a friendly merchant-farmer Jung-Stilling acquired proficiency in scientific farming and business management, as well as in Greek, Hebrew, and French. He studied Wolff and Leibnitz and was finally prepared to take up the study of medicine at the University of Strassburg in 1770. Here he enjoyed the friendship of both Herder and Goethe, who introduced him to a whole range of literary treasures, domestic as well as foreign.

Having been awarded his doctoral degree he now began the practice of medicine at Elberfeld in 1772, where he entered into friendly relations with such like-minded men as Lavater, Collenbusch, and Hasenkamp. Here he finished the first part of his remarkable *Autobiography* namely, *Heinrich Stillings Jugend*.[3] Goethe was so delighted with it that he himself worked on it and then published it without Jung-Stilling's knowledge. Needless to say, it was an immediate success, finding readers far and wide. From here on the doors of opportunity

---

1 *Johann Heinrich Jungs (genannt Stilling) Lebensgeschichte.* Abbreviated ed. of 1899, p. 52.

2 *Ibid.*, pp. 50-51.

3 His autobiography differs from others in so far as he wrote the respective parts of it soon after every major stage of his life, beginning in 1777 and ending in 1817.

were open wide for our author — a professorship of national economics at Kaiserslautern (1778), as well as at Heidelberg (1784), and in 1786 a professorship of economics and finance at Marburg. In the meantime, his fame as eye-surgeon also increased, especially so since he performed most of his cataract operations free of charge.[1] His main interests during his Marburg years, however, continued to be literary. Under the circumstances his major works, i.e., his *Heimweh*,[2] his *Szenen*,[3] his *Siegsgeschichte*,[4] and his *Der Graue Mann*[5] were produced here. His name now became a household word in both literary and pietistic circles throughout Europe. Because of his incessant writing, however, his relations with his colleagues and students suffered. Consequently he was happy to accept a pension from, as well as a position of private counselor to, the Elector of Baden, which took him to Heidelberg in 1803 and to Karlsruhe in 1806. Here he wrote his later works,[6] and at Karlsruhe his remains were finally buried in a simple grave.

Jung-Stilling was such a many-faceted genius — nationally known eye surgeon, businessman, professor of economics and finance, author of text books on economics, student of philosophy, private counselor to multitudes,[7] spiritual director, literary figure, theologian, and devotional writer — that it is almost impossible to say anything about him briefly. The historian's problem is compounded by the fact that he was, as should be expected, an immensely complicated person, who somehow managed to harmonize in the richness of his inner life the most discordant elements of his culture. Perhaps the best way, therefore, to present his impact upon the religious life of his own and subsequent ages is to look at his developing self-understanding and sense of mission as seen through his major religious works.

In the light of what has been said it is not difficult to surmise that with respect to the development of Jung-Stilling's intellectual and

---

[1] In all he is said to have performed ca. 2,000 cataract operations.

[2] *Das Heimweh*, 1794-1796, published in four volumes.

[3] *Szenen aus dem Geisterreiche*, 1795, 1801.

[4] *Siegsgeschichte der christlichen Religion*, 1799.

[5] *Der graue Mann*, 1795-1816.

[6] A very carefully gathered and full list of Jung-Stilling's large number of written pieces is found in Geiger, *op. cit.*, pp. 19-35. Letters written to Stilling by others are found on pp. 35-37. A chronologically ordered list is also found in Günther, *op. cit.*, pp. 64-65. The first edition of his works came out 1835-1837 in thirteen volumes. This was followed by others (Geiger, pp. 17-18), though a critical edition is still lacking.

[7] It has been estimated that he was forced to spend ca. 1,000 Gulden per year in order to pay for his postage.

emotional life two aspects of his cultural environment must be regarded as having been of prime importance. The first of these was the spirit of the *Sturm und Drang* movement which he, like his friend Lavater of Switzerland, absorbed from contemporaries like Klopstock, Herder, Goethe, and Wieland. The other was the philadelphic Pietism of his father, which by this time had become a mixture of the older Pietism of Halle and Bengel and the variously modified theosophical insights coming down from Boehme. In Jung -Stilling's psyche these traditions produced the tensions and dualities which were obviously there, and which our author attempted to resolve, or at least circumvent, in pursuit of a unified self-definition.

It was the *Sturm und Drang* emphasis of the most colorful personalities of his day which was responsible for many of the attitudes and values which he accepted from his environment. Ever and again in all his writings he speaks, for instance, of the joys and exhileration which result from human friendships. He almost literally lived for the friendships he formed and in them he looked for the strength and inspiration to bear life's burdens.[1] Closely associated with the need for human companionship is the sentimentality with which he regarded human relationships. Thus with "his soul melted away in tears" he kissed the pale lips of his departed wife Christine on Oct. 18, 1781. The following June there were more tears, but this time they flowed as he and his newly found bride, Selma, enjoyed the night air in the garden of a friend. "Stilling sobbed and cried—," he writes. "He kissed and hugged sometimes Mr. Schmerz and sometimes his Selma, and overflowed with feeling."[2] The relationship between Jung-Stilling and his third wife, Elise, whom he married in November 1790, is reported in similar terms.

The influence of the *Sturm und Drang* spirit upon our author, was evident, furthermore, in the anti-rationalist attitude which is evident in all of his later works. It was his deep conviction that feeling (*Empfindung*), not rational penetration, must be given the chief place in man's approach to the problem of meaning. The same spirit was evident in his extreme sensitivity to failure,[3] and conversely, in the marked success psychology which seemed to motivate his every action. It was evident, furthermore, in the patriotic concern for the welfare of

---

[1] Note the gusto with which he describes the visit of Goethe and Lavater in his *Lebensgeschichte*, *op. cit.*, p. 275f. "There is no blessedness without company," he says in his *Szenen*, in *Sämmtliche Schriften*, 1835 ed., vol. 2, p. 16.

[2] *Lebensgeschichte* in *Sämmtliche Schriften*, 1835 ed., vol. 1, pp. 390, 405.

[3] *Ibid.*, p. 338.

his fatherland, which he regarded as being seriously threatened by the French Enlightenment.[1] It was in evidence especially in his general love for life and his openness to the esthetic values in his culture. Because of this the older Pietists experienced considerable difficulty in appreciating him. They took offense at his constant converse with the literary set, at his appreciation of the theater, at his wearing of a wig, etc. On the surface, at least, his cosmopolitan deportment and his sophisticated tastes seemed to give evidence of far too much accommodation to the "world, the flesh, and the devil."

It should be remembered, of course, that during the second half of the eighteenth century the older Pietism had become both legalistic and insular in its self-understanding. For that reason, its judgement of a man like Jung-Stilling must be regarded with reservations. In actuality he never succeeded in detaching himself from the Pietism which had dominated his younger years. The tensions and inconsistencies which are apparent in his message he resolved invariably in the direction of the basic pietistic assumptions. A case in point here is his attitude toward the emphasis of his contemporaries upon happiness (*Glückseligkeit*) as man's major goal in life, which was characteristic of both the Enlightenment and the advocates of the *Sturm und Drang* mentality. At innumerable places in his writings he speaks as if he had accepted as both normal and legitimate man's primary concern for happiness. Upon closer scrutiny, however, one finds that he did not sanction at all the hedonism of his contemporaries. Against their interest in the pleasures which result from following the call of man's natural endowments he asserted the happiness which comes from doing God's will as revealed in the New Testament, a happiness which may be, and often is, made perfect in suffering. In fact, happiness, he insisted, is not likely to be the result of one's pursuit of it, but the result of the self-denial involved in spreading it among others.[2]

This leads us directly to what seems to have been the very center of his religious self-understanding. To Jung-Stilling the essence of personal religion was summed up in the concept of *Gelassenheit* which he had inherited from the mystical-pietistic tradition.[3] As far as his own conscious self-history was concerned his appreciation of the need for

---

[1] *Ibid.*, p. 474f.

[2] *Ibid.*, p. 308.

[3] For a good discussion of Jung-Stilling's rigid denial of self-will see Günther, *op. cit.*, p. 34f.

complete surrender to the divine will grew out of one of his dramatic religious experiences during his younger years.[1] It issued in the firm resolve to be absolutely obedient to God's will. Henceforth it came to be close to an obsession with him that he must never follow his own wishes or desires but that he must follow absolutely the leadings of of Providence as these become visible in everyday affairs.[2] Closely connected with this was his sense of mission. He was quite sure that he was led to the writing of each one of his books by a special providence of God, and that it was this providence, rather than his own skill, which accounted for the success which his literary work seemed to have. Under the circumstances we are not surprised to find that our author believed that there was but one truth, that he had been put in possession of that truth, and that he was under the over-riding religious obligation to help God carry through his purposes by speaking (or writing) of that truth. It was this tremendous sense of mission which caused him to regard himself as a latter-day prophet who must send forth his message at whatever cost to himself. Each of his major works, therefore, is an attempt to bring before the public a concern which he believed God had laid upon his heart.

To be specific one might begin with his *Homesickness*, which was written in imitation of Bunyan's *Pilgrim's Progress*, though the central idea of homesickness did not come from Bunyan. It was the result rather, of Jung-Stilling's basic religious orientation. Benz thinks that it was an ever recurring state of melancholia which caused him to look to the future life with heightened appreciation.[3] It is more likely, however, that we must look to his keen longing for perfection, both moral and esthetic, as the key to his inner life. This inordinate craving for the "perfection of existence,"[4] which nothing in this present world seemed to be able to satisfy fully caused him to live every moment of his life *sub specie aeternitatis*. Only the life to come, he felt, can offer to man that for which he has really been created. For that reason every enjoyment of life, exhilerating as it may be in itself, always points beyond itself. It is a reminder, as it were, of the fullness of joy which God has prepared for his children. In reading Jung-Stilling one has the feeling, therefore, that at no point in his life did he ever feel

---

[1] *Lebensgeschichte*, p. 211.

[2] *Ibid.*, p. 508.

[3] Benz, *op. cit.*, p. 23.

[4] *Lebensgeschichte*, p. 308.

himself to be fully a part of this world, though he enjoyed what it had to offer. He was always in transit, and what he experienced were transitory symbols of a reality which was to come.

Looking upon his own religious experience as being both normal and normative he wrote his *Homesickness* in the hope of helping other Christians to understand themselves and their religious aspirations more fully. To reach as many people as possible it was written in the form of a novel which, on the one hand, pictures the progress of every individual soul, and, on the other hand, the progress of God's people as a whole, toward their divinely appointed destinations. Like Jung-Stilling's other works it is based on the eschatological assumption that these are the worst of times because the end of the age is approaching and that every effort must be made to be obedient to God's will in all concrete situations of life. This is possible only if in the heart of the individual Christian, as well as in the life of the church, there is genuine homesickness. "Blessed are they who are homesick," the book begins, "for they shall reach home."[1] Presently, the reader is caught up in a certain visionary quality which is intrinsic to the whole work, and which is explained by the fact that every time the author worked on it he found himself in a near ecstatic state.[2] Gradually all of God's people, from every sect and nation, are seen gathering in the East, so as to get away from the evil influences which the Enlightenment has unleashed upon the West. The novel ends with the fervent wish that all who read it may become genuinely homesick for the land of peace.

Jung-Stilling's eschatological expectations were more explicitly set forth in his *History of the Victory of the Christian Religion* which closely follows Bengel's apocalyptical speculations. Our author was convinced, on the one hand, that Bengel's basic scheme was correct, needing only minor corrections, but that, on the other hand, the Swabian seer's timidity prevented him from applying his insights with sufficient boldness to contemporary events. These defects were to be remedied in his own discussion.[3] Under the circumstances what Jung-Stilling regarded as the evils of the time — the French Revolution, the Enlightenment with its tendency to treat biblical affirmations as myths, the advance of naturalism, materialism, and militarism, the crumbling of various

---

1 *Das Heimweh und der Schlüssel zu demselben*, in *Sämmtliche Schriften*, 1835 ed., vol. 4, p. 9.

2 *Lebensgeschichte*, p. 484.

3 *Siegsgeschichte der christlichen Religion*, in *Sämmtliche Schriften*, 1835 ed., vol. 3, preface, p. 7f.

societal structures — are regarded as proof positive that the end of the age is rapidly approaching.[1] Roughly speaking, only 38 years are left before the return of Christ (p. 271). They will indeed be times of tribulation, but then comes the first resurrection, followed by the beginning of the Millenium. The message of it all is clear. During the difficult days which are immediately ahead true believers must, on the one hand, watch, and pray and struggle so that they may not fall into temptation, while, on the other hand, they have the certain hope that God himself will soon intervene on their behalf. By the same token, however, unbelievers, and notably Enlighteners and destructive critics of the Bible, should be warned that their nefarious activities will presently be terminated by the awesome power of the Lord of history.

Jung-Stilling's *Gray Wanderer* expresses essentially the same philosophy of history and was designed, if anything, to heighten the eschatological tension produced by his other works. It was authored by himself and published in the form of a popular magazine between 1795 and 1801, and then continued by others. The major character, namely the Gray Wanderer, is the imaginary Ernst Uriel von Ostenheim, around whose activity the author's *Homesickness* was written. In the *Gray Wanderer* von Ostenheim's task is presented as that of going through the world during these last and terrible days in the hope of gathering together all true Christians. He does this by discoursing ceaselessly about the signs of the times. Thus he earnestly attempts to prepare the way for the coming of Christ, which, as has been indicated, is predicted with certainty to be only a few decades distant.

A work of a somewhat different nature is Jung-Stilling's *Scenes from the Realm of the Spirits*. Like his other writings it is didactic, of course. Instead of using his philosophy of history as a medium of instruction, however, he uses his understanding of the future life. Basic to the plan of the book is the author's belief in an intermediate state in which each departed spirit finds himself between the time of his death and the time of the general resurrection. While in that state he continues to develop in the direction set by the choices he has made during his earthly existence.[2] The body of the work consists, of a series of dramatic discourses which various departed spirits carry on with one another concerning their past and the prospects for their future. Here we find

---

[1] *Ibid.*, p. 272f.

[2] *Ibid.*, p. 376f consists of a detailed discussion of his theory regarding the intermediate state.

the naturalist,[1] the poor man,[2] the fatalist,[3] Lavater and Heinrich Hess,[4] etc. The purpose of this strange and unusual book seems to have been multi-leveled. Basically it was meant to encourage what Pietists have generally designated as religious growth, a process which is here pictured as continuing in the afterlife. At the same time, however, the author continues his perennial dialogue with the Enlighteners of his time, whose departed representatives find themselves confounded by the very fact that they are now in this state.[5] On the highest level the *Scenes* represent a courageous effort to defy the rationalistic *Zeitgeist*, which would mythologize biblical affirmations about the life to come, and to assert in popular form what the author takes to be the most sobering and meaningful reality of human existence, namely the fact of a continued personal existence which looks toward eternal rewards or punishment according to the free choices which are made.

In later life Jung-Stilling confessed one time : "I am not one of those persons whom men pass by indifferently. People must either love or hate me."[6] Of this there can be no doubt. As the chief apologist of his day for what he regarded as biblical religion he was deeply disliked by the sophisticates who regarded such religion as superstition. The remaining Orthodoxists disliked him because he was superbly indifferent to the theological problems which meant most to them. Moderates had serious reservations about his eschatological speculations. Even the older Pietists were often offended by his habit of treating them as overly legalistic.[7] Many of his literary friends were disappointed because he progressively moved away from literary to dominantly religious concerns. At the same time, however, it is evident that his books were widely read, not only in Germany but far beyond its borders. In fact, it would be difficult to deny that the eschatological tension which he greatly helped to increase contributed to the emigration of many German Pietists to Russia under Alexander I. During the evil days ahead they meant to get away from the pernicious influences of atheism, materialism, rationalism, fatalism, and naturalism which he constantly held up to censure, and because of which the wrath of God was thought

---

1 *Szenen*, p. 24.

2 *Ibid.*, p. 44.

3 *Ibid.*, p. 54.

4 *Ibid.*, p. 254f.

5 *Ibid.*, p. 55.

6 Quoted by Günther, *op. cit.*, p. 21.

7 See his preface to the second printing of his *Szenen*, p. 7.

to be about to strike the western nations. On a deeper level, in a day of dominantly this-worldly concerns it was Jung-Stilling who, perhaps more than anyone else, succeeded in keeping alive a sense of religious awe and mystery by focussing the mind of western man upon the realm of the numinous. In contrast to the older Pietism of his day he did this while he remained in close contact with the world in which he lived and while he enjoyed what he regarded as its legitimate pleasures. In so doing he, too, like Collenbusch, Urlsperger, and Lavater, helped to prepare the way for the religious revival which was soon to follow.

We have now traced the development of German Pietism through the eighteenth century. In doing so it has been noted that during the Post-Spener era it became a religious movement which began to encompass a significant segment of German Protestantism. The reason for its dynamic must be sought in its aims, which captured the imagination of the younger generation. Hence it found its way into the lecture rooms of the universities and of the theological academies. From here it was disseminated among noblemen and peasants alike by a group of highly motivated, enthusiastic pastors and laymen.

As is evident from our discussion, however, during the latter part of the eighteenth century German Pietism underwent a series of subtile changes which greatly altered its character. The most obvious external evidence of such a metamorphosis is found in the fact that it moved from the universities to the hinterland. In doing so its cultural and intellectual relevance was gradually replaced by an aura of self-satisfied insularity. Instead of taking its inspiration from a theology of hope it now sought sustenance in the myth of a golden age which was about to be destroyed by wicked innovators. Having strained at one time to change the structure of time-worn institutions, it now became fearful of change and decided to ignore it. Quite fittingly many of its adherents had permitted themselves to be convinced that the Almighty would ring down the curtain upon the doings of men in 1836. Not until the rise of the Revival Movement (*Erweckungsbswegung*) did German Pietism recapture its original vision — and then only partially.

SELECTIVE BIBLIOGRAPHY OF SECONDARY SOURCES

As indicated in the preface this is meant to be a list of only the most helpful secondary sources. Primary material, as well as most articles on a given subject, may be located through the references which are given for each chapter. Books on related subjects, though mentioned occasionally among the references, are omitted unless they are of considerable significance for this study.

General Works

Aland, K., *Kirchengeschichtliche Entwürfe*, 1960.

Beyreuther, E., *Der geschichtliche Auftrag des Pietismus in der Gegenwart*, in *Calwer Hefte*, vol. 66, 1963.

Bornkamm, H., *Mystik, Spiritualismus und die Anfänge des Pietismus im Luthertum*, 1926.

Bullock, F.W.B., *Voluntary Religious Societies, 1520-1799*, 1963.

Gass, W., *Geschichte der protestantischen Dogmatik in ihrem Zusammenhang mit der Theologie überhaupt*, 1854-1867.

Groot, K., *Die Erweckungsbewegung in Deutschland und ihr literarischer Niederschlag*, 1933.

Hirsch, E., *Geschichte der neueren evangelischen Theologie*, 1949-1954.

Kantzenbach, F.W., *Die Erweckungsbewegung. Studien zur Geschichte ihrer Entstehung und ersten Ausbreitung in Deutschland*, 1957.

Kantzenbach, F.W., *Orthodoxie und Pietismus*, in *Evangelische Enzyklopädie*, vols. 11-12, 1966.

Knox, R., *Enthusiasm*, 1950.

Kühn, J., *Toleranz und Offenbarung*, 1923.

Langen, A., *Der Wortschatz des deutschen Pietismus*, 1954.

Leube, H., *Die Reformideen in der deutschen lutherischen Kirche zur Zeit der Orthodoxie*, 1924.

Mahrholz, W., *Der deutsche Pietismus*, 1921.

Mund, F., *Pietismus — eine Schicksalsfrage an die Kirche heute*, 1936.

Nigg, W., *Das ewige Reich*, 1944.

Pinson, K.S., *Pietism as a Factor in the Rise of German Nationalism*, 1934.

Pörksen, M., *Die Weite eines engen Pietisten*, 1956.

Reinhardt, K., "Mystik und Pietismus," in *Der katholische Gedanke*, vol. 9, 1925, p. 256f.

Röbbelen, I., *Theologie und Frömmigkeit im dt. ev. luth. Gesangbuch des 17. und frühen 18. Jahrhunderts*, 1957.

Sachsse, E., *Ursprung und Wesen des Pietismus*, 1884.

Sann, Auguste, *Bunyan in Deutschland; Studien zur literarischen Wechselbeziehung zwischen England und dem deutschen Pietismus*, 1951.

Schian, M., *Orthodoxie und Pietismus im Kampfe um die Predigt*, 1902.

Schmid, H.F.F., *Die Geschichte des Pietismus*, 1863.

Schmidt, M., *Wiedergeburt und neuer Mensch*, in *Arbeiten zur Geschichte des Pietismus*, vol. 2., 1969.

Schmidt, M. and Jannasch, W., editors, *Das Zeitalter des Pietismus*, 1965.

Söhngen, O., editor, *Die bleibende Bedeutung des Pietismus*, 1960.

Stephan, H., *Der Pietismus als Träger des Fortschritts in Kirche, Theologie und allgemeiner Geistesbildung*, in *Sammlung gemeinverständlicher Vorträge und Schriften*, vol. 51, 1908.

Stephan, H., *Geschichte der evangelischen Theologie seit dem deutschen Idealismus*, 1938.

Tanner, F., *Die Ehe im Pietismus*, 1952.

Walch, J.G., *Historische und theologische Einleitung in die Religionsstreitigkeiten* etc., 1728-1736.

Weber, O. and Beyreuther, E., editors, *Die Stimme der Stillen*, 1959.

Wendland, W., "Die pietistische Bekehrung," in *Zeitschrift für Kirchengeschichte*, vol. 38, 1920.

Werner, M., *Der protestantische Weg des Glaubens*, 1955.

Chapters I and II

Aland, K., *Spener-Studien*, in *Arbeiten zur Geschichte des Pietismus*, I, 1943.

Bartz, E., *Die Wirtschaftsethik August Hermann Franckes*, 1934.

Beyreuther, E., *August Hermann Francke und die Anfänge der ökumenischen Bewegung*, 1957.

Beyreuther, E., *August Hermann Francke, 1663-1727. Zeuge des lebendigen Gottes*, 1956.

Beyreuther, E., *Selbstzeugnisse August Hermann Franckes*, 1963.

Blankmeister, F., *Der Prophet von Kursachsen*, 1920.

Büttner, D., *Der Lebenslauf des — Johann Jakob Rambachs* etc., 1736.

Cordier, L., *Der junge A.H. Francke*, 1927.

de Boer, A., *Der Pietismus in Ostfriesland*, 1938.

Dannenbaum, R., *Joachim Lange als Wortführer des halleschen Pietismus gegen die Orthodoxie*. Dissertation at Göttingen, 1952.

Deppermann, K., *Der hallesche Pietismus und der preussische Staat unter Friedrich III.*, 1961.

Duttenhofer, C.F., *Freimütige Untersuchungen über Pietismus und Orthodoxie*, 1787.

Ebelein, H., *Schlesische Kirchengeschichte*, 1952.

Engelhardt, M. von, *Valentin Ernst Löscher nach seinem Leben und Wirken*, 1856.

Fries, W., *Die Stiftungen A.H. Franckes*, 1913.

Geissendoerfer, J.T., editor, *Briefe an August Hermann Francke* etc., 1939.

Germann, W., *Ziegenbalg und Plütschau; die Gründungsjahre der Trankebarschen Mission. Ein Beitrag zur Geschichte des Pietismus*, 1868.

Guericke, H.E.F., *The Life of August Hermann Francke*, 1847.

Hartmann, R.J., *August Hermann Francke; ein Lebensbild*, 1897.

Heldmann, K., *Vierhundert Jahre hallescher Kirchen- und Kulturgeschichte*, 1923.

Hertzberg, G.F., *August Hermann Francke und sein hallesches Waisenhaus*, 1898.

Horkel, I., *Der Holzkämmerer Theodor Gehr*, 1855.

Irmer, W., *Geschichte des Pietismus in der Grafschaft Waldeck*, 1912.

Knapp, C.C. and Niemeyer, A.H., editors, *Historischer Bericht von der Stiftung der halleschen Bibelgesellschaft* etc., 1817.

Koch, E.E., *Geschichte des Kirchenlieds und Kirchengesangs* etc., vol. 2, 1852.
Krämer, G., *August Hermann Francke*, 1880.
Krämer, G., editor, *A.H. Franckes pädagogische Schriften*, 1885.
Krämer, G., editor, *Beiträge zur Geschichte August Hermann Franckes, enthaltend den Briefwechsel Franckes und Speners*, 1861.
Lother, H., *Pietistische Streitigkeiten in Greifswald* etc., 1925.
Mahling, F., Mirbt, C., Nebe, A., editors, *Zum Gedächtnis August Hermann Franckes*, 1927.
Michaelis, W., *August Hermann Francke. Vom Leben und Werk des grossen Volkserziehers*, 1938.
Niemeyer, A.H., *Die Universität Halle nach ihrem Einfluss auf gelehrte und praktische Theologie*, 1817.
Patzelt, H., *Der Pietismus im Teschener Schlesien, 1709-1730*, 1969.
Peschke, E., editor, *August Hermann Francke. Werke in Auswahl*. 1969.
Peschke, E., *Studien zur Theologie August Hermann Franckes*, 1964.
Pleijel, H., *Der schwedische Pietismus in seinen Beziehungen zu Deutschland*, 1935.
Rotermund, H.M., *Orthodoxie und Pietismus; Valentin Ernst Löschers "Timotheus Verinus" in der Auseinandersetzung mit der Schule August Hermann Franckes*, 1959.
Ruprecht, R., *Der Pietismus des 18. Jahrhunderts in den hannoverschen Stammländern*, 1919.
Sachs, W., "Schlesier in Halle," in JsKG, 1963, pp. 50-79.
Schaudig, F.P., *Der Pietismus und Separatismus im Aischgrunde*, 1925.
Schian, M., *Das kirchliche Leben der evangelischen Kirche der Provinz Schlesien*, 1903.
Schicketanz, P., *Carl Hildebrand von Cansteins Beziehungen zu Philipp Jakob Spener*, in *Arbeiten zur Geschichte des Pietismus*, vol. 1, 1967.
Selle, Götz von, *Die Georg-August Universität zu Göttingen*, 1937.
Sellschopp, A., *Neue Quellen zur Geschichte August Hermann Franckes*, 1913.
Stahl, H., *August Hermann Francke. Einfluss Luthers und Molinos' auf ihn*, in *Forschungen zur Kirchen- und Geistesgeschichte*, vol. 16, 1939.
Wachter, M., *Das psychologische Moment in der Erziehung und Unterrichtsmethode A.H. Franckes*, 1930.
Weigelt, H., *Der spener-hallesche Pietismus* in *Pietismus Studien. I Teil*, 1965.
Wendland, W., "Die pietistische Bekehrung," in ZKG, vol. 38, 1920, pp. 193-283.
Wendland, W., *Das Erwachen religiösen Lebens in Berlin*, 1925.
Winter, E., *Halle als Ausgangspunkt der deutschen Russlandkunde im 18. Jahrhundert*, 1953.
Zippel, G., *Geschichte des kgl. Friedrichskollegiums*, 1898.

Chapter III

Auberlen, K.A., *Die Theosophie Oetingers*, 1847.
Baum, F., *Johann Albrecht Bengel. Der Vater des schwäbischen Pietismus*, 1910.
Benz, E., *Die christliche Kabbala. Ein Stiefkind der Theologie*. 1958.
Benz, E., *Der vollkommene Mensch nach Jakob Boehme*, 1937.
Benz, E., *Der Mythus des Urmenschen*, 1955.
Brinton, H.H., *The Mystic Will*, 1930.
Burk, J.C.F., editor, *J.A. Bengels hinterlassene Predigten*, 1839.
Burk, J.C.F., *J.A. Bengels Leben und Wirken*, 1831.

Burk, J.C.F., editor, *Johann Albrecht Bengels literarischer Briefwechsel*, 1836.

Claus, W., *Von Bengel bis Burk*, in *Wüttembergische Väter*, vol. 1, 1887.

Claus, W., *Von Brastberger bis Hofacker*, in *Württembergische Väter*, vol. 2, 1888.

Dyrssen, C., "Hamann und Oetinger. Ein Beitrag zur Geschichte des deutschen Protestantismus," in *Zeitwende*, vol. 4, 1925.

Ehmann, K.C.E., *Friedrich Christoph Oetingers Leben und Briefe* etc., 1859.

Flatt, C.C., *Zum Gedächtnis des Jeremias Flatt*, 1822.

Flattich, J.F., *Uber Erziehung und Seelsorge*, in *Zeugnisse der Schwabenväter*, vol. 11, 1966.

Fresenius, J.P., *Zuverlässige Nachricht von dem Leben, Tod und Schriften des J.A. Bengel*, n.d.

Hartmann, F., *Personal Christianity. The Doctrines of Jakob Boehme*, 1957.

Hauck, W.A., *Das Geheimnis des Lebens. Naturforschung und Gottesauffassung Friedrich Christoph Oetingers*, 1947.

Hermann, K., *Johann Albrecht Bengel. Der Klosterpräzeptor von Denkendorf* etc., 1937.

Hermelink, H., *Geschichte der ev. Kirche in Württemberg von der Reformation bis zur Gegenwart*, 1949.

Herpel, O., *Friedrich Christoph Oetinger, die heilige Philosophie*, 1923.

Herzog, J., *Friedrich Christoph Oetinger. Ein Lebens- und Charakterbild aus seinen Selbstbekenntnissen und Schriften* etc., 1902.

Herzog, J., *Weisheit im Staube. Ein Lesebuch der Schwabenväter* etc., 1927.

Kurzer Entwurf von dem Glaubensgrund und der Entwickelung der Pregizianer Gemeinschaft, 1915.

Keller, W., *Bengel von göttlichen Dingen*, 1937.

Kolb, C., *Die Anfänge des Pietismus und Separatismus in Württemberg*, a reprint from *Württembergische Vierteljahrshefte für Landesgeschichte*, vols. 9-11, 1900-1902.

Köberle, A., *Das Glaubensvermächtnis der schwäbischen Väter*, 1959.

Knapp, A., *Altwürttembergische Charaktere*, 1870.

Ledderhose, K.F., *Leben und Schriften Flattichs*, 5. ed., 1873.

Lehmann, H., *Pietismus und weltliche Ordnung in Württemberg vom 17. bis zum 20. Jahrhundert*, 1969.

Leube, M., *Geschichte des Tübinger Stifts*, 1921, 1930.

Ludwig, W., "Neue Handschriften von Joh. Ludwick Fricker," in BwKG, vol. 56, 1956, pp. 168-171.

Mälzer, G., *Bengel und Zinzendorf*, in *Arbeiten zur Geschichte des Pietismus*, vol. 3, 1968.

Mälzer, G., *Johann Albrecht Bengel: Leben und Werk*, 1970.

Müller, G., *Christian Gottlob Pregizer. Biographie und Nachlass*, 1962.

Nanz, C.F., *C.G. Pregizers Lehre von der Seligkeit des gläubigen Christen* etc., 1843.

Nestle, E., *Bengel als Gelehrter*, 1893.

Nolte, F., *J.A. Bengel, ein Gelehrtenbild aus der Zeit des Pietismus*, 1913.

Palmer, C., *Die Gemeinschaften und Sekten Württembergs*, 1877.

Palmer, C., *J.A. Bengel, Leben und Auswahl seiner Schriften*, 1868.

Pfeil, F., *Christian Gottlob Pregizer und die Gemeinschaft der Pregizerianer*. Dissertation at Heidelberg, 1938.

Rössle, J., *Von Bengel bis Blumhardt*, 1962.

Rössle, J., editor, *Johann Albrecht Bengels: Du Wort des Vaters, rede du!* in *Zeugnisse der Schwabenväter*, vol. 6, 1962.

Rürup, R., *Johann Jakob Moser. Pietismus und Reform*, 1965.

Scholtz, H., "Evangelischer Utopismus bei Johann Valentin Andreä; geistiges Vorspiel zum Pietismus," in *Darstellungen aus der württembergischen Geschichte*, vol. 42, 1957.
Schulze, W.A., *Das androgyne Ideal und der christliche Glaube*, 1940.
Schulze, W.A., "Der Einfluss Boehmes und Oetingers auf Schelling," in BwKG, vol. 56, 1956, pp. 171-180.
Schuster, O., *Johann Albrecht Bengel, ein Mann der Schrift*, 1937.
Schuster, O., *Schwäbische Glaubenszeugen*, 1946.
Seebass, F., *Friedrich Christoph Oetinger, Denker und Seelsorger*, 1953.
Stroh, W.F., *Die Lehre des württembergischen Theosophen J.M. Hahn*, 1858, 1928.
Trautwein, J., *Die Theosophie Michael Hahns und ihre Quellen*, 1969.
Wächter, O., *J.A. Bengel. Lebensabriss, Charakter, Briefe und Aussprüche*, 1865.
Widmann, L., *Die Hahnsche Gemeinschaft. Ihre Entstehung und seitherige Entwickelung*, 1877.
Wieser, M., *Der sentimentale Mensch*, 1924.
Zinn, Elizabeth, *Die Theologie des Friedrich Christoph Oetinger*, in BFcT, vol. 36, 1932.

Chapter IV

Aalen, L., *Die Theologie des jungen Zinzendorf*, 1966.
Addison, W.G., *The Renewed Church of the United Brethren, 1722-1930*, 1932.
Baumgart, P., *Zinzendorf als Wegbereiter des historischen Denkens*, 1960.
Bechler, T., *August Gottlieb Spangenberg und die Mission*, 1933.
Becker, B., *Zinzendorf im Verhältnis zu Philosophie und Kirchentum seiner Zeit*, 1886.
Becker, B., *Zinzendorf und sein Christentum im Verhältnis zum kirchlichen und religiösen Leben seiner Zeit*, sec. ed., 1900.
Bengel, J.A., *Abriss der sogenannten Brüdergemeine* etc., 1751.
Benz, E. and Renkewitz, H., *Zinzendorf-Gedenkbuch*, 1951.
Bergmann, L., *Grev Zinzendorf eg hans Insats i Kirkens og Missionens Historie*, 1957, 1960.
Bettermann, W., *Theologie und Sprache bei Zinzendorf*, 1935.
Beyreuther, E., *Aufbruch zu Christus und zu den Brüdern bei Zinzendorf*, 1965.
Beyreuther, E., *Der junge Zinzendorf*, 1957.
Beyreuther, E., editor, *Nikolaus Ludwig von Zinzendorf in Selbstzeugnissen und Bilddokumenten*, 1965.
Beyreuther, E., *Studien zur Theologie Zinzendorfs*, 1962.
Beyreuther, E., *Zinzendorf und die Christenheit, 1732-1760*, 1961.
Beyreuther, E., *Zinzendorf und die sich allhier beisammen finden*, 1959.
Blanke, F., *Zinzendorf und die Einheit der Kinder Gottes*, 1950.
Burkhardt, G., *Zinzendorf und die Brüdergemeine*, 1886.
Cranz, D., *Ancient and Modern History of the Brethren*, 1780.
Daniel, H.A., editor, *Geistliche Lieder und Dichtungen des Grafen Nicholas Ludwig von Zinzendorf*, 1851.
Eberhard, S., *Kreuzes Theologie : das reformatorische Anliegen in Zinzendorfs Verkündigung*, 1937.
Erbe, H.W., *Zinzendorf und der fromme hohe Adel seiner Zeit*, 1928.
Fresenius, J.P., *Bewährte Nachrichten von herrnhutischen Sachen*, 1747-1751.
Gärtner, F., "Karl Barth und Zinzendorf; die bleibende Bedeutung Zinzendorfs auf Grund der Beurteilung des Pietismus durch Karl Barth," in *Theologische Existenz Heute*, N.F., vol. 40, 1953.

Gloege, G., *Zinzendorf und das Luthertum*, 1950.
Götz, W., *Zinzendorfs Jugendjahre. Ein Versuch zum Verständnis seiner Frömmigkeit*, 1900.
Hamilton, J.T., *A History of the Moravian Church*, 1900.
Haller, Mabel, *Early Moravian Education in Pennsylvania*, 1953.
Herpel, O., *Zinzendorf*, 1930.
Hirzel, S., *Der Graf und die Brüder; die Geschichte einer Gemeinschaft*, 1935.
Hök, G., *Zinzendorfs Begriff der Religion*, 1948.
Hutton, J.E., *A History of the Moravian Church*, 1909.
Kölbing, W.L., *Geschichte der Verfassung der evangelischen Brüderunität in Deutschland*, etc., n.d.
Langton, E., *History of the Moravian Church*, 1956.
Lehmann, H., *Zinzendorfs Religiosiæät*, 1903.
Lewis, A.J., *Zinzendorf the Ecumenical Pioneer* etc., 1962.
Mälzer, G. (Chapt. III).
Meyer, G., *Nikolaus Ludwig Reichsgraf von Zinzendorf und Pottendorf; eine genealogische Studie* etc., 1966.
Motel, H., *Zinzendorf als ökumenischer Theologe*, 1942.
Müller, J.T., *Hymnologisches Handbuch zum Gesangbuch der Brüdergemeine*, 1916.
Müller, J.T., *Zinzendorf als Erneurer der Brüdergemeine*, 1900.
Müller, K., *Zweihundert Jahre Brüdermission. Das erste Missionsjahrhundert*, 1931.
Nielsen, S., *Intoleranz und Toleranz bei Zinzendorf*, 1952, 1956, 1960.
Pfister, O., *Die Frömmigkeit des Grafen Ludwig von Zinzendorf*, 1910.
Plachte, K., *Die Gestalt der Kirche nach Zinzendorf*, 1938.
Plitt, H., *Denkwürdigkeiten aus der Geschichte der Brüder-Unität*, 1841.
Plitt, H., *Zinzendorfs Theologie*, 1869-1874.
Ranft, Ruth, *Das Pädagogische im Leben und Werk des Grafen Ludwig von Zinzendorf*, 1958.
Reichel, G., *August Gottlieb Spangenberg, Bischof der Brüderkirche*, 1906.
Reichel, G., *Die Anfänge Herrnhuts*, 1922.
Reichel, G., *Zinzendorfs Frömmigkiit im Licht der Psychoanalyse*, 1911.
Renkewitz, H., *Zinzendorf*, sec. ed., 1939.
Risler, J., *Leben August Gottlieb Spangenbergs, Bischofs der evangelischen Brüderkirche*, 1794.
Ruh, H., *Die christologische Begründung des ersten Artikels bei Zinzendorf*, in *Basler Studien zur historischen und systematischen Theologie*, vol. 7, 1967.
Schrautenbach, L.C. von, *Der Graf von Zinzendorf und die Brüdergemeine seiner Zeit*, ed. by F.W. Kölbing, 1851.
Schröder, J.F., *Der Graf Zinzendorf und Herrnhut*, 1863.
Seefeldt, P., *Zinzendorf als Pägadoge*, 1912.
Spangenberg, A.G., *An Exposition of Christian Doctrine, as Taught in the Protestant Church of the United Brethren* etc., 1784. A translation of Spangenberg's *Idea fidei fratrum* of 1779.
Spangenberg, A.G., *Leben des Herrn Nicolaus Ludwig — von Zinzendorf und Pottendorf* etc., 1772-1775.
Spinka, M., *John Amos Comenius; That Incomparable Moravian*, 1943.
Steinecke, O., *Die Diaspora der Brüdergemeine in Deutschland*, 1905, 1911.
Steinecke, O., *Zinzendorfs Bedeutung für die evangelische Kirche*, 1900.

Steinecke, O., *Zinzendorf und der Katholizismus*, 1902.
Uttendörfer, O., *Das Erziehungswesen Zinzendorfs und der Brüdergemeine in seinen Anfängen*, 1912.
Uttendörfer, O., *Zinzendorfs christliches Lebensideal*, 1940.
Uttendörfer, O., *Zinzendorf's religiöse Grundgedanken*, 1935.
Uttendörfer, O., *Zinzendorf und die Mystik*, 1952.
Uttendörfer, O., *Zinzendorfs Weltbetrachtung*, 1929.
Uttendörfer, O.F., *Das Tropenprinzip Zinzendorfs* etc., 1897.
Uttendörfer, O.F., *Zinzendorfs Gedanken über den Gottesdienst*, 1931.
Weinlick, J.R., *Count Zinzendorf*, 1956.
Weinlick, J.R., *The Moravian Church Through the Ages*, 1966.
Weinlick, J.R., *The Moravian Diaspora* etc., in *Moravian Historical Society Transactions*, vol. 17:1, 1959.

Chapter V

Ackermann, J.C.G., *Das Leben Johann Conrad Dippels*, 1781.
Andel, C.P. van, *Gerhard Tersteegen*, 1961.
Bedoyere, M. de la. *The Archbishop and the Lady; The Story of Fenelon and Madame Guyon*, 1956.
Barthold, F.W., *Die Erweckten im protestantischen Deutschland*, 1968.
Bender, W., *Johann Konrad Dippel. Der Freigeist im Pietismus*, 1882.
Bendiscioli, M., *Der Quietismus zwischen Häresie und Orthodoxie*, 1964.
Blankenagel, W., *Tersteegen als religiöser Erzieher*, 1934.
Büchsel, J., *Gottfried Arnold. Sein Verständnis von Kirche und Wiedergeburt*, 1970.
Delplanque, A., *Fénelon et la doctrine de l'amour* etc., 1907.
Dibelius, F., *Gottfried Arnold*, 1873.
Dörris, H., *Geist und Geschichte bei Gottfried Arnold*, 1963.
Durnbaugh, D.F., *European Origins of the Brethren. A Source Book* etc., 1958.
Govan, H.E., *The Life of Gerhard Tersteegen, With Selections from His Writings*, 1898.
Guerrier, L., *Madame Guyon; sa vie, sa doctrine, et son influence*, 1881.
Hadorn, W., *Geschichte des Pietismus in den schweizerischen reformierten Kirchen*, 1901.
Heppe, H., *Geschichte der quietistischen Mystik in der katholischen Kirche*, 1875.
Heppe, H., *Kirchengeschichte beider Hessen*, 1876.
Hinrichs, C., *Friedrich Wilhelm I*, 1941.
Hochuth, C.W.H., *Heinrich Horch und die philadelphischen Gemeinden in Hessen*, 1876.
Irmer, W. (Chapts. I and II).
Kaufmann, H.H., *Friedrich Carl von Moser als Politiker und Publizist*, 1931.
Kerlen, G., *Gerhard Tersteegen*, 1853.
Knevels, W., *Das Geheimnis der Bosheit der Ellerianischen Sekte*, 1751.
Linde, A. von der, *Antoinette Bourignon; das Licht der Welt*, 1895.
Löschhorn, A., *Ich bete an die Macht der Liebe. Gerhard Tersteegens christliche Mystik*, 1948.
MacEven, A.R., *Antoinette Bourignon, Quietist*, 1910.
May, J.L., *Fenelon*, 1938.
Mudge, J., *Fenelon : The Mystic*, 1906.
Nelle, W., *Gerhard Tersteegens geistliche Lieder mit einer Lebensgeschichte*, 1897.
Nigg, W., *Grosse Heilige*, 1946.

Pleijel, H. (Chapts. I and II).
Pourrat, P., *Christian Spirituality*, 1953-1955.
Renckewitz, H., *Hochmann von Hochenau*, 1969.
Renner, L., *Lebensbilder aus der Pietistenzeit*, 1886.
Ribadeau, D.F., *Fénelon et les saintes folies de Madame Guyon*, 1968.
Roessle, J., *Leben und Werk des Gerhard Tersteegen*, 1948.
Ruprecht, R. (Chapts, I and II).
Schaudig, F.P. (Chapts. I and II).
Schmitt, J., *Die Gnade bricht durch*, third ed., 1958.
Seeberg, E., editor, *Gottfried Arnold; in Auswahl herausgegeben*, in *Mystiker des Abendlandes*, 1934.
Seeberg, E., *Gottfried Arnold, die Wissenschaft und Mystik seiner Zeit* etc., 1923.
Seillière, E.A., *Mme. Guyon et Fénelon, précurseurs de Rosseau*, 1918.
Stählin, T., *Gottfried Arnolds geistliche Dichtung, Glaube, und Mystik*, 1966.
Thimme, L., *Kirche, Sekte und Gemeinschaftsbewegung*, 1925.
Thune, N.B., *The Behmenists and the Philadelphians*, 1948.
Voss, Karl-Ludwig, *Christianus Democritus. Das Menschenbild bei Johann Conrad Dippel*, 1970.
Wieser, M., *Peter Poiret. Der Vater der romantischen Mystik in Deutschland*, 1932.
Wolter, G., *Gerhard Tersteegens geistliche Lyrik*, 1929.
Zur Nieden, H.W., *Die religiösen Bewegungen im 18. Jahrhundert und die evangelische Kirche in Westfalen und am Niederrhein*, 1910.

Chapter VI

Aner, K., *Die Theologie der Lessingzeit*, 1929.
Benz, E., *Jung-Stilling in Marburg*, 1949.
Berkum, H. van, *Schortinghuis en de vijf nieten*, 1859.
Beyer-Fröhlich Marianne, *Empfindsamkeit, Sturm und Drang*, 1936.
Beyer-Fröhlich, Marianne, *Pietismus und Rationalismus*, 1933.
Blanckmeister, F., *Goethe und die Kirche seiner Zeit*, 1923.
Bodemann, F.W., *Johann Caspar Lavater, nach seinem Leben, Lehren, und Wirken dargestellt*, 1856.
Brockdorf, Baron Cay von, *Die deutsche Aufklärungsphilosophie* in *Geschichte der Philosophie in Einzeldarstellungen*, vol. 26, 1926.
Crocker, L.G., *An Age of Crisis*, 1959.
Dresbach, E., *Pragmatische Kirchengeschichte der preussischen Provinzen Rheinland und Westfalen*, 1931.
Dubbs, J.H., *History of the Reformed Church*, 1895.
Fischer, G., *Johann Michael Sailer und Friedrich Heinrich Jacobi*, 1955.
Gabriel, P., *Die Theologie W.A. Tellers* in *Studien zur Geschichte des neueren Protestantismus*, vol. 10, 1914.
Geiger, M., *Aufklärung und Erweckung. Beiträge zur Erforschung Johann Heinrich Jung-Stillings und der Erweckungstheologie* in *Basler Studien zur historischen und systematischen Theologie*, vol. 1, 1963.
Gessner, G., *J.C. Lavaters Lebensbeschreibung*, 1802.
Gildemeister, E.H., *Leben und Wirken des D. Gottfried Menken*, 1860.

Goeters, W., *Die Vorbereitung des Pietismus in der Reformierten Kirche der Niederlande* etc., 1911.

Good, J.I., *History of the Reformed Church of Germany*, 1894.

Guinaudeau, O., *Études sur J.C. Lavater*, 1924.

Günther, H.R.G., *Jung-Stilling. Ein Beitrag zur Psychologie des Pietismus*, sec. revised ed., 1948.

Hashagen, J., *Der rheinische Protestantismus und die Entwickelung der rheinischen Kultur*, 1924.

Heppe, H., *Kirchengeschichte beider Hessen*, 1876.

Heussi, K., *Johann Lorenz von Mosheim. Ein Beitrag zur Kirchengeschichte des 18. Jahrhunderts*, 1906.

Janensky, C., *J.C. Lavater*, 1928.

Kantzenbach, F.W., *Protestantisches Christentum im Zeitalter der Aufklärung*, 1965.

Kantzenbach, F.W., *Theismus und biblische Uberlieferung; Beobachtungen zur Theologie der Erweckung*, 1965.

Kleiss, W., *Sturm und Drang*, 1966.

Knappert, L., *Geschiedenis der Nederlandsche Hervormde kerk gedurende de 16e en 17e eeuw*, 1912.

Kolb, C., *Die Aufklärung in der württembergischen Geschichte*, 1908.

Krause, R., *Die Predigt der späten Aufklärung, 1770-1805*, 1965.

Kromsigt, J.C., *Wilhelmus Schortinghuis*, 1904.

Krug, F.W., *Die Lehre des Doctor Collenbusch* etc., 1846.

Krüger, G., *Die Religion der Goethezeit*, 1931.

Lanko, T., *Jung-Stilling und Russland*. Dissertation at Marburg, 1954.

Lavater-Showmann, Mary, *Genie des Herzens*, 1939.

McCoy, C.S., *The Covenant Theology of Johannes Coccejus*. Dissertation at Yale, 1956.

Morax, R., *Le docteur H. Stilling, sa vie et ses ourvres*, 1914.

Nordmann, H., *Die Theologie Johann Joachim Spaldings*, 1929.

Ruprecht, R. (Chapts. I and II).

Schattenmann, P., *Georg Adam Michel, Generalsuperintendent in Oettingen, und sein gelehrter Briefwechsel*, 1962.

Schmitt, J., *Der Kampf um den Katechismus in der Aufklärungsperiode Deutschlands* 1935.

Schobert, H., *Der pietistische Einfluss Urlspergers auf das Bildungswesen Augsburgs*, 1940.

Schollmeier, J., *Johann Joachim Spalding. Ein Beitrag zur Theologie der Aufklärung*, 1967.

Severijn, J., *Spinoza en de gereformeerde theologie zijner dagen*, 1919.

S.P.C.K., *Henry Newman's Salzburger Letterbook*. Transl. by G. Fenwig James, 1966.

Stecher, G., *Jung-Stilling als Schriftsteller*, 1913.

Stephan, H., rev. by Schmidt, M., *Geschichte der deutschen evangelischen Theologie seit dem deutschen Idealismus*, 1960.

Stolzenburg, A.F., "Die Theologie des Jo. Franc. Buddeus und des Chr. Matth. Pfaff. Ein Beitrag zur Geschichte der Aufklärung in Deutschland," in *Neue Studien zur Geschichte der Theologie und der Kirche*, vol. 22, 1926.

Thelemann, O., *Friedrich Adolf Lampe. Sein Leben und seine Theologie*, 1868.

Thirsch, H.W.J., *Lavater; ein Vortrag*, 1881.

Thrändorf, E., *Pietismus und Aufklärung*, 1912.

Tiessmeyer, L., *Die Erweckungsbewegung in Deutschland während des 19. Jahrhunderts*, 1901-1907, vol. 1.
Vömel, A., *J.C. Lavater, ein Lebensbild*, 1927.
Weigelt, H., *Johann August Urlsperger. Ein Theologe zwichen Pietismus und Aufklärung*, 1961.
Weigelt, H., *Der spener-hallesche Pietismus*, in *Pietismus-Studien*, I Teil, 1965.
Wenig, O., *Rationalismus und Erweckungsbewegung in Bremen*, 1966.
Zur Nieden, H.W., (Chapt. V).

INDEX

Adiaphora 18, 70, 76, 95
Alardin, Johann 224
Alexander I of Russia 264
Altdorf, University of 207
Ames (Amesius), William 224, 233
Analogia fidei, 48, 51, 99
Andrea, Johann Valentin 2, 90, 97
Anne, Queen of England 35
Anton, Paul 43, 48, 50, 95, 134
Arndt, Johann 2, 9, 18, 23, 30, 33, 53, 73, 81, 82, 85, 90, 95, 168, 174, 177, 195, 206
Arnold, Daniel Heinrich 252
Arnold, Gottfried 66, 67, 128, 175-182, 183, 185, 186, 192, 197, 198, 200, 202, 203, 206
Augsburg Society for the Promotion of Active Christianity 253

Backmeister, Lukas 83
Baier, Johann Wilhelm 43
Balthasar, Jacob Heinrich von 78
Barclay, Robert 206
Basel, University of 1
Baumgarten, Siegmund Jacob 74, 238, 247
Bayle, Pierre 143
Becker, O.H. 84
Bemer, Johann Hermann 163
Bengel, Johann Albrecht 94-107, 108, 111, 112, 113, 116, 117, 119, 120, 125, 126, 128, 129, 163, 187, 232, 243, 259, 262
Berleburger Bibel 108, 214
Bernard Ludwig, Duke of Württemberg 89
Bernieres-Louvigny, Jean de 196, 197, 200
Bertram, Johann Friedrich 82
Betkius, Joachim 171
Beverley, Thomas 205
Biblia pauperum 98
Bilfinger, Georg Bernhard 238, 246, 247
Black Death 41
Boehme, Anton Wilhelm 34, 35
Boehme, Jakob 108-111, 112, 113, 119, 120, 123, 125, 128, 152, 168, 169-171, 173, 174, 175, 177, 178, 188, 197, 206, 209, 249, 254, 259
Bogatzky, Carl Heinrich von 81
Börner, Friedrich 80
Bourignon, Antoinette 172, 173, 174
Bradacius, Michael 137
Brakel, William à 227, 228
Brastberger, Immanuel Gottlob 105
Breckling, Friedrich 171, 206
Breithaupt, Joachim Justus 42, 43, 45, 46 47, 48, 49, 50, 53, 59, 60, 61, 62, 67, 70 95
Bremen, Academy of 225, 234
Brenneysen, Enno Rudolf 82
Brenz, Johannes 96
Bromley, Thomas 209
Brorson, H. A. 84
Brückner, Hieronymus 84
Brunnquell, Ludwig 109
Brüske, Conrad 211
Buchfelder, Ernst Wilhelm 224
Buddeus, Johann Franz 53, 54, 80, 83, 238
Burk, Philipp David 106, 107
Busskampf 8, 14, 15, 19, 28, 49, 50, 150, 206
Buttlar, Eva von 62, 211

Cabbala 102, 108
Callenberg, Clara Elizabeth von 213
Calvin, John 15, 18, 46, 98, 200, 228
Canstein Bible House 36, 55
Canstein, Carl Hildebrand von 36, 55, 56 132
Canz, I. G. 238, 246, 247
Carl, Dr. Johann Samuel 210, 214
Carpzov II, Johann Benedict 4, 7, 59, 79
Christian IV of Denmark 82, 84
Christophilus Wohlgemut (Christian Weiss mann) 189
Clauder, Israel 85
Coccejus, Johann 97, 226, 227, 228, 232
Collenbusch, Samuel 243-246, 252, 257, 265

Comenius, Bishop Johann Amos 137
Conventicles 23, 74, 81, 82, 84, 88, 93, 96 104, 120, 121, 125, 127, 128, 129, 194, 219, 222
Copenhagen, University of 105
Cranz, David 142
Crasselius, Bartholomäus 85
Cyprian, Ernst Salomo 180, 181
Cyprian, Johann 4

Dannhauer, Johann Konrad 2, 53
David, Christian 137, 138, 139, 140, 165
Deism 237
Descartes, René 237
Detry, Peter Friedrich 233
Deutschmann, Johann 72
Diecmann, Johann 83
Dieterici, Wilhelm 224
Dilfeld, Georg Conrad 58
Dippel, Johann Conrad 62, 66, 67, 182-191, 192, 195, 197, 198, 201, 202, 203, 206, 207, 213, 243, 245
Dithmar (Dittmar), Johann 211, 212
Dorlich, Susanna 138
Dornfeld, Johann 4
Dyke, Daniel 5, 57

Edzardus, Esdras 3
Egeler, Anton 123
Eisler, Tobias 208
Elsner, Samuel 74
Enlightenment 52, 66, 74, 88, 100, 129, 144 163, 166, 187, 198, 224, 237f.
Erfurt, University of 2, 3, 59
Evenius, Sigismund 1
Evertson, Engelbert 201
Eytel, Johann Jacob 125, 127

Fabricius, Johann Jakob 85
Fell, John 51
Fichte, Johann Gottlieb 240
Flatt, Jeremias 253
Förtsch, Michael 92
Formula of Concord 66
Francke, August Gotthilf 77, 132, 133, 135
Francke, August Hermann 1-87, 149, 177, 203, 207
Franeker, University of 225, 226, 227
Frank, Sebastian 206
Frederick I of Prussia (1688-1701 Frederic III, Elector of Brandenburg) 34, 40, 42, 60, 71, 75, 76, 184
Frederick II of Prussia (Frederick the Great) 40
Frederik Wilhelm, Elector of Brandenburg 39
Frederick Wilhelm I of Prussia 34, 40, 41, 77
Fresenius, Johann Philipp 163
Freylinghausen, Johann Anastasius 47, 50, 51, 56
Fricker, Johann Ludwig 118-119, 243
Frommann, Johann Andreas 91
Froreisen, Johann Leonard 163
Füssli, Heinrich 239

Gebhardi, Brandanus Heinrich 78
Gebhard, Frau 211
Gehr, Theodor 75
Geistliche Fama 210, 214
Gerhard, Johann 95
Gerhard, Paul 106
German Society of Active Promoters of Pure Doctrine and True Godliness 251, 252
Gerstorff, Henrietta von 80, 132
Gichtel, Johann Georg 171, 177
Giessen, University of 97, 163, 176, 183
Gifftheil, Ludwig Friedrich 171
Glassius, Salomo 2
Gloxin, Anton Henry 3, 5
Gmelin, Sigismund Christian 92
Goethe 240, 242, 254, 257, 259
Göttingen, University of 83, 97
Götz, Christian Gottlieb 98
Grävenitz, Wilhelmine von 98
Greifswald, University of 78
Groningen, University of 234
Grossgebauer, Theophilus 24, 90, 91
Gruber, Eberhard Ludwig 207, 214
Guyon, Madam de la Mothe 152, 172, 173, 174, 196, 197

Hackenberg, Johann Kaspar von 211
Haferung, Johann Caspar 80
Hahn, Johann Michael 121-124, 125, 126, 127
Hahn, Philipp Matthäus 118, 119-120
Hahnische Gemeinschaft 121-124

Halle 1-87, 92, 95, 96, 97, 99, 101, 103, 107, 112, 126, 132, 133, 134, 135, 150, 154, 163, 171, 179, 181, 187, 189, 199, 203, 207, 208, 214, 234, 235, 238, 246, 247, 250, 252, 253, 259
Hamann, Johann Georg 240
Hase, Cornelius de 227
Hasenkamp, Johann Gerhard 243, 257
Hattem, Pontian van 220, 221, 223, 233
Hattemists 221, 222
Haug, Johann Friedrich 210
Hedinger, Johann Reinhard 93, 98, 128
Hedwig Sophie, Countess von Wittgenstein-Berleburg 204, 213
Hegel, Georg Wilhelm Friedrich 240
Heidelberg, University of 235, 258
Heiler, Günther 77
Heitz, Johann Georg 138
Hellmund, Egidius Günther 85
Helmstädt, University of 97
Herder, Johann Gottfried 240, 254, 257, 259
Herrnhut 108, 138, 139, 140, 151, 158, 162, 163, 214
Herrnschmidt, Johann Daniel 43, 57
Hess, Heinrich 239, 264
Heumann, Christian 248
Hiller, Philipp Friedrich 105
Hinckelmann, Abraham H. 5
Hochenau, Ernst Christoph Hochmann von 195, 202, 203-204, 206, 213, 214
Hochstetter, Andreas Adam 93, 95
Hochstetter, Johann Andreas 91, 93, 97, 98, 128
Hoffmann, Christoph 139
Hoffmann, Gottfried 92
Hoffmann, Wilhelm 194, 195, 196, 197, 202, 204
Hofmann, Carl Gottlob 163
Hofmann, J. C. K. 246
Hohburg, Christian 171
Horb, Johann Heinrich 5, 61
Horch(e), Dr. Heinrich 204-206, 208, 210, 236
Hottinger, Johann Heinrich 235
Hülsemann, Johann 4
Huss, John 137

Jablonski, Daniel Ernst 140
Jäger, Wolfgang 90, 93, 97
Jaenicke, Johann 74
Jaschke, Michael 138
Jena, University of 73, 80
Joch, Johann Georg 80, 85
Jung-Stilling, Johann Heinrich 253-265

Kaiser, Dr. Johann 211
Kaiserslautern, University of 258
Kant, Immanuel 74, 240, 242, 249
Karl Alexander, Duke of Württenberg 89
Karl Eugen, Duke of Württemberg 89
Kasimir, Count of Wittgenstein-Berleburg 184
Kiel, University of 3
Klopfer, Balthasar Christoph 205, 208
Klopstock, Friedrich Gottlieb 240, 254,259
Knoblach, Johann Heinrich 62
Knorr, Christian 211
König, J.F., 53
König, Samurl 208, 213
Königsberg, University of 1, 74, 75, 76, 77, 234
Korthold, Christian K. 3, 5
Kottwitz, Ernst von 74
Krafft, Johann Melchior 62
Krüger, Johann Sigismund 138
Kuhlmann, Quirinius 171

Labadie, Jean de 220
Lampe, Friedrich Adolph 218, 222, 224-236
Lange, H. D. 207
Lange, Joachim 43, 45, 47, 48, 50, 54, 55, 58, 62, 63, 64, 66, 67, 68, 69, 73, 97, 163, 189, 238
Lavater, Johann Caspar 253-256, 257, 259, 264, 265
Leade, Mrs. Jane 209, 210, 212
Leibnitz, Gottfried Wilhelm von 36, 74, 108, 112, 237, 254, 255, 257
Leipzig, University of 4, 5, 6, 7, 59, 72, 79, 80
Lessing, Gotthold Ephraim 255
Leyden, University of 226
Lilienthal, T.C. 77, 252
Locke, John 236

Lodensteyn, Jadocus van 223, 225, 227
Löscher, Valentin Ernst 15, 41, 58, 63, 64, 65, 66, 67, 68, 69, 70, 135
Lorija, Jizchak 108
Louis XIV of France 89, 94, 212, 214
Ludolf, Heinrich Wilhelm 35
Luther, Martin 2, 8, 9, 11, 12, 14, 15, 16, 17, 18, 20, 22, 52, 61, 62, 96, 98, 142, 145, 151, 154, 178, 208
Lysius, Heinrich 75, 76

Mack, Alexander 214
Mager, Martin 123
Mai, Johann Heinrich 86
Malebranche, Nicolas 110
Marburg, University of 234, 258
Marsay ,Charles Hector de 213
Mayer, Christoph 207
Mayer, Johann Friedrich 6, 61, 62, 78
Mel, Conrad 233-235, 236
Melanchthon, Philipp 52, 96, 178
Menken, Gottfried 244
Merker, Johann 85
Michaelis, Johann Heinrich 43, 62
Michel, Georg Adam 253
Molinos, Miguel de 5, 9, 171, 172, 197
Müller, Heinrich 180
Müller, Michael 92
Münchhausen, Frau von 82
Mühlenberg, Henry Melchior 83

Natzmer, D. G. von 71
Neander, Joachim 208, 223, 235
Neisser, August 138, 165
Neisser, Jakob 138, 165
Neology 218, 139f.
Nethenus, Samuel 223
Neumeister, Erdmann 189
Newton, Sir Isaac 112, 236
Nicolai, Friedrich 249, 250
Nitschmann, Georg 139
Nitschmann, Melchior 139, 140
Noailles, Cardinal 135
Novalis 240

Oberberger, Johann Kaspar 108
Oder, Georg Ludwig 163
Oechslin, J. 92
Oetinger, Friedrich Christoph 107-120, 123 125, 126, 169, 243, 245, 249
Olearius, Gottfried 79
Olearius, Johann 4, 53, 79
Olevianus, Dr. Caspar 212
Oppenheim, Süss 89
Osiander, Lucas II 2, 90
Oxford Greek Testament 97

Pelagianism 2, 16, 220
Perkins, William 233
Peter the Great of Russia 34
Petersen, Dr. Johann Wilhelm 103, 128, 203, 205, 210
Petersen, Johanna Eleanore 210
Pfaff, Christoph Matthias 93, 246
Pfeiffer, Johann Gottlob 80
Philadelphianism 103, 160, 161, 175, 177, 205, 206, 208-216, 259
Philadelphus, Nathanael (Christian F. Knorr) 211
Philadelphus, Timotheus (Dr. Johann Kaiser) 211
Plütschau, Heinrich 35
Poiret, Peter 61, 128, 172, 173, 174, 194, 196, 197
Pordage, John 209
Porst, Johann 72, 73
Praetorius, Stephan 125, 126
Pregizer, Christian Gottlob 124-127
Puritanism 5, 10, 21, 49, 66, 209, 224

Quakers 61
Quand, Johann Jakob 74, 75, 76
Quietism 4-5, 9, 22, 171-175, 196, 197, 198, 199, 200, 201, 222

Raab, Johann Adam 206
Radical Reformation 52
Raith, Balthasar 90, 91
Rambach, Johann Jacob 44, 47, 50, 53, 54, 56, 57
Rebstock, J. 92
Rechenberg, Adam 4, 79, 80
Raimarus, Hermann Samuel 255
Reinbeck, Johann Gustav 41, 73, 238
Reitz, Johann Heinrich 208
Reuchlin, Christoph 93, 95

Reuss, Countess Erdmunthe Dorothea 137
Reuss, Jeremias Friedrich 105
Rieger, Georg Conrad 105
Rinteln, University of 97
Ritschl, Albrecht 8, 17, 73, 142, 167, 196
Rock, Johann Friedrich 108, 214
Roëll, Hermann Alexander 233
Römeling, Christian Anton 233
Rogall, Georg Friedrich 76
Roos, Magnus Friedrich 105
Rosenbach, Johann Georg 67, 109, 206-208
Rosenroth, Knorr von 108
Rostock, University of 1, 3, 5
Rothe, Albrecht Christian 59, 60, 61, 62
Rothe, Johann Andreas 136, 138, 139
Rousseau, Jean Jacques 237

Saint Bernard 73
Sandhagen, Caspar Hermann 6
Sassov, Theodor 62
Schade, Johann Kaspar 62, 72
Schäffer, Martin 122
Schelling, Friedrich Wilhelm 240
Schiller 240
Schimmeyer, Johann Christoph 78
Schlegel, Friedrich 240
Schleiermacher Friedrich 240
Schmid, Johann Laurentius 73
Schmidt, Johann Heinrich 83
Schortinghuis, Wilhelmus 218, 222, 223, 233, 236
Schrader, J. K. 84
Schrautenbach, L. C. von 142
Schubart, C. F. D. 120
Schultz, Franz Albert 76, 77, 252
Schwartze, Christoph Gottlob 86
Schweinitz, Baron von 132
Schwenckfeld, Caspar 69
Schwiechelt, Eleonore Charlotte von 82
Seckendorf, Ludwig Veit von 60, 61
Serpilus, Christian 62
Seven Years War 40
Shaftesbury, Lord 236, 239
Silberschlag, Johann Esaias 74
Silchmüller, Johann Christoph 87
Society for the Promotion of Christian Knowledge (SPCK) 247, 251
Society for the Propagation of the Gospel in Foreign Parts 234
Sommer, Heinrich 194
Sonthom, Immanuel 5, 95, 206
Spalding, Johann Joachim 239-240, 254
Spangenberg, August Gottlieb 108, 134, 142, 165
Spener, Philipp Jakob 1-87, 88, 91, 95, 99, 103, 132, 139, 150, 154, 157, 176, 177, 179, 181, 203, 206, 214, 232, 245, 265
Spinoza, Baruch 222
Sprögel, Anna 177
Sprögel, Johann Heinrich 78
Stargard Bible 78
Stolberg, Christian Ernst von 82
Stolberg, Sophie Charlotte von 82
Storr, Johann Christian 207
Strassburg, University of 257
Storr, Johann Philipp 207
Sturm und Drang 143, 240, 241, 243, 253, 254, 255, 259, 260
Swedenborg, Emmanuel 118, 245

Teellinck, William 222, 224, 227
Tennhardt, Johann 103, 208
Tersteegen, Gerhard 119, 172, 191-202, 208, 222, 236, 245
Thirty Years War 1, 39, 41, 88
Thomasius, Christian 42, 59, 246
Tieck, Ludwig 240
Toland, John 236
Trescho, S. F. 252
Tuchtfeld, Victor Christoph 211, 213
Tübingen, University of 2, 90, 91, 92, 93, 97, 108, 118, 124, 128, 238, 246

Untereyck, Theodor 204, 208, 218, 223, 227, 234, 235, 236
Urlsperger, Johann August 246-253
Urlsperger, Samuel 246, 252, 265
Utrecht, University of 225, 226

Verschuir, Jacob 220, 221, 223, 233
Vitringa, Campegius 97, 227
Voetius, Gisbertus 226, 227
Volk, Alexander 163

Waeyen, Johannes van der 227

Wagner, Friedrich 189
Wagner, Tobias 90
Walch, Johann Georg 173
Weck, Wilhelm 202
Weigel, Valentin 108
Weissmann, Christoph Eberhard 93
Wernsdorf, Gottlieb 135
Wertheim Bible 73, 74
Wesley, John 101, 119
Wetzel, Frau 211
Whitefield, George 119
Wieland, Christoph Martin 259
Winckler, Johann W. 5, 31, 86
Witsius, Hermann 227
Wittenberg, University of 66, 70, 80, 134, 135, 142, 176
Wolf, Abraham 76
Wolff, Christian 73, 74, 76, 77, 108, 112, 237, 238, 247, 252, 257
Voltaire, Francois Marie Aruet de 237
Woltersdorf, Ernst Gottlieb 81
Wolterdorf, Theodor Carl Georg 74
Wuppermann, Dorothea 245

Ziegenbalg, Bartholomäus 35
Zierold, Wilhelm 77, 78
Zimmermann, Johann Jacob 109, 254
Zinzendorf, Nikolaus Ludwig von 79, 87, 131-167, 184, 187, 187, 188, 199, 204, 213, 243
Zollinger, Johann Christoph 202
Zwingli, Ulrich 98, 228